Risk Sharing in Finance

The Islamic Finance Alternative

Risk Sharing in Finance

The Islamic Finance Alternative

HOSSEIN ASKARI
ZAMIR IQBAL
NOUREDDINE KRICHNE
ABBAS MIRAKHOR

John Wiley & Sons (Asia) Pte. Ltd.

Other Wiley Editorial Offices

John Wiley & Sons, 111 River Street, Hoboken, NJ 07030, USA

John Wiley & Sons, The Atrium, Southern Gate, Chichester, West Sussex, PO19 8SQ, United Kingdom

John Wiley & Sons (Canada) Ltd., 5353 Dundas Street West, Suite 400, Toronto, Ontario, M9B 6HB, Canada

John Wiley & Sons Australia Ltd., 42 McDougall Street, Milton, Queensland 4064, Australia

Wiley-VCH, Boschstrasse 12, D-69469 Weinheim, Germany

Library of Congress Cataloging-in-Publication Data

ISBN 978–0–470–82966–0 (Hardback)
ISBN 978–0–470–82960–8 (ePDF)
ISBN 978–0–470–82967–7 (Mobi)
ISBN 978–0–470–82961–5 (ePub)

Typeset in 10/12pts Sabon Roman by MPS Limited, a Macmillan Company
Printed in Singapore by Markono Print Media Pte. Ltd.

10 9 8 7 6 5 4 3 2 1

In the Name of Allah, the All Merciful, the All Beneficent

Contents

Preface   ix

Acknowledgments   xvii

Glossary   xix

PART ONE

THE HISTORY AND CAUSES OF FINANCIAL CRISES

CHAPTER 1
A Brief History of Financial Crises and Proposed Reforms   3

CHAPTER 2
Financialization and the Decoupling–Recoupling Hypotheses   31

PART TWO

RISK SHARING AND THE ISLAMIC PARADIGM

CHAPTER 3
A Brief History of Risk-Sharing Finance   49

CHAPTER 4
Risk Sharing and the Islamic Finance Paradigm   69

CHAPTER 5
Risk Sharing in the Islamic Financial System: The Building Blocks   95

CHAPTER 6
Risk Sharing and Vibrant Capital Markets in Islamic Finance   115

CHAPTER 7
Portfolio Theory and Asset Pricing   **133**

CHAPTER 8
**Complementary Role of Intermediaries and Markets in
Promoting Risk Sharing**   **159**

PART THREE

MOVING FORWARD

CHAPTER 9
**Enhanced Access to Finance, Social Welfare, and Economic
Development under a Risk-Sharing System**   **181**

CHAPTER 10
The Role of Institutions and Governance in Risk Sharing   **201**

CHAPTER 11
Gaps between the Theory and Practice of Islamic Finance   **225**

CHAPTER 12
Concluding Remarks   **247**

References   **259**

Index   **277**

Preface

The financial crisis that erupted in the United States in 2007 and quickly permeated many of the advanced industrial countries is undoubtedly the most serious financial and economic crisis since the Great Depression of the 1930s. Its severity has invoked more debate than the run-of-the-mill financial crisis that seems to occur about once every 10 or so years; and rather than calling for minor reforms, some academics, practitioners, and policymakers have been questioning the fundamental stability of the modern conventional financial system.

The suggested reasons for this financial crisis have been many:

- wholesale and foolhardy deregulation;
- inadequate and failed supervision;
- unregulated and unsupervised financial institutions;
- an inadequate level of capital;
- an extended episode of low interest rates;
- excessive risk taking;
- the emergence of a parallel banking sector (the repo market);
- rapid and uncontrolled financial innovations (derivatives);
- mark-to-market accounting;
- the consolidation of the financial sector and the emergence of institutions that are deemed "too big to fail";
- shortcomings of the credit rating agencies and, especially, the conflict of interest in their operations;
- excessive assumption of debt and leveraging;
- increased international capital mobility; and
- human greed, fraud, and Ponzi finance.

The list is long and could be lengthened even further.

Depending on which of these reasons one considers the culprit(s), recommendations for reform have also been numerous. As to be expected, reforms are little more than a "bandaging" of the current financial system: higher levels of capital; breaking up of financial institutions; re-regulation to include all financial institutions; measures to limit risk taking and to increase transparency, and more. But it is difficult to see how any of these changes will eliminate the likelihood of future financial crises. Higher capital requirements, for instance, would reduce bank lending, money creation, and leveraging, but there is always the chance that bad loans could still wipe out a bank's capital. Similarly, limiting the size of financial institutions would reduce, but not eliminate, systemic risk and the need for bailouts. Increasing transparency in the packaging, pricing, and settling of derivatives would afford investors more information on pricing and reduce, but again not eliminate, systemic risk. And on and on.

The conventional banking system is a fractional reserve banking system that is based predominantly on debt financing and, by its structure, creates money and encourages leveraging. The embedded risk of such a system is that money and debt creation, and leveraging, could be excessive. Safeguards such as deposit guarantee schemes—for instance, the Federal Deposit Insurance Corporation (FDIC) in the United States—and the classification of some banks as "too big to fail" are the implicit government subsidies that reduce funding costs and create moral hazard, encouraging mispricing and excessive assumption of risk by financial institutions. The mispricing of loans and assumption of excessive risk, in turn, threaten the liquidity and solvency of financial institutions. Systemic risks that are inherent in the system, such as the linkages and the interdependencies of institutions, as well as the prominence of "too big to fail" institutions, create financial instability and threaten the entire financial and real economy. To enhance financial stability, regulators would have to adopt policies and practices that eliminate moral hazard and excessive debt creation and leveraging.

One way to ensure the stability of the financial system is to *eliminate* the type of asset–liability risk that threatens the solvency of all financial institutions, including commercial banks. This requires commercial banks to restrict their activities to two: (i) cash safekeeping; and (ii) investing client money, as in a mutual fund. Banks would accept deposits for safekeeping only (as, for example, in a system with a 100 percent reserve requirement) and charge a fee for providing this service and for check-writing privileges. In their intermediation capacity, banks would identify and analyze investment opportunities and offer them to clients; they would charge a fee for this service, much like a traditional investment bank. The bank would not be assuming any asset–liability risk on its balance sheet; instead, gains or losses would accrue directly to client investors. However, the bank could at the same time invest its own equity capital in these and other investment projects, as could its client investors. In this case, the bank would not be assuming any asset–liability exposure, just a potential loss of some (but not all) of its capital, which would not endanger the bank's solvency.

In other words, in this example of a financial system, there would be no debt financing by institutions, only equity financing; and there would be no risk shifting, only risk sharing. Banks would not create money, as they do under a fractional reserve system. Financial institutions would be serving their traditional role as intermediaries between savers and investors but with no debt on their balance sheets, no leveraging, and no predetermined interest rate payments as an obligation.

Proposals along these lines are not new. Financial systems in some such form or other have been practiced throughout recorded history (see Chapter 3). Recently, such an approach was recommended in the "Chicago Plan." This reform plan was formulated in a memorandum written in 1933 by a group of renowned Chicago professors, including Henry Simons, Frank Knight, Aaron Director, Garfield Cox, Lloyd Mints, Henry Schultz, Paul Douglas, and A. G. Hart, and was forcefully advocated and supported by the noted Yale University professor Irving Fisher in his book titled *100% Money*. Noting the fundamental monetary cause underlying each of the severe financial crises in 1837, 1873, 1907, and 1929–34, the Chicago Plan called for a full monopoly for the government in the issuance of currency and forbade banks from creating any money or near money by establishing 100 percent reserves against checking deposits. Investment banks would play the role of broker between savers and borrowers and act as financial intermediators. Hence, under such a system, the inverted credit pyramid, highly leveraged financial schemes (such as hedge funds), and monetization of credit instruments (for example, securitization) are excluded. The credit multiplier is far smaller and is determined by the savings ratio instead of the reserves ratio.

As stated by Irving Fisher: "The essence of the 100% plan is to make money independent of loans; that is to divorce the process of creating and destroying money from the business of banking. A purely incidental result would be to make banking safer and more profitable; but by far the most important result would be the prevention of great booms and depressions by ending chronic inflations and deflations which have ever been the great economic curse of mankind and which have sprung largely from banking." According to Fisher, the creation of money depends on the coincidence of the double will of borrowers to borrow and of banks to lend. Keynes deplored this double want coincidence as a source of large swings in the circulating medium. Why? In times of recession, borrowers are over-indebted and see narrower profit prospects, and thus become less willing to borrow; while banks are saddled with impaired assets and are less willing to lend. Jointly, they cause a contraction of money and, in turn, an aggravation of the downturn in the economic cycle. Irving Fisher wrote: "I have come to believe that that plan is incomparably the best proposal ever offered for speedily and permanently solving the problem of depressions; for it would remove the chief cause of both booms and depressions."

More recent than the Chicago Plan, Laurence Kotlikoff (2010) has made a proposal along similar lines, coining it "Limited Purpose Banking (LPB)." Henry and Kotlikoff, writing in *Forbes* (2010), said of the Kotlikoff approach:

> *Were we really serious about fixing our financial system, there's a very simple alternative—Limited Purpose Banking. LPB would transform all financial intermediaries with limited liability into mutual fund companies. Under LPB a single regulatory agency— the "Federal Financial Authority"—would organize the independent rating, verification, custody and full disclosure of all securities held by the mutual funds. Voilà, by dint of competition and transparency, "liar loans," off-balance sheet gimmickry, and toxic assets would all disappear. LPB would let the financial sector do only what Main Street needs it to do—connect lenders to borrowers and savers to investors. The financial sector's job is not to take taxpayers to the casino and collect the winnings.*

There are many reasons why reform along this, or similar lines, has not entered the political and financial mainstream until the recent financial turmoil. For starters, there is the opposition of the powerful financial sector. The lobbying of the financial sector against fundamental financial reform in the United States is well documented and its interest is evident. Starting in the 1970s, the financial sector has gained relative to the real sector, as measured by its growing share of gross domestic product (GDP), aggregate corporate profits, and salaries and bonuses. The financial sector will not readily give up activities and instruments that have allowed it to establish such a dominant position and to accumulate such gains.[1] When risk transfer is combined with high leverage, the growth of interest-based debt contracts and their pure financial derivatives—those with little or no connection to real assets— outpace the growth of the real sector leaving the liabilities in the economy a large multiple of real assets needed to validate them. This phenomenon has been coined "financial decoupling" or "financialization," whereby finance is no longer anchored to the real sector.

A second popular concern is the "assumed" impact on economic growth and prosperity if debt financing is significantly reduced or eliminated. Although most observers attribute a significant role to the explosion of debt and leveraging in bringing about financial crises, at the same time some argue that the reduction, let alone elimination, of debt financing and bank money creation would reduce economic growth. This is an empirical issue that deserves careful estimation—how would growth over the long haul compare under each regime? And what would be the attendant social benefits and costs under each regime? While many have prejudged the result, we are not sure that booms and busts are superior to steady growth. To our mind, much of the assumed contributions of finance over the last 30 or so years (as indicated by its growing share of the economy), and thus debt financing and leverage, have been only a mirage. Under an equity-based (risk-sharing) financial system, investment demand by the private sector should be similar to the conventional financial system as long as debt and equity receive the same tax treatment; this result would readily follow from the Modigliani-Miller theorem. Government demand would also be similar as long as vibrant capital markets allowed the government to finance its investment projects through equity-based financing (see Chapter 7). The only difference would be consumer demand. However, in an equity-based system, the reduction in uncertainty and risk affords its own impetus to economic growth. And social gains may dwarf loss in economic output, if any, under an equity-based system. Social gains come in two forms. In an equity-based system, there would be more interaction between investors and entrepreneurs, in turn bringing the parties closer together. Even more apparent, steady economic and employment growth would avoid the social upheavals and family pressures that the unemployed face. Again, any valid comparison must be comprehensive and accumulative—that is, made over the long haul.

A third reason for inaction on fundamental reform is that politicians are by nature and temperament "incrementalists," always with an eye on the next election. They invariably put off wholesale and fundamental reforms until they have no other option. In many instances, fundamental reform eventually comes, but at a much higher cost and when there are no other easier options and no more room for maneuver. Realistically, we may have to experience a few more bouts of financial instability, possibly a total financial meltdown, before regulators and politicians take the need for fundamental reform seriously. While the United States adopted sweeping financial reforms (the Dodd-Frank Wall Street Reform and Consumer Protection Act) in July 2010, the contents of this Act do not even get close to addressing the fundamental issues that have fueled financial instability.

Henry and Kotlikoff judge the Dodd-Frank Act and give their reason why fundamental reform may have been sidestepped yet again:

> *This kind of "cowboy capitalism" is far too dangerous to maintain. But Dodd-Frank does precisely this, albeit with many more regulatory cops on the beat. In contrast, LPB would put an end to Wall Street's gambling with taxpayer chips. Since mutual funds are, in effect, small banks with 100% capital requirements in all circumstances, they can never fail. Neither can their holding companies. Under LPB, financial crises and the massive damage they inflict on*

*the entire (global) economy would become a thing of the past.
Of course, there would be losers. Some Wall Street executives might
have to find employment in Las Vegas or offshore banks. Some
lobbyists, lawyers, credit analysts and accountants might need to
find higher callings. Some politicians might even have to solicit
more support from Main Street. Alas, Dodd-Frank bears no resemblance to Limited Purpose Banking. But bad laws don't always last,
and this one may eventually lead us to LPB by showing us precisely
what not to do—if we ever get another chance.*

While the Chicago Plan or LPB are two approaches that may be used to
alleviate financial booms and busts, Islam long ago recommended a financial
system that incorporates equity financing (risk sharing) and prohibits debt
financing, its attendant interest payments, and the risks that accompany
excessive debt creation and leveraging. This is, essentially, a two-tiered
banking system: one that handles deposits for safekeeping only; and the
other that acts much like an investment bank. These investment banks invest
directly in real projects with investor capital, as well as with their own capital,
and share directly in the risks of the project. They invest directly in every
segment of the economy (except activities that are prohibited, such as gambling and alcohol). Given the central role of risk sharing in such a financial
system, vibrant capital markets are essential for these institutions to fulfill
their central role as intermediaries as envisaged in Islamic finance.

Although Islamic finance has a long history, it had been largely
pushed aside until its revival beginning in the 1970s, when Muslims
began to rediscover their heritage. As a result, what is today "popularly
classified" as Islamic finance has grown rapidly over the last three or
four decades. Islamic financial institutions have emerged in Muslim and
non-Muslim countries, and conventional banks have also embraced the
practice. In some Muslim and non-Muslim countries the legal system
has been modified to accommodate Islamic finance, enabling more level
competition with conventional finance.

While a number of indicators point to rapid growth in the practice of
Islamic finance, much of this growth, to our mind, has been superficial. Two
factors have limited more fundamental progress in establishing an Islamic
financial system in a country or region. First, with money to be made selling
Islamic financial products, the focus has been to quickly develop and market
profitable instruments. Financial institutions have installed their own board
of *Shari'ah* scholars to sanction as "*Shari'ah* compliant" the financial products that they have developed for marketing to Muslims. Unfortunately, in
the race to make money, expected shortcuts may have compromised the
basic Islamic requirements of risk sharing and prohibition of a predetermined

interest rate. Second, in the race to develop *Shari'ah*-compliant instruments and reap financial rewards, there has been little, or no, effort to develop a comprehensive system of Islamic finance to compete with conventional finance. No country, with the recent possible exception of Malaysia, has even attempted, let alone succeeded, to establish a comprehensive Islamic financial system; with the only difference across countries, Muslim and non-Muslim, being the traded value of questionable *Shari'ah*-compliant instruments sold to Muslims.

Our goal in this book is to make a modest contribution in developing the building blocks of a complete Islamic financial system and elaborating on its implementation as a comprehensive system for any country or region. In the process, we hope to highlight the characteristics, operations, and benefits of a comprehensive risk-sharing financial system for long-term economic and social prosperity. In Part One, we begin by taking a brief look at the history of financial crises and how they may be minimized. In Part Two, we examine the history of risk-sharing finance, the Islamic finance paradigm, and the role of vibrant stock markets. We then look more broadly at how money markets and capital markets could promote risk sharing; and we conclude by looking at how risk sharing could advance social development. In Part Three, we look ahead and assess the needed elements to establish a complete Islamic financial system in a country. Finally, with an eye towards the future, we present our concluding remarks.

ENDNOTE

1. The significant increase in credit to the sub-prime sector and the housing bubble that ensued may have masked the rapidly growing income and wealth disparity in the United States since the mid-1970s. The housing bubble was accompanied by increased home ownership and availability of home equity loans, which in turn enabled homeowners to increase their consumption without an increase in their disposable income.

Acknowledgments

We acknowledge the valuable contribution of editor Robyn Flemming, and the continuing support of John Wiley & Sons (Asia) in promoting the development of Islamic finance literature. We are also indebted to Professor Robert Merton for taking the time from his busy schedule to write an endorsement to our book, and are grateful to Amirhossein Najafi for compiling the reference list. As always, we are grateful to our families for their understanding and encouragement.

Glossary of Arabic terms

A

ajar: Reward for doing good.
akhlaq: Personality disposition stemming from individual character.
akl amwal alnas bi al-batil: Enrichment through non-permissible means.
al-adl: Justice.
al-amal: The concept of work.
al-bay': Exchange.
al-ihsan: Behaving with full consciousness of the Supreme Creator.
al-khiyar/khiyar: Option.
al-mal: Wealth or property.
al-Mo'meneen: Active believers.
amanah: Trust.
aqidah: Binding principles of faith.
awqaf (sing. *waqf):* Endowments.

B

bai' bithamin ajil (BBA): Sales contract where payment is made in installments after delivery of goods. Sale could be for the long term and there is no obligation to disclose profit margins.
barakah: An invisible but "material" blessing whose results can be observed by any believer who engages in righteous conduct.
bashar: Man. This concept refers to the physical/outward attributes, rather than the inner character.
bay': Contracts of exchange.
bay' al-arabun: A portion of the full sale price paid in good faith as earnest money (could be considered as a non-refundable down payment).
bay' al-dayn: Sale of debt or liability.
bay' al-istisna': Sale on order (usually manufactured goods).
bay' al-muajjil: Deferred-payment sale, either by installments or a lump sum.
bay' al-salam (also *salaf):* Sale in which payment is made in advance by the buyer and the delivery of the goods is deferred by the seller.

D

dayn: Debt.
dharoora: Necessity.

F

fadl: Addition.

faqih (pl. fuqaha'): Jurist who gives rulings on various issues in the light of the Qur'an and the *sunnah*.

fatwa: Religious verdict by *fuqaha'*.

fiqh: Corpus of Islamic jurisprudence. In contrast to conventional law, *fiqh* covers all aspects of life—religious, political, social, commercial, and economic. *Fiqh* is based primarily on interpretations of the *Qur'an* and the *sunnah* and secondarily on *ijma'* and *ijtihad* by the *fuqaha'*. While the *Qur'an* and the *sunnah* are immutable, *fiqhi* verdicts may change in line with changing circumstances.

fiqhi: Relating to *fiqh*.

G

ghabun: The difference between the price at which a transaction is executed and the fair price (unjustified exploitation, loss).

gharar: Literally, "deception, danger, risk, and excessive, unnecessary uncertainty (ambiguity)." Technically, it means exposing oneself to excessive risk and danger in a business transaction as a result of either having too little information or asymmetric information about price, quality and quantity of the counter-value, the date of delivery, the ability of either the buyer or the seller to fulfill their commitment, or ambiguity in the terms of the deal—thereby, exposing either of the two parties to unnecessary risks.

H

hadia/hibah: Gifts.

hadith (pl. ahadith): Oral tradition of the Prophet Muhammad (pbuh) as narrated by his companions.

hajj/umra: The pilgrimage to Mecca.

hajr: Blocking the use of a resource.

haram: Prohibited.

hawala: Bills of transfer.

hifz al-mal: Protection of wealth or property.

hila (pl. hiyal): Refers to strategies in applying juristic rules to ease constraints on a particular transaction that would have been non-permissible otherwise.

I

'ibada (pl. ibadat): Adoration of Allah (*swt*) through rule compliance.

ijarah: Leasing. The sale of the usufruct of an asset. The lessor retains the ownership of the asset with all the rights and responsibilities that go with ownership.

ijarah sukuk: Instrument issued on the basis of an asset to be leased. The investors provide funds to a lessor (say, an Islamic bank). The lessor acquires an asset (either existing or to be created in future) and leases it out if it is not already leased out. They are issued by the lessor in favor of the investors, who become owners of the leased asset in proportion to their investment. These entitle the holders to collect rental payments from the lessee directly. Can also be made tradable in the stock exchange.

ijarah wa "qtinah": Hire-purchase agreement.

ijma: The consensus of jurists.

ijtihad: Exertion of personal effort to understand the wisdom behind the pre-scribed rules and/or efforts to extend juristic rulings to new situations based on study of the *Qur'an* and *hadith*.

ikrah: Coercion.

iman: Active belief.

insan: This concept refers to a "human being" who is fully conscious of the human state in relation to the Supreme Creator. cf. *bashar*.

israf: Overspending.

istihsan: Judicial preference.

istisna' (short form for *bay' al-istisna'):* A contract whereby a manufacturer (con-tractor) agrees to produce (build) and deliver well-described products (or prem-ises) at a given price on a given date in the future. The price need not be paid in advance and may be paid in installments in step with the preferences of the parties, or partly at the front end and the balance later on, as agreed.

itlaf: Waste.

itraf: Opulent and extravagant spending.

J

jo'alah: Performing a given task for a prescribed fee in a given period.

K

kanz (pl. konooz): Treasure(s). Refers to wealth held in the form of gold, silver, and other precious metals.

khalifa: Vicegerent, trustee.

khawf: Fear of the consequences of thoughts and actions.

khilafah: Trusteeship, stewardship.

khisarah: Loss.

khums: One-fifth of income payable for the purpose of redeeming the rights of others.

kifala: Taking responsibility for someone else (see also *takaful*, which is derived from this).

M

ma'aad: The ultimate return of everything to the Creator for the final account-ability and judgment.

madhahib: School of thought.

manafaah al-ikhtiyarat: Gains from taking options.

manfaa maal/ manfa' ah: Usufruct. Benefit flowing from a durable commodity or asset. Also, gains from transaction.

maqasid al-Shari'ah: Basic objectives of the *Shari'ah*: the protection of faith, life, progeny, property, and reason.

maslahah: Literally, "benefit." Technically, it refers to any action taken to protect any one of the five basic objectives of the *Shari'ah*.

mithaq: A covenant.

muamalat: Interpersonal transactions.

mubaya'a: Contract between the ruler and the community that he will be faithful in discharging his duties in compliance with the rules prescribed by Allah (*swt*).

mudarabah: Contract between two parties—a capital owner or financier (*rabb al-mal*) and an investment manager (*mudarib*). Profit is distributed between the two parties in accordance with the ratio upon which they agree at the time of the contract. Financial loss is borne only by the financier. The investment manager's loss lies in not getting any reward for his labor services.

mudarib: Investment manager.

muhtasib: A market supervisor.

murabahah: Sale at a specified profit margin. This term, however, is now used to refer to a sale agreement whereby the seller purchases the goods desired by the buyer and sells them at an agreed marked-up price, the payment being settled within an agreed time frame, either in installments or as a lump sum. The seller bears the risk for the goods until they have been delivered to the buyer. Also referred to as *bay' mu'ajjal*.

musharakah: Partnership. Similar to a *mudarabah* contract, the difference being that here both partners participate in the management and the provision of capital and share in the profit and loss. Profits are distributed between the partners in accordance with the ratios initially set, whereas loss is distributed in proportion to each one's share in the capital. Also, this contract is more suitable for longer-term partnership contracts and long-gestating projects.

musharakah 'aqd: The contract of *musharakah*.

musharakah mulk: Specification of property rights of partnership.

musharakah mutanaqisah: "Diminishing partnership."

mysir: Gambling or any game of chance.

N

nafaqa: Expenditure.

nafs: The psyche (sometimes translated as "soul").

nisab: A level of wealth beyond which levies are due.

niyyah: Intention.

Q

qard: A loan.

qard-ul-hassan: Loan extended without interest or any other compensation from the borrower. The lender expects a reward only from Allah (*swt*).

qimar: Gambling.

qist: Social (inter-relational) justice.

qiyas: Analogy.

Qur'an (also written as *al-Qur'an*): The Holy Book of Muslims, consisting of the revelations made by Allah (*swt*) to the Prophet Muhammad (pbuh). Prescribes the rules of social and personal behavior, compliance with which guarantees social solidarity, economic growth and development.

R

rabb al-mal: Capital owner or financier.

rahn: A pledge (also translated as "collateral").

riba: Literally, "increase," "addition," or "growth." Technically, it refers to the "premium" that must be paid by the borrower to the lender along with the principal amount as a condition for the loan or an extension in its maturity. Interest, as commonly understood today, is regarded by a predominant majority of *fuqaha'* to be equivalent to *riba*.

ribh: Profit.

S

sadaqat: Payments to redeem others' rights (also translated as "charity").

safih: A person of weak understanding.

sarf: An exchange contract.

sarrafs: Exchange dealers.

Shari'ah: The corpus of Islamic law based on Divine guidance, as given by the *Qur'an* and the *sunnah*, and embodies all aspects of the Islamic faith, including beliefs and practices.

shirakah: Partnership.

suftaja: Bills of exchange.

sukuk: Negotiable financial instruments.

sunnah: The second-most important source of the Islamic faith after the *Qur'an* and refers to the Prophet's (pbuh) operationalization and explication of the rules prescribed by Allah (*swt*) in the *Qur'an* in words and action.

surah: A chapter of the *Qur'an*.

T

tabdhir: Squandering.

takaful: An alternative to the contemporary insurance contract. A group of persons agree to share a certain risk (for example, damage by fire) by collecting a specified sum from each. Any loss is met from the collected funds.

taqwa: Awe/fear that comes with consciousness of the presence of Allah (*swt*).

tawarruq: Reverse *murabahah*. Buying an item on credit on a deferred-payment basis and then immediately reselling it for cash at a discounted price to a third party.

tawhid: The Unity and Oneness of the Creator.

tijaarah/tirajah: Contracts of trade.

U

urf: Customs.

W

wa'd: A time-bound promise to deliver on terms contracted.

wadia: Trust or safekeeping.

wikalah: Contract of agency in which one person appoints someone else to perform a certain task on his behalf, usually for a fixed fee.

wali: A protective, loving friend.

waqf (pl. *awqaf):* Endowment.

Z

zakah/zakat: Amount payable by a Muslim on his net worth as a part of his religious obligations to redeem the rights of others.

The History and Causes of Financial Crises

A Brief History of Financial Crises and Proposed Reforms

The historic quest for financial stability is motivated by a desire to avoid the ever-recurring cost of financial instability, and in turn to sustain real economic growth, full employment, price stability, social equity, and growing international trade and prosperity.

In this chapter, we present a brief history of financial crises to establish the attraction of a financial system based on equity finance and risk sharing, as opposed to a system based on debt, a predetermined fixed rate of interest, and risk shifting. While there have been a number of proposals and ideas that are based on the benefits of risk sharing (mentioned above in the Preface), such as the "Chicago Plan" of 1933 and Kotlikoff's "Limited Purpose Banking," an Islamic financial system is totally premised on risk sharing and equity finance.[1] An Islamic financial system prohibits debt financing, interest, and speculation. In this chapter, we hope to show that debt—that is, the transfer of risk—and fixed rate of interest have been at the foundation of financial crises in the past and will likely continue to be so in the future unless radical change in financial structure is introduced; that a system based on risk sharing and equity finance is immune to instability; and that such a system requires no bailouts and does not lead to social injustices, such as privatizing gains and socializing losses.

We argue that the conventional system is inherently unstable, often shaken by periodic crises and requiring massive bailouts, for essentially two reasons: (i) it is a debt- and interest-based system; and (ii) it creates excessive debt (mispriced) and leveraging through the credit multiplier and, in turn, faces sudden withdrawal of deposits when confronted with default by borrowers on their payments, and thus requires some form of deposit guarantee support by the government to reduce liquidity crises and bank failures.[2] Sovereign countries default on their debt interest and principal payments, let alone sub-prime borrowers. Increased regulation after each severe financial crisis has not prevented the recurrence of even more severe crises.

Regulations have been subverted by financial innovations, with regulators and supervisors invariably always in a catch-up role. Financial innovations have in turn led to financialization of the economy, whereby the relative importance of the financial sector to the real sector has increased, leading to a number of other developments. The number of unregulated financial institutions in the form of money funds has mushroomed along with the number of financial products. Speculation and debt trading have intensified, creating asset bubbles, excessive volatility, heightened uncertainty, and costly exchange rates instability. The inverted credit pyramid has become over-leveraged and vulnerable with even a small shock sending the credit pyramid tumbling into bankruptcies with a freezing of the entire banking and financial system.

With financialization, the frequency, contagion, and severity of crises have increased. Financial instability has been accompanied by abnormal exchange rate instability with implied disruption to international trade. In view of the tremendous economic losses inflicted by recurring financial crises, price distortions, inflation tax, and social inequities, the quest for financial stability has become ever more urgent. By briefly examining the history of financial crises, we hope to show that a financial and banking system that is founded on equity financing and risk sharing can deliver stability and enable the integration, or reintegration, of finance and the economy.

In Section I, we argue that the conventional banking system is inherently unstable. In Section II, we define the essence of a financial crisis. In Section III, we present a brief history of financial crises. In Section IV, we present the anatomy of financial crises; and in Section V, we argue that increasing regulation has not prevented the recurrence of financial crises. In Section VI, we elaborate on the role of central banks in financial instability; and in Section VII, we note the contagious effect of financial instability. In Section VIII, we provide some concluding remarks.

I. THE INHERENT INSTABILITY OF CONVENTIONAL BANKING

Conventional banking is a system based on interest-bearing debt. This is in contrast to an equity-based system, which is a profit–loss arrangement. Historically, debt-based banking has been prone to bouts of instability, threatening its very existence in the absence of massive government guarantees, subsidies, and bailouts.

By definition, commercial banks that do not maintain 100 percent of their assets in the form of reserves are theoretically vulnerable to withdrawals of deposits. More practically, a bank that keeps about 10 percent of its assets in the form of reserves is vulnerable to sudden panic withdrawals of deposits by depositors. It can be immunized from such panic withdrawals and runs if deposits are guaranteed by the government or by a quasi-government agency, invariably on a subsidized basis. It was for this reason that deposit insurance, after a number of such destructive panics, became part and parcel of conventional banking. While deposit insurance can deter runs on solvent banks that may be temporarily facing a liquidity crisis from an asset–liability mismatch, banking crises come about also because of insolvency (loan losses exceeding bank capital) resulting from bad (mispriced) loans, speculation, and even fraud on the part of banks. Insolvencies can either be allowed to run their course, leading to bankruptcy and loss of shareholder value and creditor loans, or the government can bail out its banks. Bailouts could be ominous and shift bank losses to the taxpayers, workers, pensioners, and the poor.[3] Bailouts have required two essential ingredients: costless paper money, and a central bank or direct government funding. Under the gold standard, bailouts were non-existent as they resulted in a loss of gold for the central bank. With paper money, bailouts have often turned into bouts of inflation as the central bank finances them by printing paper money, with the frequent result of price distortions and resource misallocation. Bailouts redistribute wealth, via a heavy inflation tax, in favor of banks and debtors at the expense of taxpayers, creditors, workers, and pensioners.

The need for bailouts has become imbedded in the interest-based system. It has been implemented by governments with a view to protecting banks (especially banks that are deemed "too big to fail" as they might threaten the entire financial system and in turn the broader economy) and debtors, and to reinflating asset prices to their pre-crisis levels. Recent reassurances about bailouts, which became known as the Greenspan put,[4] created moral hazard and led financial institutions to indulge in risky speculation or a dangerous degree of asset–liability mismatch. Consequently, bailouts have become all too frequent. The necessity of bailouts was explicitly stated by Bagehot in *Lombard Street* (1873); namely, when the banking system is hit by a crisis, the central bank has to print money freely and lend freely to banks that can no longer settle their payments. Minsky (1986) called upon the government to stem economic crises that necessarily follow a financial crisis (as aggregate demand falls following bankruptcies and loss of wealth). Keynes (1936) called for a prompt intervention of the government in expanding public expenditures in order to increase aggregate demand.[5]

A financial crisis could be defined as a crash in asset prices following a speculative asset boom, which can come in many forms (Tulip Bulb Mania, South Sea Bubble, Mississippi Bubble, Great Depression), or a banking crisis following a liquidity shortage and an impairment of bank assets, or both. A financial crisis causes defaults that affect the banking system in a country or across countries, followed by the financial ruin of depositors (to the extent that they do not have deposit insurance) and companies and a sharp decline in economic activity and employment.[6] As a web of cash flows and money incomes links banks, firms, and consumers, a spending of one is the income of another. Default by some economic agents may freeze the payments system and trigger general default and loss of money incomes. A bank may face a sudden massive withdrawal of deposits, just as in the past goldsmith houses faced a sudden withdrawal of gold. A bank may face default on its loans and sharp depreciation of its assets, and may then be unable to settle its liabilities and so face bank runs. During financial crises, either banks have suspended redemption of deposits into gold and currency, or simply failed, or both.[7]

Financial crises, in the form of asset price crashes or bank and business failures, have been frequent throughout time and across countries. They were as frequent in the 18th and 19th centuries as in the past century. Kindleberger and Aliber (2005) have shown that the frequency of financial crises has even increased since 1970. They have occurred both in highly advanced countries, where banks may number in the thousands, as well as in low-income countries, where there may be only three or four banks.

The diagnoses of the causes of financial crises have been numerous and diverse. Often causes are analyzed as effects, and effects are analyzed as causes. Each school of thought has laid the blame for a particular crisis on a different set of factors. For instance, the anti-gold standard and inflationist school attributed crises in the 19th century to gold fetters, liquidity shortages, and the inability of central banks operating under the gold standard to print money freely in order to bail out banks. They accused the gold standard of being liquidationist—that is, it liquidated troubled banks. The recommendation of this school, summarized by Bagehot (1873), was for the central bank to print and lend money freely during a financial crisis. The currency school, spearheaded by David Ricardo (1817), blamed financial crises on cheap money, low interest rates, and speculation. Their recommendation was to restrain credit expansion and tie currency issues to gold flows or a strict money rule (Simons, 1948). This recommendation led to the Peel Act in 1844, following the suspension of convertibility of banknotes into gold by the Bank of England between 1797 and 1820 and the severe financial crises of 1825 and 1836–39.

Irving Fisher (1933) attributed financial crises to over-indebtedness by companies and households, followed by deflation of asset prices and bankruptcies. Friedrich Hayek (1931) explained the origin of the business cycle in terms of central bank expansion and its transmission over time in terms of capital misallocation caused by artificially low interest rates. Hayek claimed that past instability of the market economy is a consequence of the exclusion of the most important regulator of the market mechanism, money, from itself being regulated by the market process.

Peter Temin (1991) blamed the Great Depression on government fiscal policy and its failure to undertake countercyclical expenditures to step up demand when an economic boom had slowed down and consumer spending had fallen. Financial crises have been blamed on poor harvests, as in the case of England in 1847, resulting in large gold outflows to finance food imports. Because of the Peel Act, gold outflows could not be sterilized through credit expansion. Financial crises have also been blamed on traders in stock markets and their manipulations of stock prices, "talking up" stock returns to push stock prices to high speculative levels. Such was the case with the South Sea Company in England in 1720 and the Mississippi Company in France in 1720. Similar swindle schemes have recurred across time and space. For instance, the bankers' panic of 1907 was precipitated by an attempt to corner stocks; the failed cornering depressed share prices by a further 50 percent in 1907, inflicting losses on banks and precipitating bank runs.[8] A financial crisis was blamed on banks using deposits to lend to brokerage firms, stock speculators and investors, mortgage borrowers, or even trading directly in assets, in violation of prudential banking. Barings Bank (1762–1995) fell as a result of speculation in asset markets. When asset prices collapse, depositors suffer losses. Prudential rules would require banks to finance trade and production operations without creating mismatching maturities and prohibiting speculative asset purchases.

Marx (1894) attributed financial crises to low wages for labor and large surplus value for capitalists and entrepreneurs. Low-wage incomes afforded to labor would not enable labor to buy the output of goods being produced, leading to over-production. Owners of capital would stimulate the working class to buy more and more in the way of expensive goods, houses, and durable goods, pushing them to take on more and more expensive credit, until their debt becomes unbearable. The unpaid debt would lead to bankruptcy of banks and thus to a financial crisis.

The most recent financial crisis of 2007–10 has produced its own share of explanations. Some have blamed regulators for being asleep on the job as events unfolded. Many experts and politicians have faulted bankers and financial markets such as hedge funds, mutual funds, and equity funds for excessive risk taking and the inability of regulators to understand, much less regulate, complex financial derivatives. Securitization of illiquid assets such as mortgages and multiplication of derivatives in a deregulated financial industry were faulted for debt trading, excess leverage, and a highly inflated credit pyramid. Other analysts have attributed the crisis to the increasing number of institutions that were deemed too big to fail. Others have faulted the credit rating agencies for their incestuous relationship with the entities that they rated. Still others (Gorton, 2010) put the blame on the run on banks, not by individual depositors, as in past crises, but by institutional investors, in what he calls the parallel banking sector (in the repo market because of the sharp decline in the price of collateral assets in the fire sale that ensued).[9] This and other credit quality concerns, in turn, motivated banks to withdraw from the interbank loan market.[10]

The meltdown of sub-prime credit in 2007 led to millions of foreclosures and inflicted devastating losses on leading investment banks. The crisis was considered by many a "Minsky moment." Minsky (1986, 1992) established instability as an endogenous feature of the conventional financial and banking system. He postulated two theorems of financial instability. The first theorem is that the economy has financing regimes under which it is stable, and others under which it is unstable. The second theorem is that over periods of prolonged prosperity, the economy transits from financial relations that make for a stable system to those that make for an unstable system. In particular, over a protracted period of good times, capitalist economies tend to move from a financial structure dominated by hedge finance entities to one increasingly prone to entities engaged in speculative and Ponzi finance. The hypothesis maintains that, historically, business cycles are compounded out of (i) the internal dynamics of capitalist economies, and (ii) the system of interventions and regulations that are designed to keep the economy operating within reasonable bounds.

II. DEFINITION OF A FINANCIAL CRISIS

Regardless of the absence of consensus on the causes of financial crises, they can be invariably described by observed facts. The consequences of a financial crisis are financial chaos and collapse, financial losses, and a period of economic decline and impoverishment.[11] In the case of a stock market crash or the bursting of a speculative asset bubble, a large part of financial wealth is wiped out when asset prices collapse. In the case of a banking crisis, the banking system is suddenly impaired: banks or debtors default or the market value of debt depreciates. Crises have been marked by bankruptcies of many firms, millions of foreclosures, large losses for depositors, bursting of bubbles and asset price deflation, and failures of banks. A debtor can always default if he chooses intentionally to fail on his commitment to pay his debt. Goldsmith houses, finance houses, and modern banks often run into a liquidity shortage in order to meet their short-term liabilities. The Asian financial crisis (1997–98) was due to a mismatch of assets and liabilities. Asian banks had invested short-term foreign capital in long-term assets, in real estate, and in industrial projects; consequently, they were not able to satisfy the withdrawal and repatriation of this capital. A company may default when its cash flow is mismatched; for instance, it has longer-term assets, in the form of supplier loans or unsold inventories, but short-term liabilities. The company may also default if it faces a drop in its sale prices or adverse exchange rate fluctuations. A debtor may default because of a liquidity mismatch, reduced capital basis, or insufficient income for servicing his debt or when expected payoffs do not materialize. A government may default on its commitments when it does not have enough revenues to service its debt. A Ponzi speculator may default when his speculative asset has depreciated.

Default by isolated debtors, for whatever reason, may not undermine a bank or a whole banking system. For instance, default by a single bank and a run on that bank by depositors to withdraw their deposits may not undermine the banking system unless it has a powerful contagion effect and undermines confidence in other banks. In order to have a financial crisis, the default or debt devaluation has to be on a large scale in relation to the banking system and the cause has to be systemic, affecting numerous debtors and their lender banks. A speculative crash in stock markets, asset markets, or exchange rates could be a systemic shock that triggers a financial crisis as ominous as the Great Depression and as drawn out as the Japanese crisis in the 1990s.

An often-cited cause of a systemic crisis is the multiplication of credit and the ability of banks to create an inverted debt pyramid, a "house of cards," to such a degree that it becomes vulnerable to even small shocks, such as a change in the expectations of entrepreneurs or the collapse of a speculative bubble in stock or housing markets. In fact, banks have a great ability to multiply credit and attain excessive leverage in relation to their capital or reserve basis, since credit is created by the stroke of a pen. The credit ratios have varied from country to country, demonstrating the ability of banks to multiply loans. Before the 2007 financial crisis, the credit to GDP ratios stood at 254 percent in Japan, 223 percent in the US, 164 percent in the UK, 108 percent in Norway, 128 percent in Thailand, 122 percent in Korea, 53 percent in Indonesia, and 47 percent in Mexico. A credit boom could turn into a systemic default. The higher the amount of credit in relation to the underlying capital and income levels, the higher the probability of default. A liquidity shortage and a credit freeze may affect most of the banking system and cause a financial crisis.

III. HISTORY OF FINANCIAL CRISES

Financial crises in the past have called for increased regulation of asset markets and the banking sector. Yet, in spite of strengthened regulation, financial crises have recurred in more devastating and prolonged forms. The US Federal

Reserve Bank, created in 1913, was seen by its founders as an institution that would prevent the recurrence of severe crises as witnessed in 1907, 1893, and 1873. Yet, the Fed did not prevent the Great Depression and might have even been a source of the crisis, as contested by a number of economists (for example, Hayek, 1931; Friedman and Schwartz, 1963; Currie, 1934). A study of the history of financial crises should uncover their varied nature, the forces that led to them, and why they have continued to occur despite both the dramatic consequences of previous crises in terms of deep losses of capital, economic turmoil, and unemployment, and the regulations and prudential guidelines introduced following each crisis. Our purpose in this section is to present general facts about financial crises, and to show that they can arise in different contexts, at different times, in different countries, in advanced as well as developing countries, and despite increased regulation of capital markets and the banking industry.

Financial institutions in the form of banks, trust institutions, and gold-smith houses existed during medieval times and the Renaissance in many European cities and Mediterranean trading centers. They catered to inter-national trade, performing payments and exchange settlements, and lent to monarchs and merchants. They were often stricken by financial crises in the form of runs on gold deposits or defaults of their debtors. However, absent a central bank and government bailouts, banks failed and could not be rescued. Medieval financial institutions remained at an embryonic stage and could not reach a stage of full development as witnessed by modern banks. The widespread use of metallic monies and very limited use of paper money was a constraint on the development of medieval banking. A central bank could exist, and government bailouts become feasible, only under a regimen of paper money. A central bank or a government cannot use gold to bail out banks. The purpose of bailout is to shift losses, by printing paper money, away from banks to the private sector, workers, pensioners, and the poor.

With the establishment of joint stock companies in Europe in the 16th century, the stock market became one of the most important sources of financing for companies and an important part of financial intermediation. It allowed businesses to be publicly traded, or to raise additional capital for expansion by selling shares of ownership of the company in a public market. The liquidity that an exchange provides affords investors the ability to quickly and easily sell securities. This is an attractive feature of invest-ing in stocks, compared to other less liquid investments such as real estate. The price and volume of shares and other assets is an important part of the dynamics of economic activity, and can influence or be an indicator of economic activity. An economy where the stock market is on the rise is considered to be a booming economy. In fact, the stock market is often con-sidered a leading indicator of a country's economic outlook. Rising share prices, for instance, tend to be associated with favorable expectations and increased business investment. (The reverse applies to falling prices.) Share prices also affect the wealth of households and their consumption.

Stock markets have been strongly affected by bank credit. Often, an expansion of credit has led to an economic boom with higher profits and, in turn, higher share prices; and in such an environment banks advance loans for purchasing shares, further fueling the price rise in shares. Stock markets have also been vulnerable to manipulations, swindles, and speculative mania. Swindle schemes such as those perpetrated by Bernie Madoff's wealth management firm have not been uncommon. In the panic of 1907, attempts to corner stocks led to losses for banks that financed these attempts and resulted in a run on banks. In 1720, stocks of the South Sea Company were pushed very high through swindle schemes that inflated the returns of the company.[12] In 1720, a similar swindle scheme was carried out by the Mississippi Company in France. The bursting of these two bubbles left many banks, as well as investors who had purchased the companies' shares, in ruins.

Stock prices could often be pushed upward by speculative euphoria orchestrated by swindlers and condoned by the government. Stock prices keep rising until the price-to-earnings ratios reveal low dividend return, or until speculators and investors find it an opportune time to sell off and earn large capital gains. A selling wave triggers more selling and a rapid fall in prices as buyers refrain from buying, allowing prices to reach bottom levels. Speculators may engage in short selling with a view to buying shares at a lower price. A general collapse of stocks would cause loss of capital for investors and a wave of bank failures. Central banks intervene, lowering interest rates and injecting massive quantities of money to reinflate stock prices. Their intervention increases moral hazard, intensifies speculation, and paves the ground for a more severe financial disorder and inflation in the future.

Swindles in the stock markets or a market crash may have little impact on the economy when the stock market is small, where there are few listed companies, and where stocks are a negligible part of banks', firms', or households' assets. However, if stocks are a significant part of their portfolios, stock market crashes can wipe out a large part of the financial wealth of banks, firms, and households.[13] In countries without stock and mortgage markets, financial crises may affect the banking sector and result in the failure of banks. Many developing countries have seen their banks collapse because of bad loans; however, the impact on the economy was limited because financial intermediation was too shallow in these countries.

In industrialized countries, financial crises have simultaneously involved the banking sector and capital markets because of the deep relationships between the two and the importance of asset markets such as stocks, bonds, and mortgages. The transmission channels between these two sectors have become highly interconnected. An expansion of credit may create an economic boom, higher profits, and an appreciation of share prices. Similarly, an abundance of liquidity and low interest rates may lead to higher demand for shares or real estate and, therefore, an appreciation of asset prices. Stock markets play a great role in financial intermediation; similarly for bonds and mortgage markets. Rarely has a financial crisis occurred without simultaneously affecting the banking and asset markets. For instance, the end of the railroad boom in England and a correction of stock markets caused the financial crisis of 1847 and the bankruptcy of many companies and financing houses.

The Great Depression of 1929–35 provided an example of close interaction between the stock market, or asset markets, and the banking sector. Banks were highly exposed to stock markets, financing the speculative drive by affording credit to brokerage firms and share buyers, called broker loans or call money. Hence, they were using deposits in ways that were not appropriate, to finance or engage in speculative operations. Stocks were subject to the same speculative financing as in the South Sea Company Bubble, when they were sold on credit and buyers then sold them to repay loans and earn capital appreciation. Speculators and investors were essentially making gains from price appreciation and not from dividends, based on self-financing strategies.[14] Stock prices were appreciating at 30 percent per year during 1925–29. The Dow Jones Industrial Average rose from 100 in October 1924 to a peak of 381 in September 1929 (see Figure 1.1). The rate of appreciation far exceeded the annual interest rate of 4 percent. The speculative drive was left unchecked and was fueled with abundant liquidity and cheap loans collateralized by stocks until the bubble burst. Without credit, or swindle by traders, the speculative drive cannot be sustained. The degree of involvement of banks in the speculative drive was illustrated by losses suffered by banks, bank runs, and the failure of about 8,000 banks during 1930–33. To prevent more failures and bank runs, a bank holiday was imposed in many states, followed by a nationwide bank holiday. Stock prices continued their downturn until they hit 41.2 in July 1932. As was to be expected, the consequences in terms of decline in output and unemployment were onerous.

IV. ANATOMY OF FINANCIAL CRISES

Despite the rich literature on financial crises, policymakers and central bankers have consistently failed to predict or prevent the recurrence of financial crises, even though arguably all financial crises are years in the making. Policymakers tend to adopt rapidly expansionary monetary policies that allow asset bubbles to develop until they burst on their own with dramatic consequences for financial and banking stability, and more generally for the

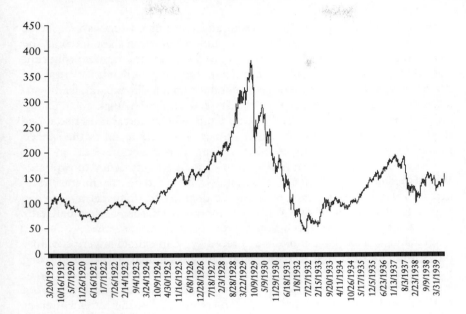

FIGURE 1.1 Dow Jones Industrial Average Index, 1919–39
Source: Dow Jones.

real economy. Rarely have financial tremors occurred without policymakers adopting a dominant role in furthering the crisis. The South Sea Company investigation revealed the close involvement of influential government officials in the speculative drive. Policymakers at times pretend that they cannot recognize an asset bubble until it bursts. Yet, there are many typical features of monetary policy, fiscal policy, credit, and asset prices that preceded every financial crisis. These typical patterns have been widely discussed in the literature and imply that a financial crisis is forecastable and that certain types of policies are likely to lead to financial instability.

Low interest rates

An extended period of low interest rates has been shown to be a main cause of monetary instability by a number of renowned economists, including Thornton (1802), Ricardo (1817), Marx (1894), Wicksell (1898), and Hayek (1931). With the advent of central banking, money interest rates are set by the central bank through its rediscount rate and open market operations. Thornton and Wicksell developed the doctrine of two interest rates, the money market rate and the natural rate of interest. The latter rate could be defined as the rate of profit in relation to invested capital, and depends on innovation, factor prices, and product prices, and may rise and decline with these factors. The money rate of interest is the cost of borrowed capital. The rate of profit cannot be observed and can only be estimated. On the one hand, if the rate of profit exceeds the interest rate, the demand for credit will expand, leading to a credit and economic boom. Prices will rise, setting off a Wicksellian cumulative inflationary process. On the other hand, when interest rates rise above the rate of profit, because of tighter money or simply a fall in the rate of profit, the demand for credit contracts and prices may decline.

Keynes (1936) advanced the notion of marginal efficiency of capital.[15] When the marginal efficiency of capital is higher than the interest rate, investment demand expands, as does the demand for loans to finance the higher level of investments. When the marginal efficiency of capital falls below the rate of interest, the demand for credit contracts.

Financial crises have often been preceded by an extended period of low interest rates that stirred a credit boom, rising economic growth, and rising prices (Hayek, 1931). For instance, the Great Depression was preceded by an epoch of low interest rates in the US and England. Interest rates fell from 8 percent in 1920 to 3 percent in 1924, and remained low thereafter. Different explanations were offered for these low rates. One such explanation was support by the US Fed for the Bank of England to maintain the pound sterling at its pre-war gold parity level. Hence, low interest rates in the US would not encourage migration of capital out of England. Low interest rates were also explained in terms of political pressure to protect farmers against high interest rates at a time when agricultural prices were depressed, and to preserve an economic boom. Consequently, economic growth was very high in the US, reaching 13 percent in 1923 and averaging 5 percent per year during 1922–29.

An extended period of low interest rates can also encourage speculative activities. Low interest rates reduce the cost of borrowing and thus the cost of speculation. Moreover, as low interest rates reduce the income of institutions and individuals that rely on fixed income revenues, invariably some institutions are encouraged to take on more risk in order to enhance revenues. At the same time, an extended period of low interest rates can freeze up the interbank market, especially lending to small local banks, and be accompanied by declining credit to medium businesses, or banks having to access alternative funding with higher interest expense, or both.

Credit expansion

Fisher (1933) argued that over-indebtedness precedes major financial crises. Enterprises borrow and expand capacity on the basis of expectations of higher profits. Credit expansion is a multiplicative process. A person who receives credit will not keep it idle while paying interest on it. The borrower will spend it immediately to earn profits. The seller of goods, services, and assets will deposit the proceeds of their sales in a bank. Hence, the loan becomes a deposit in a bank and creates excess reserves. Banks attempt to increase their loans and reduce their excess reserves by loaning the new deposits. Credit expansion takes place through the credit multiplier.[16] Credit expansion may be accompanied by an economic boom and resurging speculation. Both lead to higher demand for credit and renewed credit multiplication. Banks have turned to different innovations for increasing credit volume. They have issued promissory notes and bills of exchange that circulate as a means of payment and are settled in clearing houses. The amount of these loan documents increases rapidly during a credit boom. Securitization became a new innovation for increasing the amount of loans. Securitization consists of rendering long-term loans liquid by selling them in the form of marketable securities and bonds to investors. They enable a bank to issue new loans, manage liquidity, and tap investors' money without relying solely on traditional depositors' money. The bank gains in terms of loan commissions and fees, and on interest rate differentials between issued loans and issued securities.

Although credit is essentially based on scriptural money and is created by a stroke of the pen, banks may feel the pinch for liquidity when a maturity mismatch occurs as a result of higher-than-expected payments. They have recourse to interbank money markets using repo transactions. Increased reserve tightness will cause an increase in the interbank money markets. Banks may have recourse to rediscount at the central bank. The central bank has the option of taking away the "punch bowl," to use an expression of William McChesney Martin, Jr., US Fed chairman (1951–70), and forcing a credit deceleration, or it may expand the monetary base and accommodate the credit expansion through open market operations and rediscounts. Often, central banks have been reluctant to decelerate a credit boom, especially in the face of political pressures. In examining US Fed history, arguably only two chairmen, Martin and Volcker, adopted policies that were opposed by the party in power. Policymakers have generally allowed the boom to spiral into a systemic bankruptcy. Following the collapse of a credit boom, the central bank has to expand its monetary base even further in the form of bailouts of the banking system.

Asset price inflation: Share and real estate price inflation

Often, a financial crisis in an advanced banking system has been preceded by a speculative rise in the price of shares, commodities, and real estate. The Great Depression was preceded by a real estate boom, speculation in stock markets, and rapid appreciation of asset prices on the basis of easy broker loans collateralized by shares. The Japanese crisis of 1992–2000 was preceded by virulent speculation in asset and real estate markets and large appreciation of asset prices. The same developments were noted for Norway, Sweden, Thailand, South Korea, and many other countries that suffered financial tremors. The bursting of asset price bubbles would cause dramatic loss in financial wealth and, therefore, a loss for banks and individual wealth holders. Monetary policy in leading industrial countries has been geared to reinflate the asset bubble of the late 1990s and prevent a loss of wealth that could prove to be disruptive for the economy. However, the policy of low interest rates during 2001–04, while aimed at reinflating asset price bubbles, in part fostered the most severe crisis of the post-World War II period.

Commodity price inflation

Credit expansions and speculation have often sparked commodity price inflation. With the development of futures markets in industrialized countries, speculation has intensified in the commodity markets. A period of easy money would encourage speculation in commodities, especially during an economic boom when demand for raw materials by manufacturers and builders is rising. Classical economists have often cited inflation as a prelude to an economic crisis. In view of the limited size of stock markets, commodity price inflation was a main feature of the study of financial crises by classical economists. In an economic boom, the demand for goods increases. Demand is initially satisfied from inventories without a price rise. However, as inventories become low, companies are encouraged to increase their prices. Moreover, labor markets may become tight, and employers may compete for labor by increasing wages. Under a cost mark-up theory, higher wages would lead to higher prices. With the passing of the economic boom and the onset of credit contraction, prices and wages are depressed. Such is the typical trade cycle studied by classical economists, marked by fluctuations in business and sales, employment, and goods prices, with the economy gyrating from booms to recessions.

Fiscal deficits

Many of the financial crises in the past could be related to large fiscal deficits caused by wars or expansionary government spending. Wars have caused monetization of deficits, money printing, and high inflation. The gold standard ended in 1914 with the outbreak of World War I and the incipient monetization of large deficits. Wars caused financial disorders in the 18th, 19th, and 20th centuries. For instance, the Napoleonic Wars caused financial disorders in England and the suspension of convertibility of banknotes into gold. Large fiscal deficits absorb savings, constrain economic growth, and may cause governments to default on their debt or inflate their way out of debt by debasing money. The US fiscal deficits in the 1960s were seen as a source of monetary disorders in the 1970s. They could also be seen a source of instability that has led to the recent financial crisis of 2007–10. The monetization of the deficit and a regime of low interest rates to reduce interest payments on public debt provide liquidity and stimulate demand for credit.

Balance of payments deficits and exchange rate instability

Often, credit expansion translates into an external deficit. Under the gold standard, gold outflows, if not sterilized, would lead to a contraction of credit. If the central bank chooses to sterilize gold outflows through foreign borrowing or rediscount and open market operations, it would keep credit growing and external deficits widening. Countries that have reserve currencies run external deficits without tears and lose no real resources. There is no automatic stabilizer. External deficits in the case of a reserve currency are multiplicative. Holdings of US dollars by foreigners are repatriated and invested in US banks, leading to a further expansion of credit and, therefore, to even greater external deficits. Under the gold standard, a country cannot run increasing deficits. The US external deficits exerted pressure on US gold holdings, forcing the US to exit the Bretton Woods system in 1971 (which required the convertibility of the dollar into gold by the United States). The alternatives were to lose gold or force a credit contraction and an economic recession.

Exchange rate instability has frequently been a prelude to financial instability. The combination of low interest rates and growing external deficits may lead to a significant depreciation of a currency. A depreciating exchange rate would lead to higher inflation and instability. Under fixed exchange rates, an overvalued exchange rate could be a source of instability. The setting of the pound at pre-war parity was considered by Keynes as a source of instability and led to England's exit from the gold standard in 1931. The misalignment of exchange rates was seen as a source of instability that contributed to the Great Depression. Competitive devaluations intensified trade rivalry during the interwar period and antagonized relations among industrial countries. The appreciation of the Japanese yen in the late 1980s led the central bank to lower interest rates, with a protracted financial crisis following thereafter.

The anatomy of a crisis affords warning indicators for a crisis that may be brewing. Not all indicators of a financial crisis may be evident. For instance, the ongoing Japanese financial crisis occurred in the context of current account surpluses. In countries without asset markets, a financial crisis may occur even without credit expansion. Simply, the portfolios of a few banks were not sound. Policymakers may face a dilemma as to which indicators to monitor. Modern central banking has narrowed price indices to core price inflation, which excludes food and energy prices. The stability of this indicator at a low rate was considered a measure of success for a central bank in reining in inflation. This supposed success led to the 2000–08 era being dubbed an era of "Great Moderation," in contrast to the "Great Inflation" of the 1970s. Policymakers discarded housing price inflation, commodity price inflation, large external deficits, and exchange rate instability as a threat to financial stability. Some central bankers have even denied any relationship between low interest rates and housing price inflation. The core inflation essentially measures the price of industrial products. The rates of technical progress and productivity gains are high in many industrial lines. For instance, in electronics, the price of personal computers has fallen by 80 percent, a result not of lower profits but higher profits and technological change; cost, performance, and quality have improved in a fashion that is not commensurate with the first generation of personal computers. If the annual rate of technological progress in manufacturing were 10 percent, in order to have an inflation rate of 2 percent per annum in core inflation, the actual rate of inflation would have to be 12 percent.

The conflicting evolution of financial indicators was notorious prior to the Great Depression. The prices of shares and real estate were rising at a fast rate, while the Consumer Price Index (CPI) was flat and agricultural product prices were depressed. Policymakers were more worried about depressed farm prices than rising speculative share prices. It was deemed more important to ease monetary policy with a view to helping farmers, inflating agricultural prices, and preserving the economic boom than reining in stock market speculation. Similarly, central banks deliberately ignored asset price bubbles prior to the recent crisis of 2007–10, claiming that price stability, measured by core inflation, had been achieved and that tighter monetary policy would disrupt economic growth. With the bursting of asset price bubbles, central banks have adopted the most unorthodox monetary policies in the form of near-zero interest rates and expansion of the monetary base with a view to reinflating housing and share prices to their pre-crisis levels.

International history of financial crises

Reinhart and Rogoff (2009) and Reinhart (2010) have assembled and analyzed individual country data on financial crises over a period of eight centuries. Their main conclusions, in this very impressive study, are as follows:[17]

- Serial default is a widespread phenomenon across emerging markets and several advanced economies.

- Prior to World War II, serial banking crises in the advanced economies were the norm; as the larger emerging markets developed a financial sector in the late 1800s, these economies joined the "serial banking" crisis club.
- There is a similar serial pattern in International Monetary Fund (IMF) programs.
- Private debts typically surge prior to a banking crisis.
- Public debts may or may not surge ahead of a banking crisis.
- Banking crises most often either precede or coincide with sovereign debt crises.
- Public debts follow a repeated boom-bust cycle; much (if not most) of the bust phase involved a debt crisis in the emerging markets. Public sector borrowing surges as the crisis nears.
- Debts continue to rise after default, as arrears accumulate, and GDP contracts markedly.
- Short-term debts (public and private) escalate on the eve of the banking crisis and sovereign defaults.
- Private debts become public debts after the crisis.

Debt is at the core of all of these banking and financial crises. Banking and financial crises, in turn, have led to inflation and hyperinflation. Hyperinflation has invariably led in turn to a crisis in the real economy.

V. MORE REGULATION HAS NOT PREVENTED FINANCIAL CRISES

Financial tremors have, over time, devastated economic activity and forced governments to renew their search for stronger regulations that would avert the repeat of crises. The recent global financial crisis has again renewed the drive of governments to strengthen their supervisory and regulatory systems. Some have dubbed the modern financial system a "Grand Casino." Besides the traditional and regulated banking system, there are thousands of financial institutions such as hedge funds, mutual funds, and equity funds that are unregulated and do not fall under banking or any other regulatory system. The regulated and non-regulated financial institutions compete for profit opportunities and are prone to excessive risk taking. Non-regulated intermediaries do not face capital requirements and may indulge in excessive leverage. In addition to the multiplication of non-regulated intermediaries, there is a far-reaching multiplication of increasingly complex and exotic financial products. The multiplication of financial intermediaries and products is one facet of this financialization. Speculation has become a dominant activity, and volatility and uncertainty have reached unprecedented historical levels, heightening the risk of sizeable losses from asset price and exchange rate instabilities. While Schumpeterian technical innovations are conducive to greater economic growth, financial innovations have at times turned out to be conducive to greater instability, volatility, and economic uncertainty and disruption.

The debate for banking reform has contrasted the 18th- and 19th-century schools of thought: the Currency School, which has among its proponents David Ricardo; and the Banking School, whose proponents include John Law. The Currency School is so called for tying the issuance of currency to gold and premising its theory on the Quantity Theory of Money, relating the price level to the quantity of money in circulation. In contrast, the Banking School argued that the issuance of currency could be naturally restricted by the desire of bank depositors to redeem their notes for gold, and that the central bank should accommodate business needs for credit. Their theory is based on the "real bills doctrine," mainly that credit is extinguished once firms pay advances made by their banks. Following severe financial crises in England, the Currency School's recommendations, advocated by Lord Overstone, led to the 1844 Bank Charter Act, which had been passed by the Conservative government of Robert Peel. The Act separated the Bank of England into two departments: an issue department and a banking department. The issue of money became tied to gold flows, and not to banking and discount operations. As can be expected, the Act ended an era of easy money, causing an explosion of interest rates and a wave of bank failures in 1847. Under political pressure, the Act was suspended in 1848, allowing for easy money, low interest rates, and a series of financial crises in 1857, 1866, 1873, 1883, and 1890.

In the US, the bankers' panic of 1907 led to the establishment of the US Federal Reserve System in 1913 with a view to preventing the recurrence of financial crises of the past. Unfortunately, the Fed was not able to prevent the worst financial crisis in modern history—namely, the Great Depression. In the wake of financial collapse, hallmark reforms were introduced with the renewed objective of restoring financial stability. The National Credit Corporation (1931) and the Reconstruction Finance Corporation (1932) were created to provide loans to banks, for mortgages, agriculture, and industry. The 1933 Glass-Steagall Act, repealed in 1999, separated deposit and investment banking and created the Federal Deposit Insurance Corporation. Without government deposit insurance, banks were no longer able to attract depositors. The US Securities and Exchange Commission (SEC) was created in 1934 to regulate stock and derivative markets. The 1933 Banking Act, transferring policymaking from the New York Fed to the Federal Reserve Board in Washington, established the Federal Open Market Committee. The convertibility of the dollar was ended after the dollar was devalued relative to gold in 1934. These reforms were considered to have afforded the US financial system a long period of stability until the mid-1960s, when the early signs of financial instability began to reappear. Instability grew in the 1970s with the failures of Real Estate Investment Trusts (REITs), and built further momentum in the 1980s with the failure of savings and loans associations and a number of banking corporations. The number of bailouts became ominous. For instance, the bailouts of the savings and loans associations cost taxpayers about US$130 billion, resources that could have been invested by the government in health, education, and productive infrastructure enhancing social welfare and growth. The re-emergence of increasing instability since the mid-1960s, in turn, led Hyman Minsky (1986) to qualify the banking system as inherently unstable, with long-term stability building the stage for instability, which he called "unstable stability."

Despite far-reaching structural changes in the banking system, the drive to reform the system in the early 1930s fell short of the proposal, coined the "Chicago Reform Plan." It called for ending the monetary policy discretion of monetary authorities and proposed the adoption of rules for monetary policy (Fisher, 1936; Simons, 1948). The Chicago Plan addressed the essence of financial instability. It recognized two distinct roles of money: (i) as a medium of exchange and store of value; and (ii) for financial intermediation between savings and investment. Banks theoretically have the power to create and destroy money through the credit multiplier. The expansion of credit and money is coupled with rising prices and activity. The contraction of credit and money is coupled with bankruptcies, loss of wealth, deflation, and economic crisis. Such was the typical pattern of bank credit and monetary cycles in the past two centuries. Consequently, the Chicago Plan sought to isolate the money function of money from its intermediation function. The money function is carried by 100 percent reserve banking (thus, banks do not create money but accept it for safekeeping), and intermediation is carried by investment banking (such as mutual fund opportunities in a variety of companies and business ventures) with close matching of assets and liabilities. Thus, financial bankruptcy and illiquidity are totally sidestepped.

Over time, the authors of the Chicago Plan have gained followers, as the same factors that precipitated the Great Depression continue to remain in play; uncertainty and volatility have gone beyond tolerable limits, making investment decisions very difficult. With innovations such as securitization, the powers to create money and leverage have become boundless. Financialization in the form of multiplication of unregulated money funds and of complex financial products has been diverting huge wealth in favor of speculators and others in the financial sector, and at the expense of real producers and workers. Large financial gains have led to large and obscene pay packages and bonuses in the financial industry.

The immediate reaction to the recent devastating crisis was to strengthen the regulatory apparatus with the objective of achieving financial stability and preventing a recurrence of the crisis. In May 2010, the US Senate passed the bank reform bill titled "Restoring American Financial Stability," or the "Dodd-Frank Bill," which was designed to strengthen the regulation of banks and non-bank financial institutions, create a sound economic foundation for job growth, protect consumers, rein in Wall Street, end the policy of "too big to fail," and, ultimately, prevent another financial crisis. The bill introduced the Volcker Rule, which will force deposit-taking banks to spin off their proprietary trading arms (trading on their own account) and sell ownership interests in hedge funds and private equity firms. After a Senate–House conference committee ironed out differences between the two houses of Congress, President Obama, on July 21, 2010, signed into law the Dodd-Frank Wall Street Reform and Consumer Protection financial overhaul bill. The major provisions of the bill are: a new consumer watchdog; a financial early warning system; breakup authority of financial institutions; a tighter leash on financial firms; and mortgage reform. In our opinion, the bill, which has been hailed as the most significant set of financial reforms since World War II, fails to address the future of Fannie Mae and Freddie Mac and, most importantly, does little to prevent the next financial crisis.

VI. THE ROLE OF CENTRAL BANKS IN FINANCIAL INSTABILITY

The reform drive in the wake of the recent crisis has largely sidestepped the role of central banks in financial crises. Counterfactual questions would be: would the crisis have occurred if the US Fed had maintained the federal funds rate at 6 percent or higher and restrained the monetary base, instead of forcing interest rates to 1 percent and expanding the monetary base? The debate on the issue of monetary reforms has been diverse and conflicting in respect to central banking and monetary policy, and has been dominated by both political and economic views. A dominant strand has empowered central banks with the mandate of creating jobs and ensuring full employment. In pursuing this objective, the stability of the financial system may become a secondary consideration. In the US, the Full-Employment Act of 1946 obligates the US central bank to pursue the full-employment objective. Supporters of this doctrine have advocated a discretionary monetary policy, which can be summarized by the Taylor rule: The central bank reduces interest rates inversely with the unemployment rate, so that the higher the unemployment rate, the lower the interest rate. The central bank injects as much liquidity as is required to force interest rates to the targets decided by the central bank, irrespective of the quality of credit and risk for banks.

In contrast to discretionary monetary policy is the doctrine of fixed money rule (Simons, 1948; Friedman, 1959), whereby the central bank controls monetary aggregates without exceeding a ceiling implied by a fixed growth rate or a target zone for credit and money supply. The advocates of this doctrine claim that the central bank can control only monetary aggregates and not unemployment or interest rates. Its primary objective is to safeguard the soundness of the banking system. Their argument is that a fixed rule will not totally eliminate instability; however, it will preserve the financial system from uncontrolled growth of credit and violent instability as experienced during frequent financial crises.

Besides achieving the objective of full employment, some modern central banks operate as if they have also been assigned the objective of reinflating asset price bubbles to prevent a loss of financial wealth. The aggressive role of central banks during 2001–04 in reinflating stock prices and preserving employment succeeded in inducing an economic boom, but at the same it intensified speculation and precipitated financial chaos and the even bigger financial crisis that exploded in 2007. Trillions of dollars in bailouts and the loss of employment and growth may far outweigh the short-lived gains of an economic boom. This is, in the end, an empirical question, which requires careful investigation.

Those that advocate a fixed money rule see the setting of the interest rates by the central bank as a form of price control, which can cause significant distortions in the economy. A prolonged period of low interest rates and monetary expansion necessarily promotes speculation and over-leveraging, just as cheap beer and meat promotes drunkenness and gluttony. Speculation becomes entrenched in the asset and commodity markets when speculators are no longer constrained by liquidity. Real estate, commodities, equities, and exchange rates become subject to speculation. The quality of credit deteriorates as more credit is pushed to sub-prime markets or when borrowers face no limit on their borrowing. The structure of demand is altered in violation of Say's law of markets: demand is no longer equal to income flows arising from the production process; rather, it exceeds income by the amount of fictitious credit that is not backed by savings. Industries and sectors that face rising demand plan to expand their production capacity; however, when the credit boom is bankrupted, they find themselves with excess capacity and high production costs and have to resort to layoffs.

In addition to price distortions and the misallocation of resources, cheap monetary policy causes a far-reaching redistribution of wealth in favor of borrowers and speculators, and amounts to an inflation tax. The latter can reach disproportionate levels, such as in 2007–10, and may trigger energy and food riots when these vital products become too expensive for the average person.

Although a laudable and certainly prime objective of economic development, employment should not be a mandate of a central bank. Employment depends in large part on capital accumulation and technical change in the economy. Education and training are essential elements of any employment strategy. The structure of the labor market evolves with technical change and economic development. New skills are needed as new industries appear. Cyclical unemployment results from a number of sources, including a financial crisis. Hayek (1931) contended that such cyclical unemployment could not be repaired through expansionary policies. The pre-crisis demand for consumption and investment was distorted by fictitious and abnormal credit that could not be repaid. If the state hires workers to dig holes, such an approach will not solve cyclical unemployment in the car industry. Similarly, if the central bank reduces interest rates and forces loans on households for buying houses and durable goods, these loans cannot be serviced and repaid. In other words, there are serious dangers and implications for an economy when the financial sector and the real sector become de-linked and go their separate ways. This, we believe, is a major source of economic crisis and will be discussed in greater detail in Chapter 2 and throughout this book.

VII. INTERNATIONAL FINANCIAL INSTABILITY

Countries are linked through trade and capital flows. Instability in one country is transmitted to other countries via trade and capital flows, and sometimes through labor movements and remittances.

The devastating effects of exchange rate instability during the Great Depression led to reform of the international payments system in 1944, which established the Bretton Woods fixed exchange rates system and created the International Monetary Fund. The objective of the Bretton Woods agreement was to impose policy discipline on countries, avoid competitive devaluations, and provide temporary balance of payments finance for countries facing external deficits without resorting to disruptive adjustments and devaluations. The pursuit of full-employment and growth objectives in reserve currencies led to unduly high expansion of fiscal and external deficits. For the Bretton Woods system to work, countries had to coordinate policies or readily change the parity of their currencies relative to gold and thus to the US dollar. However, countries were reluctant to follow the economic policies adopted by the United States, a necessity for fixed exchange rates to be maintained; and the US was unwilling to change its policies to satisfy the economic and financial needs of other countries, mainly Western Europe and Japan. This had led again to competitiveness and currency speculation, and forced frequent currency devaluations in the 1960s. The fixed exchange rate system collapsed with the exit of the US from the Bretton Woods system in 1971.

The floating exchange rate system that replaced the Bretton Woods system has led to greater financial and exchange rate instability. It contributed to high commodity price inflation in the 1970s, as well as to high inflation rates in leading industrial countries. Countries have again become entangled in competitive devaluations and beggar-thy-neighbor policies. Expansionary policy in one country is met by countervailing monetary expansion in a rival country. The rapid depreciation of the US dollar following the 1985 Plaza Accord eroded Japan's external competitiveness. Japan responded by reducing its interest rates and adopting an expansionary monetary policy with a view to depreciating its currency and restoring its external competitiveness, as its economy was heavily dependent on exports. Low interest rates led to powerful speculation in real estate and stock markets, followed by bankruptcies and bailouts. The Japanese crisis affected the advanced Asian countries. The Asian crisis in turn affected the Russian economy, which led to the collapse of LTCM (Long Term Capital Management). Contagion then spread to the US, causing a downturn in share prices.

Exchange rate instability increased with aggressive monetary policies around the world during 2001–10. The financial crisis that followed these policies was contagious and affected many leading industrial countries simultaneously. Although its epicenter was the meltdown of sub-prime credit in the United States, the crisis mutated into a public debt crisis in a number of developed countries, such as Greece, Ireland, Portugal, and Spain.

Numerous reforms have been advocated for the international payments system. Proposals made by Triffin (1960) led to the creation of the special drawing rights (SDR) as a reserve currency to supplement other reserve currencies. Rueff's (1964) proposals called for simply restoring the gold standard as it had prevailed before 1914. Keynes (1943) called for creating a world currency, called the bancor, emitted by an international clearing union. Other proposals have called for creating a world currency pegged to the price of a basket of internationally traded commodities. The 2007–10 crisis has led to a number of efforts towards reform. However, none of these recent reforms addresses the international payments system, the reform of which is a pressing concern. Exchange rate instability inflicts large losses on firms that export or import, investors, and immigrant workers when exchange rates go into wide gyrations. Absent substantial reform of the system, international financial instability is likely to grow.

VIII. CONCLUSION

In this chapter, we have presented a brief history of financial crises and an overview of the theories put forward to explain them. The anatomy of financial crises shows that crises are generally predictable and are in the making for a number of years before they erupt. Crises are invariably preceded by typical developments such as low interest rates, fast credit expansion, rapid asset price increases that defy fundamental explanations, asset bubbles, and exchange rate instability that can only culminate in a financial crisis. Debt and its uncontrolled growth are invariably at the core of banking and financial crises.

Policymakers are cheered by the short-lived success of expansionary monetary policy; however, they seem to be unaware of the chaos that is almost certain to follow. A bull market is cheered on by the media and policymakers and is considered a policy success. But when this is followed by attempts to restrain credit expansion, it is invariably met by strong opposition from politicians and financial markets. Bubbles burst on their own. The recurrence of financial crises led Minsky to qualify the conventional system as inherently unstable. By pushing debt to high levels, banks face imminent and unavoidable losses on their assets. Additional regulations have not prevented the recurrence of financial crises. Financial innovations have subverted regulations and turned into a financialization of the economy.

The future cannot be very different from the past if we continue just to patch up our current financial system. The vicious circle of financial instability, which is centuries old, is likely to continue into the future if we try the same old standard remedies that have proven ineffective. Patching up the present system will solve very little. If this is what we do, then we are bound to be classified as insane if one accepts the definition of that term proposed by Benjamin Franklin: "Insanity is doing the same thing over and over and expecting different results."

Each financial crisis inflicts a heavy toll in terms of loss of wealth and lowered economic growth, followed by high unemployment and all the human and social suffering that goes with it, invariably leading to high inflation down the road, mounting bailouts that tend to socialize private losses, with a large segment of the population having to pay for sins they did not commit and a tremendous burden placed on future generations, and transmitting instability to much of the world through diminished trade and long-term capital flows. Yet, we keep going down the same road and patching up the system that we have: "better" and "more" regulation; "better" and "more" supervision; prohibiting instruments and practices that are "newly" discovered to be disruptive; slapping the wrists of a few sacrificial culprits; marginally increasing some safety standards (such as capital), and the like.

But still conventional finance continues to survive from crisis to crisis because of strong government subsidies and support in terms of money creation, bailouts, and deposit insurance. Why? Entrenched special interests will not permit a full and fundamental examination of our financial system. Others argue that the conventional financial system is most conducive to enhancing economic growth. Yet this is an empirical question that has not been studied. What is the trade-off of a financial system with rapid growth, followed by a financial crisis and all that comes with it, versus a financial system that is immune to crises but induces slower and steady economic growth?

A risk-sharing financial system—one that is based on equity finance as opposed to debt—is, in our view, substantially immune to the financial crises that plague the conventional financial system. This is the case simply because it is free of the causes that have led to crises in the conventional system: interest, excessive debt creation and leverage, and speculation. The substitution of equity financing (and risk sharing) for debt and predetermined interest removes the fodder of financial crises. In a risk-sharing financial system, banks cannot create and destroy money; there is no credit multiplication. Since there is no interest rate, the remuneration of capital is determined by the rate of profit and cannot be distorted by central banks, as in conventional finance. In a risk-sharing system, the financial sector and the real sector are seen as closely linked, with both having to grow in tandem. Although the control of debt creation does not require 100 percent reserve banking (as in the Chicago Plan), 100 percent reserve banking is one approach that effectively controls debt multiplication and leveraging. Economic growth and employment are sustained and stable, and do not go through booms and busts. Investors and savers are brought more closely together, while preserving social justice. We believe that cumulative economic growth will be proven to be higher than that under the boom-and-bust cycle of the conventional system.

In the following chapters, we hope to show the desirability of a financial system based along the lines advocated in Islam. We hope also to address a related issue—namely, the increasing divergence of the financial and real sectors in the conventional system and the increasing dominance of the financial sector through what has been coined financialization. Finally, we will describe how a complete financial system can be developed along the lines advocated in Islam.[18]

ENDNOTES

1. A number of the best economic minds in the United States created this reform plan. Although the principal author was Henry Simons, he was supported in his efforts by Paul Douglas, and by a number of other renowned economists from other universities such as Irving Fisher, Frank Graham, and Charles Whittlesley. The plan was in fact broadly supported by a majority of the US academic

economists who studied it. More recently, in 1948, Maurice Allais published a book in support of the Chicago Plan; and Milton Friedman endorsed the plan in various forums, including congressional testimony, in 1975. The plan would replace the fractional reserve banking system by a 100 percent (in announced step increases of reserves requirement) reserve system of banking on checking accounts, eliminating the ability of banks to create money through the money multiplier; instead, banks would be warehousing and transferring money and would charge a fee for their services. The lending activity of banks would be separated, and banks would no longer be exposed to an asset–liability management conundrum (borrowing short and lending long), as lending would be matched by savings (investment) deposits of similar maturity; thus the distinction between money and credit would become clearly established.

2. The instability of the conventional system is firmly established in the *Qur'an*. Many verses have made interest strictly forbidden. In Chapter 2, verse 276, Allah says: "Allah will destroy interest and will give increase to charity and alms." In 2:278–9, "O you who believe, be conscious of Allah and give up what remains due to you from interest if you are believers. And if you do not do it, then take a notice of war from Allah and His Messenger."

3. For instance, the bailout of the savings and loan associations in the US in the late 1980s cost taxpayers US$130 billion. Such vast resources could have been spent directly on enhancing education, health, and productive infrastructure, which in turn would have increased welfare and economic growth.

4. Greenspan injected massive liquidities in 1987 following a stock market crash to reinflate share prices, sparking inflation in the late 1980s. He repeatedly injected liquidity in support of asset prices, bailed out banks, and organized the rescue of the hedge fund Long Term Capital Management. In 2001–04, he forced interest rates to record lows in order to reinflate share prices. For this reason, his bailouts and monetary policy became known as a put option, or portfolio insurance, whereby traders feel secure in the sale price of their assets.

5. Keynes did not analyze the structure of demand. The component of demand that has imploded was demand financed by credit, such as cars, houses, durable goods, and investment goods. Government expenditures may succeed in increasing demand for wage-goods, but not the demand that was previously inflated by credit, such as demand for housing, durables, and capital goods. The sectors that relied on credit for the sale of their products may continue to suffer unemployment and excess capacity even in the presence of an expansionary fiscal policy. Their demand can be restored only through credit expansion, which will lead to renewed crisis. For instance, since 2007 the housing industry in the US has remained depressed despite record fiscal deficits and unorthodox monetary policy.

6. Loss of deposits was common before the enactment of the government deposit insurance schemes.

7. Governments in many countries now provide deposit insurance. For instance, the Federal Deposit Insurance Corporation in the US was created in 1933 following devastating losses by depositors. The creation of deposit insurance became necessary to re-establish confidence in the banking system and allow it to grow.

8. The crisis was triggered by the failed attempt in October 1907 to corner the market on stock of the United Copper Company. When this bid failed, banks that had lent money to the cornering scheme suffered runs that later spread to affiliated banks and trusts, leading a week later to the downfall of the Knickerbocker Trust Company—New York City's third-largest trust. The collapse of the Knickerbocker spread fear throughout the city's trusts as regional banks withdrew reserves from New York City banks. Panic extended across the United States as vast numbers of people withdrew deposits from their regional banks.

9. "The important points are:
   - As traditional banking became unprofitable in the 1980s, due to competition from, most importantly, money market mutual funds and junk bonds, securitization developed. Regulation Q that limited the interest rate on bank deposits was lifted, as well. Bank funding became much more expensive. Banks could no longer afford to hold passive cash flows on their balance sheets. Securitization is an efficient, cheaper, way to fund the traditional banking system. Securitization became sizable.
   - The amount of money under management by institutional investors has grown enormously. These investors and non-financial firms have a need for a short-term, safe, interest-earning, transaction account like demand deposits: repo. Repo also grew enormously, and came to use securitization as an important source of collateral.
   - Repo is money. It was counted in M3 by the Federal Reserve System until M3 was discontinued in 2006. But, like other privately-created bank money, it is vulnerable to a shock, which may cause depositors to rationally withdraw en masse, an event which the banking system—in this case the shadow banking system—cannot withstand alone. Forced by the withdrawals to sell assets, bond prices plummeted and firms failed or were bailed out with government money.
   - In a bank panic, banks are forced to sell assets, which causes prices to go down, reflecting the large amounts being dumped on the market. Fire sales cause losses. The fundamentals of subprime were not bad enough by themselves to have created trillions in losses globally. The mechanism of the panic triggers the fire sales. As a matter of policy, such firm failures should not be caused by fire sales.
   - The crisis was not a one-time, unique, event. The problem is structural. The explanation for the crisis lies in the structure of private transaction securities that are created by banks. This structure, while very important for the economy, is subject to periodic panics if there are shocks that cause concerns about counterparty default. There have been banking panics throughout U.S. history, with private bank notes, with demand deposits, and now with repo. The economy needs banks and banking. But bank liabilities have a vulnerability." See Gorton (February 2010).

10. Bloomberg, June 1, 2010.

11. Following the bursting of the South Sea Bubble, Sir Isaac Newton lost £20,000 and lamented: "I can calculate the motions of the heavenly bodies but not the madness of people." The Bishop of Norwich more polemically

wrote that: "[T]he collapse was divine judgment on the universal inclination of all ranks of men and women too to excessive gaming which led to the occasion of bringing such a curse and blast upon us, as never was felt before by this Nation; by which we have been all of a sudden strangely impoverished in the midst of plenty, our riches having made themselves wings, and flying away nobody knows whither, and more families and single persons have been undone and ruined than hardly ever were known to have been so, by the most tedious and lingering war." Fearing the disastrous effects of an unstable banking system, the US President Thomas Jefferson wrote in 1802: "I believe that banking institutions are more dangerous to our liberties than standing armies. If the American people ever allow private banks to control the issue of their currency, first by inflation, then by deflation, the banks and corporations that will grow up around the banks will deprive the people of all property until their children wake-up homeless on the continent their fathers conquered."

12. The South Sea Bubble provided an example of inflating share price through talking up the profit potential of the South Sea Company and through a wave of "speculating frenzy." The share price had risen from £128 in January 1720, to £175 in February, £330 in March, and £550 in May. The price finally reached £1,000 in August and the level of selling was such that the price started to fall, dropping back to £100 per share before the end of 1720, triggering bankruptcies among those who had bought shares on credit, and increased selling of shares. Company failures extended to banks and goldsmiths, as they could not collect loans made on the stock, and thousands of individuals were ruined. Investigation in 1721 revealed widespread fraud among the company directors and corruption in the cabinet of the government in power.

13. The Souk-Al-Manakh stock market crash in Kuwait in 1982 caused financial losses of about US$73 billion and devastated the portfolios of banks and households, pushing the Kuwaiti economy into a deep economic recession.

14. Irving Fisher (1936) compared the broker loans to Liberty bonds. Subscribers to Liberty bonds make no payments when they purchase a bond. The bond is used as collateral for bank credit to finance the bond. The subscriber to the bond earned an interest differential between the bond and loan interest rates, and capital gains when and if the bond appreciated.

15. Marginal efficiency of capital, or equivalently, internal rate of return, is introduced by Keynes in *The General Theory of Employment, Interest, and Money* (1936), p. 135. It is defined as the discount rate that would equate the present value of the returns of an investment equal to the cost of the investment.

16. The credit multiplier, m, is defined as $m = 1/r$ where r is the ratio of reserves to deposits.

17. See pp. 10–13.

18. It should be noted that neither the *Qur'an* nor the Tradition of the Prophet (pbuh) stipulates anything about fractional reserve banking. The requirement is instead for risk sharing and the prohibition of interest-based debt.

CHAPTER 2

Financialization and the Decoupling–Recoupling Hypotheses

I. DEFINITION OF FINANCIALIZATION

The financial crisis that originated in the United States in 2007 and quickly spread to most of the other industrial countries is, undoubtedly, the most severe financial and economic crisis to affect the global economy since the Great Depression of the 1930s. The US and European financial systems may have been saved from total collapse and disintegration by costly bailouts, by government treasuries and central banks, and by unorthodox fiscal and monetary policies in the form of record fiscal deficits, near-zero interest rates, and the purchase of toxic assets financed by printing money. While the direct cost of the bailouts has been largely passed on to average taxpayers, the fallout of the financial crisis is not limited to financial bailouts and government stimuli. Lost economic output, and social pain and dislocation, will continue to have immeasurable consequences for a number of advanced economies and for future generations.

The crisis has been explained by some as a culmination of a long process of "financialization" of industrial economies that was left unchecked, despite numerous warnings in the previous three decades and especially beginning in the 1990s. The concept of financialization has been defined in various ways that emphasize three basic elements or characteristics: (i) fast expansion of financial institutions and products outside traditional banking and traditional instruments, without which financialization could not have thrived;[1] (ii) a significant expansion of the financial sector relative to the real sector as reflected in a number of variables such as share in GDP, share of corporate profits, higher rate of return on equity, and the like; and (iii) an expansion that was not beneficial to the broader economy and may have even turned out to be harmful for longer-term economic growth. In fact, besides bringing on the worst financial crisis since the Great Depression, the economic consequences of financialization may be summarized as: (i) a drop in the share of wages and non-financial profits in the national income; (ii) a consequent drop in fixed capital investment in the non-financial sectors of the economy; (iii) tepid economic growth of the real economy; (iv) intensification of speculation; (v) increased bankruptcies; (vi) increased economic distortions; (vii) significant economic and financial uncertainty; and (viii) increased and more diverse social inequities, including a worsening of income distribution.

The financial sectors of leading industrial countries have become dichotomized. These financial systems embrace, on the one hand, traditional instruments such as shares and bonds; and on the other hand, non-traditional instruments such as financial derivatives. They include traditional banking and unregulated banking. The latter comprises money market funds, institutional investors, hedge funds, mutual funds, equity funds, finance companies, and insurance companies. The competition for financial resources (such as deposits) and for income opportunities between traditional and non-regulated financial intermediaries has become intense, leading both segments of the financial system to devise innovations that increase their access to resources and to income-earning assets, and at times promoting unwarranted speculation and risk taking.

Financialization has fueled an explosion of financial activities in the form of non-regulated financial institutions, and phenomenal growth of financial engineering and complex financial products, incorporating the power to create money through debt (leveraging) with little regard for risk standards. Besides its traditional and beneficial role of intermediation between savers and investors, the financial sector has sprawled its activities into proprietary trading and speculation and in the process has become dangerously over-leveraged. Financialization has led to the development of shadow banking, securitized or parallel banking, the purpose of which is to increase the availability of resources for the traditional banking sector. This shadow banking includes: (i) bank conduits—namely, special investment vehicles (SIVs), special purpose vehicles (SPVs), and limited purpose finance corporations (LPFCs); and (ii) securitizations that cover asset-backed securities (ABSs), residential mortgage-backed securities (RMBS), commercial mortgage-backed securities (CMBS), auto-loans-backed securities, collateralized loan obligations (CLOs), collateralized bond obligations (CBOs), and collateralized debt obligations (CDOs). Derivatives such as credit default swaps (CDSs) were invented in order to spread risk and push traditional banks into higher-risk lending and related activities. Securitization has created derivatives based on existing debt with the purpose of increasing and tapping dormant liquidity. However, in the end it turned into the practice of selling toxic loans to investors using fraudulent practices, such as rating contaminated and risky CDOs as AAA securities. Opacity replaced transparency, and investors could not know the "fair" price of the securities they were trading.

In short and more broadly, financialization is a process whereby financial markets, financial institutions, and financial elites gain greater influence over economic policy and economic outcomes. Financialization transforms the functioning of economic systems at both the macro and micro levels. There are reasons to believe that financialization may put the economy at risk of debt deflation and prolonged recession. To Epstein (2005), financialization refers to the increasing importance of financial markets, financial motives, financial institutions, and financial elites in the operation of the economy and its governing institutions, both at the national and international level. Krippner (2005) defined financialization as a pattern of accumulation in which profit making occurs increasingly through financial channels, rather than through trade and commodity production. Palley (2007) contended that the notion of financialization covers a wide range of phenomena: (i) the deregulation of the financial sector and the proliferation of new financial instruments; (ii) the liberalization of international capital flows and increasing instability on exchange rate markets; (iii) a shift to market-based financial systems; (iv) the emergence of institutional investors as major players on financial markets and the cycle of boom and bust on asset markets; (v) shareholder value orientation and changes in corporate governance of non-financial business; and (vi) increased access to credit by previously "under-banked" groups or changes in the level of real interest rates.

The process of financialization, it is argued, expands access to finance, thus relaxing and reducing the role and importance of financial constraints. Financialization transforms illiquid financial assets into asset classes that are traded in various asset markets. When a financial sector is dominated by interest rate-based debt contracts, the financialization process creates more and more debt as it expands throughout the economy, converting equity in real assets into debt. This was the case in the early stages of the housing boom in the United States, where excess liquidity and low interest rates created an incentive for homeowners to cash out equity built up in their homes through refinancing. The cashed-out equity was largely used to support a consumption boom and masked the deteriorating income distribution in the US. By emphasizing debt multiplication and relaxing risk standards, financialization has resulted in rapidly growing corporate debt-to-equity ratios and household debt-to-income ratios, acceleration of dominance of the financial sector relative to the real sector, income transfer from the real sector to the financial sector, deterioration of income distribution and increased income inequality, and changes in the economy from a saving–investment– production–export orientation to a borrowing–debt–consumption–import orientation.

II. THE ANATOMY OF FINANCIALIZATION

A number of interrelated factors have promoted financialization in the advanced economies and, most poignantly, in the United States, including deregulation, lax supervision and enforcement, implicit government subsidies, and accommodating monetary policies.

Financial deregulation in the form of the Gramm-Leach-Bliley Act (also referred to as the Financial Services Modernization Act) in 1999 opened the floodgates of the "anything goes" mentality to the financial sector. Principally, the Glass-Steagall Act was repealed, thus enabling commercial banks, investment banks, and insurance companies to form any combination of these activities, hitherto separated, into one entity. For example, banks were now able to take investment banking risk and investment banks to accept deposits. As the financial sector became deregulated, supervision and enforcement, which should have become more vigilant, became instead more relaxed. A number of financial entities took unwarranted risks and leveraged their capital to unprecedented multiples. The assumption of risk was in part promoted by the emergence of higher funding costs that resulted from interest-bearing deposit options (such as money market funds) for depositors and the resulting competition for funding. At the same time, as low interest rates reduced banking profits, banks took on added risk to enhance their revenues.

While calculated risk might have been tolerated, financial institutions resorted to even illegal financial practices to increase their profits. Although these practices may have temporarily increased the profits of financial institutions and threatened the stability of the entire financial system, governments have allowed all manner of financial mergers to create mega-institutions and then provided these large financial institutions with an implicit subsidy to balloon their profits even more. The subsidy has been afforded to the large financial institutions that are referred to as "too big to fail." This implicit subsidy, guaranteeing the financial institution its solvency no matter the level of risk it assumes, has created moral hazard, effectively reducing the funding costs of these institutions and creating an important barrier to entry and thus to competition in the financial sector. As a result of these and other practices, for example, the return to equity achieved by British banks has increased from an average of 7 percent between 1921 and 1971 to an average of 20 percent today.[2] In addition, many categories of financial institutions, such as hedge funds, escaped all regulations while benefiting from the above-mentioned implicit government subsidy. In the case of hedge funds, in addition to escaping regulation and receiving the protection of "too big to fail," they have been afforded preferential tax treatment in the United States. Namely, the managers of hedge funds and private equity firms are allowed to treat a significant part of their compensation as capital gains (taxed at 15 percent) as opposed to ordinary income (taxed at 35 percent). The special treatment of the financial industry in the US and attendant benefits were promoted and protected by intense lobbying.

A defining feature of financialization has been an increase in the volume of debt via proliferation of unregulated intermediaries and rapid expansion in the trading of derivatives. There has been no apparent, or perceived, limit to the increasing ratio of debt to GDP, as if any higher and higher levels of debt could be easily serviced. In other words, a savings rate, say at 10 percent of GDP, could service any level of debt that could be many times the size of GDP. Data for the US show that non-financial sector debt rose from 140 percent of GDP in 1978 to 243 percent in 2009. Total debt of the non-financial and financial sector rose from 158 percent of GDP in 1978 to 353 percent in 2009. The debt of the financial sector rose from 18 percent of GDP in 1978 to 110 percent in 2009. The financial sector debt represents non-deposit liabilities of financial institutions. It represents essentially bonds, securitization, and commercial paper issued by financial institutions. Household debt rose from 48 percent of GDP in 1978 to 95 percent in 2009, after peaking to 98 percent of GDP in 2007.

Such an expansion of debt could not be innocuous. It changed macroeconomic equilibrium in a very profound way and caused widespread distortions in the broader economy. For example, the increasing assumption of debt enabled households to spend far above their incomes. Consumption, both public and private, rose at very high rates. Data for the US showed that household saving rates fell to close to zero in 2007, while net national savings—defined as savings of households, business, and government, excluding depreciation charges—became largely negative in 2009, at about 2.5 percent of GDP. The difference between consumption and national output required external borrowing. Thus the US current account deficit widened to 6–7 percent of GDP during 2005–07, remained at 4 percent in 2009, and was expected to be ominous for the US for many years into the future (Bergsten, 2009). At the macroeconomic level, the era of financialization has been associated with generally tepid economic growth. Gross investment spending as a share of GDP has exhibited a declining trend. When "speculation dominates enterprise," as Keynes put it, investment is often poorly allocated and society is poorly served. Consequently, real economic growth has slowed down in most industrial countries, with a long stagnation in countries that used to be strong growth performers such as Japan. Subsequent to the financial crisis in 2007, real economic growth became negative in most industrial countries. Thus the financial and real sectors significantly parted ways some time ago. There is today little or no association between the growths of the two sectors. And the financial sector has become pre-eminent.

Another inherent feature of financialization is speculation and ensuing bubbles, both supported by a loose monetary policy. Without speculation and high price volatility, financial intermediaries cannot extract profits from the real sector. The unlimited expansion of debt and credit led to pressure on prices, particularly on asset prices such as stocks, housing, commodities, and exchange rates. The demand for goods and assets is financed by abundant credit at low interest rates, not from income, with the result that pressure builds up in asset prices.

Thus, financialization has been associated with destructive bubbles in the 1980s, 1990s, and 2000s. A number of key factors leading to these bubbles can be identified: (i) as postulated by Keynes and Minsky, the inherent nature of financial markets leads to speculation, herding, and instability; (ii) the increasing importance of the privatization of the savings system, which leads individual investors to search for higher returns and take on riskier investments, increases their susceptibility to rumors and misinformation; (iii) the increasing role of institutional investors and the role of mutual funds increases the concentration of information and incentives for herding; (iv) the "Greenspan Put," by which the Federal Reserve appeared to place a floor under equities; (v) the rise to power of a faction of financial capital, Wall Street Finance, who are able to influence regulatory and central bank policy to keep the bubble going; and (vi) macroeconomic theory, which has supported an optimistic view of financial markets through q-theory (Brainard and Tobin, 1977).[3]

In the early stages of the growth of a debt-dominated financial system there is a tenuous relationship between financing and real sector investment as entrepreneurs compare the expected rate of return to the investment project and the rate of interest. As financialization proceeds and debt securitization grows in sophistication, the relationship becomes progressively less important. As the financial sector grows to dominate the real sector, layer upon layer of securitization weakens the connection between the two to the point where an inverted pyramid of debt is supported by a very narrow base—that is, the real sector's output. Overwhelming dominance of the financial sector over the real sector can be discerned by noting that the ratio of global financial assets to the annual global output of goods and services grew from 109 percent in 1980 to 316 percent in 2005. Similarly, while total world GDP was about US$48 trillion in 2006, the value of global financial assets in the same year was US$140 trillion (nearly three times as much). As of 2007, the global liquidity market was estimated to be 12.5 times global GDP. Financial derivatives constituted 80 percent of this liquidity.

The warning signs of such an eventual implosion had been around long before the recent crisis of 2007–10. Indeed, five years before the event, it was observed (Mirakhor, 2002):

While the financial innovations of the 1990s in the conventional system have led to mobilization of financial resources in astronomical proportions, they have also led to equally impressive growth of debt contracts and instruments. According to the latest reports, there are now US$32 trillion of sovereign and corporate bonds alone. Compare this (plus all other forms of debt, including consumer debt in industrial countries) to the production and capital base of the global economy, and one observes an inverted pyramid of huge debt piled up on a narrow production base that is supposed to generate income flows that are to serve this debt. In short, this growth in debt has nearly severed the relationship between finance and production. Analysts are now worried about a "debt bubble." For each dollar worth of production there are thousands of dollars of debt claims.

The succeeding five years made this picture far more ominous, as debt grew further with a growth rate that dwarfed that of global real economic output. For example, by 2007, credit default swaps alone had grown to more than US$50 trillion, as compared to the total US GDP of US$14 trillion.

In short, financialization has transformed productive economic activities into pursuits that resemble participation in a gambling casino, as Keynes remarked, using real resources but producing no real output, and no productive investment (Hirshleifer, 1971). Such an economy produces "rolling bubbles" in financialized assets. As one bubble bursts, finance moves to another. Such has been the case over the past three decades, as bubbles were created and then imploded in emerging market debt, dotcoms, real estate, and commodities markets. Investments in real productive activities were not the primary objective of debt and credit expansion in any of these financial bubble-building episodes. It was the expectations of higher prices of financial assets that attracted participants in droves as they speculated to build bubbles that were destined to burst. That this would happen was analytically demonstrated as early as the 1980s. For example, Flood and Garber (1980) demonstrated that rational individuals participate in asset price bubbles if they have expectations of rising asset prices. Growth in liquidity, low interest rates, higher leverage, and rapidly expanding credit, combined with regulatory–supervisory forbearance and passivity, accelerate the emergence and growth of bubbles.

III. INCOME DISTRIBUTION

During the last three or so decades, many observers have commented on the stagnation in the real incomes of a majority of Americans and the widening gap between rich and poor to levels not seen since the days of the "Robber Barons" in the late 19th and early 20th centuries. Financialization may have played an important role in the growing income and wealth disparity in the US. As far as income distribution is concerned, financialization means an increase in the income share of rentiers—in particular, a rise in rentiers' income from dividends—at the expense of firms' retained profits or wage income. Today, the US has the most unequal income distribution among industrial countries. Emmanuel Saez (2010) provides what is arguably the most respected analysis of the changing income distribution in the US. Briefly taking from a popularized version of his results:

> In 2008, the top decile [10 percent of income earners] includes all families with market income above $109,000. The overall pattern of the top decile share over the century is U-shaped. The share of the top decile is around 45 percent from the mid-1920s to 1940. It declines substantially to just above 32.5 percent in four years during World War II and stays fairly stable around 33 percent until the 1970s. . . . After decades of stability in the post-war period, the top decile share has increased dramatically over the last twenty-five years and has now regained its pre-war level. Indeed, the top decile share in 2007 is equal to 49.7 percent, a level higher than [in] any other year since 1917 and even surpasses 1928, the peak of [the] stock market bubble in the "roaring" 1920s. In 2008, the top decile share fell to 48.2 percent, approximately its 2005 level, and is still higher than any other year before 2005 (except for 1928). . . . the top percentile has gone through enormous fluctuations along the course of the twentieth century, from about 18 percent before WWI, to a peak [of] almost 24 percent in the late 1920s, to only about 9 percent during the 1960s–1970s, and back to almost 23.5 percent by 2007, and then to 20.9 percent in 2008. Those at the very top of the income distribution therefore play a central role in the evolution of US inequality over the course of the twentieth century.[4] But such dramatic movements towards more unequal income distribution may have in part been masked by inflating housing prices, access to home equity finance and increased indebtedness of the household sector.

Figures on wealth concentration, a more meaningful and stable indicator of income distribution, are even more alarming. In 2007, the richest

20 percent of Americans owned more that 85 percent of the country's wealth (1 percent owned 35 percent), meaning that the bottom 80 percent of Americans owned about 15 percent.[5]

Financialization may also be accompanied by rising management salaries at the expense of the wages of ordinary workers. Assuming different propensities to save from rentier, management, and worker incomes, redistribution in turn will affect consumption, and investment through different channels. Thus, the distributional effects of financialization may have a significant impact on growth. The era of financialization has witnessed a disconnection of wages from productivity growth, raising serious concerns regarding wage stagnation and widening income and wealth inequality. Data for the US showed that from 1959 to 1979 wages grew roughly in line with productivity, but thereafter the two have diverged, with wages flat while productivity has continued to grow. Wages of US production and non-supervisory workers, who constitute over 80 percent of the employed, have become detached from productivity growth during the era of financialization.

Crotty (2005) reported that, for the United States, the profits of financial institutions rose dramatically relative to those of non-financial corporations after 1984. In the case of the US economy, Crotty argued that financialization has had a profound and largely negative impact on the operations of US non-financial corporations (US NFCs). This is partly reflected in the increasing incomes extracted by financial markets from these corporations. For example, Crotty showed that the payments US NFCs paid out to financial markets more than doubled as a share of their cash flow between the 1960s and the 1970s, on the one hand, and between the 1980s and 1990s on the other. As NFCs came under increasing pressure to make payments, they were also under pressure to increase the value of their stock prices. Financial markets' demands for more income and more rapidly growing stock prices occurred at the same time as stagnant economic growth, and increased product market competition made it increasingly difficult to earn profits. Non-financial corporations responded to this pressure in three ways, none of them healthy for the average citizen: (i) they cut wages and benefits to workers; (ii) they engaged in fraud and deception to increase apparent profits; and (iii) they moved into financial operations to increase profits. Crotty argued that financialization in conjunction with neo-liberalism and globalization has had a significantly negative impact on the prospects for economic prosperity. Epstein and Jayadev (2005) presented a profile of similar distributional issues in a larger group of countries. They showed that rentiers—financial institutions and owners of financial assets—have been able to greatly increase their shares of national income in a number of OECD countries since the early 1980s.

In an article in *The Economist* a related question was framed in the following words: "How has finance done so well for itself and why haven't its returns been competed away?"[6] The answer that is given comes from a number of papers in a report published by The London School of Economics (LSE) (July 2010).[7] Quoting one of the authors, the magazine reports that the success of finance has been "as much mirage as miracle." The summary answer in *The Economist* is not at all surprising: "The financial industry has done so well for itself, in short, because it has been given a licence to make a leveraged bet on property. The riskiness of that bet was underestimated because almost everyone from bankers through regulators to politicians missed one simple truth: that property prices cannot keep rising faster than the economy or the ability to service property-related debts. The cost of that lesson is now being borne by the developed world's taxpayers." In other words, the financial sector's contribution to financial intermediation has not been enhanced in recent years. If this had been the case, it would have been reflected in economic performance indicators, such as more rapid growth. Instead, the financial sector has grabbed a bigger slice of the economic pie through leveraged speculation that has been supported by governments and ultimately paid for by ordinary taxpayers.

The financialization thesis is that these developments regarding increased debt, changes in the functional distribution of income, wage stagnation, and increased income inequality are in large measure due to changes wrought by financial sector interests. These changes concern the structure of the economy, economic policy, and the behavior of corporations. The growth effects of increased indebtedness, increases in the share of profits, shifts in income away from workers, and lower retained profits of corporations will tend to reduce the long-run equilibrium growth rate. However, this conclusion is sensitive to assumptions concerning the response of aggregate demand to changes in the share of profits. In particular, if investment responds strongly to an increased share of profits and consumption is little affected by a lower share of wages, then growth can increase as a result of a higher share of profits.

While the distributional aspects of financialization may be largely confined to the advanced countries, it may have enabled redistribution of wealth and income from developing and emerging countries to developed countries. Speculation in commodity markets pushed the prices of staple commodities to record highs, extracting real incomes from consumers, many in developing countries. Demonstrations against exorbitant food and energy prices in 2007–08 were a clear sign that financialization has operated large profits in favor of speculators. The wealth redistribution was exemplified by huge losses of sovereign funds that had invested in contaminated derivatives.

IV. FINANCIALIZATION AND THE INTERNATIONAL MONETARY SYSTEM

The process of financialization may have in part been facilitated by the demise of the gold standard and the adoption of flexible exchange rates. Rueff (1964) argued that reserve currency countries could run external deficits without losing real resources. In turn, the surplus of non-reserve currency countries is reinvested in the reserve currency countries in the form of bonds and shares and constitutes a basis for further credit expansion. As reserve currency countries, principally the United States, ran large deficits in the financial crisis that erupted in 2007, banks had to devise innovations in order to create credit and push more debt to consumers and corporations. The fast expansion of debt has been met with widening external deficits for the US, whose currency, the dollar, is still the most important reserve currency.

Dickens (2005) attributed financialization of the world economy to the rise of the Eurodollar market and the breakdown of the Bretton Woods system in the late 1960s and its collapse in the early 1970s. Dickens contended that a complex interaction of powerful forces helped to foster capital mobility and financialization, including: (i) competition between US and UK banks; (ii) the US need to finance the Vietnam War; and (iii) the re-emerging political power of financial institutions.

This international monetary system, based on the creation of liabilities and aggregate demand by the US as importer of last resort, is not sustainable, according to Jane D'Arista (2005), who contends that the US must continue to run up a large international debt that will eventually undermine confidence in the US dollar. Alternatives to US external deficits, such as currency blocs and further dollarization, will only increase the degree of instability. D'Arista has proposed taking a page from Keynes: an international clearing system that can provide the basis for an "open international trading system in an institutional framework that promotes more egalitarian participation by all countries in the global economy."

V. FINANCIALIZATION AND THE RECOUPLING–DECOUPLING HYPOTHESES

The financialization process has gained momentum in a number of advanced countries in addition to the United States. In large part because of rapidly rising international capital mobility after the demise of the Bretton Woods system and the absence of capital controls, financial institutions, sovereign wealth funds, and ordinary investors became interconnected through a web of debt, securities, and cash flows. Debt was pushed not only on households and corporations in the US but also on households, corporations, and governments in a number of other advanced countries. Equity and housing bubbles developed in many countries. Many banks around the globe bought derivatives such as collateralized debt obligations and mortgage-backed securities. With the outbreak of the crisis in 2007, a number of large European banks incurred significant financial losses in the form of toxic assets, deposits, and loans at failed US banks. The fast depreciation of toxic securities inflicted losses on sovereign funds and banks outside of the US. The contagion of the crisis was fast and deep. A number of banks in Europe, Japan, and emerging market countries had to be bailed out by their respective central banks and governments. The failure of investment banks, most prominently Lehman Brothers, and the ensuing credit crunch curtailed trade financing.

The recoupling hypothesis is stated as follows: when the US sneezes, the rest of the world catches a cold. The recoupling hypothesis implied that contagion from US banks and the freezing of trade credit would hamper the financial system in emerging countries. It thus implied that an economic recession in the US would reduce exports of emerging countries to the US and would, therefore, end up decelerating their economic growth. The decoupling hypothesis postulates that the emerging market economies are less vulnerable to financial contagion and could grow without relying on growth in industrial countries by stimulating their own domestic demand and gaining markets in developing countries. They could draw on their sizeable international reserves, supported by current account surpluses, for increasing consumption and investment. A slump or economic recession in major industrial countries such as the US, Japan, or a country in the Eurozone would not by itself cause a slump in emerging market countries.

The credit freeze and the curtailment of trade loans led the Group of 20 (G-20) to re-energize the IMF and increase its resources by US$1.1 trillion, a sum which included a new Special Drawing Rights allocation in the amount of US$250 million to supplement the reserves of member countries and maintain their import capacity. The IMF was also instructed to relax its conditionality and issue loans to member countries facing shortfall in reserves to finance their imports. Hence, the IMF was considered as an appropriate vehicle to push debt on to emerging and developing countries to keep world demand buoyant and afford export outlets for industrial countries that faced serious domestic economic downturns. Some of this debt extended by the IMF could become non-performing in the future when vulnerable countries are not able to service their debt, as exemplified by the Greek debt crisis in 2010–11.

The decoupling–recoupling hypotheses applied with nuances to a number of countries. Some countries suffered more from contagion than others.

The financial crisis has deepened in the Eurozone, causing a significant drop in real economic growth and high unemployment. Eurozone banks have incurred considerable losses and their books have remained saddled by assets that still have to be written down as non-performing loans. Japan suffered deep contraction in 2008 and 2009; however, it recovered somewhat in 2010. China, India, and other Asian emerging market countries showed great resilience and maintained high economic growth in spite of the curtailment of exports to the US and Europe. Similarly, for emerging market countries in Latin America, the crisis has had a moderate impact, much less severe than anticipated under the recoupling hypothesis. An explanation for this resilience was that banks in emerging countries suffered limited losses from exposure to toxic securities, continued to function in a normal fashion, and provided credit to businesses. Moreover, export markets have not disappeared for these countries, as demand remained robust outside the industrial countries that were severely shaken by the financial crisis and have continued to be burdened by a sharp increase in unemployment. Countries such as China and India have followed a diversified export strategy based on competitiveness and a currency peg or devaluation. They were able to make forays in many countries other than the US and Europe. Their exports were sufficiently diversified—ranging from food products to manufacturing and services—and less vulnerable to demand shocks.

Largely because of the degree of capital mobility and integrated capital markets, the financialization process has affected banks and investors in advanced and emerging countries. The contagion of the crisis affected countries with varying degrees of damage. Although most of the emerging countries were negatively impacted in 2008–09, they nonetheless recovered at a faster pace than anticipated under the recoupling hypothesis. Their recovery was led by expansion of their domestic demand as well as by a diversified export strategy. Emerging countries seem to have learned their lesson; following their huge losses associated with toxic securities, their investments in securitization have dropped to negligible levels and are once again limited to traditional securities, such as equities and government bonds. The financialization process may thus be weakened in the future, as a number of newly devised financial instruments will have more limited demand in industrial and emerging market countries.

VI. CONCLUSION

Financialization has been defined as an over-expansion of the financial sector that turned out to be a drag on the real sector. It has unraveled the inherent instability of conventional finance. It illustrated the power of the financial system to create money, push debt, and create bubbles and volatility in the quest to earn greater wealth. It created distortions that led to changes in income distribution in favor of the financial sector, and to long-term economic stagnation as exemplified in Japan and in the drawn-out recession in the US and Europe during 2007–10. By creating speculative bubbles in assets and commodity markets, the financial sector has excised income from the real sector. Without volatility in asset prices and exchange rates, financialization could not remunerate speculators with huge gains. The profits of the financial sector remained private and its losses were socialized through government and central bank bailouts.

Financialization has had an international dimension by its propagation to leading industrial countries as well as emerging countries. A number of trends associated with financialization have caused concern. These include unsustainable and unproductive increase in debt, a fall in non-financial sector shares in national income, growing income disparities, and declines in growth of per capita income.

More regulation has been proposed as a way to tackle the undesirable effects of financialization. Reform proposals have varied. They have called for regulating the unregulated financial institutions, regulating derivatives, imposing special taxes on the profits of financial institutions, and prohibiting proprietary trading. In the conventional fractional reserve banking system, regulators have injected moral hazard through various implicit subsidies such as deposit insurance schemes and the notion that some institutions are "too big to fail." Thus, conventional banks have created excessive debt via the money multiplier by mispricing loans, speculating, and otherwise engaging in activities that strain their ability to implement effective asset–liability management. At the same time, central banks may have unknowingly promoted financialization through excessive money creation and support for the prevailing international monetary system.

In this book, we contend that financial instability can be virtually eliminated only if risk sharing (equity finance) replaces risk shifting (debt creation).

ENDNOTES

1. Many developing countries have a limited number of financial institutions and a very small number and narrow range of financial products. Banks finance mainly trade and real investment operations and do not extend consumer loans. In these countries, the concept of financialization is largely inapplicable. The latter applies essentially to economies such as the US, UK, Japan, and Europe, as well as a number of other countries that have highly advanced financial systems and a considerable number of financial products, with commercial banks and non-bank institutions competing for both corporate and consumer loans.

2. "Time for a Rent Cut: Controlling the Finance Sector's Excess Returns," *The Economist*, June 3, 2010.

3. "q" represents the ratio of the market price of capital to its replacement cost, and the q-ratio supposedly provides firms with a signal that efficiently directs investment and capital accumulation. Thus, when q is greater than unity, the market price exceeds the replacement cost. That sends a signal that capital is in short supply and profitable investment opportunities are available, and firms respond by investing.

4. Emmanuel Saez, "Striking it Richer: The Evolution of Top Incomes in the United States," March 15, 2008, www.docstoc.com/docs/48716353/Striking-it-Richer-The-Evolution-of-Top-Incomes-in-the-United-States.

5. G. William Domhoff, "Wealth, Income, and Power," *Who Rules America?*, September 2005, http://sociology.ucsc.edu/whorulesamerica/power/wealth.html.

6. Buttonwood, "A Mirage, Not a Miracle: The Banks' Contributions to the Economy Have Been Overstated," *The Economist*, July 17, 2010, p. 66.

7. *The Future of Finance: The LSE Report* contains the collection of papers that were presented at a one-day conference at LSE on July 14, 2010.

Risk Sharing and the Islamic Paradigm

A Brief History of Risk-Sharing Finance

Risk sharing has been an integral part of human activity since long before the formation of modern-day corporations banks, and other financial institutions. It has been a natural activity whereby parties find it profitable to pool resources, be it financial, entrepreneurial, or technical, and requiring other inputs, as opposed to operating individually. The sharing of risk is undertaken with the expectation that the combination of numerous participants (investors, entrepreneurs, scientists, and those from many other professions and walks of life), larger resources, and diversified skills and technologies would result in greater output and larger profits than operating individually; and in some instances, projects that for a variety of reasons would not have been undertaken would be developed and pursued. Partners in business ventures have contractual arrangements that define the contribution of each party, including the financing, managerial, technical, and other contingencies that could arise, and the distribution of the fruits of their undertaking. Risk-sharing enterprises have evolved over the centuries into the modern corporate structure, which has diversified equity ownership and is the dominant source of economic output and employment in most advanced economies.

Brouwer (2005) traced the evolution of the modern-day corporation in Europe. She described how the equity-based "*commenda*" organizations supported trade in medieval Europe. The *commenda* organization, which was especially popular in Pisa and Venice, has over the centuries evolved into the limited liability corporation of today. It was based on equity financing, as opposed to debt financing, and became the most popular organizational form of maritime ventures in medieval Italy. It has been shown that the *commenda* was directly adopted from Islamic sources (Udovitch, 1970a; Mirakhor, 1983). Weber (2003) has described the evolution of these organizations into limited liability companies with autonomous management, then into corporations with many investors and a managing partner, and evolving into widely held share ownership to become the prominent corporations of today.

Islam has long endorsed risk sharing as the preferred organizational structure for all economic activities, specifically the most comprehensive application of risk sharing and going beyond anything put forward by modern theories. On the one hand, Islam prohibits—and without any exceptions—explicit and implicit interest-based contracts; on the other hand, it lauds risk sharing in all its forms as the structure for economic activity. It goes even further to require mandatory risk sharing with the poor, the deprived, and the handicapped based on its principles of property rights, which specify a right for the less able to share in the income and wealth of the more able, as the latter use more resources to which all are entitled. Through its redistributive mechanisms, such as *zakat*, Islam incorporates the duty of sharing into all economic relations. In other words, Islam prescribes that the more able have the duty to share in the risks faced by the poor and vulnerable social classes. As part of its incentive structure, the *Qur'an* promises that these sharing arrangements, far from reducing income and wealth of the more able, increase income and wealth by multiples.[1]

In this chapter, we review the history of risk-sharing finance in both Islamic and conventional systems. We hope to show how in past centuries financing based on mutual trade and risk sharing led to successful economic development in Islamic societies. We also assess (in the empirical literature) the important contributions of equity financing (stock markets) in the conventional financial system for economic growth and development.

We begin by briefly discussing the foundation and structure of Islamic finance. In Section II, we outline the evolution of risk sharing in Islamic finance. In Section III, we briefly trace the development of conventional finance as an activity that focuses on risk management. We then take a brief look at how the relationship between Islamic and conventional finance may evolve in the future, before presenting our conclusions in Section V.

I. THE FOUNDATIONAL STRUCTURE OF ISLAMIC FINANCE[2]

The central proposition of Islamic finance is the prohibition of transactions that embody rent for a specific period of time as a percentage of the loaned principal without the transfer of the property rights claims, thus shifting the entire risk of the transaction to the borrower. As the *Qur'an* prohibits interest rate-based debt contracts, it simultaneously ordains an alternative. The alternative to debt-based contracts is *al-bay'*—that is, a mutual exchange in which one bundle of property rights is exchanged for another, thus allowing both parties to share production, transportation, and marketing risks. It further allows both parties to an exchange to reduce the risk of income volatility and to allow consumption smoothing, which is a major outcome of risk sharing and increases the welfare of the parties to the exchange.

The emphasis on risk sharing is evident from one of the most important verses in the *Qur'an* regarding economic behavior. The verse states that: ". . . they say that indeed *al-bay'* is like *al-riba*. But Allah has permitted *al-bay'* (exchange contract) and has forbidden *al-riba* (interest-based debt contract). . ." (2:275). This verse can be considered as the cornerstone of the *Qur'an*'s conception of an economy, since from this verse flows major implications of how the economy should be organized. One of these implications relates to the nature of these two contracts. Etymologically, the first *al-bay'* is a contract of exchange of one commodity for another where the property rights over one good are traded for those of another. In the case of contracts of *riba*, a sum of money is loaned today for a larger sum in the future without the transfer of the claim over property rights (or the principal) from the lender to the borrower. Not only does the lender retain property rights over the sum lent, but also over the additional sum paid as interest, which is transferred from the borrower to the lender. The verse renders exchange and trade of commodities (and assets) the foundation of economic activity.

Important implications follow: exchange requires that the parties be free to enter into contracts. This in turn implies freedom to produce, which calls for clear and well-protected property rights that would permit production. Moreover, to freely and conveniently exchange, the parties need a place— that is, a market. To operate successfully, the market needs rules, norms, and procedures to allow information to flow smoothly; trust to be established among buyers and sellers; competition to take place among sellers, on the one hand, and buyers, on the other; and transactions costs, as well as costs to third parties resulting from the adverse impact of exchange, to be reduced.

Risk is a fact of human existence. The exposure of income to risk is important and can play havoc with a person's livelihood. Reduction in income risk is therefore welfare enhancing, by lowering volatility to allow smoothing of consumption. This is accomplished by risk sharing and risk diversification, which are facilitated by trade and exchange. By relying on exchange, the *Qur'an* promotes risk sharing. Arguably, it can be claimed that through its rules governing just exchange, distribution, and redistribution, the entire Qur'anic position on economic relations is oriented toward risk sharing. This is perhaps the reason why in the *Qur'an* there is more emphasis placed on rules governing exchange distribution and redistribution— to effect a balanced risk sharing—than on production.

The *Qur'an* strongly suggests that risk sharing, along with other prescribed behavioral rules such as cooperation (*Qur'an*, 5:2), promotes human solidarity by bringing humanity closer to unity, which in itself is a corollary of Islam's central axiom: the Unity of the Creator. An Islamic philosophic axiom declares that from One Creator only one creation can issue. The *Qur'an* itself unambiguously declares: "Neither your creation (was) nor your resurrection (will be) other than as one united soul" (*Qur'an*, 31:28; see also 4:1; 6:99). In a series of verses, the *Qur'an* exhorts humankind to take individual and collective actions to achieve social unity and cohesion and then strive to preserve and protect collectivity from all elements of disunity (for instance, 3:103). Unity and social cohesion are so central among the objectives of the *Qur'an* for humankind that all conducts prohibited may be regarded as those that cause disunity and, conversely, those prescribed to promote and protect social cohesion. It is a natural consequence of such a system to require risk sharing as an instrument for social integration. Therefore, promoting maximum risk sharing is, arguably, the ultimate objective of Islamic finance. It is for this reason that Muslim scholars consider profit–loss sharing and equity participation as first best instruments of risk sharing (Iqbal and Mirakhor, 2007; Mirakhor and Zaidi, 2007). In this way, social integration is enhanced.

Indeed, there is some evidence that stock markets and social interaction are related (Hong et al., 2004; Huberman, 2001). Shiller (2003) has recognized the potential benefits of risk sharing for humankind and points out: "Massive risk sharing can carry with it benefits far beyond that of reducing poverty and diminishing income inequality. The reduction of risks on a greater scale would provide substantial impetus to human and economic progress."

Arguably, the most meaningful human progress would be achieved when all distinctions among human beings on the basis of race, color, creed, income, and wealth are obliterated to the point where humanity truly views itself as one. The *Qur'an* (4:1) unambiguously calls attention to the fact that, despite all apparent multiplicity, humans are fundamentally of one kind and rejects all bases for distinction between and among them except righteousness (*Qur'an*, 49:13). The objective of the unity of mankind could well be promoted by financial globalization since it could promote risk sharing across geographic, racial, national, religious, cultural, and language boundaries. The same potential holds for Islamic finance if progress follows the trajectory envisioned by Islam, which specifies preconditions for the successful operation of financial arrangements within its framework firmly anchored on a network of norms and rules of behavior (institutions) prescribed for individuals and collectivities (Iqbal and Mirakhor, 2002). This network includes, but is not limited to, those institutions that modern scholarship considers crucial for financial development, integration, and globalization (Garretsen et al., 2003).

Among the institutions prescribed by Islam are property rights, contracts, trust, and governance. The word "property" is defined as a bundle of rights, duties, powers, and liabilities with respect to an asset. In the Western concept, private property is considered the right of an individual to use and dispose of a property, along with the right to exclude others from the use of that property. Even in the evolution of Western economies, this is a rather new conception of property that is thought to have accompanied the emergence of the market economy. Before that, however, while a grant of the property rights in land and other assets was the right to use and enjoy the asset, it did not include the right to dispose of it or exclude others from its use. For example, the right to use the revenues from a parcel of land, a corporate charter, or a monopoly granted by the state did not carry the right of disposing of the property. It is thought that the development of the market economy necessitated a revision of such a conception of property because it was seen as difficult, if not impossible, to reconcile this particular right with a market economy. Hence, of the two earlier property rights principles—the right to exclude others, and the right not to be excluded by others—the latter was abandoned and the new conception of property rights was narrowed to cover only the right to exclude others. In Islam, however, this right is retained without diminishing the role of the market as a resource allocation and impulse transmission mechanism (Iqbal and Mirakhor, 2007).

The first principle of Islamic property rights is that the Supreme Creator is the ultimate owner of all properties and assets, but in order that humans can become materially able to perform duties and obligations prescribed by Allah, they have been granted a conditional right of possession of property; this right is granted to the collectivity of humans. The second principle establishes the right of the collectivity to created resources. The third principle allows individuals to appropriate the products that they produce by combining their labor with the provided resources, without the collectivity losing its original rights either to the resources or to the goods and services that are produced by individuals. The fourth principle recognizes only two ways in which individuals accrue rights to property: (i) through their own creative labor; and (ii) through transfers—via exchange, contracts, grants, or inheritance—from others who have gained property rights title to a property or an asset through their labor. Fundamentally, therefore, work is the basis of the acquisition of rights to property. Work, however, is not performed only for the purpose of satisfaction of wants or needs; it is considered a duty and obligation required from everyone.

Similarly, access to and the use of natural resources for producing goods and services is everyone's right and obligation. So long as individuals are able, they have both the right and the obligation to apply their creative labor to natural resources to produce goods and services needed in the society. However, if individuals lack the ability, they no longer have an obligation to work and produce without losing their original right to resources.

Therefore, an important principle, called "immutability or invariance of ownership," constitutes the fifth principle of property rights in Islam and confirms the duty and obligation of sharing. Before any work is performed in conjunction with natural resources, all members of the society have an equal right and opportunity to access these resources. When individuals apply their creative labor to resources, they gain a right of priority in the possession, use, or market exchange of the resulting product without nullifying the rights of the needy in the sale proceeds of the product. As a result, the sixth principle imposes the duty of sharing the monetary proceeds after the sale of the property. This principle regards private property ownership rights as a trust held to effect sharing. The seventh principle imposes limitations on the right to dispose of the property. Individuals have an obligation not to waste, destroy, squander, or use property for unlawful purposes. Once the specified property obligations are appropriately discharged, including that of sharing in the prescribed amount and manner, property rights are held inviolate—that is, no one can appropriate or expropriate their rights.

While the above principles strongly affirm people's natural tendency to possess—particularly products resulting from an individual's creative labor—the concomitant private property obligations give rise to interdependence among the members of society. Private initiative, choice, and reward are recognized but are not allowed to subvert the obligation of sharing. The inviolability of appropriately acquired private property rights in Islam deserves emphasis. As observed by a legal expert (Habachy, 1962), given the divine origin of Islam:

> . . . *its institutions, such as individual ownership, private rights, and contractual obligations, share its sacredness. To the authority of law, as it is understood in the West, is added the great weight of religion. Infringement of the property and rights of another person is not only a trespass against the law; it is also a sin against the religion and its God. Private ownership and individual rights are gifts from God, and creative labor, inheritance, contract, and other lawful means of acquiring property or entitlement to rights are only channels of God's bounty and goodness to man. . . . All Muslim schools teach that private property and rights are inviolable in relations between individuals as well as in relations with the state. . . . It is not only by their divine origin that the Muslim institutions of private ownership and right differ from their counterpart in [the] Western system of law; their content and range of application are more far-reaching. . . . If absolutes can be compared, it can be safely said that the right of ownership in Muslim law is more absolute than it is in [the] modern*

system of law. . . . The Muslim concept of property and right is less restricted than is the modern concept of these institutions.

In a terse, unambiguous verse, the *Qur'an* exhorts the believers to "be faithful to contracts" (5:1). This command, buttressed by other verses (2:282; 6:151–153; 9:4; 16:91–94; 17:34–36; 23:8), establishes the observance of and faithfulness to the terms of contract as the central anchor of a complex relationship between: (i) the Creator and His created order, including humans; (ii) the Creator and the human collectivities; (iii) individuals and the state, which represents the collectivity; (iv) human collectivities; and (v) individuals. The concept of contracts in Islam transcends its usual conception as a legal institution "necessary for the satisfaction of legitimate human need." It is considered that the entire fabric of the Divine Law is contractual in its concept and content. Contract binds humans to the Creator, and binds them together. As Habachy suggests:

This is not only true of private law contacts, but also of public law contracts and international law treaties. Every public office in Islam, even the Imamate (temporal and spiritual leadership of the society), is regarded as a contract, an agreement (áqd) that defines the rights and obligations of the parties. Every contract entered into by the faithful must include a forthright intention to remain loyal to performing the obligations specified by the terms of contract.

The fulfillment of contracts is exalted in the *Qur'an* to rank it with the highest achievements and noblest virtues (2:172).

The divinely mandated command of faithfulness to the terms and conditions of contracts, and abiding by its obligations, is built on the equally strong and divinely originated institution of trust (Iqbal and Mirakhor, 2007; Kourides, 1970). There is strong interdependence between contract and trust; without the latter, contracts become difficult to enter into and costly to monitor and enforce. When and where trust is weak, it is expensive to enforce contracts. Accordingly, the *Qur'an*, in a number of verses, proclaims trustworthiness as a sign of true belief and insists on the obligation to remain trustworthy in fulfilling the terms and conditions of contracts as an absolute requirement before entering into a contract. Conversely, untrustworthiness and betrayal of trust are considered a clear sign of disbelief (2:27; 2:40; 2:80; 2:177; 2:282–283; 3:161; 4:107; 4:155; 6:153; 7:85; 8:27; 8:58; 9:12; 9:75; 9:111; 11:85; 13:20; 16:91; 16:94; 16:95; 17:34; 23:8). Moreover, the *Qur'an* makes clear that fulfilling the obligations of a contract or a promise is mandatory. In short, the *Qur'an* makes trust and trustworthiness, as well as keeping faith with contracts and promises, obligatory and has rendered them inviolable except in the event of an explicitly permissible justification. In addition, there are numerous prophetic sayings that supplement the Qur'anic verses on trust. For example, it is reported that the Prophet (pbuh) was asked: Who is a believer? He replied: "A believer is a person to whom people can trust their person and possession." It is also reported that he said: "The person who is not trustworthy has no faith, and the person who breaks his promise has no religion." Also, "keeping promises is a sign of faith," and "there are three [behavioral traits] if found in a person, then he is a hypocrite even if he fasts, prays, performs big and small pilgrimages, and declares 'I am a Muslim': when he speaks, he lies; when he promises, he breaches; and when trusted, he betrays" (Payandeh, 1984; Iqbal and Mirakhor, 2007).

There are other behavioral rules and norms that strengthen the governance structure of the state and firms, including transparency, accountability, voice, and representation. Nevertheless, the three basic institutions—property rights, contracts, and trust—give a flavor of the strength of governance in Islam. The rule of law governs the behavior of state rulers no less stringently than that of individuals. As two Western legal experts (Anderson and Coulson, 1958) observe: "Islam is the direct rule of God. His Law, the *Shari'ah*, is the sole criterion of behavior," and "the authority of the temporal ruler is both derived and defined by this law." Under the rule of law, "the ruler is by no means a free agent in the determination of the public interest," and the decisions that the ruler makes "must not be arbitrary, but rather the result of conscientious reasoning on the basis of the general principles of the *Shari'ah* as enunciated in the authoritative texts." These legal experts also assert that, based on their consideration of Islamic legal texts, the command to observe contracts and covenants faithfully "appl[ies] to the ruler acting in a public capacity" just as severely as to individuals. "Indeed, when considerations of expediency and public interests are taken into account, [such commands] apply even with greater force to the actions of the ruler."

The same principles of governance under which a ruler or a state should function apply also to firms. Iqbal and Mirakhor (2004) argue that within the Islamic framework a firm can be viewed as a "nexus of contracts" whose objective is to minimize transaction costs and maximize profits and returns to investors, subject to constraints that these objectives do not violate the property rights of any party whether it interacts with the firm directly or indirectly. In pursuit of these goals, the firm honors all implicit or explicit contractual obligations. It is incumbent on individuals to preserve the sanctity of implicit contractual obligations no less than those of explicit contracts. By the same token, firms have to preserve the sanctity of implicit and explicit contractual obligations by recognizing and protecting the property rights of stakeholders, community, society, and state. Since the firm's behavior is shaped by that of its managers, it becomes their fiduciary duty to manage the firm as a trust for all stakeholders in ensuring that the behavior of the firm conforms to the rules and norms specified by the law.

The institutions ordained by Islam reduce uncertainty and ambiguity to ensure predictable behavior. Islam also prescribes rules regarding income and wealth sharing to promote income-consumption smoothing. Arguably, sharing of economic risks in the society is of great concern to Islam. The *Qur'an* emphasizes distributive justice through *zakat*, as well as additional exhortation for voluntary economic assistance to those less able; all of which are insurance against income risk. However, these institutions are exceptional by their absence in many, if not all, Muslim countries (Chapra, 2000; Abed and Davoodi, 2003).

II. THE EVOLUTION OF RISK SHARING IN ISLAMIC FINANCE

In 1958, Franco Modigliani and Merton Miller showed that, in the absence of frictions, a firm's financial structure would be indifferent between debt and equity. In the real world, there are a number of frictions that bias financial structures in favor of debt and debt-based contracts, with the two most important being tax and information. The tax treatment of equity returns and interest in industrial countries is heavily biased against equities. Informational issues (information asymmetry and the subsidies and policies that encourage moral hazard and adverse selection) are conceived in favor of debt or debt-based contracts. Broadly speaking, legal–financial systems in advanced countries are structured in favor of debt and debt-based transactions.

In the West, debt and debt-based financing has long been the dominant form of finance. We have to go all the way back to the Middle Ages to trace this evolution. Before the beginning of the 20th century, economic historians of the Middle Ages all but ignored the importance of trade and financial relations between Europe and the rest of the world, which were crucial to the economic development of the West before the 15th century (Udovitch, 1967). Abu-Lughod (1994) contends that this was due to the belief held by the Eurocentric scholarship that globalized trade became relevant only after the "rise of the West" in the late 15th century. According to Abu-Lughod, an advanced globalized system of trade "already existed by the second half of the Thirteenth Century, one that included almost all regions (only the 'New World' was missing). However, it was a world-system that Europe had only recently joined and in which it played only a peripheral role." Abu-Lughod maps growing global trade flows between 737 and 1478, demonstrating that trade flows first centered in Mesopotamia and spread rapidly over the next eight centuries throughout the then-known world to become global (Frank, 1990; Gills and Frank, 1994a).

Beginning with Postan (1928), economic historians have indicated that these trade flows were supported by a financial system sustained by an expanding risk-sharing credit structure based on *commenda* and *maona*. *Commenda* is identical to *mudarabah*, and *maona* partnerships are either *musharakah* or *mudarabah*,[3] depending on the nature of activity undertaken by the partners. Postan's paper was path-breaking as it demonstrated that: (i) economists and historians had, until then, underestimated the growth of the volume of credit in the Middle Ages; and (ii) the bulk of this credit was either *commenda* or *commenda*-like joint risk-sharing partnerships, even if they were "miscalled or modified" as loans (Postan, 1928, 1957). There is little doubt that the institutions of *commenda* and *maona* originated in the Islamic world (Udovitch, 1962, 1967, 1970a and 1970b). These institutions, along with financial instruments such as *hawala* and *suftaja*, were brought to Europe and to other regions. Jewish scholars and merchants brought them to the Jewish Diaspora (Fischel, 1933, 1937), and Islamic sources did the same via Spain through trade and scholastic borrowing (Mirakhor, 2003). Goitein has examined the documents known as the Geniza records and reached the conclusions (Goitein, 1954, 1955, 1962, 1964, 1967) that: (i) trade in the Middle Ages was both extensive and intensive, financed by risk-sharing partnerships; (ii) partnership was used in industrial, commercial, and public administration projects; (iii) Mediterranean and Indian trade, as revealed by the Cairo Geniza, were largely not based on cash benefits or legal guarantees, but on the human qualities of mutual trust and friendship; and (iv) even a cursory examination of the Geniza material proves that lending money for interest was not only shunned religiously, but was also of limited economic significance.

Studying both the Geniza records as well as Islamic *Fiqh* sources, Udovitch reaches the following conclusions: (i) "there is remarkable symmetry between the Hanafite legal formulations of the late-8th Century and the documented commercial practices of the 11th and 12th Centuries' Geniza merchants" (Udovitch, 1962, 1967); and (ii) he reaffirms Goitein's conclusion that researching "the extensive commercial records of the Geniza, we found comparatively little evidence of usurious transactions" (Udovitch, 1970a and 1970b). Moreover, research by medieval historians demonstrated the extensive use of risk-sharing partnerships (Adelson, 1960; Arfoe, 1987; Ashtor, 1975, 1976, 1983; Byrne, 1920, 1930; Exenberger, 2004; Laiou, 2002; Lieber, 1968; Lopez, 1951, 1952, 1955). While risk-sharing techniques continued to prevail in Europe until the mid-17th century, beginning in the mid-16th century, the institution of interest-based debt financing also began to be used more widely and extensively throughout Europe (Munro, 2003). The initial utilization of this method of financing and its dominance over risk-sharing methods can be attributed to a combination of several factors, including: (i) the demise of the scholastic prohibition of usury (Munro, 2003; Sauer, 2002); (ii) the appearance and rapid growth of fractional reserve banking, which led to specialization of finance by intermediaries who preferred to provide financing to agent-entrepreneurs at fixed interest rates based on contracts enforceable by law and the state in order to reduce monitoring and transaction costs; (iii) the inflow of vast amounts of gold and other riches into Europe from the colonies in the Americas and elsewhere, which reduced the incentive for the elite classes to continue financing trade on the basis of risk sharing, preferring fixed interest debt contracts; (iv) the emergence of nation-states whose governments needed finance for wars or other state activities, but could not raise resources except by means of fixed interest rate contracts according to which an annuity was paid in perpetuity without the need for governments to repay the principal (Michie, 2007); and (v) most importantly, the innovation of the process of securitization in the 14th century created a revolution in mobilizing financial resources. It is likely, however, that the breakdown of trust in Europe and elsewhere was a major factor for the loss of dominance of risk-sharing finance by the end of the Middle Ages.

Risk-sharing finance is trust intensive, and trade financing during the Middle Ages was based on risk sharing, which, in turn, was based on mutual trust (Goitein, 1964). Alesina and La Ferrara (2002) have shown that catastrophic and traumatic experience contributes to the breakdown of trust in a community and among its members. The Middle Ages witnessed continuous and extensive traumas, including four Crusades, three Mongol invasions, numerous wars in Europe, and the Bubonic plague of the mid-15th century, which spread rapidly throughout the then-known world along well-established and intensively traveled trade routes (Abu-Lughod, 1994).

More recently, interest in the practice of *Shari'ah*-compliant business activities was sparked by the expansion of conventional "interest-based" commercial banking in the Arab and Muslim world. In the late 19th century, a formal critique and opposition to the element of "interest" started in Egypt when Barclays Bank was established in Cairo to raise funds for the construction of the Suez Canal. Further, a formal opposition to the institution of "interest" can be found as early as 1903 when the payment of interest on post office saving funds was declared contrary to Islamic values, and therefore illegal, by *Shari'ah* scholars in Egypt. During the first half of the 20th century, there were several attempts to highlight the areas where the emerging conventional financial system conflicted with Islamic values. By the 1950s and 1960s, as several Muslim countries became independent of their colonial masters, they attempted to rediscover their Islamic heritage. In 1953, Islamic economists offered the first description of an interest-free bank. By the start of the 1960s, there was sufficient demand for *Shari'ah*-compliant banking to justify the establishment of the Mit Ghamr Local Savings Bank in Egypt in 1963 by the noted social activist Ahmad-al-Najjar. Around the same time, there were parallel efforts in Malaysia to develop a saving scheme for Muslims wishing to undertake the Hajj (pilgrimage to Mecca).

The concept of Islamic finance was put into practice in the 1970s when the first commercial Islamic bank, Dubai Islamic Bank, was launched, followed by the establishment of the Jeddah-based multilateral development institution the Islamic Development Bank (IDB) in 1975. Since then, the Islamic finance industry has enjoyed consistently high growth. There are more than 300 institutions in more than 65 countries engaged in some form of Islamic finance. Oil revenues of the 1970s offered strong incentives for creating suitable investment outlets for Muslims wanting to comply with the *Shari'ah*. Interest-free or Islamic banking, which was only a conceptual idea in the early 1970s, was given a strong business foundation. Both domestic and international bankers, including some of the world's leading conventional banks, exploited this business opportunity.

The IDB was established along the lines of other regional development institutions with the objective of promoting economic development in Muslim countries, as well as offering development finance according to the rules of the *Shari'ah*. Since its inception, the IDB has played a key role in expanding Islamic modes of financing and in undertaking valuable research in the area of Islamic economics, finance, and banking. The 1980s proved to be the beginning of a trend of rapid growth and expansion of an emerging Islamic financial services industry. The major developments of the time included academic research on the conceptual and theoretical level, constitutional protection in three Muslim countries, and the involvement of conventional bankers in offering *Shari'ah*-compliant services. The Islamic republics of Iran, Pakistan, and Sudan announced that they would transform their overall financial systems to make them compliant with the *Shari'ah*. Other countries such as Malaysia and Bahrain started Islamic banking within the framework of the existing system.

In the 1980s, Islamic banks faced a dearth of quality investment opportunities, allowing conventional Western banks to act as intermediaries to deploy Islamic banks' funds according to the guidelines given by the Islamic banks. Western banks realized the importance of the emerging Islamic financial markets and started to offer Islamic products through "Islamic windows" in an attempt to attract clients directly, without having an Islamic bank as intermediary. The number of conventional banks offering "Islamic windows" grew, and several leading conventional banks, such as the Hong Kong and Shanghai Banking Corporation (HSBC) and Citicorp, began marketing their products. By the early 1990s, the market had attracted the attention both of policymakers and of institutions interested in introducing innovative products. Citibank was one of the early Western banks to have established a separate Islamic bank—Citi Islamic Investment Bank (Bahrain), in 1996. HSBC has a well-established network of banks in the Muslim world. With the objective of promoting Islamic asset securitization and private equity and banking in OECD countries, HSBC Global Islamic Finance (GIF) was launched in 1998. With the growth of Islamic products and services, the need for regulation and standards increased, resulting in the establishment of a self-regulatory agency—Accounting and Auditing Organization for Islamic Financial Institutions (AAOIFI)—in Bahrain.

By the late 1990s and early 2000s, an increasing number of countries began to embrace the concept that a system without interest (interest-bearing debt-based contracts) is workable. This was probably attributable to two factors. First, during its history of more than 30 years, no major Islamic bank had failed; on the contrary, these banks proved to be as efficient and profitable as their conventional counterparts. Although there were cases of bank failures, they were attributed to bad governance and the lack of risk management. In none of the failed banks was the issue of Islamic financial products or the design of financial intermediation ever questioned. This success over a period of three decades gave confidence and trust to customers and skeptics. Second, the advancement of conventional and Islamic financial theory has been supportive. In particular, it has been shown that a system without interest can be designed; and, under certain conditions, such a system may prove to be more stable than the conventional system.

As the science of financial engineering developed, its application to Islamic finance also led to innovations. The first wave of innovation came in the form of Islamic funds where a portfolio of commodities, equities, Islamic leases, and other Islamic products were established. In the case of equities, special screenings and filters were developed to comply with *Shari'ah*, and research showed that the application of such screens or filters does not impact the benefit of diversification. The other significant breakthrough came in the form of *sukuk* (Islamic bonds), where a pool of *Shari'ah*-compliant financial instruments is securitized in the form of a fixed-income security. The issuers of *sukuk* include both sovereign and corporate entities, and the success of *sukuk* is evident by the high growth this market has enjoyed. *Sukuk* have also proved to be a bridge between Islamic and conventional markets and have led to the gradual development of capital markets, as discussed in the following section. As the demand for infrastructure increased in the region, innovative structures for financing infrastructure projects were introduced.

Another noticeable development has been the awareness of Islamic finance in non-Muslim countries and the acceptance of Islamic products at major financial centers in the West. Leading Western financial intermediaries were engaged in Islamic transactions from the early stages, although the majority of the deals were done discreetly. However, by the mid-2000s, competition had increased and both Islamic and conventional financial institutions began to position themselves aggressively to capture market share. Islamic finance gained attention in academic circles, with academics writing books, and universities developing courses and certificate and degree programs, in the area.

More recently, there has been a second wave of interest in Islamic finance. Similar to the 1970s, the recent surge was stimulated by higher oil revenues in the Middle East. Whereas during the 1970s, interest in Islamic finance was limited to the high net worth class, the more recent and ongoing growth is the result of demand by a much wider group, including small investors and retail consumers. Several countries where Islamic finance was dormant are experiencing a sudden surge in demand for *Shari'ah*-compliant products. One example is Saudi Arabia: where for a long time there was skepticism of Islamic finance and no encouragement for its growth, the country has suddenly seen increasing public pressure to embrace Islamic finance. For example, Saudi Arabia's largest bank, National Commercial Bank, has converted its entire branch network to *Shari'ah* principles. Saudi Arabia has also issued three new licenses for *takaful* (Islamic insurance) companies.

Bahrain and Malaysia have taken an active role in the development of Islamic finance and made serious efforts to establish world-class financial centers in order to promote it. The government of Malaysia has taken a phased approach to developing this industry, and its approach can be used as a possible roadmap for others. An Islamic banking Act was enacted in 1983, which led to the establishment of the first Islamic bank—Bank Islam Malaysia Berhard—in 1983. *Shari'ah*-compatible investment certificates were introduced to supplement the liquidity needs of the Islamic banking sector. In the second phase, three conventional banks were allowed to open "Islamic windows." In January 1994, Bank Negara Malaysia established the Islamic Interbank Money Market to allow Islamic institutions to adjust their portfolios according to their short-term financing needs. In the third phase, in the late 1990s, some conventional banks with a sufficient critical mass of Islamic customers transitioned to a full-fledged Islamic bank. Finally, the government began to promote the development of Islamic capital markets, Islamic insurance businesses, and other supporting institutions.

Notwithstanding these advances in the development of Islamic finance, as mentioned in the preface, much of its growth could still be seen as superficial. Two factors have limited more fundamental progress in establishing an Islamic financial system in a country or region. First, with money to be made selling Islamic financial products, the focus has been to quickly develop and market profitable instruments; and in the race to make money, expected shortcuts may have compromised the basic Islamic requirements of risk sharing and prohibition of a predetermined interest rate. Second, there has been little, or no, effort to develop a comprehensive system of Islamic finance at the national level to compete with conventional finance.

III. THE DEVELOPMENT OF CONVENTIONAL FINANCE AND RISK MANAGEMENT

Modern conventional finance as a separate field has a relatively short history in the field of economics. Financial markets were seen as important in affording savers the instruments to attract their savings, and as a channel for allocating savings to investors in the most efficient way. Thus, finance was not treated as an important and separate field of endeavor. Finance was seen as a means to advance the real economy. As a result, it could be assumed that the real and financial sectors were perceived as moving in tandem. The appreciation of risk as central to financial theory was the important building block in the development of modern finance. Early in the 20th century, Irving Fisher was one of the first to appreciate the importance of risk in the functioning of financial markets. In the 1930s a number of economists—including Keynes, Hicks, and Marschak—recognized the importance of risk in portfolio selection; but even then its role was largely limited to its effect on expected capital gains and speculative and hedging activities. This led to results covering the relationship of futures prices and expected spot prices (normal backwardation) and the price stabilizing effect of speculation.

Harry Markowitz, in the early 1950s, saw the critical role of risk in assessing future income streams. Based on these developments and on von Neumann-Morgenstern's theory of expected utility, Markowitz developed what is today referred to as portfolio theory; in essence, the trade-off between risk and return, with portfolio diversification reducing the overall risk of a portfolio. James Tobin expanded Markowitz's work by adding money (risk free) as an asset and attributing the different portfolio selection (money as the riskless asset and various combinations of risky assets) of individuals to differing attitudes toward risk. However, the practical application of the Markowitz-Tobin (M-T) approach was difficult, with the benefits of diversification only identified after estimating the covariance of returns for every pair of assets. To overcome this operational limitation, in the early 1960s William Sharp and John Lintner developed the Capital Asset

Pricing Model (CAPM). They showed that calculating a more limited number of covariances or betas—the covariance of every asset return relative to the market index—could duplicate the M-T approach.

In the mid-1970s, Stephen Ross moved away from the risk–return comparison basis of CAPM and used pricing by arbitrage to develop his Asset Pricing Theory. He further suggested that arbitrage-based reasoning was the fundamental feature of all finance. His assertion is confirmed by the Black-Scholes-Merton option-pricing model and the Modigliani-Miller Theorem. In the case of option pricing, if a portfolio of other assets can reproduce the return from an option, then the price of the option must be equal to the value of the portfolio; if not, there will be arbitrage opportunities. The Modigliani-Miller Theorem also uses arbitrage reasoning to examine the impact of corporate financial structure in arriving at a market value for a firm. If the production outlook of two firms (with differing financial structures) is the same, then the market value of the firms must be the same; if not, there is an arbitrage opportunity.

Another important development in the theory of modern finance was the Efficient Markets Hypothesis. The empirical finding that sparked this hypothesis was that commodities and asset prices behaved randomly. In the case of US stock prices, Alfred Cowles confirmed this result in the 1930s. Economists could make little sense of this result, however, until Paul Samuelson came up with the explanation that has become known as the Efficient Markets Hypothesis. Samuelson reasoned that asset prices had to be random; if not, arbitrageurs could exploit the opportunity to make a profit. For asset prices to behave randomly, all available and relevant information would have to be immediately translated into asset price changes in markets that behaved "efficiently." Eugene Fama in 1970 further developed the theory and connected it to the Rational Expectations Hypothesis.

In sum, the appreciation of the importance of risk, arbitrage pricing, and efficient markets formed the relatively recent foundations of conventional finance. At its core, conventional finance is seen today as the management of risk. At the same time, it is important to recognize that Islamic finance is built on the foundation that risk must be *shared* between parties in any endeavor, as opposed to being all assumed by one party or the other. On the face of it, modern finance should provide practitioners of Islamic finance with added tools to achieve their central goal of better risk sharing. Moreover, as Islam prohibits financial gain without the assumption of some measure of risk, on the one hand, it would appear that efficient markets and the random walk behavior of financial assets and commodities are implicitly, if not explicitly, assumed in Islamic teachings.

IV. ISLAMIC AND CONVENTIONAL FINANCE: WHAT LIES AHEAD?

In today's world, as we have repeated a number of times already, there are numerous frictions that bias the global financial structure in favor of debt and debt-based contracts. The two most important of these are tax and information. The tax treatment of equity returns and interest, informational issues, and legal systems in industrial countries, which dominate the world of finance and the present structure of capital flows, are heavily biased against equities. However, as financial market developments progress, legal and institutional developments across the world accelerate, and information technology advances, the informational problems will diminish. Whether tax and legal treatment of equity versus debt will become less biased is a policy question. What is clear is that as informational problems decline, it will become increasingly difficult to maintain legal, institutional, and tax policy impediments to level the playing field between equity and debt. Consequently, it is not unreasonable to expect a process of decreasing dominance of the financial system by debt and debt-based instruments, which has not been without costs, including severe financial crises.

It is well known that the full-scale adoption of a financial system based on fixed interest, with a fractional reserve-banking sector at its core, has a major deficiency; the system is inherently fragile (Minsky, 1982; Khan, 1987; Posen, 2001).[4] In the late 1970s and early 1980s, the existence of financial intermediaries in general, and banks in particular, was justified due to their ability to reduce transaction and monitoring costs, as well as to manage risk. However, minimal attention was paid to reasons why banks operated on the basis of fixed, predetermined interest-rate-based contracts—that is, on a fixed interest basis, which rendered the system fragile and unstable, requiring a lender of last resort to regulate it.

Generally, interest rate theories explain the rate as an equilibrating mechanism between the supply of and demand for finance, which is a rate that prevails in the market as a spot price and not as a price determined *ex ante* and fixed, tied to the principle and the period covered by the debt contract. Bhattacharya (1982) has argued that: ". . . with risk-neutral preferences, when the choice of risk level is unobservable, then any sacrifice of higher mean asset payoff constitutes an inefficient choice. The classical model of intermediaries existing to save on transactions/monitoring costs in asset choice does not explain why their liability structure should not be all equity." With the development and growth of information economics and agency literature, another explanation was added to the list of reasons for the existence of intermediaries. They served as delegated monitoring as well as signaling agents to solve the informational problems, including asymmetric information existing between principals and agents. Based on the findings of the developing field of information economics (see, in particular, Stiglitz and Weiss, 1981), it has been argued that adverse selection and moral hazard effects in a banking system operating on the basis of fixed-fee contracts in the presence of asymmetric information—particularly in cases where this problem is acute—means that some groups will be excluded from the credit market even when the expected rate of return for these groups may be higher than for those with access to credit. Furthermore, risk–return sharing contracts—for instance, equity—are not subject to adverse selection and moral hazard effects, as "the expected return to an equity investor would be exactly the same as the expected return of the project itself" (Cho, 1986).

Stiglitz (1988) underlined the fragility of a financial system operating on the basis of a fixed, predetermined interest rate. He argued:

> [The] interest rate is not like a conventional price. It is a promise to pay an amount in the future. Promises are often broken. If they were not, there would be no issue in determining creditworthiness. Raising interest rates may not increase the expected return to a loan; at higher interest rates one obtains a lower quality set of applicants (adverse selection effect) and each one's applicants undertake greater risks (the adverse incentive effect). These effects are sufficiently strong that the net return may be lowered as banks increase the interest rates charged: it does not pay to charge higher interest rates.

The findings of the new field of information economics strengthened the arguments of Minsky (1982) and others that a debt-based financial system with fractional reserve banking—operating with a fixed, predetermined interest rate mechanism at its core—is inherently fragile and prone to periodic instability. Stiglitz's findings underlined Minsky's arguments that, as returns to banks decline, unable to raise interest rates on their loans, they enter a liability-management mode by increasing interest rates on their deposits. As this vicious circle continues to pick up momentum, the liability management transforms into Ponzi financing and eventually bank runs develop (Posen, 2001).

The last two decades of the 20th century witnessed a number of global bouts with financial instability and debt crises, with devastating consequences for a large segment of humanity, thus raising consciousness regarding the vulnerability and fragility of the financial systems which are based, at their core, on fixed-price debt contracts. As previously emphasized, legal and institutional developments, along with good governance and adoption of standards of best practice in transparency and accountability at the level of individuals, firms, and the state, buttressed by information technology advances, will mitigate the informational problems and lead to less reliance on debt-based contracts. It is on the basis of such reasoning that we see an increasingly prominent role for equity finance, and thus for risk sharing, not only in Islamic countries, but the world over.

V. CONCLUSION

It is important to recognize that there is nothing magical about the recent historical prominence of debt financing. Before the rise of debt financing, equity financing was pre-eminent. But a host of factors and developments catapulted debt financing to the forefront. Early on in the last century, economic historians indicated that trade flows in Europe were based on a risk-sharing credit structure. The institutions, along with financial instruments, that supported this trade were brought to Europe and to other regions.

Risk-sharing finance is trust-intensive, and trade financing during the Middle Ages was based on risk sharing, which, in turn, was based on mutual trust. Recent research indicates that catastrophic and traumatic experiences contributed to the breakdown of trust in communities and among their members. While risk-sharing techniques continued to prevail in Europe until the mid-17th century, beginning in the mid-16th century, the institution of interest-based debt financing also began to be used more widely and extensively throughout Europe. The initial reasons for using this method of financing and for its emerging dominance included developments such as the process of securitization in the 14th century and the breakdown of trust in Europe and elsewhere.

But the regular frequency of financial crises in the advanced countries that rely heavily on debt financing, and especially the financial instability and turmoil that started in 2007, may favor equity financing in the future. Bank failures and the leveraging of debt have made this crisis the worst in memory, with a significant impact on the real sector and economic growth to be expected for a number of years to come; and with a growing number of specialists recognizing debt as the essential source of financial instability. At the same time, Islamic financial institutions have been relatively unscathed by the crisis, and with their reputation intact. Islamic finance, based on risk sharing, has a much shorter history than conventional finance.

In just a few years, benefiting in part from conventional financial research and innovation, Islamic finance has expanded rapidly from a small base in Islamic countries and also internationally. Historical developments and a comparison of the recent and future evolution of conventional and Islamic finance portend an increased importance of Islamic finance in global financial markets, as well as at the national level.

We must conclude by repeating that, in our opinion, modern Islamic finance has not been developed on a solid Islamic foundation with the necessary scaffolding to enable its adoption as a complete financial system in a country or region. We hope that, in the following chapters, we can make a modest contribution to the development of Islamic finance as a comprehensive financial system that could be adopted in a country in the not-too-distant future.

ENDNOTES

1. "Allah will destroy *al-riba* and will reward in multiples deeds of sharing (through redistributive mechanisms provided; acts that confirm and affirm belief and rule compliance). . ." (*Qur'an*, 2:276)
2. For more detailed discussions, see Askari et al. (2008), and Askari et al. (2010).
3. For a full discussion of Islamic financial instruments, see Iqbal and Mirakhor (2007).
4. For further details, see Askari et al. (2010).

CHAPTER 4

Risk Sharing and the Islamic Finance Paradigm

I slamic finance is basically a financial system structured on risk sharing. The notion of risk has many dimensions. In general, it means the possible occurrence of an event that leads to a loss—an event such as an accident, fire, or sickness. Economic agents who face such common risks try to transfer and reduce their risk exposure through insurance.

In a company, or in any business entity, risk sharing normally takes the form of purchasing shares or stock in the business venture. The sharing of risk in international capital markets is invariably accomplished by buying shares in foreign companies. The risks of accident, fire, unemployment, and natural disasters are not systemic risks; they are essentially idiosyncratic. In economic and financial activities, the notion of risk denotes the variability of an economic or financial variable such as output, prices, returns, and incomes. If an economic outcome has a large variability, it is said to be "risky." Risk is inherent in most economic activities. The size and quality of next year's agricultural crop—be it sugar, wheat, or anything else—is subject to risk. Output may be affected by a number of factors, including rainfall, climate, and the presence of insects and disease. For a company, profits are subject to risk. They may rise or fall, depending on prices for raw materials, change in demand, change in technology, sale orders, and competition from other firms.

In finance, risk is broadly divided into two types: price and credit risk. Finance has developed numerous concepts and measures for measuring and pricing financial risk (or variability). The most common and the most frequently used measures are the variance or the standard deviation of an economic or financial variable. The higher the variance of a variable, the higher the risk associated with that variable.[1] A stock that has high variance is said to be a risky stock. Risk is also measured by third moment (skewness) and fourth moment (kurtosis). When assessing the risk of a portfolio of financial assets, value at risk (VaR) is frequently used. VaR is the maximum likely loss over some target period—or the most an investor expects to lose over that period, at a specified probability level. For instance, it would say that on 95 days out of 100, say, the most an investor can expect to lose is $10 million or some other dollar sum. The so-called expected tail loss (ETL)—or expected shortfall—is another measure of risk. The ETL is the loss an investor can expect to make if he or she incurs a loss in excess of VaR. There are other methods for measuring market risk, including the margin system SPAN (standard portfolio analysis of risk) developed by the Chicago Mercantile Exchange, and the margin rules of the US Securities and Exchange Commission. Higher margins are required for risky assets acquired by investors. The market price of risk is defined as the risk premium per one unit of standard deviation.[2]

The "sharing of risk" has many possible meanings depending on how risk sharing is organized. All forms of organized risk sharing have a "mutuality" dimension in their activities. The most familiar are cooperatives of various forms to share risk faced by their members. Producer, consumer, and farm cooperatives allow members to share risks of production, consumption, crop output, and related activities. In the case of Islamic insurance such as *takaful*, meaning mutual care, a group pools its resources to insure its members against risk. Ordinary insurance, where a person buys an insurance contract for a fee (indicated by a premium), is not an example of risk sharing but of "risk transfer," where for a fee the insured transfers part of his or her idiosyncratic risks to a firm willing to provide protection against possible contingencies. What is missing here is the element of mutuality. Each policyholder deals directly with the insurance company without the need to know any other policyholder. For instance, if a plant catches fire, the owner does not have to bear the full cost of rebuilding the plant. The insurance company can cover this because it pools the resources of a large number of such policyholders. Since fires do not occur simultaneously in all insured firms, an insurance company is expected to be financially in a position to replace one or a number of destroyed plants.

It may be worth noting that over the last few decades, the Islamic *takaful* industry has had a fast pace of growth. Companies in the *takaful* business tend to be organized as conventional insurance companies with the exception that they are not engaged in interest-based debt contracts in their financial dealings and that they do not insure businesses that are prohibited in Islam, such as gambling. However, while *takaful* companies pool risks, the mutuality element, or risk sharing, is absent. Risk sharing is a contractual or societal arrangement whereby the outcome of a random event is borne collectively by a group of individuals or entities involved in a contract, or by individuals or entities in a community. In a company, all shareholders share in the risk inherent in the operations of the company. In finance, risk sharing is an essential feature of equity financing, where the risks of loss and gain are shared, as opposed to interest-based debt financing, where the lender does not share in the risk of losses; thus, all the risk of loss is shifted to the borrower.

The last five decades have witnessed the development and innovation of many instruments of risk management, such as futures, options, and swaps. A futures contract allows two counterparties to agree today on the price of a commodity or an asset for delivery at some future date. An option, on the other hand, gives the purchaser the right, but not the obligation, to buy or sell an asset or a commodity at a stated price (the strike price) during a fixed time period. In a swap contract, two parties swap an asset or a liability today, with the agreement to reverse the swap at some specified future date. But in all three cases—futures, options, and swap contracts—the risk associated with a change in price of the underlying asset is shared between the two parties to the contract. The field, or activity, of risk management essentially entails risk sharing between buyers and sellers of insurance contracts.

Islamic finance encourages risk sharing in its many forms but generally discourages risk shifting or risk transfer—in particular, interest-based debt financing. It is in part so designed to promote social solidarity by encouraging finance to play an integrating role. This form of finance would be inclusive of all members of society and all entities, especially the poor, in terms of enjoying the benefits of economic growth and bringing humankind closer together through the sharing of risk. Since risk sharing is the foundation and a basic activity in Islamic finance, it is governed by rules that, if and when observed, lead to lower transaction costs than in conventional finance.

Our plan in this chapter is as follows. In Section I, we review the theoretical basis of risk sharing and the role of securities in the allocation of risk. In Section II, we present the model for risk sharing in consumption. In Section III, we define risk sharing in consumption. In Section IV, we present various empirical findings about risk sharing in consumption. In Section V, we define Islamic finance as a risk-sharing, equity-based finance. In Section VI, we describe the evolutionary process of equity finance in Islamic finance. In Section VII, we examine the balance between short-term, less risky, liquid assets and long-term, higher risk, and illiquid assets, and introduce the concept of a vibrant stock market in Islamic finance (to be discussed in detail in the subsequent chapter). We present our conclusions in Section VIII.

I. THE ROLE OF SECURITIES IN RISK SHARING AND IN THE ALLOCATION OF RISK

All societies face the crucial question of how to allocate economic risks that are an everyday fact of life. Kenneth Arrow, one of the pioneers of conventional modern finance, provided (1964) an answer: risks in the economy should be shared according to the risk-bearing ability of the participants. More fundamentally, he (along with Gerard Debreu) proposed the design of instruments that could accommodate risk sharing according to the risk-bearing desires of participants. His contribution became the foundational theory for pricing assets and derivatives through the notion of primitive securities, also commonly referred to as Arrow-Debreu (AD) securities.

Arrow's contribution can be summarized as follows. If the state of the world in a future period is described by S states, $s=1,2,...,S$, then an AD security of the s type pays \$1 if state s occurs and nothing if other states occur. If the forward price for an asset is \$100, the state of the world is described by the spot prices of the assets at the delivery date. Let the s state be given by an asset price of \$110; the payoff for a long trader would be \$10. A long trader can achieve this payoff by buying a bundle of 10 AD securities. If the price of AD security of type s, denoted by q_s, is known, then the price of any risky asset, at time t_0, can be computed as a weighted sum of payoffs in each state at time T:

$$p_0 = \sum_{s=1}^{S} q_s \cdot p_{T,s} = \sum_{s=1}^{S} q_s \cdot \left(payoffs\right)_{T,s} \tag{1}$$

where p_0 is the price of a risky asset at time t_0, $p_{T,s}$ is the payoff of the asset at time T in state s, and q_s is the price of a primitive AD security (also called the state price). The crux for pricing an asset is, therefore, to compute q_s.[3] The risk is shared through the securities market. There is a buyer of a security and a seller of a security. The price paid by the buyer to the seller is q_s. The Arrow pricing model has been generalized as:

$$p_0 = E_{t_0}\left(m_T \cdot p_T\right) \tag{2}$$

where E_{t_0} is the expectation operator with the expectation computed at time t_0, m_T are stochastic discount factors, and p_T are payoffs at time T.

Arrow's model on the role of securities in the optimal allocation of risk is essentially an extension of the model of the Walrasian auctioneer operating under uncertainty in an exchange economy.[4] In the one-period certainty setting, the equilibrium allocation computed by the auctioneer has the property of being a Pareto Optimum allocation—that is, an allocation where it is not possible to increase the well-being of one trader without reducing that of another trader. In the two-period uncertainty setting, traders enter into risky contractual arrangements in time t_0 that will become legally binding in T with payoffs dependent on the state of the world in T. Uncertainty in Arrow's model is described by the state of the world in time T. As in an exchange economy, there are I traders, $i = 1, 2, ..., I$, and C commodities, $c = 1, 2, ..., C$. The risk is described by the fact that traders do not know which state will prevail in the future; however, they know the exact payoff or endowment in each state when a particular state s occurs. Hence, the endowment $x_{c,s}$ of commodity c in state s is known at time t_0. Similarly, the income of each trader i in each state s, $y_{i,s}$ is known at time t_0. Further, let $x_{i,c,s}$ be the amount of commodity claimed by traders i if state s occurs. These claims are limited by available resources, so that:

$$\sum_{i=1}^{I} x_{i,c,s} = x_{c,s} \tag{3}$$

Each trader has an income in t_0 equal to y_i. Total money income in the economy at time t_0 and T is:

$$\sum_{i=1}^{I} y_i = y \tag{4}$$

If there is a market for claims on commodities at t_0 with delivery in period T, then the economy will be similar to an exchange economy with SC claims instead of C commodities in the certainty model. Each trader will have a budget constraint:

$$\sum_{s=1}^{S} \sum_{c=1}^{C} \bar{p}_{s,c} x_{i,s,c} = y_i \tag{5}$$

where $\bar{p}_{s,c}$ is the price in time t_0 of a unit claim on commodity $x_{c,s}$. With uncertainty, the auctioneer in the same fashion computes prices $\bar{p}_{s,c}$ as prices p_c in the case of operating under certainty.

Arrow observed that, in the real world, risk bearing is not allocated by the sale of claims against specific commodities. A simplified picture would be the following: securities are sold and paid for in cash, the amount depending on the state s that has actually occurred. This concept is obvious for stocks. A stock is a security that pays a dividend according to the state of the world. For bonds, there is a possibility of default if a certain state s occurs. When the state s occurs, the money transfer determined by the securities takes place, and then the allocation of commodities takes place through the market in the ordinary way, without further risk bearing. Each trader knows at t_0 his payoff $y_{i,s}$ in state s. He buys a bundle of securities of type s in a number equal to $y_{i,s}$ at a price of q_s per security. The budget constraints for a trader i for purchasing securities is:

$$\sum_{s=1}^{S} q_s y_{i,s} = y_i \tag{6}$$

$$\sum_{i=1}^{I} y_{i,s} = y \tag{7}$$

The allocation $x_{i,c,s}$ in state s is computed according to the budget constraint:

$$\sum_{c=1}^{C} p_{c,s} x_{i,c,s} = y_{i,s} \tag{8}$$

The prices $p_{c,s}$ take place in period T, while the prices $\bar{p}_{s,c}$ take place at time t_0; they are related by a discount factor, which is q_s according to:

$$q_s \cdot p_{c,s} = \bar{p}_{s,c} \tag{9}$$

The primitive security price also verifies the relationships:

$$q_s = \frac{\sum_{i=1}^{I} \sum_{c=1}^{C} \bar{p}_{c,s} x_{i,c,s}}{y} \tag{10}$$

$$\sum_{s=1}^{S} q_s = 1 \tag{11}$$

Prices q_s have the property of adding up to unity. Although q_s are not probabilities, they are called risk-neutral probabilities. The securities market is essentially made up by traders that buy and sell securities, and it operates in close relationship with the commodities market to determine the prices of securities, as described in equation (9). For instance, in option pricing, q_s are computed in such a manner that the stochastic process of the underlying asset is a martingale. Socially, the significance of Arrow's model is that it permits economizing on markets; only $S + C$ markets are needed to achieve the optimal allocation, instead of the SC markets implied in the markets for claims on commodities. Arrow proved that the allocation of risk bearing in competitive security markets is in fact optimal.

II. RISK SHARING IN CONSUMPTION

Perfect risk sharing (PRS) in consumption is defined as a case where there is perfect correlation of an individual's consumption with aggregate consumption. Hence, this is the case when individual consumption is not affected by idiosyncratic income shocks. When a laborer is unemployed, his consumption is not impaired and is related directly to aggregate consumption through risk sharing. The model for PRS in consumption is based on the standard intertemporal optimization problem for the representative consumer:

$$\max_{c_t, A_t} E_0 \left\{ \sum_{t=0}^{\infty} \beta^t U(c_t) \right\} \tag{12}^5$$

Subject to the following constraints:

$$A_t = (1+r) A_{t-1} + y_t - c_t \tag{13}$$

$$\lim_{t \to \infty} E_0 \left(\frac{A_t}{(1+r)^t} \right) = 0 \tag{14}$$

where y is disposable income, c is consumption, A is wealth yielding a return of r, and U is a utility function with intertemporal separability.[6] The parameter β describes the rate of the intertemporal preferences of the representative consumer, who has an infinite time horizon and does not face any liquidity constraints. Therefore, such a consumer can run negative balances of A in any period with the only constraint that the present discounted value of his wealth at time t approaches zero as t approaches infinity (that is, the transversality condition). Lastly, we denote the expectation formed conditionally upon the information set available at time 0 by E_0. Finding the maximum of the Lagrangian function solves the intertemporal optimization problem:

$$L = \max_{c_t, A_t} E_0 \left\{ \sum_{t=0}^{\infty} \beta^t H_t \right\} \tag{15}$$

where:

$$H_t = U(c_t) + \lambda_t \left(A_t - (1+r) A_{t-1} - y_t + c_t \right) \tag{16}$$

and λ_t is the Lagrangian multiplier. The Lagrangian multiplier can be written as:

$$L = \max_{c_t, A_t} E_0 \left\{ H_0 + \beta H_1 + ... + \beta^t H_t + \beta^{t+1} H_{t+1} + ... \right\} \tag{17}$$

with:

$$H_{t+1} = U\left(c_{t+1}\right) + \lambda_{t+1}\left(A_{t+1} - \left(1+r\right)A_t - y_{t+1} + c_{t+1}\right) \tag{18}$$

Replacing H_t and H_{t+1} by their expressions in L yields:

$$L = \max_{c_t, A_t} E_0 \left\{ \begin{array}{l} H_0 + \dots + \beta^t \left[U\left(c_t\right) + \lambda_t \left(A_t - \left(1+r\right)A_{t-1} - y_t + c_t\right)\right] \\ + \beta^{t+1} \left[U\left(c_{t+1}\right) + \lambda_{t+1}\left(A_{t+1} - \left(1+r\right)A_t - y_{t+1} + c_{t+1}\right)\right] + \dots \end{array} \right\} \tag{19}$$

Taking the derivatives with respect to c_t and A_t yields:

$$\frac{\partial L}{\partial c_t} = E_0 \left[\beta^t \left(\frac{dU}{dc_t} + \lambda_t \right) \right] = E_0 \left[\left(\beta^t \left[U_t' + \lambda_t \right] \right) \right] = 0 \tag{20}$$

$$\frac{\partial L}{\partial A_t} = E_0 \left[\beta^t \lambda_t - \beta^{t+1}\left(1+r\right)\lambda_{t+1} \right] = 0 \tag{21}$$

where $U_t' = \dfrac{dU}{dc_t}$.

Solving the above equations yields:

$$E_0 U_t' = -E_0 \lambda_t \tag{22}$$

$$E_0 \lambda_t - \beta\left(1+r\right)E_0 \lambda_{t+1} = 0 \tag{23}$$

Replacing this in the previous expression yields the Euler equation:

$$-E_0 U_t' + \beta\left(1+r\right)E_0 U_{t+1}' = 0 \tag{24}$$

The latter expression can be expressed as:

$$\frac{E_0 U_{t+1}'}{E_0 U_t'} = \frac{1}{\beta\left(1+r\right)} \tag{25}$$

The ratio $\dfrac{U_{t+1}'}{U_t'}$ is the intertemporal marginal rate of substitution (IMRS), also referred to as the rate of growth of marginal utility of consumption. The Euler condition states that the expected rate of growth of the marginal utility of consumption is equal to $\dfrac{1}{\beta\left(1+r\right)}$. The Euler condition is extensively used in pricing assets and is formulated in a most general form as:

$$E_0\left[\beta\frac{U'_{t+1}}{U'_t}R_{t+1}\right]=1 \tag{26}$$

where R_{t+1} is the return from holding assets. For measuring welfare gains, consumption-based models have assumed a utility function of the form of constant relative risk aversion (CRRA), namely:

$$U(c_t)=\frac{c_t^{1-\gamma}}{(1-\gamma)} \tag{27}$$

where γ is the coefficient of relative risk aversion. The derivative with respect to c_t is $U'_t=c_t^{-\gamma}$. The Euler condition can be written as:

$$E_0\left(\frac{1}{\beta(1+r)}c_{t+1}^{-\gamma}-c_t^{-\gamma}\right)=0 \tag{28}$$

This model has served as a main framework for testing risk sharing in consumption. It implies that, *ex post* the growth of consumption c_{t+1}/c_t has to be the same for all agents sharing in consumption.

III. DEFINITION OF RISK SHARING IN CONSUMPTION

With complete markets, individuals can be fully insured against idiosyncratic income shocks. If all households have access to a complete set of securities the resulting allocations will be Pareto Optimal. A complete market is defined as one where the number of securities is equal to the number of states. A well-known implication of complete markets is efficient risk sharing—namely, that the change in (the log) marginal utility is common to all households and individual consumption is proportional to aggregate consumption. Efficient risk sharing leads heterogeneous agents to act in a manner equivalent to that of a single representative agent. Agents will share a common intertemporal marginal rate of substitution equal to the common marginal rate of transformation. Thus, consumption growth differs across households *only* because of measurement error. The perfect risk-sharing condition can be stated, *ex post*, as:

$$\frac{U'_{t+1}}{U'_t}=\frac{\lambda_{t+1}}{\lambda_t} \tag{29}$$

This equation provides a clear illustration of perfect risk sharing: the growth of marginal utility of all households (on the left-hand side) should only be a function of the aggregate variables (the right-hand side).

With limited insurance markets, however, the variability of individual consumption may exceed that of the aggregate, and the implied asset prices may differ significantly from those predicted by a representative consumer model. Idiosyncratic shocks can be buffered by trading in financial securities, but the extent of trade is limited by borrowing, short-sales constraints, and transaction costs.[7] Agents reduce consumption variability by trading in stock and bond markets to offset idiosyncratic shocks, but transaction costs in both markets limit the extent of trade. Incomplete markets in the form of an inability to borrow against risky future income or to buy contingent claims and insurance contracts have been proposed as an explanation for the poor predictive performance of the standard consumption-based asset pricing model.

At the international level, full consumption risk sharing means that agents across countries will equalize the intertemporal marginal rates of substitution state by state. This fundamental condition states that the international ratio of marginal utilities from consuming any good must be constant across states of nature. In statistical terms, this condition states that the national marginal utilities from consuming any good are positively and perfectly correlated across countries. Without an international contingency claims market, risk sharing cannot be achieved among countries. Opening the stock market to foreign investors enables domestic agents in a small open economy to share risk with the rest of the world. Assuming constant relative risk aversion utility as in equation (27) and taking logarithms, the condition for perfect risk sharing can be expressed as:

$$\ln\left[\frac{C_{t+1}^H}{C_t^H}\right] = \ln\left[\frac{C_{t+1}^F}{C_t^F}\right] = -\frac{1}{\gamma}\ln\left[\frac{1}{\beta}\frac{\lambda_{t+1}}{\lambda_t}\right] \tag{30}$$

where C_t^H is home country consumption, C_t^F is foreign country consumption, γ denotes risk aversion that is common across both economies, and β is the rate of time preference. The expression implies that consumption growth rates are perfectly correlated internationally. A corollary, explored in the vast literature, is that consumption growth in each country varies only with world factors.

IV. EMPIRICAL FINDINGS ON RISK SHARING IN CONSUMPTION

The main test of perfect risk sharing is to estimate a relationship of the type delineated in equation (30) above, which equates intertemporal marginal rates of substitution among households, and then to determine if any idiosyncratic variable is correlated with the resulting error term.

There is an empirical rejection of perfect risk sharing—the hypothesis that individuals can insure against all idiosyncratic shocks and are thus able to equate the growth rate of their marginal utilities to one another. A number of empirical studies have found household consumption growth (or, more precisely, the growth in their marginal utility) to be correlated with certain idiosyncratic shocks—and income shocks, in particular—violating the premise of perfect insurance. Mace (1991) and Cochrane (1991), in early attempts, employed micro data to test if risk sharing was complete across households. In sharp contrast to the macro studies, however, they considered household idiosyncratic shocks and concluded that complete risk sharing was generally not supported by the data. At the level of the individual, Mace used the US Consumer Expenditure Survey, regressing individual consumption growth on average consumption growth and individual income growth and found that income growth is significantly correlated with some, but not all, categories of consumption. Using the US Panel Study of Income Dynamics (PSID), Cochrane found that the distribution of food consumption shifts across individuals who are unemployed for more than 100 days due to illness and involuntary job loss. Since information asymmetry problems, such as moral hazard and adverse selection, make it difficult for households to insure perfectly for pure household-specific risk, these results may not be surprising. Townsend (1994) investigated whether consumption allocations among villages might not exhibit full insurance. While he found quite a considerable amount of insurance, he rejected the hypothesis of full insurance; household consumption responded to idiosyncratic income shocks.

Guvenen (2002) analyzed the extent of risk sharing among stockholders to see whether stockholding provided perfect risk sharing. In the US, wealthy households play a crucial role in many segments of economic life because of the significant concentration of wealth in a relatively few hands. Hence, to evaluate the empirical importance of market incompleteness, it is essential to determine if idiosyncratic shocks are important for the wealthy, who also have better insurance opportunities as compared to average households. Because of this, Guvenen used a dynamic structural model, where in each period households compared the benefits of holding stocks (with a per period trading cost) to decide whether to participate in the stock market. Using data from the Panel Study of Income Dynamics, he strongly rejected perfect risk sharing for stockholders; however, perhaps surprisingly, he found no evidence against it among non-stockholders.

Hess and Shin (1999) estimated the extent to which idiosyncratic and disaggregated macro shocks (such as regional and industry shocks) were not shared in the economy. Comparing the degree to which idiosyncratic and disaggregated macro shocks were not shared allowed a deeper understanding of why there was an absence of risk-sharing arrangements in specific sectors and could indicate areas where risk-sharing capability could be enhanced. Using household data from the Panel Study of Income Dynamics, they found that a negligible amount of risk (around 10 percent) was shared in the aggregate, about 50 percent was shared within regions and industries, while the remaining 40 percent was not shared with other households. Their findings suggested that given the low level of national risk sharing, increased international integration may not lead to a significant increase in international risk sharing.

At the international level, two approaches have been used to assess the gains from international risk sharing. One approach, based on a general equilibrium framework, starts from the observation that the perfect risk-sharing hypothesis implies that country-specific consumption growth should be perfectly correlated across countries, while it should be uncorrelated with country-specific income growth. However, these theoretical relationships are generally rejected in regression-based tests. Whether the imperfect risk-sharing outcome is surprising or not depends on the size of the potential gains from international risk sharing. A second approach, based on a partial equilibrium capital asset pricing model (CAPM) framework, starts from the observation that there is a strong home bias in international stock and bond portfolios. The portfolio approach attempts to assess the welfare gains resulting from maximizing the expected utility of a portfolio made of country-specific securities that follow exogenously given stochastic processes. National stock market indices and GDP-based securities have been typically taken as proxies for country-specific securities. In these models, the welfare gains from diversification result from changes in both the mean and the variance of the optimal portfolio compared to the portfolio that is held. Gains from diversification have typically been estimated to be much larger under the portfolio-based approach than under the consumption-based approach.

Fratzscher and Imbs (2009) tested the perfect sharing hypothesis that consumption growth rates in home and foreign economies should only depend on a world factor, and in particular not on country-specific income, as postulated in equation (30). They used the model proposed by Lewis (1996) to test this claim in a panel of countries, estimating δ in:

$$gc_t^i = \alpha_t + \delta gy_t^i + \varepsilon_t \tag{31}$$

where gc_t^i and gy_t^i are consumption and income log growth rates in country i, respectively; α_t captures the world factors embedded in the Lagrangian multiplier and the discount rate; and ε_t denotes measurement error or preference shocks. Perfect risk sharing implies $\delta = 0$ with consumption growth independent of domestic income. Lewis's model is a test for multilateral risk sharing because its findings say nothing about the partner with which a particular economy shares risk. Lewis obtained significant and large estimates of δ in her sample of 72 countries, and in each G-7 economy taken in isolation, indicating a rejection of perfect risk sharing.

Fratzscher and Imbs argued that the introduction of asset-specific transaction costs must result in estimates of δ further away from zero. This is intuitively straightforward; transaction costs render risk sharing more difficult, and thus idiosyncratic consumption growth becomes more dependent on idiosyncratic income changes. Transaction costs in international investment can simply reflect different tax treatments, intermediation fees, or liquidity premiums across countries and asset classes. They could also arise from information frictions. Information asymmetries matter less for standardized financial assets such as Treasury bonds than for information-sensitive equity or corporate bonds. Fratzscher and Imbs emphasized that transaction costs in international investment alter standard consumption risk-sharing relations. Financial assets that entail large transaction costs are associated with little international risk sharing, in the sense that the representative investor's consumption plans remain significantly correlated with his idiosyncratic income. Diversification could be hampered by restrictions on international capital flows. Countries that trade financial assets also appear to be diversified, in that they manage to unhinge domestic consumption from domestic production, in some cases perfectly. The bulk of risk sharing is related to the international holdings of equities and bonds. By contrast, portfolios heavy in foreign direct investment or bank loans do not appear to provide much diversification, at least on the basis of observed aggregate consumption behavior.

Crucini (1999) analyzed the international and national dimensions of risk sharing. Specifically, he found that more than two-thirds of the fitted annual variation in regional consumption is common to all regions, compared to less than one-third in the case of G-7 countries. In testing the null hypothesis of complete risk sharing, researchers have effectively computed the probability that average consumption growth explains all of the variance of fitted individual consumption growth. Taken together, these studies present substantial evidence against full insurance. Risk-sharing theory produces full consumption insurance only under stringent assumptions (that contracts can be written and enforced at zero cost, for example). More generally, the theory predicts that individuals will choose to pool risk to the extent that the costs and benefits are equal. Given that the costs and benefits of risk sharing may differ across individuals, and indeed across different contingencies, individuals will choose different levels of risk sharing or choose different groups with whom they pool risk. Once it is recognized that risk sharing may be imperfect, test results of consumption risk sharing would be expected to depend on the groups included in the test and the extent to which shocks occurring over the period of observation are fully, partially, or not at all insured. Tests of the null hypothesis of complete insurance are not equipped to uncover these differences. One robust prediction of imperfect risk sharing is that, after controlling for common income shocks, consumption should move together more closely across individuals that engage in more risk sharing.

Models have been developed to assess how transaction costs in international investment affect conventional tests of consumption risk sharing, both in a multilateral and a bilateral setting. Tests were implemented using novel international data on bilateral holdings of equity, bonds, foreign direct investment (FDI), and bank loans. High foreign capital holdings are associated with international consumption risk sharing. This is especially true of investment in equity or in bonds, but not in FDI or bank loans. The implication is that transaction costs are higher for FDI and international loans. The discrepancy could reflect technological differences, but also the prospect of expropriation, perhaps most stringent for FDI or loans. The detrimental impact of poor institutions is muted in open economies, where the possibility of subsequent exclusion from world markets deters expropriation of foreign capital. The implied effects of institutions prevailed in both the cross-section of consumption risk sharing and in observed international investment patterns. Holdings of foreign assets with high transaction costs delivered little consumption risk sharing. As a result, domestic consumption did not decouple from domestic resources, as it would under complete markets and perfect risk sharing. This result was true in the conventional multilateral setup, and extended to a bilateral framework. In particular, institutional quality conditioned the extent of consumption risk sharing.

The expansion of global financial market activity has inspired a large body of empirical research into the forces linking the financial markets of individual countries. Findings about the nature and strength of these forces are important for their implications about public policy toward international capital movements. A basic finding was that the direct welfare gains from cross-border portfolio diversification—from the international pooling of national consumption risks—were likely to be quite small. This thesis led to the following coherent interpretation of observed financial relationships among industrialized countries. When the gains from international diversification are small, even minor impediments to asset trade can wipe them out. Similarly, minor trade impediments can wipe out small gains from consumption-smoothing intertemporal exchanges. The welfare loss from prohibiting international diversification would unlikely exceed a tiny percentage of average national product per year, even at high levels of risk aversion.

Appreciation of the importance of risk, arbitrage pricing, and efficient markets provides the relatively recent foundations of conventional finance. At the same time, Islamic finance is built on the foundation that risk must be shared between parties in any endeavor, as opposed to being all assumed by one party or the other. On the face of it, modern finance should provide practitioners of Islamic finance added tools to achieve their central goal of better risk sharing. Moreover, as Islam prohibits financial gain without the assumption of some measure of risk, it would appear that efficient markets and the random walk behavior of financial assets and commodities are implicitly, if not explicitly, assumed in Islamic teachings. Today, even after years of rapid innovation, conventional finance only embraces risk management of private sector equity. Shiller (2003) has emphasized that risk management, the basic focus of modern conventional finance, is still in the early stages of its development. Risk management, especially across borders, has a very long way to go. Future developments in risk management could dramatically reduce individual risk and increase economic output and welfare.

V. ISLAMIC FINANCE IS EQUITY-BASED AND RISK-SHARING FINANCE

The foundational principle of Islamic finance is the prohibition of interest (*riba*) and interest-based contracts. This prohibition has been stated in many verses in the *Qur'an* and was explicated in many sayings of the Prophet (pbuh). In the *Qur'an*, 2:275, Allah says: "Those who devour *riba* will stand except as stands one who the evil one by his touch has driven to madness. That is because they say exchange is like *riba*; but Allah has permitted exchange and forbidden *riba*." There is no rule violation in the *Qur'an* more serious than charging interest (see 2:276), which is considered an act of injustice. An economic understanding of the essence of these verses—that interest-based debt contracts have to be replaced by contracts of exchange—requires analysis of the particularities of the two contracts.

Interest rate-based debt contracts have two major characteristics. First, they are instruments of risk shifting, risk shedding, and risk transfer. Second, in interest-based debt contracts, the creditor attains a property rights claim on the debtor, equivalent to the principal plus interest and whatever collateral may be involved, without losing the property rights claim to the money lent. This is a violation of Islamic property rights principles. The most important of these principles are that: (i) the Creator has ultimate property rights on all things; (ii) He has created resources for all mankind and no one can be denied access to these resources; (iii) work (and voluntary transfer) is the only means by which individuals gain rightful possession of property when they combine their physical or mental abilities with natural resources to produce a product; (iv) since resources belong to all mankind, a right is created in the products produced by the more able for the less able—in effect, the less able are silent partners in the products, income, and wealth produced by the more able whose shares have to be redeemed; (v) all instantaneous property rights claims, such as theft, bribery, interest, and gambling, are prohibited; and (vi) a person can transfer a property rights claim to another via exchange, inheritance, or the redemption of the rights of the less able. Interest rate-based debt contracts create an instantaneous property rights claim for the creditor against the debtor regardless of the outcome of the objective for which the two sides entered the contract. The creditor obtains this property rights claim without commensurate work.

Ordaining exchange to replace interest rate-based debt contracts has significant economic implications. First, before parties can enter into a contract of exchange they must have property rights in what they are going to exchange. Second, the parties need a place or a forum to consummate the exchange: a market. Third, the market needs rules for its efficient operation. Fourth, market rules need enforcement. Exchange facilitates specialization and allows the parties to share production, transportation, marketing, sales, and price risk. Therefore, exchange is above all a means of risk sharing. From an economic standpoint, therefore, by prohibiting interest rate-based contracts and ordaining exchange contracts the *Qur'an* encourages risk sharing and prohibits risk transfer, risk shedding, and risk shifting. In a typical risk-sharing arrangement such as equity finance, the parties share the risk as well as the reward of a contract. In an interest rate-based debt contract the risk is transferred from the financier to the borrower, with the financier retaining not only the property rights claim to the principal and interest but also that of any collateral that has guaranteed the financing arrangement. In a risk-sharing arrangement, such as equity participation, the asset is invested in remunerative trade and production activities, the returns to the asset are not known at the time of investment, and are therefore a random variable making equities risky assets. In equity investment, owners of money and physical assets and entrepreneurs share the risk; their income is random, depending on the performance of the equity investment. The randomness of income is explained by the fact that equity shares are contingent claims whose payoff, defined as the sum of change in price and dividends, depends on the state of the world, as described in Section I.

An important performance dimension of risk-sharing finance in general, and of Islamic finance in particular, is whether it is more or less vulnerable than conventional finance (which relies heavily on debt finance) to principal–agent and informational issues. Agency issues arise because of asymmetric information between agents (entrepreneurs) and principals (investors) and the possibility that the agent's utility maximization may not maximize the utility of the principal. The agency problem is normally addressed by incorporating incentive structures in contracts for the complete sharing of information and for the agent to behave in a way to maximize rewards for the principal.

Informational and agency problems have been discussed in the context of one risk–reward sharing instrument: equity. On the one hand, for example, Stiglitz (1989) suggests that there are two informational problems in the case of equities: (i) adverse signaling effect, which leads good firms not to issue as much equity for fear that it may signal poor quality; and (ii) an adverse incentive effect problem, which suggests that equity finance weakens the incentive for the entrepreneurs (agents) to exert their maximum effort for the highest maximum joint returns for themselves and their shareholders (principals). This happens because once the project is financed, the entrepreneur knows that the net return will have to be shared with the financier (the principal) and, therefore, may not have a strong motivation to work as hard as when the return is not shared. On the other hand, there are also agency and informational problems in interest rate-based debt financing. Stiglitz points out that there is an inherent agency conflict in debt financing in that the entrepreneur (the agent) is interested in the high end of the risk–return distribution. The lender (the principal), on the other hand, interested in safety, focuses on the low end of the risk–return distribution, and therefore discourages risk taking. This, Stiglitz asserts, has "deleterious consequences for the economy." He further suggests that "from a social point of view equity has a distinct advantage: because risks are shared between the entrepreneur and the capital provider, the firm will not cut back production as much as it would with debt financing if there is downturn in the economy."

The agency problem has been generalized to bank lending. Banks, being highly leveraged institutions that borrow short (deposits) and lend long, are exposed to an asset–liability mismatch that creates potential for liquidity shocks and instability. Stiglitz suggests that to protect their financial resources, banks generally discourage risk taking. Additionally, their behavior toward risk often creates informational problems that lead to phenomena that can be classified as market failure, such as credit rationing. In contrast to Stiglitz's position, Hellwig (1998) argues that there is an oft-neglected informational problem in the lending behavior of banks, which he refers to as "negative incentive effects on the choice of risk inherent in the moral hazard of riskiness of the lending strategy of banks." This risk materialized dramatically in the period of run-up to the recent financial crisis (see Askari et al., 2010; Sheng, 2009).

Based on the above background, the question is whether Islamic contracting is better suited to solving this contractual dilemma through its reliance on risk–reward sharing under conditions where interest-based debt financing is prohibited. In the presence of informational problems such as asymmetric information (where only one side of the contract, usually the agent, has information not available to the other parties), there is transaction cost as well as the cost of monitoring the agent's activities and the project(s). It could be plausibly argued that in Islamic contracts asymmetric information issues would be minimized. This assertion is supported by the strict rules governing contracts, exchange, and trade enunciated in the *Qur'an* and in the Tradition of the Prophet (pbuh). These include the need for written contracts that fully and transparently stipulate terms and conditions, the direct and unequivocal admonition that commitments to the terms and conditions of contracts must be faithfully carried out, and strong emphasis on trust, cooperation, and consultation. Rules governing market behavior also create incentives—both positive and negative—to enforce honest, transparent, and compliant behavior on the part of participants. Hence, risk-sharing contracts designed under Islamic rules would mitigate informational problems (Khan and Mirakhor, 1987; Presley and Sessions, 1994) and could be better structured than interest-based debt contracts with incentives to maximize both parties' expected joint rewards.

At the same time, it should be noted that there is an important moral dimension to Islamic risk sharing, as it strengthens social solidarity by enhancing cooperation among all economic agents, which would also go some way in easing the coordination problem.[8] Moreover, when risk is spread by means of risk–reward sharing contracts, closer coordination is forged between the real and financial sectors of the economy. Risk transfer by means of interest-based debt contracts, in contrast, weakens that linkage. Particularly when risk transfer is combined with high leverage, the growth of interest-based debt contracts and their pure financial derivatives—those with little or no connection to real assets—outpaces the growth of the real sector, leaving the liabilities in the economy a large multiple of real assets needed to validate them. This phenomenon is called "financial decoupling" (Menkoff and Tolkorof, 2001) or financialization (Epstein, 2006; Palley, 2007), whereby finance is no longer anchored in the real sector. The result is financial instability leading to frequent crises. Reinhart and Rogoff (2009) have catalogued the high frequency of historical occurrences of crises in the conventional interest-based system and have clearly shown that all crises, whether classified as a currency or banking crisis, have been at their core a debt crisis.

In comparing risk-sharing financing and debt financing, Presley and Sessions propose to consider:

> . . . *a single project undertaken by a single manager, the outcome of which is determined by the level of capital investment, the level of managerial effort, and the state of nature, which we envisage in terms of some random shock to demand or technology. We examine the situations where capital is financed through* riba *[debt] and* mudarabah *[profit–loss] based contracts respectively. . . . The manager is assumed to have superior information to investors in two respects: First, having signed a contract with investors the manager is able to observe the demand or productivity conditions affecting the project before committing to production decisions; and second, he alone observes his personal level of effort. Such an asymmetry is not unusual and, indeed, rationalizes the manager's involvement in the project. But whilst the manager's relative informational expertise suggests that he should be delegated some authority over production decisions, the exploitation of this expertise is problematic. Since effort is private information, the manager cannot be compensated directly for its provision. A revelation problem therefore arises with the manager's preferences over productive inputs only coinciding with those of investors if he personally bears the entire risk of adverse shocks. . . .*

In this situation, Presley and Sessions show that a profit–loss (*mudarabah*) contract between the agent and a group of investors may result in a more efficient revelation of any informational advantage possessed by the agent over the principals. Again, and as mentioned a number of times above, it should be noted that there is an important moral dimension to Islamic risk sharing, strengthening society by enhancing cooperation between principals and bringing agents and principals closer together.

Not all debt contracts are forbidden in Islam. Contracts have to be free of an interest rate. Because they are not remunerative, debt contracts cannot play a significant economic role in financing trade and investment in Islamic finance. But the case of the needy and the poor is an exception and has a special place in Islam. Before Islam, and also in medieval Europe, the poor used to borrow by pledging their property as collateral. As default was a common event, the poor risked the loss of all their property with the consequence that often they were forced into serfdom or slavery. As a direct consequence of the principles of property rights in Islam, the poor, orphans, and the needy have a prescribed and mandatory share in the earnings of assets; essentially amounting to the provision of a social safety net.

The rich are required to share in the risk of livelihood faced by the poor, the needy, orphans, and the disabled. Prohibition of interest and the obligation of *zakat* and other prescribed duties levied on those that are materially blessed are often stated together, and not separately, in both the *Qur'an* and the *sunnah*. When members of society who are in an economically strong position shirk their duty of redeeming the rights of the needy, the needy will have to borrow or fall into abject poverty. The existence of widespread poverty in a society is *prima facie* evidence of shirking in the duty of sharing.

While, in our opinion, Islamic finance would be inherently stable because it is structured on a foundation of equity financing and risk sharing, conventional finance, a debt-and-interest-based system, has proven to be unstable. Minsky has dubbed the instability of conventional finance as endogenous instability because conventional finance experiences a three-phased cycle: relative calm, speculation and fictitious expansion, and then crisis and bankruptcy. Bankruptcy in conventional finance is not limited to the private sector, as governments can also face bankruptcy. Again, recent historical analysis has demonstrated that all financial, banking, and currency crises are at their core a crisis arising from debt (Reinhart and Rogoff, 2009). In the recent past, the widespread bankruptcies of many developing countries has entailed debt cancellation or forgiveness. This is often because governments that borrowed at what were considered reasonable debt levels (normally as measured by debt/GDP) later found themselves in an unsustainable debt spiral as a result of increased debt service obligations. In the aftermath of the recent global financial crisis, the IMF and regulators in industrial countries have called for capital surcharges on banks and for strengthened regulation and supervision to make conventional banking less crisis prone and thus more stable and safe.

VI. ISLAMIC FINANCE AND THE EVOLUTIONARY PROCESS OF EQUITY FINANCING

In an Islamic financial system, modeled with no risk-free assets, where all financial assets are contingent claims and in which there are no interest rate-based debt contracts, it has been shown that the rate of return to financial assets is determined by the rate of return in the real sector (Askari et al., 2010). Output is divided between labor and capital. Once labor is paid, the profit is then divided between entrepreneurs and equity owners. Since profits are *ex post*, returns on equities cannot be known *ex ante*. It is demonstrated that in such a system there is a one-to-one mapping between finance and the real economy, and that an equity-based finance is stable as assets and liabilities adjust to shocks, and therefore, the system is immune to banking crises and disruption in the payments mechanism.

In addition to a strict prohibition of interest-based and speculative transactions, Islamic finance is an equity-based system under which Islamic banks own real assets and participate directly in production and trade activities. Islamic finance is essentially a two-tier system, composed of deposit safekeeping banking and long-term investment banking. While in the first banking activity deposits remain highly liquid and checking services are fully available at all times, the second activity is an investment activity whereby deposits are considered as longer-term savings and banks engage directly in risk taking in trade, leasing, and productive investment in agriculture, industry, and services. The most important characteristic of this activity is that it is immune to the unbacked expansion of credit. An Islamic bank is assumed to match deposit maturities with investment maturities (with no need for asset–liability management). Short-term deposits may finance short-term trade operations, with the bank purchasing merchandise or raw materials and selling to other companies; liquidity is replenished as proceeds from sales operations are generated. For longer-term investment, longer-term deposits are used. Liquidity is replenished as amortization funds become available. In all these investments, an Islamic bank is a direct owner of the investment in a project or in a business, which is awarded through the normal due-diligence process. In such a system, a financial institution therefore participates directly in the evaluation, management, and monitoring of the investment process. Returns to invested funds arise *ex post* from the profits or losses of the operation, and are distributed to depositors as if they were shareholders of equity capital. Since loan default is absent, depositors do not face the risk of loss of their assets.

As opposed to the conventional financial system, an Islamic financial institution is prohibited from making a loan at a fixed or floating interest rate. It has to engage in real trade or production activities. An Islamic bank may, however, engage in short-term operations. It may, for instance, undertake trade operations, or it may finance crop transactions. It may buy goods on behalf of a trader, for resale at a profit. The possession of goods takes place in a physical form, and not in the form of financial or speculative contracts; in effect, there is complete transfer of property rights claims. For example, when it finances a crop transaction, the bank cannot act as a pure financier and assume no risk in its financing activities. It has to be a full partner; it buys fertilizer on behalf of farmers and makes available financing for operating costs; it participates in the marketing activity of crops. The financing institution is involved directly in all phases of the transaction on a profit–loss-sharing basis; it faces directly the risk of price and exchange rate fluctuations. It may lose part of the capital if the proceeds of sales fall short of the amount of capital. It may also incur operating losses. The invested capital is repaid from the proceeds of crop sales. Net profits are distributed according to an agreed formula. The growth of Islamic finance is thus strictly determined by real economic growth, rather than by credit and the stroke of a pen independent of the production of goods and services.

Equity financing has been an essential mode of financing of trade and industry throughout the centuries. It continues to be employed as a mode of financing in many developing countries where it has evolved with the introduction of business enterprises and stable economic growth. Historically, enterprises were established with share ownership and were recorded as share-owned or anonymous enterprises. Shares were not necessarily offered to the public through formal stock markets and were primarily private contributions of founders of the company. In many countries, share-owned companies continue to be formed without necessarily resorting to stock market public offerings. Nonetheless, with the spread of equity-financed firms, stock markets as a form of organized exchanges became an integral part of financial intermediation for channeling savings to long-term investment. Stock markets, considered as the first-best instruments of risk sharing (provided there are no short sales and limited leverage), offer liquidity for listed shares in that the owners of shares may sell them when the need for liquidity arises. Moreover, liquidity and attractiveness of stocks have been enhanced via the proliferation of derivatives such as options and futures that allow portfolio insurance against bear markets. For instance, a protective put provides protection against stock downturns. While stock markets have been vulnerable to speculative bubbles, and crashes have been ruinous to savers and to pension funds, the main reason for these adverse developments has often been informational problems, self-dealings such as insider trading, unregulated short sales that promote unnecessary speculation, lack of protection of minority shareholder rights, weak regulation and supervision, and even weaker enforcement of contracts and regulations. Many developing countries have tried to develop conventional banking to enhance their financial infrastructure; however, a large number of these countries have experienced repeated bouts of severe banking and currency crises and have failed in their effort to develop a deep and stable financial system. Economic growth and employment in these countries thus continue to be severely constrained. Developing long-term, equity-based banking and efficient stock markets could be a promising alternative for financing growth and employment creation.

VII. BALANCING SHORT-TERM, LESS RISKY LIQUID ASSETS AND LONG-TERM, HIGHER RISK, AND LESS LIQUID ASSETS: THE VIBRANT STOCK MARKET APPROACH

For Islamic finance to achieve its expected potential, it has to emphasize long-term investment and economic growth and not be confined to short-term, highly liquid, safe commodity trade, and cost-plus sale financing contracts. The focus on these short-term instruments may provide a profitable business opportunity for bankers and *Shari'ah* experts, but it achieves little in establishing a complete Islamic financial system. Long-term investments are more risky than short-term ones, as the more distant the payoffs of an investment the riskier they are. Risk increases with time. Concomitantly, long-term investments have higher expected payoffs. Nonetheless, stumbling blocks to long-term finance are liquidity, informational problems, the absence of a level playing field between equity and debt financing, weak regulation and enforcement, and non-protection of minority shareholder rights. The liquidity problem has been addressed by developing secondary markets where securities can be traded. The liquidity of equity shares is enhanced through two channels. The first channel is over-the-counter trade, where deposits in investment accounts held at an Islamic bank are transferred to a new owner who redeems the previous owner for the amount being deposited in long-term equity accounts. The second channel is organized stock market exchanges, where listed shares can be traded at low cost in liquid markets.

Risk sharing and equity finance have been emphasized in a recent paper, the focus of the next chapter, as a means to enhance Islamic finance with a view to promoting growth and employment (Mirakhor, 2010). In this paper, it is noted that the first best instrument of risk sharing is a vibrant stock market, the most sophisticated market-based risk-sharing mechanism. Developing an efficient stock market can effectively complement and supplement the existing and to-be-developed array of other Islamic finance instruments. It would provide the means for business and industry to raise capital. Such an active market would reduce the dominance of banks and debt financing where risks become concentrated, creating system fragility. In the current evolution of Islamic finance, the emphasis should be on long-term investment contracts that allow the growth of employment and income and expansion of the economy. Moreover, through holding diversified stock portfolios, investors can eliminate idiosyncratic risks specific to individual investors as well as to firms. Diversification can allow reduction in portfolio risk.

VIII. CONCLUSION

Islamic finance, based on risk sharing, has had a long history, particularly in the Middle Ages when it was the dominant form of financing investment and trade. Even today, venture capital financiers use techniques very similar to Islamic risk-sharing contracts such as *mudarabah*. Conventional banking, which began with the goldsmiths' practice of fractional reserve banking, has received strong financial subsidies from central banks as lenders of last resort, from government deposit insurance schemes, and from tax treatments, rules, and regulations which have heavily favored debt-based contracts over risk-sharing contracts. For these and other reasons, risk sharing is still at an early stage of development in all countries, to say nothing of its even more modest international application.

These developments have helped the perpetuation of a system that a number of renowned economists, such as Keynes, have deemed detrimental to growth, development, and equitable income and wealth distribution. More recently, a growing literature and proposed reforms have argued that the stability of a financial system can only be assured by limiting credit expansion and leveraging; this, in turn, requires the elimination of subsidies that fuel moral hazard, such as subsidized deposit insurance schemes and guarantees that support "too large to fail" institutions, and restrictions to limit the creation of money through the fractional reserve conventional banking system. Islamic finance, based on risk sharing and limiting fractional reserve banking, has been shown to be inherently stable and socially more equitable. In such a system, there is a one-to-one mapping between the growth of financial and real sector activities, meaning that credit cannot expand or contract independently of the real sector, as in the conventional system. In other words, the real and the financial sectors are closely connected and cannot be decoupled as in conventional finance.

To foster the development of Islamic finance, there is a need to emphasize its risk-sharing foundation, remove biases against equity finance, reduce the transaction costs of stock market participation, create a market-based incentive structure to minimize speculative behavior, and develop long-term financing instruments as well as low-cost efficient secondary markets for trading equity shares. These secondary markets would enable better distribution of risk and achieve reduced risk with expected payoffs in line with the overall stock market portfolio. Absent true risk sharing, Islamic finance may provide a false impression of being all about developing debt-like, short-term, low-risk, and highly liquid financing without manifesting the most important dimension of Islamic finance: its ability to facilitate high growth of employment and income with relatively low risk to individual investors and market participants.

In the next chapter, we follow up our discussion of risk sharing by explaining in some detail the important role of vibrant capital markets comprising asset-based securities and equity markets for promoting risk sharing. We envisage stock markets that go beyond the private sector and include shares issued by governments to finance their budgets, including diverse long-term investment projects.

ENDNOTES

1. The variance is an essential variable for pricing assets and derivatives. Many models are used for its estimation and forecast. These are the ARCH-GARCH (autoregressive conditional heteroskedasticity) models and stochastic volatility models.
2. Let the expected return of an asset be denoted as $E(R)$, its standard deviation be σ_R, and the risk-free rate of interest be R_f; the market price of risk is then defined as: $\left[E(R) - R_f\right] / \sigma_R$.
3. In option pricing, q_s are found through computing a martingale process for the underlying asset price.
4. A Walrasian auction (named after the French economist Leon Walras) is an auction where participants submit their demand at every price to the auctioneer. The auctioneer then announces the price that equates supply and demand. Equilibrium in such an auction is reached in little steps by repeating this procedure.
5. An alternative form of equation (12) is $\max_{c_t, A_t} \left\{ \sum_{t=0}^{\infty} \beta^t \sum_{s=1}^{S} \pi(s) U(c_t(s)) \right\}$ where s denotes the state at time t, $s = 1, ..., S$, and $\pi(s)$ is the probability of state s with $\sum_{s=1}^{S} \pi(s) = 1$.
6. Two variables are said to be "separable" from a third if the marginal rate of substitution between the first two is independent of the third.
7. Transaction costs can have two effects on asset prices. First, gross rates of return on securities may be altered because agents require higher returns to compensate for transaction costs. A second indirect effect of transaction costs is that they limit the ability of agents to use asset markets to self-insure against transitory shocks, so that individual consumption does not move directly with the aggregate. The implied equity premium could rise in response to increases in transaction costs alone.
8. For details of these and other rules governing the economy, see Mirakhor and Askari (2010, pp. 158–70); and Mirakhor (2010, pp. 8–19).

CHAPTER 5

Risk Sharing in the Islamic Financial System: The Building Blocks

The primary role of a financial system is to create incentives and mechanisms for an efficient allocation of financial and real resources in order to achieve competing aims and objectives across time and space. A well-functioning financial system promotes investment by: (i) identifying and funding the best business opportunities; (ii) mobilizing savings; (iii) monitoring the performance of managers; (iv) enabling the trading, hedging, and diversification of risks; and (v) facilitating the exchange of goods and services. These functions ultimately lead to the efficient allocation of resources, rapid accumulation of physical and human capital, and faster technological progress, which, in turn, stimulate economic growth.

Within a financial system, financial markets and banks perform the vital functions of capital formation, monitoring, information gathering, and facilitation of risk sharing. An efficient financial system is expected to perform several functions. First, the system should facilitate efficient financial intermediation to reduce information and allocation costs. Second, it must be based on a stable payment system. Third, with increasing globalization and demands for financial integration, it is essential that the financial system offers efficient and liquid money and capital markets. Finally, the financial system should also provide a well-developed market for risk trading, where economic agents can buy and sell protection against event risks as well as financial risks.

Research on financial intermediation and financial systems in the past two decades has enhanced our understanding of why the financial system matters, and of the crucial role it plays in economic development and growth. For example, studies have shown that countries with higher levels of financial development grow by about an additional 0.7 percent per year. Between 1980 and 1995, 35 countries experienced some degree of financial crisis. These were, essentially, periods during which their financial systems stopped functioning; consequently, their real sectors were adversely affected, leading to economic downturns and recessions. Although strong evidence points to the existence of a relationship between economic development and growth and a well-developed financial system that promotes efficient financial intermediation through a reduction in information, transaction, and monitoring costs, this linkage and the direction of causation is not as simple and straightforward as it may at first appear. The form of financial intermediation, the level of economic development, macroeconomic policies, and the regulatory and legal framework are some of the factors that can complicate the design of an efficient financial system.

I. FUNCTIONAL VIEW OF A FINANCIAL SYSTEM

A financial system may be better understood when viewed as the set of functions it performs in an economy. In contrast to the traditional view that restricts the role of a financial system to capital mobilization, a functional view is based on an expanded role for the financial system. Most poignantly, by restricting the financial system to capital mobilization, the deeper role of a financial system under uncertainty, where risk allocation becomes critical, is ignored. In addition, given information asymmetries and incentive issues, capital markets may offer more efficient contracting.[1] Another factor favoring a functional view of a financial system is that its functions do not change significantly over time and space, while the forms and functions of institutions and intermediaries are subject to change.

Although the most fundamental role of a financial system is still financial intermediation, the following are the core functions of an efficient financial system (Ul-Haque, 2002):

- **Efficient capital mobilization.** The ultimate function of a financial system is to perform efficient resource allocation through capital mobilization between savers and users of capital. This function is performed efficiently when the economic agents have access to capital through a liquid market for funding of varied maturity structures—that is, from the very short to the very long term. Access to capital has to be easy, transparent, and cost-effective, with minimal transaction costs and free of information asymmetries.
- **Efficient risk allocation.** Under volatile market conditions, risk sharing, risk transfer, and risk pooling become critical in a financial system. In the absence of such functionality, the financial system will discourage high-risk, high value-added projects. The function of "insurance" is vital in any financial system, and efficient risk-sharing facilities promote diversification and allocational efficiencies.

- **Pooling of resources and diversification of ownership.** A financial system provides a mechanism for the pooling of funds to undertake large-scale indivisible investments that may be beyond the scope of any one individual. They also allow individual households to participate in investments that require large lump sums of money, by pooling their funds and subdividing the shares in the investment. The pooling of funds allows for a redistribution of risk, as well as the separation of ownership and management (Merton and Bodie, 1995; Levine, 1997).
- **Efficient contracting.** A financial system should promote financial contracting that minimizes incentive and agency problems arising from modern contractual arrangements among owners, managers, regulators, and other stakeholders. Both financial institutions and financial markets have distinct incentive problems due to a diverse set of conflicting interests between investors, managers, owners, and regulators.
- **Transparency and price discovery.** A financial system should promote efficient processing of information such that all the information pertaining to the value of an asset is available at the lowest cost and is reflected in the value or price of the asset. This price discovery function leads capital to be allocated to the most productive use in the most efficient manner.
- **Better governance and control.** Advances in modern finance have highlighted the importance of good governance, especially with respect to financial institutions and markets. A financial system should facilitate transparency in governance and promote discipline in management through external pressures or threats, such as takeovers, so that misallocations and misappropriations are minimized.
- **Operational efficiency.** A financial system should provide smooth operation of financial intermediaries and financial markets by minimizing any operational risk due to failure in processes, settlement, clearing, and electronic communication. Smooth and transparent execution of financial transactions develops a good reputation and "trust" among economic players and is therefore beneficial in attracting external resources. This is especially poignant in emerging economies that are eager to attract foreign investors.

II. BUILDING BLOCKS OF THE ISLAMIC FINANCIAL SYSTEM

A financial system comprises different sub-systems such as the banking system, financial markets, and capital markets, and is underpinned by legal and commercial infrastructure. We now turn to a discussion of the theoretical design of the form of banking, financial intermediation, and capital markets operating on the basis of a *Shari'ah* legal system. When compared to the conventional system, the Islamic financial system has two distinct features: (i) as discussed previously, prohibition of *riba* (interest) results in the elimination of debt from the system, which ultimately removes leveraging; and (ii) the financial system promotes risk sharing through modes of transactions which are designed to share risks and rewards on an equitable basis. Because of the risk-sharing nature of the Islamic system, stock markets play a vital role and are expected to represent a large segment of the financial market. The conventional system is dominated by the debt market, followed by the banking sector and the stock market. Researchers have argued that an active and vibrant market of securitized assets, which has some resemblance to the conventional asset-based debt market but has its own distinct features, replaces the debt market and behaves and operates differently.

The banking system

The *Shari'ah* provides a set of *intermediation contracts* that facilitate efficient intermediation and is sufficiently comprehensive to provide a wide range of typical intermediation services such as asset transformation, a payment system, custodial services, and risk management. The box below briefly describes the key intermediation contracts. Both *mudarabah* (a principal–agent profit-sharing contract) and *musharakah* (an equity partnership) are cornerstones of financial intermediation in the Islamic financial system.

KEY FINANCIAL INTERMEDIATION CONTRACTS IN THE ISLAMIC FINANCIAL SYSTEM

Mudarabah (principal–agent profit-sharing assets management)

In a *mudarabah* contract, an economic agent with capital develops a partnership with another economic agent who has expertise in deploying capital into real economic activities with an agreement to share the profits. *Mudarabah* partnerships perform an important economic function by combining the three most important factors of production—capital, labor, and entrepreneurship. Typically, the contract of *mudarabah* involves an arrangement in which the capital owner entrusts his or her capital or merchandise to an agent (*mudarib*) to trade with it and then return to the investor the principal plus a previously agreed-upon share of the profits. As a reward for the agent's labor and entrepreneurship, the agent (*mudarib*) receives the remaining share of the profit. Any loss resulting from the exigencies of travel or from an unsuccessful business venture is borne exclusively by the investor. More formally, a *mudarabah* contract is a contract of partnership between the investor (principal) and the entrepreneur who acts as an agent of the investor to invest the money in a fashion deemed suitable by the agent with an agreement to share the profits. This contract is usually limited to a certain period of time at the end of which the profits are shared according to their pre-agreed profit-sharing ratios.

Musharakah (equity partnership)

The *musharakah* contract is a versatile contract with different variations to suit different situations. *Musharakah* is a hybrid of *shirakah* (partnership) and *mudarabah*, combining the act of investment and management. *Musharakah* or *shirakah* can be defined as a form of partnership where two or more people combine either their capital or labor in order to share the profits and losses, and where they have similar rights and liabilities.

Wikalah (principal–agent representation)

The contract of *wikalah* is the designation of a person or legal entity to act on one's behalf or as one's representative. It has been a common practice to appoint an agent (*wakil*) to facilitate trade operations. A *wikala* contract gives a power of attorney or an agency assignment to a financial intermediary to perform a certain task. In the case of *mudarabah*, the *mudarib* has full control and freedom to utilize funds according to their professional knowledge; in the case of *wikalah*, the agent (*wakil*) does not have similar freedom. A *wakil* (agent) acts only as a representative to execute a particular task according to the instructions given.

Amanah (trust) and *wadia* (deposits)

Amanah and *wadia* contracts are all concerned with placing assets in trust with someone. These contracts are utilized in facilitating a custodial relationship between investors and the financial institutions. *Wadia* (deposit) arises when a person keeps his or her property with another person for safekeeping and also allows him or her to use it without the intention of receiving any return from it. The term *amanah* (trust deposit) is a broad term where one party is entrusted with the custody

(Continued)

(Continued)

or safekeeping of someone else's property. In the context of interme-diation, *amanah* refers to a contract where a party deposits assets with another for the sole purpose of safekeeping. Unlike *wadia*, where the keeper of the asset is allowed to use the asset, an *amanah* deposit is purely for safekeeping and the keeper cannot use the asset. Demand deposits of an Islamic bank are offered through *amanah* contracts.

Kifala (suretyship)

The contract of *kifala* refers to an obligation in addition to an existing obligation in respect of a demand for something. In the case of finan-cial obligations, it refers to an obligation to be met in the event of the principal debtor's inability to honor his or her obligation. In financial transactions, under the contract of *kifala*, a third party becomes a surety for the payment of a debt or obligation if it is not paid or ful-filled by the person originally liable.

Jo'ala (service fee)

The contract of *jo'ala* deals with offering a service for a predeter-mined fee or commission. A party undertakes to pay another party a specified amount of money as a fee for rendering a specified service in accordance with the terms of the contract stipulated between the two parties. *Jo'ala* allows contracting on an object not certain to exist or come under a party's control.

Although committed to carrying out their transactions in accordance with the rules of the *Shari'ah*, Islamic banks are expected to perform the same essential functions as banks in the conventional system. That is, they act as the administrators of the economy's payments system and as financial inter-mediaries. The need for them in the Islamic system arises precisely for the same reason as in the conventional system. That is, generally, their *raison d'être* is the exploitation of the imperfections in the financial markets. These imper-fections include imperfect divisibility of financial claims, transaction costs of search, acquisition, and diversification by the surplus and deficit units, and the existence of expertise and economies of scale in monitoring transactions.

Permissible contracts for trade, and for the exchange of goods and ser-vices, coupled with intermediation contracts, offer a comprehensive set of instruments with varying financing purposes, maturities, and degrees of risk to satisfy the needs of diverse groups of economic agents in the economy. This set of instruments can be used to design a formal model for an Islamic financial intermediary (IFI) or an Islamic bank that can perform the typical functions of resource mobilization and intermediation. By utilizing this set of intermediation contracts, an IFI will be able to offer a wide array of commercial- and investment-banking products and services.

Formally, three theoretical models have been suggested for the structure of Islamic financial intermediation and banking. The first model is based on *mudarabah* and is commonly referred to as the "two-tier" *mudarabah* model, while the second model is known as the "two-windows" model. A less-used model is the *wikala* model, which is based on the principal–agent model but with defined restrictions. As mentioned earlier, a *mudarabah* is a principal–agent contract, where the owner of the capital (investor or depositor) forms a partnership with the entity that has the specialized skill (professional manager or bank) to invest capital and to share profits and losses from the investment.

"Two-tier" *mudarabah* **model**   This model is called "two-tier" because the *mudarabah* contract is utilized on each side of the bank's balance sheet. The first model, relying on the concept of profit sharing, integrates the assets and liabilities sides on the basis of the principle called "two-tier" *mudarabah*. This model envisages depositors entering into a contract with a bank to share the profits accruing to the bank's business. The basic concept of this model is that both fund mobilization and fund utilization are on the same basis of profit sharing among the investor (depositor), the bank, and the entrepreneur (the user of the funds). The first tier of the *mudarabah* contract is between the investor (analogous to a depositor) and the bank, where investors act as suppliers of funds to be invested by the bank as *mudarib* on their behalf. The investors share in the profits and losses earned by the bank's business related to the investors' investments. Funds are placed with the bank in an investment account.

The liabilities and equity side of the bank's balance sheet thus shows the deposits accepted on a *mudarabah* basis. Such profit-sharing investment deposits are not liabilities (the capital is not guaranteed and they incur losses if the bank does), but are a form of limited-term, non-voting equity. In this model, in addition to investment deposits, banks accept demand deposits that yield no returns and are repayable on demand at par and are treated as liabilities. This model, though requiring that current deposits must be paid on the demand, has no reserve requirement.

The second tier represents the *mudarabah* contract between the bank as the supplier of funds and the entrepreneurs who need funds and agree to share profits with the bank as stipulated in the contract. The bank's earnings from all its activities are pooled and are then shared with its depositors and shareholders according to the terms of their contract. Thus the profit earned by the depositors is then a percentage of the total banking profits. A distinguishing feature of the "two-tier" model is that, by design, the assets and liabilities sides of a bank's balance sheet are fully integrated, which minimizes the need for active asset–liability management; this, in turn, provides stability against economic shocks. The model does not feature any specific reserve requirements on either the investments or the demand deposits.

"Two-windows" model   The "two-windows" model also features demand and investment accounts, but takes a different view from the "two-tier" model on reserve requirements. The "two-windows" model divides the liabilities side of the bank balance sheet into two windows, one for demand deposits (transactions balances) and the other for investment balances. The choice of the window is left to the depositors. This model requires a 100 percent reserve for the demand deposits but stipulates no reserve requirement for the second window. This is based on the assumption that the money deposited as demand deposits is placed as *amanna* (safekeeping) and must be backed by 100 percent reserves, because these balances belong to depositors and do not give a bank the right to use them as the basis for money creation through fractional reserves. Money deposited in investment accounts, on the other hand, is placed with the depositors' full knowledge that their deposits will be invested in risk-bearing projects, and therefore no guarantee is justified. Also in this model, depositors may be charged a service fee for the safekeeping services rendered by the bank. In this model, the provision of interest-free loans to those who may need them is limited to the funds deposited in such accounts by the depositors who think that the bank may be better equipped for this purpose. No portion of the deposits in the current accounts or investment accounts will be required to be used for this purpose.

Wikalah model   A third but less-known model for an Islamic bank has also been suggested. This model is based on the contract of *wikalah*, where an Islamic bank acts purely as *wakil* (agent or representative) of the investors and manages funds on their behalf on the basis of a fixed fee. The terms and conditions of the *wikalah* contract are to be determined by mutual agreement between the bank and the clients.

Figure 5.1 shows a simplified version of how a typical Islamic bank can be structured to mobilize funding from the deposits and how the funds are invested in different instruments. The bank's relationship with the depositors could be on the basis of a *mudarabah, amanah, wikalah*, or *wadia* contract on its liabilities side. However, on the assets side, the bank has more freedom and choices in investing depositors' funds. Islamic banks carry

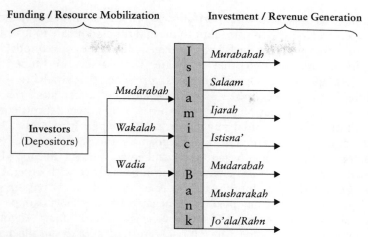

FIGURE 5.1 Islamic Financial Intermediation

murabahah, ijarah, istisna', mudarabah, and *musharakah* investments on their assets side.

Banks in the Islamic financial system can be reasonably expected to exploit economies of scale, as do their counterparts in the conventional system. Through their ability to take advantage of these imperfections, they alter the yield relationships between surplus and deficit financial units and thus provide financing at a lower cost and a higher return than would be possible with direct financing. Just as in the conventional financial system, the Islamic depository enables financial intermediaries to transform the liabilities of business into a variety of obligations to suit the preferences and circumstances of savers. Their liabilities consist of investments or deposits, and their assets consist mainly of instruments of varying risk–return profiles. These banks are concerned with decisions relating to such issues as the nature of their objective functions, portfolio choice among risky assets, liability and capital management, reserve management, the interaction between the asset and liability sides of their balance sheets, and the management of off-balance sheet items—such as revolving lines of credit, standby and commercial letters of credit, and bankers' acceptances.

Moreover, as asset transformers, these institutions can assess risk and serve as filters to evaluate signals in a financial environment with limited information. Their deposit liabilities serve as a medium of exchange, and they have the ability to minimize the cost of transactions that convert current income into an optimal consumption bundle. One major difference between the two systems is that, due to the prohibition against taking interest and the fact that they have to rely primarily on profit sharing, Islamic banks have to offer their asset portfolios of primary securities in the form of risky open-ended investments (akin to mutual funds) for sale to investors or depositors. In contrast to the Islamic system, banks in the conventional system keep title to the portfolios they originate. These assets are funded by the banks through issuing deposit contracts, a practice that results in solvency and liquidity risks, since their asset portfolios and loans entail risky pay-offs or costs of liquidation prior to maturity, while their deposit contracts are liabilities that are often payable instantly at par. In contrast, Islamic banks act as agents of investors or depositors and therefore create pass-through intermediation between savers and entrepreneurs. In short, Islamic financial intermediaries are envisioned to intermediate with an embedded notion of risk sharing. Intermediation is performed on a "pass-through" basis such that the returns (positive or negative) on the assets are passed to the investors or depositors. The intermediary applies financial engineering to design assets with a wide range of risk–return profiles to suit the demands of investors on the liabilities side of its balance sheet.

The conventional banking system is a fractional reserve banking system that is predominantly based on debt financing and, by its struc-ture, creates money and encourages leveraging. The embedded risk of such a system is that money and debt creation and leveraging could be excessive. Safeguards such as deposit guarantee schemes along the lines of the FDIC in the United States, and the classification of some banks as "too big to fail," are the implicit government subsidies that reduce funding cost and create moral hazard, encouraging mispricing and excessive assumption of risk by financial institutions. The mispricing of loans and the assumption of excessive risk, in turn, threaten the liquidity and solvency of financial institutions. Systemic risks that are inherent in the system, such as the link-ages and the interdependencies of institutions as well as the prominence of "too big to fail" institutions, create financial instability and threaten the financial and real economy. To enhance financial stability, regulators would have to adopt policies and practices that eliminate moral hazard and exces-sive debt creation and leveraging, or a clear separation between retail and investment banking (along the lines proposed in 2011 by the Chancellor of the Exchequer in the UK).

One way to ensure the stability of the financial system is to *eliminate* the type of asset–liability risk that threatens the solvency of all financial institutions, including commercial banks. This would require commercial banks to restrict their activities to two: (i) cash safekeeping; and (ii) investing client money, such as in a mutual fund. Banks would accept deposits for safekeeping only (as, for example, in a system with a 100 percent reserve requirement), and would charge a fee for providing this service and check-writing privileges. In their intermediation capacity, banks would identify and analyze investment opportunities and offer them to clients; the bank would charge a fee for this service, much like a traditional investment bank. The bank would not be assuming any asset–liability risk on its balance sheet; instead, gains or losses would accrue directly to the client investors. In other words, there would be very little debt financing by banks, only equity financing; and no risk shifting, only risk sharing. Banks would not create money as under a fractional reserve system. Financial institutions would be serving their traditional role of intermediation between savers and investors but with no debt on their balance sheets, no leveraging, and no predetermined interest rate payments as an obligation.

Proposals along these lines are not new. Financial systems in some such form or other have been practiced throughout recorded history. As mentioned earlier, such an approach was recommended in the "Chicago Plan," and more recently Laurence Kotlikoff (2010) has made a proposal along similar lines, calling it "Limited Purpose Banking." Henry and Kotlikoff, writing in *Forbes* (2010), said of the Kotlikoff approach:

> *Were we really serious about fixing our financial system, there's a very simple alternative—Limited Purpose Banking. LPB would transform all financial intermediaries with limited liability into mutual fund companies. Under LPB a single regulatory agency— the "Federal Financial Authority"—would organize the independent rating, verification, custody and full disclosure of all securities held by the mutual funds. Voilà, by dint of competition and transparency, "liar loans," off-balance sheet gimmickry, and toxic assets would all disappear. LPB would let the financial sector do only what Main Street needs it to do—connect lenders to borrowers and savers to investors. The financial sector's job is not to take taxpayers to the casino and collect the winnings.*

Henry and Kotlikoff suggest why fundamental reform may have been sidestepped yet again:

> *This kind of "cowboy capitalism" is far too dangerous to maintain. But Dodd-Frank does precisely this, albeit with many more regulatory cops on the beat. In contrast, LPB would put an end to Wall Street's gambling with taxpayer chips. Since mutual funds are, in effect, small banks with 100% capital requirements in all circumstances, they can never fail. Neither can their holding companies. Under LPB, financial crises and the massive damage they inflict on the entire (global) economy would become a thing of the past. Of course, there would be losers. Some Wall Street executives*

might have to find employment in Las Vegas or offshore banks. Some lobbyists, lawyers, credit analysts and accountants might need to find higher callings. Some politicians might even have to solicit more support from Main Street. Alas, Dodd-Frank bears no resemblance to Limited Purpose Banking. But bad laws don't always last, and this one may eventually lead us to LPB by showing us precisely what not to do—if we ever get another chance.

Distinct features of the Islamic mode of intermediation and banking

Financial intermediation and banking in the Islamic financial system differ from conventional banking in a number of important ways:

- **Nature of fiduciary responsibilities.** With financial intermediation in Islam, the intermediary simply "passes through" the performance of its assets to the investors or depositors on its liability side. There is an element of risk sharing present in the contractual agreement between the financial intermediary and the depositors or investors. Assets on the asset side of the balance sheet could be in the form of over-the-counter assets financed by the Islamic bank or direct investments in marketable securities of *Shari'ah*-compliant assets—that is, equities or asset-linked securities. In the case of Islamic banks, there is more diversity of contractual agreements as the bank may be acting as a trustee in one mode of intermediation and as a "partner" in another. Islamic banks also enter into a principal–agent model on both sides of the balance sheet.
- **Profit–loss sharing.** The profit-and-loss-sharing concept implies a direct concern for the profitability of the physical investment on the part of the creditor (the Islamic bank). The conventional bank is also concerned about the profitability of the project, because of concerns about potential default on the loan. However, the conventional bank puts the emphasis on receiving the interest payments according to set time intervals, and so long as this condition is met, the bank's profitability is not directly affected by whether the project has a particularly high or low rate of return. In contrast, the Islamic bank has to focus on the return on the physical investment, because its own profitability is directly linked to the real rate of return.
- **Enhanced monitoring.** Islamic financial contracting encourages banks to focus on the long term in their relationships with their clients. However, this focus on long-term relationships in profit-and-loss-sharing

arrangements means that there might be higher costs in some areas, particularly in regard to the need for monitoring the performance of the entrepreneur. Conventional banks are not obliged to oversee projects as closely as Islamic banks, because the former do not act as if they were partners in the physical investment. To the extent that Islamic banks provide something akin to equity financing as opposed to debt financing, they need to invest relatively more in managerial skills and expertise in overseeing different investment projects. This is one reason why there is a tendency among Islamic banks to rely on financial instruments that are acceptable under Islamic principles, but which are not the best in terms of risk-sharing properties, because in some respects these financial instruments are closer to debt than to equity.

- **Asset–liability management.** Theoretically, Islamic banks offer their asset portfolios in the form of risky open-ended "mutual funds" to investors or depositors. By contrast, banks in the conventional system finance their assets through issuing time-bound deposit contracts. This practice results in solvency and liquidity risks, since their asset portfolios and loans entail risky payoffs and/or liquidation costs prior to maturity, while their deposit contracts are liabilities that are often payable instantly at par. In contrast, Islamic banks act as agents for investors or depositors and therefore create a pass-through intermediation between savers and entrepreneurs, eliminating the risk faced by conventional banks. One of the most critical and distinguishing features of financial intermediation by Islamic banks is the inherent design by which the assets and liabilities sides of the Islamic bank's balance sheet are matched. In the case of a conventional bank, deposits are accepted at a predetermined rate irrespective of the rate of return earned on the assets side of the bank. This instantaneously creates a fixed liability for the bank without the certainty that the bank would be able to earn more than it promised or was committed to paying to the depositors. Since the return on the asset depends on the bank's ability to invest the funds at a higher rate than the one promised on the liability side, and this rate is unknown, it can lead to the classical mismatch between assets and liabilities. In contrast, there is no predetermined rate on the deposits or investments and the depositors' share in the profits and losses on the assets side of the Islamic bank; therefore, the asset–liability mismatch problem does not arise. It has been argued that because of this pass-through nature of the business and the closely matched assets and liabilities, financial intermediation by Islamic banks contributes to the stability of the Islamic financial system.

Capital markets

Conventional capital markets can be broadly divided into three categories: (i) debt markets; (ii) equities or stock markets; and (iii) markets for structured securities, which are hybrids of either equity or debt securities. Debt markets dominate the conventional capital markets, and debt is considered the major source of external funding for the corporate and public sectors. As a result of financial innovations and the application of financial engineering, large numbers of financial products have been developed for resource mobilization. Most of these innovations are variations of the plain-vanilla debt or equity securities with added optionalities or customization. In comparison, Islamic capital markets have two major categories: (i) stock markets; and (ii) securitized "asset-linked" securities. Due to the prohibition of interest, the financial system will be free of any debt market and there will be a clear preference for risk-sharing securities, such as an exchange-traded stock market. After the stock market, a market for securitized securities issued against a pool of assets, which has the risk–return characteristics of the underlying assets, would be the major source of capital.

Stock market   With the prohibition on interest and the preference for partnerships to share profits and losses, equity markets hold a significant place in the Islamic financial system. Therefore, Islamic scholars have pointed out the necessity, desirability, and permissibility of a stock market in the Islamic financial system in which transactions in primary capital instruments such as corporate stocks can take place. The conditions for operating these markets, in accordance with the rules of the *Shari'ah*, are much like those that must prevail in markets for goods and services. For example, in such markets the rules are intended to remove all factors inimical to justice in exchange and to yield prices that are considered fair and just. Prices are just or equitable not on any independent criterion of justice, but because they are the result of bargaining between equal, informed, free, and responsible economic agents. To ensure justice in exchange, the *Shari'ah* has provided a network of ethical and moral rules of behavior for all participants in the market and requires that these norms and rules be internalized and adhered to by all. Given that a proper securities underwriting function is performed by some institutions in the system—for instance, the banks—the firms could then directly raise the necessary funds for their investment projects from the stock market, which would provide them a second source of funding other than the banks.

If we assert that Islamic finance is all about risk sharing, then the first-best instrument of risk sharing is a stock market, "which is arguably the most sophisticated market-based risk-sharing mechanism" (Brav et al.,

2002). Developing an efficient stock market can effectively complement and supplement the existing and to-be-developed array of other Islamic finance instruments. It would provide the means for business and industry to raise long-term capital. A vibrant stock market would allow risk diversification necessary for the management of aggregate and idiosyncratic risks. Such an active market would reduce the dominance of banks and debt financing where risks become concentrated and lead to system fragility (Sheng, 2009).

A stock market operating strictly in accordance with Islamic rules is envisioned to be one in which the disposal of investible funds is based on the profit prospects of enterprises, in which relative profit rates reflect the efficiencies between firms, and in which profit rates (as signals coming from the goods market) are not distorted by market imperfections. Such a market might be expected to allocate investible funds strictly in accordance with expected investment yields—that is, resources would be allocated in order to finance higher return projects. Stock markets would also be capable of improving allocation of savings by accumulating and disseminating vital information in order to facilitate comparisons between all available opportunities, thus reflecting the general efficiency in resource allocation expected from a system that operates primarily on the basis of investment productivity.

Stock markets and their role in risk sharing in an Islamic financial system are discussed in depth in the next chapter.

Securitized "asset-linked securities" market In addition to the standard stock market, there is another capital market that provides a platform for trading asset-linked securities. The idea behind tying capital or financing closely and tightly to a real asset (that is, what is being financed) encourages the issuance of securities against a portfolio of assets.

III. DERIVATIVE MARKETS

No discussion of financial systems can be complete without a mention of derivative markets. Derivative markets perform three major functions in a financial system:

- **Risk reduction and redistribution.** It is widely accepted that the primary function of the derivatives market is to facilitate the transfer of risk among economic agents. Financial derivatives unbundle the risks associated with traditional domestic and cross-border investment vehicles, such as foreign exchange, interest rate, market, credit, and liquidity risks. Derivatives facilitate the decomposition of risks and the redistribution of these risks from those who do not want or are not capable of hedging them to those who are in a better position to do so.

- **Price discovery and stabilization.** The existence of derivatives markets for futures and options is expected to increase information flows into the market and is known to lead to a price-discovery function in the financial sector.

- **Completeness of markets.** The derivatives markets enable individuals and firms to customize and monetize payoffs that might not otherwise be possible without considerable transaction costs.

Research on the scope of derivative securities and trading of risk in an Islamic financial system is in its early stages. *Shari'ah* scholars are working on assessing the permissibility of derivatives such as forwards, futures, options, and swaps. Unlike financing and investment instruments, which have been in existence for several centuries and, therefore, have been taken up by *Shari'ah* scholars, financial derivatives as independent financial contracts that can be traded have no precedents in classical Islamic jurisprudence. As a result, the research in this area is still evolving, without concrete conclusions.

The majority view of *Shari'ah* scholars is that an option is a promise to sell or purchase a thing at a specific price within a stipulated time, and such a promise cannot be the subject of a sale or purchase. As the resolution of the Islamic Fiqh Academy, Jeddah, asserts:

> *Option contracts as currently applied in the world financial markets are a new type of contract which do not come under any one of the* Shari'ah *nominate contracts. Since the subject of the contract is neither a sum of money nor a utility nor a financial right which may be waived, the contract is not permissible in* Shari'ah.

These objections are based on the prohibition of *maysir* and *gharar*. The *Qur'an* prohibits *maysir* (speculative risk), warning the faithful to avoid games of chance with asymmetrical probabilities, where the probability of a loss is much higher than the probability of a gain. Conventional finance asserts that speculators play an important role in price discovery and price stabilization, but it omits the fact that excessive and large-scale speculation can become a factor for instability in the system. In Islam, gambling of any form is strictly discouraged on the grounds that it does not create value in society and an addiction to gambling is detrimental to economic growth.

In short, debate on derivatives will continue in Islamic finance, but at present they have very limited acceptability and it is unlikely that the practice of derivatives will be as widespread as seen in conventional markets any time soon. However, as Islamic finance grows, its own version of hedging mechanisms and financial products with embedded options will emerge. Prohibition of derivatives, however, does not preclude an Islamic financial intermediary from designing a risk-sharing or risk-mitigating scheme. This can be achieved through the creation of a risk-mitigating instrument synthetically using existing instruments. As was shown in the previous chapter, Islamic financial instruments promote risk sharing, which implies that there will be risk sharing across the system and that there will be opportunities for financial intermediaries to utilize these contracts and the freedom to contract in designing products and services to hedge against exposures.

IV. PRIMARY, SECONDARY, AND MONEY MARKETS

The development of a secondary market is important and essential to the development of a primary market. All savers, to some degree, have a liquidity preference. This liquidity preference, although perhaps to a different extent and magnitude, can exist in an Islamic system or in any other system. To the extent that savers can, if necessary, sell securities quickly and at low cost, they will be more willing to devote a higher portion of their savings to long-term instruments than they would otherwise. Since the probability is high that primary securities in the Islamic system would be tied to the projects and management of particular enterprises, there are various risks that must enter into the portfolio decisions of savers. The risks regarding the earning power of the firm and of its default are examples of these types of risks.

There is another class of risk that is closely tied to the secondary market for a given security issued by firms. If two securities are identical in all respects except that one has a well-organized secondary market while the other has a poorly organized one, an investor in the latter runs the risk of liquidating his or her securities holdings at depressed prices as compared to the prices offered for the security with the well-organized secondary market. Moreover, the degree of this marketability risk is directly related to factors such as the extent of the knowledge of the participants, as well as the number of traders in the market, which determine the depth and resilience of the secondary markets.

In an Islamic system, perhaps more than in any other, both the primary and secondary markets require the active support of the government, the central bank, and regulators, not only in their initial development and promotion but also in their supervision and control, in order to ensure their compliance with the rules of the *Shari'ah*. Particularly in the case of the secondary markets, the traders and the market makers need the support and supervision of the central bank if these markets are to operate efficiently. For secondary markets to be able to transform an asset into a reliable source of cash for an economic unit whenever the latter needs it, they must be dealer markets, in which there is a set of position users who trade significant amounts of assets. In the traditional interest-based system, these position takers are financed by borrowings from banks, financial intermediaries, and other private cash sources. Since in the Islamic system refinancing on the basis of debt is not permitted, reliable and adequate sources of funds must be provided by the central bank. There will have to be arrangements through which the central bank and the financial regulator can, at least partially, finance secondary markets and supervise them fully.

In a conventional interest-based system, the money market becomes a means by which financial institutions can adjust their balance sheet and finance positions. Short-term cash positions, which exist as a result of imperfect synchronization in the payment period, become the essential ingredient for the presence of the money markets. The money market, in this case, becomes a source of temporary financing and an abode of excess liquidity in which transactions are mainly portfolio adjustments and no planned or recently achieved savings need be involved.

In an Islamic financial system, the liabilities that an economic unit generates are, by necessity, closely geared to the characteristics of its investment. On the other hand, the liabilities that financial intermediaries generate are expected to have nearly the same distribution of possible values as the assets they acquire. Hence, given that debt instruments cannot exist, money market activities will have different characteristics from their counterparts in the conventional system. As stated earlier, the existence of a poorly organized money market combined with a poor structure of financial intermediation leads to a situation where money becomes more important as a repository of wealth than would be the case with more active financial intermediation.

The existence of broad, deep, and resilient markets where assets and liabilities of financial intermediaries can be negotiated is a necessary feature of supportive money markets. Additionally, to the extent that money markets lower the income elasticity of demand for cash and finance investment projects, their importance in an Islamic financial system cannot be overlooked. Even in this system, money markets will enable financial units to be safely illiquid, provided they have assets that can be efficiently exchanged for cash in the money market. In this system, too, the basic source of the money in the market is the existence of pools of excess liquidity. One main activity of money markets in this system is to make arrangements by which the surplus funds of one financial institution are channeled into profit-sharing projects of another. It is conceivable that, at times, excess funds may be available with some banks, but no assets, or at least assets attractive enough in terms of their risk–return characteristics, on which they can take a position. On the other hand, there may be banks with insufficient financial resources to fund all available opportunities, or with investment opportunities requiring commitments of what the banks may consider excessive funds in order for them to take a position and for which they may prefer risk sharing with surplus banks. In such a case, the development of an interbank funds market is a distinct possibility. It may also be possible for some banks to refinance a certain position that they have taken by agreeing to share their prospective profits in these positions with other banks in the interbank funds market. Finally, since most of the investment portfolios of banks will contain equity positions of various maturities, it is also possible that a sub-set of their asset portfolios comprising equity shares can be offered in the money market in exchange for liquidity.

Here, too, effective and viable money markets in an Islamic system will require active support and participation by the central bank, particularly at times when the investment opportunities or the risk–return composition of projects and shortages of liquidity in the banking system may require a lender of last resort. Such money markets must be flexible enough to handle periods of cash shortage for individual banks, based on some form of profit-sharing arrangement. The challenge for money markets, as well as for the secondary markets, in an Islamic financial system is the development of instruments that satisfy the liquidity, security, and profitability needs of the markets while, at the same time, ensuring compliance with the rules of the *Shari'ah*—that is, provision of *uncertain and variable rates of return on instruments with corresponding real asset backing.*

V. CONCLUSION

In this chapter, we have provided an outline of the Islamic financial system and its role in the broader economy. The functions of the Islamic financial system in the economy are similar to those of the conventional system. However, because of the prohibition of interest and debt in Islam, the Islamic system is based on risk sharing as contrasted with risk shifting, which is the case with debt. As such, Islamic finance relies heavily on equity finance. In turn, this calls for well-developed stock markets and other secondary capital markets for equity finance to motivate savers to provide financing and to supply entrepreneurs with sufficient resources for their projects. The building blocks of the Islamic financial system are readily identified and require important government regulations and supervision to be effective and efficient.

ENDNOTE

1. In contrast, the market-based or market-dominated view highlights the growth-enhancing role of well-functioning markets through: (i) fostering greater incentives to research new firms and to profit from this information by trading in large and liquid markets; (ii) facilitating corporate control by easing takeovers and linking managerial compensation to firm performance; and (iii) enabling risk trading.

CHAPTER 6

Risk Sharing and Vibrant Capital Markets in Islamic Finance

Because of the prohibition of risk-shifting interest rate-based debt contracts and their replacement by risk-sharing equity contracts, Islamic finance is essentially an equity-based financial system requiring vibrant capital markets for its successful operation. In order to fit into this framework, Islamic banking has been envisioned as a two-tier banking system: (i) a banking system that accepts deposits for safekeeping, thus protecting the payment system of the economy while concurrently limiting the credit-creating ability of the banking system, and thereby obviating the need for a deposit guarantee as in the conventional fractional reserve system; and (ii) an investment component that functions as a classical financial intermediary, channeling savings to investment projects, and where deposits in investment banks are considered as equity shares with no guarantees for their face value at maturity and subject to the sharing of profits and losses. These banks invest directly in real projects in every segment of the economy (except in activities that are prohibited, such as gambling and alcohol) and share in their attendant risks. Vibrant capital markets are essential for these institutions to fulfill their central role as intermediaries as envisaged in Islamic finance.

Recently, Mirakhor (2010) has argued that an important element for promoting risk sharing is a vibrant capital market. Specifically, he has recommended that Islamic finance would more readily achieve its envisioned objective of promoting risk sharing through more comprehensive stock markets. Many developing countries have a banking system but do not have a stock market. One reason could be the very limited entrepreneurial capacity in creating productive projects, and also the limited amount of real savings available for investment. Moreover, many of these markets suffer from informational problems and governance issues that create high transaction costs. Developing a stock market could be a major channel for mobilizing savings for productive investment. The primary objective of the stock market is to enhance financial intermediation through a non-banking channel, primarily stock exchanges and over-the-counter markets. Stock markets have been instrumental in the development process of most industrial countries. Their main contributions have been to raise venture and equity capital and provide liquidity for investors. Equity capital is the normal source of funding for business enterprises in all countries throughout history, with the equity owned individually or by business associates. Investors in stocks could be the initial founders of the enterprise. Their aim is not speculative or short-term. Their purpose is to establish a productive firm that would produce real goods and services, provide employment, and be expected to stay in business indefinitely, commonly referred to as "a going concern." Investors may be individuals and entities looking for investments; they may be institutional investors, such as pension funds and endowment funds; or, in fact, they could be anyone looking for viable investments that entail risk sharing.

In the natural development of a successful firm, growth requires increasingly diversified sources of capital that may have to be shared by a larger number of stakeholders. Some firms may go public and allow their shares to be traded on the stock market. Going public affords the company access to a wider and more diversified pool of capital and gives its shareholders enhanced liquidity. The importance of a national stock market depends on many factors, including the general business climate and the quality of institutions, economic performance, economic size, the availability of entrepreneurial talent, the size of the savings pool, and the number of listed firms. As an economy grows, develops, and creates public companies, the more important becomes the stock market as the instrument for financing projects and corporate operations. The primary function of a stock market is the financing of companies and their projects, which in turn is intimately connected to the real economy—the production of goods and services demanded by consumers, institutions, and governments.

In this chapter, we examine stock markets as a fundamental driver of Islamic finance. We hope to show that an Islamic stock market is endogenously stable and is not vulnerable to the instability that has periodically undermined conventional stock markets, turning them into veritable "casinos." Periodic crashes of stock markets have ruined investors and banks, and resulted in deep economic recessions. The inherent stability of an Islamic stock market is akin to the inherent stability of an Islamic banking system. It is due basically to the prohibition of interest rate-based debt contracts and speculation, and the existence of rules governing the behavior of participants, such as trust, faithfulness to the terms and conditions of contracts, clear property rights, and effective enforcement. Ensuring stability and reducing transaction costs would enhance efficiency and increase participation in a stock market.

I. STOCK MARKETS IN ISLAMIC FINANCE

Islamic finance is based on risk sharing and a market where residual shares in firms in the form of stocks are traded, short sales are limited and regulated, and the probability of leverage is minimized. Stock markets are such effective tools for risk sharing because each share represents a contingent residual equity claim. Particularly in the case of open corporations, their common stocks are "proportionate claims on the pay offs of all future states" (Fama and Jensen, 1983). These returns are contingent on future outcomes. Stock markets that are well organized, regulated, and supervised are efficient from an economic point of view because they allocate risks according to the risk-bearing ability of the participants. The Arrow-Debreu model of competitive equilibrium provides a solution to the problem of how best the risks of an economy can be allocated (see Chapter 4). According to this model, efficient risk sharing requires that economic risks be allocated among participants in accordance with their "respective degree of risk tolerance" (see Hellwig, 1998, and Chapter 4). Governments could also access stock markets as a vehicle for equity-based financing of their investment projects.

Thus the first-best instrument of risk sharing is a stock market, ". . . arguably the most sophisticated market-based risk-sharing mechanism" (Brav et al., 2002). Developing an efficient stock market can effectively complement and supplement the existing and to-be-developed array of other Islamic financial instruments. It would provide the means for business and industry to raise long-term capital. A vibrant stock market would allow risk diversification necessary for the management of aggregate and idiosyncratic risks. Such an active market would reduce the dominance of banks and debt financing where risks become concentrated, creating in turn system fragility.

A large number of theoretical and empirical studies over recent decades have focused on the investment-employment-growth benefits of stock markets (see the reference list in Askari et al., 2010). When risk is spread among a large number of participants through an efficient stock market, closer coordination between the financial and real sectors is promoted, as well as better sharing of the benefits of economic growth and financial system stability. Risk transfer through debt instruments, in contrast, along with high leverage, weakens the link between the financial and real sectors, thus posing a threat to financial sector stability. As the growth of pure financial instruments—that is, those with little connection to real assets—outstrips the real sector, a phenomenon emerges called decoupling (Menkoff and Tolkorof, 2001) or financialization (Epstein, 2006; Palley, 2007), whereby finance is no longer anchored in the real sector. As we have stated earlier, the result is financial instability leading to frequent crises. Again, Reinhart and Rogoff (2009) have demonstrated the high frequency of crises in the history of the conventional system, which crises are invariably connected to excessive increases in debt financing. All too often, financial sector crises have required large government interventions and massive bailouts. Thus, while private financiers enjoy the gains of robust pure financial innovations, which ultimately lead to decoupling, the society at large suffers the pain of saving the real sector from the vagaries of financial sector crises. This is what Sheng (2009) has aptly called "privatizing the gain, socializing the pain."

Empirical studies have also demonstrated that countries with robust stock markets rely more on equity and long-term financing and less on banks and short-term debt. Firms place greater reliance on external capital than on internally generated funds. With a strong stock market, venture capitalists can recoup their capital investment in a project through an initial public offering, thus promoting faster rollover of venture capital to make it available more frequently to finance other productive real sector projects. Not only can individuals and firms benefit from the existence of a vibrant and robust stock market that provides risk-sharing opportunities, but also countries can benefit from risk sharing with one another. A large body of empirical research in recent years, in the area of international risk sharing, has demonstrated that there are gains to be made by countries when they trade in each other's securities. For example, Kim et al. (2005) looked at the potential welfare gains of 10 East Asian countries through sharing risk among them and separately with the OECD. Indonesia and Malaysia had the lowest level of risk sharing and, therefore, the largest potential for welfare gains from improving the sharing of risk between them and other East Asian countries. The magnitude of gains was even higher through increased risk sharing with the OECD. These results would in all likelihood be replicated in other areas and regions.

Governments should also become active in stock markets, as they generally share risks with their citizens. They share risks with individuals, firms, and corporations through their tax and spending policies. They also share the risk of livelihood of their poor and disadvantaged citizens through social expenditures. They provide natural disaster relief. They share in financial system risk through monetary policy and deposit guarantee. They could choose to finance part of their budget, at least their development spending, through risk sharing and direct ownership of development projects with their citizens. In this way, they would also reduce their budgetary debt burden; the attendant reduction in government borrowing would in turn reduce the burden on monetary policy. Governments undertake public goods projects because the characteristics of these goods—especially their indivisibility and non-exclusivity characteristics—prohibit their production by the private sector. However, the social rate of return of public goods is substantial and is likely to be much higher than private rates of return. Some have made suggestions that these projects should be undertaken jointly with the private sector, hence the Public Private Partnership (PPP) label. The proposal has a number of problems—market distortion, and informational and governance problems being just three.

Financing a portion of a government's budget through the stock market, instead of resorting to debt financing, as is the practice the world over, has a number of advantages:

1. It can energize a stock market, provided that all preconditions—in terms of human capital, and the legal, administrative, and regulatory frameworks—are met, and can also help to strengthen market credibility.
2. It deepens and broadens the stock market.
3. It demonstrates that stock markets can be used as a tool of risk and financial management.
4. It reduces the reliance of the government budget on borrowing, thus imparting greater stability to the budget and mitigating the risk of "sudden stops."
5. It has a positive distributional effect in that the financial resources that would normally go to service public debt can now be spread wider among the people as returns to the shares of government projects.
6. It enhances the potential for financing of a larger portfolio of public goods projects without the fear of creating an undue burden on the budget.
7. It makes the task of monetary management simpler by limiting the amount of new money creation.
8. It promotes ownership of public goods by citizens, which should have a salutary effect on the maintenance of public goods as it creates an ownership concern among the people and to some extent mitigates the "tragedy of the commons."
9. It has the potential to strengthen social solidarity.
10. It also has the potential to promote better governance by involving citizens as shareholder–owners of public projects.
11. It provides an excellent risk-sharing instrument for financing of long-term private sector investment.
12. It is also an effective instrument for firms and individuals to use to mitigate liquidity and productivity risks.
13. By providing greater depth and breadth to the market and minimizing the cost of market participation, governments convert the stock market into an instrument of international risk sharing, enabling investors from other countries to participate in their stock market.

14. It will help demystify Islamic finance and create an environment of cooperation and coordination within international finance.

The design of risk-sharing instruments to be issued by governments is not difficult. It could start by equity financing of the development budgets, usually 20–40 percent of the total budget. These instruments can be traded in the secondary market if the shareholders experience liquidity or idiosyncratic shocks. Their rate of return can be structured as an index of return tied to the rate of return of the stock market. If the domestic stock market is not deep, then an index of regional or international stock market returns, or both, can be developed. The argument is that since the social rate of return to public goods is higher than to privately produced goods and services, investment in public goods should have a rate of return at least as high as the return to the stock market index in order to promote efficient resource allocation. Since the risks associated with governments are usually less than for their corporate counterparts, the rate of return to government-issued shares has to be adjusted downward to take account of governments' risk premium. Depending on the country and the interest rate its government pays on debt, it is unlikely that the rate of return the government would pay to holders of its equity shares—adjusted for the credit rating of the government as reflected in lower risk premiums—would be any higher than the interest rate on its debt. Even in the unlikely event that the rate is a few basis points higher than on its debt, the trade-off is worthwhile considering the positive contributions that equity financing would make to society and to the economy in general.

Besides long-term investment, stock markets provide liquidity for stockholders. Idiosyncratic risks impact the liquidity of shareholders when they materialize. While some individual idiosyncratic risks can be mitigated through the purchase of insurance policies, such as health, life, and accident, there are potentially a large number of unforeseen, and therefore unpredictable, personal or family risks that are not as of yet insurable and for which no insurance policy can be purchased—for instance, risks to a person's livelihood. An individual can buffer against uninsurable risks by buying shares of stocks in good times and selling them when, and if, a liquidity shock is experienced. Similarly, stock markets can be used to diversify the risk of shock to asset returns. Firms can also reduce their liquidity risk through active participation in the stock market. They can also reduce the risk associated with the rate of return on their own operation—such as productivity risk—by holding a well-diversified portfolio of shares of stocks. Thus, incentives are created for investment in more long-term productive projects. Moreover, an active and vibrant stock market creates strong incentives for a higher degree of technological specialization, in turn increasing the overall productivity of the economy. This happens because, without sufficiently strong risk sharing in the financial system through the stock market, firms avoid deeper specialization, fearing the risk from sectoral demand shocks (Saint-Paul, 1992).

Islamic financial markets have developed an array of short-term, liquid, and reasonably safe instruments that are considered *Shari'ah* compatible. However, there is no stock market that operates in accordance with Islamic precepts. There is a missing market for Islamic instruments for which there is a substantial demand. In a sense, there has been a financial market failure. This deficiency has been addressed and is likely to be changed in Malaysia. The government of Malaysia has made a considerable commitment of resources and has put its credibility on the line to organize this missing market. Specifically, the Malaysian government's role in developing an Islamic stock market would suggest that the same kind of intense dedication and commitment could successfully generate the ways and means of pushing the agenda of Islamic finance forward in terms of developing medium- to long-term investment instruments of risk sharing. As a result of the Malaysian government's commitment of significant resources, and of its credibility, innovations and development of the needed instruments could be energized and facilitated. In this context, one strategy would be for governments to develop the long-term, high-return, riskier end of the spectrum of financial instruments for risk sharing, and to market them through a deepened stock market. This would create the needed incentive for the private sector to design and develop instruments in between the short-term liquid end of the market on the one hand and the longer-term government instruments on the other.

While vibrant stock markets are recommended, stock markets may be characterized by low participation of investors and hence the emergence of the equity premium and international risk-sharing puzzle. The prime reason for this is a low trust level and, a related factor, the cost of entering the market. Empirical evidence (Guiso et al., 2005; Erbas and Mirakhor, 2007) suggests that one reason for low participation of the population in a stock market is the fact that people generally do not trust stock markets. Low level of trust, in turn, is explained by institutional factors and education. Moreover, high transaction costs—especially information and search costs, as well as the high cost of contract enforcement—are crucial factors inhibiting stock market participation. These factors also stem from the institutional (rules of behavior) framework in the economy. Stiglitz (1989) suggests that disadvantages of equity finance stem from two informational problems: (i) the adverse signaling effect, which leads good companies not to issue as many equity shares for fear that it may signal poor quality; and (ii) an adverse incentive effect problem, which suggests that equity finance weakens the incentive for entrepreneurs to exert their maximum effort for the highest possible joint return. This happens because once the project is financed, the entrepreneur knows that net returns have to be shared with the financier and may, therefore, not be motivated to work as hard as when the returns would not be shared. While the idea has intuitive appeal, empirical evidence does not support it.

Conditions for a vibrant, robust stock market have been analyzed in the literature. Allen and Gale (2007) suggest that a successful, deep, and active stock market requires that information, enforcement, and governance costs be eliminated or at least minimized. Once this happens, the cost of entry into the equity market becomes low and "there is full participation in the market. All investors enter the market, the average amount of liquidity in the market is high, and asset prices are not excessively high." Lucas (1990) has proposed the abolition of capital gains tax as a way to promote investment through stock markets. "I now believe that neither capital gains nor any of the income from capital should be taxed at all." If the Islamic rules of market behavior—such as faithfulness to the terms and conditions of contracts, trust, and trustworthiness—are in place in a society, the informational problems and transaction costs, governance, and enforcement issues either would not exist or would be at low levels such as not to create a deterrence to stock market entry.

There is, however, a paradigm gap between what Islam teaches and actual market behavior. For this reason, government actions (and the institutions they create) to remedy the deficit in informational, enforcement, and governance behavior and reduce the cost of participation in stock markets have to be stronger and more comprehensive than exist today. These policies, actions, and institutions should have the competence, efficiency, and enforcement capabilities such that they can elicit the kind of behavior that replicates, or closely approximates, those expected if market participants behaved in compliance with Islamic rules. Such actions, policies, and institutions would include, *inter alia*: (i) developing a level playing field for equities to compete fairly with debt-based instruments (this means removing all legal, administrative, economic, financial, and regulatory biases that favor debt and place equity holdings at a disadvantage); (ii) creating positive incentives for risk sharing through the stock market; (iii) investing in a massive public education campaign to familiarize the population with the benefits of stock market participation—the kind of campaign that Prime Minister Margaret Thatcher's government ran in the UK in the 1980s, increasing stock market participation substantially in a short span of time; (iv) investing in human capital to produce competent, well-educated, and trained reputational intermediaries—lawyers, accountants, financial journalists, and *Shari'ah* scholars— which means investing in the creation of world-class economics departments, business schools, and law schools; (v) limiting leverage (including margin operations) of non-bank financial institutions and the credit-creation ability of banks through prudential rules that effectively cap the total credit the banking system can create; (vi) instituting thoughtful securities laws and regulations; (vii) developing strong and dynamic regulatory and supervisory systems for stock exchanges that not only continuously monitor the behavior of markets and participants, but stay a few steps ahead of those with a penchant and motivation to use regulatory arbitrage to get around rules and regulations; (viii) finding ways and means of regulating and supervising reputational intermediaries, or at least mandating that they become self-regulating to ensure minimization of false reporting or misreporting under the threat of liability to market participants; (ix) ensuring completely transparent and accurate reporting of the day's trade by all exchanges; and (x) instituting legal requirements for the protection of the rights of minority shareholders. While the above policies and institutions are crucial in reducing the cost of participation in stock markets and thus promoting widespread risk sharing, governments need to do more: they must lead by example. And it goes without saying that a strong financial sector goes hand-in-hand with a strong real economy, which is in turn largely dependent on good institutions, including the rule of law.

To Taj El-Din (2002), Islamic *Shari'ah* recognizes, in principle, stock markets as vehicles for investment and also encourages existing non-interest modes of investment that are based on the pooling of numerous sources of capital through floatation of stock subscriptions under specified rules and conditions. However, he notes that the exchange of financial claims is more vulnerable to hazard and the lack of information, both contrary to Islamic rules of exchange. He examined the efficiency criteria of conventional stock markets and concluded that the dominance of speculative motives versus those of real investment and the nature of interaction among "professional" and "non-professional" market players deprived these stock markets of internal stabilizers and undermined their efficiency. Efficiency in the financial market cannot be ensured by laissez-faire policies. It is necessary to reinforce Islamic rules. A regulatory framework is therefore indicated, with the aim of organizing the stock market on an Islamic basis that controls speculation and information asymmetry.

Along the same lines, Maurice Allais (1989) called for radical reforms of conventional stock markets. He noted that stock markets were true casinos where big poker games were being played. The wide gyrations in stock prices were transmitted to the real economy, leading to economic crises. According to Allais, the stock market system is fundamentally non-economic, inefficient, and unfavorable to the smooth functioning of economies. It can be advantageous only to a small minority of speculators. Allais called for the elimination of hedge funds and institutional intermediaries, other than brokers, whose activity was only trading in shares. He proposed the elimination of all financing of stock market operations through credit, and the adoption of a high-margin requirement for forward operations to be paid in cash and not through loans. In addition, he called for the continuous quotation of stocks to be dismantled and replaced by one daily quotation; and for the elimination of automatic trading programs for sales and purchases, and of speculation on indices and derivatives.

Finally, we should note that monetary policy has a direct bearing on the stability of stock markets. Central banks have often fueled stock market bubbles by creating excessive liquidity. When stock prices become over-inflated in relation to fundamentals, the market eventually crashes. Central banks at times try to re-inflate the bubble. Some governments have seen stock market bubbles as a sign of a buoyant economy and opposed attempts to arrest them. A regulatory framework for stock markets cannot be conceived independently of monetary policy. Criteria have to be developed for measuring and preventing bubbles and determining how far stock prices have departed from their fundamentals. Triggers have to be put in place to arrest euphoria and speculation and prevent ruinous crashes.

Idiosyncratic risks impact the liquidity of individuals when they materialize. With an active stock market, individuals can buffer idiosyncratic liquidity shocks by selling equity shares they own on the stock market. Firms can also reduce their liquidity risk through active participation in the stock market; and they can reduce risk to the rate of return to their own operation—such as productivity risk—by holding a well-diversified portfolio of shares of stocks. Thus, incentives are created for investment in more long-term, productive projects. Importantly, by actively participating in the stock market, individuals and firms can mitigate the risk of unnecessary and premature liquidation of their assets due to liquidity and productivity shocks. Moreover, an active and vibrant stock market creates strong incentives for a higher degree of technological specialization through which the overall productivity of the economy is increased. This happens because, without sufficiently strong risk sharing in the financial system through the stock market, firms avoid deeper specialization fearing the risk from sectoral demand shocks (Saint-Paul, 1992).

II. THE SECURITIZED "ASSET-LINKED SECURITIES" MARKET

In addition to the standard stock market, there is another capital market that provides a platform for trading asset-linked securities. The notion in Islamic finance of binding capital or financing closely and tightly to a real asset that is financed encourages the issuance of securities against a portfolio of assets.

For example, an asset financed through *ijarah* (lease) or *istisna'* can be used as collateral to issue securities linked to the payoffs and cash flows generated by the underlying assets. The assets of an Islamic financial intermediary based on *ijarah* or *istisna'* have interesting features. First, a wide range of maturity structures can be provided—that is, from short-term trade financing to medium-term lease-based assets. The second, and equally important, feature is that the risk profiles of such assets carry relatively low credit risk because the payoffs are directly linked to the predetermined cash flows. Finally, predetermined cash flows and fixed maturities make these securities a close substitute for fixed-income securities, which could be demanded by some investors. A portfolio of such assets can be securitized to create a financial security, which can be traded on an organized capital market, both primary and secondary. The securitization technique has been criticized in the conventional system in the aftermath of the financial crisis of 2007–08, where securitized securities with complex embedded derivatives led to the meltdown. A serious post-mortem of the crisis will probably exonerate the process of "securitization" as such and put the blame elsewhere. The technique of securitization by which a marketable security is developed that is backed by the payoffs of the underlying asset has a number of merits. As will be discussed below, a judicious application of securitization can lead to the development of a vibrant market for "asset-linked' securities which can play a critical role in the financial system.

Securitization involves collecting homogeneous assets with a known stream of cash flows into a pool, or portfolio, which is independent of the creditworthiness of the financier. This pool of assets is used to issue securities, which can be marketed to different classes of investors, from the individual to the institutional. The securities are structured in such a way that all payoffs in terms of risks and returns are "passed through" to the investors or the holders of the securities. The net result is that it is as if the investor has the direct ownership of the underlying assets, shares the returns of the assets, and, finally, is exposed to all the associated risks. These securities are, in turn, traded and negotiated freely on organized exchanges. This is readily and directly applicable to the development of securitized securities in a risk-sharing financial system. The point of departure from the conventional system depends on the way the returns and risks are shared with, or "passed on" to, the investors. A securitized security in the conventional system is referred to as an asset-backed security because, in most cases, the security owner is exposed to credit risk of the guarantor and not necessarily to the risks of the underlying portfolio or, in other words, the risks–returns of the underlying assets do not fully "flow" back to the security owner. Although the security is "backed" by the assets in the pool, its payoffs are not "linked" to the security risk–return profile. Due to this distinction, we argue that securitized security in Islamic finance will be by design linked to the payoffs of the underlying asset and, therefore, we refer to such securities as "asset-linked" securities. Figure 6.1 shows the process of securitization of asset-linked securities. Different financial intermediaries and economic agents will be holding assets that qualify for pooling, and the holders of these assets may desire

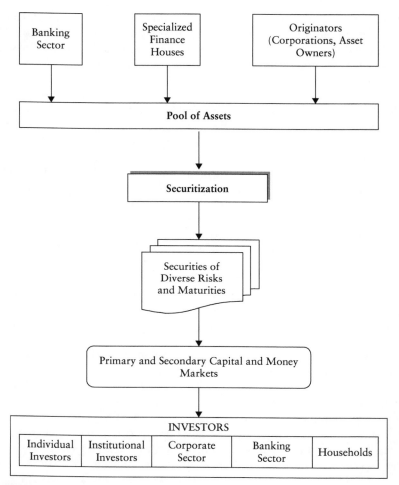

FIGURE 6.1   Structuring of Asset-Linked Securities

to sell these assets in the market for various valid reasons. For example, an Islamic bank may have accumulated a portfolio of leases (*ijarah*), which it can sell through securitization to free up its investable funds. Similarly, a specialized finance house or a corporation can offer assets to be securitized.

The pool of assets is converted into marketable securities through the process of securitization, which can be carried out by either specialists in securitization or Islamic financial intermediaries. The process of securitization ensures that the security is structured to match the risk–return profile demanded by diverse groups of investors. For example, some investors may have a low risk appetite, while others may be looking for longer maturities. The structuring of the security will ensure that it is attractive to investors, fitting in their portfolio and affording them with portfolio management and diversification benefits.

These "asset-linked" securities are traded in the market through competitive bidding by a pool of investors, which includes individuals, Islamic banks, institutional investors such as pension funds or insurance funds, and corporate treasuries. Such investors trade these securities in primary and secondary markets. There is no reason to believe that the targeted investors will be limited to Islamic investors, and the securities will be available also to conventional investors who may be attracted to their risk–return profile. The great interest in mortgage-backed securities in the conventional system indicates the significant appetite for securitized products.

In Table 6.1, we list the main differences between conventional and Islamic securitized securities. In the case of conventional securitization, the resultant security is invariably a debt security with a predetermined stream of coupon payments with the principal guaranteed (often through formal credit guarantees). In the case of an Islamic asset-linked security, the security's cash-flow stream will depend on the stream of cash flow of the underlying asset, and the principal will not necessarily be guaranteed. It is possible that in some cases, depending on the underlying asset, the security owner may have a high certainty of repayment of the principal in full, but it may not be guaranteed.

A security holder in the conventional asset-backed security does not own the underlying asset, but the ownership control in the asset-linked security will be higher. The asset ownership is also dependent on the degree of recourse the security owner has to the underlying asset. A major difference between the two types of securities is the variables that are used in their pricing. If we take the example of a conventional mortgage-backed security, the typical pricing model uses variables such as probability of prepayment or refinancing, which depends on the expected interest rate levels in the future, the loan-to-debt ratio, the credit score of the borrower, and so on. Since the principal of the security is guaranteed through credit-enhancing mechanisms, the security is priced like a coupon-bearing debt security with an early prepayment option. In the case of an Islamic security, on the other hand, the price will depend on typical variables determining the expected periodic cash flows in the future, but in addition it will have to factor in the expectation of future market value or the residual value of the underlying asset. In the absence of any guarantee of the principal, the redemption value of the security will depend on the expected market value of the asset at the time of maturity of the security.

TABLE 6.1   Comparison of Conventional and Islamic Securitized Securities

	Conventional Asset-Backed Security	Islamic Asset-Linked Security (Theory, but not current practice)
Security type	Fixed income (debt-based).	Hybrid depending on the contract and the underlying assets. Could be quasi-fixed income or risk sharing, or both.
Ownership	Security holder does not own the asset, but owns a security against the asset.	Security holder has an ownership interest in the underlying asset.
Recourse	Security holder does not have recourse to the asset in the event of distress.	Security holder has recourse to the underlying asset in the event of distress.
Pricing variables	Based on expected yields, current interest rates, and other variables influencing the asset owner's decision whether to prepay or refinance. The creditworthiness of the asset owner or the guarantor influences prices.	Based on expected yields, current levels of return, market value of the underlying assets, and the expected value of the underlying asset at maturity.
Linkage with asset value	No direct link to the market value of the underlying asset. Indirect variables such as the loan-to-value (LTV) ratio are used as a proxy.	In general, final or other payoffs may be linked to the market value of the underlying asset.
Principal protection	Principal is protected irrespective of the value of the underlying assets.	Principal is linked to market value of the underlying assets.
Risk shifting	Risk transfer.	Risk sharing.

Finally, for a conventional asset-backed security the risks are transferred to a third party in the event of a default because of multiple layers of origination and credit enhancements. Risk sharing is minimized, and investors are protected from the performance of underlying assets but are still exposed to the creditworthiness of the guarantor. In an asset-linked security, the price of the security will incorporate the riskiness of the underlying assets and the investor will be sharing the risk through fluctuations in the price of the security. Investors will be exposed to the risks associated with the portfolio of assets and will share the losses, rather than being exposed to the creditworthiness of the guarantor. This will put greater emphasis on the need for prudent selection of the underlying assets and close monitoring of the assets' performance, and will motivate securitization specialists to structure good-quality securities that offer valuable and secure investment opportunities.

Given that the foundation of Islamic capital markets is based on a vibrant stock and asset-linked securities market, the door is open for investors to apply portfolio management techniques to develop optimized portfolios with an unlimited number of risk–return profiles. Whereas a stock market may have higher volatility, an asset-linked securities market is expected to exhibit less variance and thus provide vast diversification benefits. Both markets complement each other, have different investor characteristics, and serve as venues for resource mobilization.

Table 6.2 provides a comparison of stock market and asset-linked securities.

TABLE 6.2 Comparison of Common Stock and Asset-Linked Securities

	Stock Market Security	**Asset-Linked Security**
Risk	Business risk.	Asset risk. Credit risk.
Collateral	Business assets (tangible and intangible). Equity capital.	Underlying assets.
Returns	Depends on business growth and earnings; residual claim on assets.	Depends on underlying assets' cash flows.
Cash flows	Less predictable.	Deterministic.
Volatility	Medium to high, subject to sector or business volatility.	Mostly low, but could be medium to high depending on the nature of securitization and the degree of risk sharing.
Contractual agreement	Equity share. Capital ownership.	Diverse, ranging from leases (rental) to equity (risk sharing) Could be amortizing or rental stream, or pass-through.
Recourse	None. Last claim on residual assets.	Ownership of underlying assets.
Pricing	Based on the expected growth and the earnings of the business.	Creditworthiness of asset holder and the market value of underlying assets.

The success of an asset-linked securities market will largely depend on the supply and variety of assets, and on the ability to innovate security structures with distinct features such as return, risk, maturity, credit-worthiness, geographical exposure, sector (technology, manufacturing, and so on) exposure, and currency exposure. One can argue that as the underlying pool of Islamic assets expands, a vibrant market for securitized securities will develop; and that, in its fully developed form, such a market will offer significant opportunities for portfolio and risk management to all classes of investors.

The following conclusions can be drawn about capital markets from the above discussion:

- The elimination of debt markets will not deprive investors of diverse investment opportunities.
- Asset-linked securities offer a better value proposition than the plain debt security.
- With the application of financial engineering or spanning, capital markets can develop securities and financial products with the full spectrum of risk profiles.

III. CONCLUSION

While risk management is arguably at the core of both conventional and Islamic finance, Islam addresses this directly by placing risk sharing as the foundational principle of Islamic finance. Stock markets have been seen as a vehicle to promote risk sharing among investors; shares are contingent claims whose payoff depends on the state of the world. However, most stock markets are conventional markets; an Islamic stock market that promotes risk sharing and operates according to Islamic teachings has still to be developed. In this chapter, we have advocated the concept of risk sharing in Islamic finance and expressed the need for an Islamic stock market that operates on risk sharing and is based on Islamic teachings. We have argued that for a complete Islamic financial system, we cannot simply develop short-term liquid assets and neglect long-term investment instruments that are more supportive of economic growth. To develop long-term investment and venture capital financing, we have advocated not only the vehicle of investment banking but also that of a vibrant stock market. Developing financial markets require private resources for their operation and government resources for their regulation, monitoring, and supervision. In order to develop an Islamic stock market, there is a need for both types of resources, and especially for the government to take an active role in building the institutional and regulatory framework required for capital markets to flourish. An Islamic stock market would provide investment opportunities for investors in a non-interest economy, and its role would be to promote long-term real investment and at the same time afford liquidity for investors. Governments should also become active in stock markets for risk sharing by choosing to finance part of their budget through risk sharing and direct ownership of development projects with their citizens. In this way, they would also reduce their budgetary debt burden. Governments undertake public goods projects because the characteristics of these goods—especially their indivisibility and non-exclusivity characteristics—prohibit their production by the private sector.

Ever since Keynes (1936) dubbed stock markets "casinos," a major concern with conventional stock markets has been the predominance of speculative and liquidity considerations and the limited emphasis on their role in allocating resources toward productive long-term investments. Most long-term investments have been financed through retained earnings or debt. The volume of new issues destined for long-term investment was low. An Islamic stock market has to avoid the main shortcomings of conventional stock markets and ensure financing of long-term investment while preventing speculation. Its regulatory framework must be designed to prevent the excesses of conventional stock markets, ruinous crashes, and large transaction costs, and protect the interests of investors against the vagaries of modern stock markets. An efficient Islamic market would enable mobilization of savings, promote risk sharing, and generate attractive returns for investors, provided that the required institutional scaffolding prescribed by Islam is in place.

An Islamic stock market should be inherently stable and not suffer from the systemic risks that have periodically undermined the stability of conventional stock markets and their associated economies. This stability derives from the institutional structure prescribed by Islam, which includes the prohibition of interest and speculation. The latter two factors have been sources of instability in conventional financial markets. Stability will be essential for enhancing participation in stock markets and risk sharing. The role of central banks in stock market instability should not be minimized. Bubbles have been fueled by low interest rates and abundant credit. The stability of stock markets cannot be disassociated from the stability of monetary policy.

Empirical work has not provided a clear-cut conclusion as to the efficiency of conventional stock markets. However, in view of their speculative component, the large resources devoted to speculation, and the recurrent bubbles, conventional markets could not be deemed as fully efficient. Equity premiums and interest rate puzzles were major price distortions caused by inefficiencies and deviations from the competitive setting of asset returns.

The presence of high risk and high transaction costs associated with stock ownership results in a high risk premium and a higher cost of equity capital, thus making the financing of long-term investment through issuing shares much more expensive than debt financing. The financialization of advanced economies is indicative of inefficiency in the financial and capital markets.

The development of a vibrant Islamic stock market is necessary to complete the Islamic financial system. In fact, the development of a stock market has been part of the proposals of monetary reform that have sought to reduce the money-creation power of banks and eliminate interest rate-based contracts. Nonetheless, there is considerable work in terms of institution building that needs to be done. Regulations have to be all-encompassing in order to limit damage to the system due to rule non-compliance behavior that leads to instability.

Developing an active and efficient stock market can promote international as well as domestic risk sharing, which will render the economy and its financial system resilient to shocks. In a sense, the absence of equity instruments within the menu of Islamic finance instruments is akin to a market failure; a strong ground for government intervention. The introduction of Islamic finance at the global level could present a remedy for the failure of financial markets to meet a strong demand for Islamic instruments. It took a top-down, government commitment, dedication, and investment of resources, particularly in the case of Malaysia, to correct this market failure. Once again, government intervention can remedy the current failure of the market to develop long-term, more risky, higher-return equity instruments.

Some 65 years ago, Evsey Domar and Richard Musgrave (1944) argued: "if the government fully shared in gains and losses, it can actually encourage risky investment" (Stiglitz, 1989). Governments can do this by developing a stock market with the characteristic of low entry cost to ensure the widest possible participation of investors. In doing so, governments could also ensure that stock markets would have limitations on short-selling and leverage operations by establishing market-based regulatory measures. Creating such a stock market would represent a leap forward by providing an effective instrument for domestic and international risk sharing and long-term equity investment. Governments can enhance the credibility and appeal of the stock market by financing part of their budgets through issuing tradable equity shares. They can also mount public information campaigns to educate the population about the risk-sharing characteristics of the stock market. This strategy has been adopted elsewhere with considerable success. Islamic finance has developed instruments to serve the low end of the time–risk–return profile of its transactions menu, and the stock market can serve the high end, with private investors filling the intermediate range.

CHAPTER 7

Portfolio Theory and Asset Pricing

Assuming that the institutional structure required by Islam is in place in the economy, portfolio and valuation analyses apply to Islamic capital markets. In such markets, a benchmark rate of return reflecting the return to the real sector of the economy would replace the interest rate in the conventional financial system, as there is no debt financing in an Islamic economy. The optimal growth path, equilibrium, and stability of such a system can be demonstrated utilizing traditional neoclassical theory. The most important advantage of such a system would be the fact that the rate of return to the real sector would drive the rate of return in the financial sector because of the close relationship between the two sectors. As such, the probability that "decoupling" or "financialization" would become factors would be insignificant.[1]

In Section I of this chapter, we review portfolio diversification theory and show how it relates to Islamic finance. In Section II, we discuss the relationship between risk and expected return and asset pricing. In Section III, we discuss the equity premium and interest rate puzzles and show that these puzzles demonstrate inefficiency and price distortions in conventional markets—in other words, in conventional finance there is a wedge between the rate of interest and return to equities that Islamic finance can exploit. The efficiency hypotheses of stock markets are of paramount importance and are discussed in Section IV. In Section V, we discuss the theoretical stability of an Islamic stock market, which we claim does not face systemic risk. And in Section VI, we present our conclusions.

I. PORTFOLIO DIVERSIFICATION THEORY AND ISLAMIC FINANCIAL SYSTEM

The pricing of assets, and in particular of stocks, is an important area of finance and offers analytical tools for investors in an Islamic stock market. Prior to the pioneering contribution of Markowitz on portfolio diversification (1952), investors were assumed to demand a stock that had the best performance, as defined by high dividends and low risk. In developing his portfolio theory, Markowitz demonstrated that an investor may not restrict his or her portfolio to high-performing stocks and may combine stocks with different performances by choosing a portfolio composition that minimizes variance (risk) for a target (that is, given) expected return or maximizes the expected return for a target risk. In the Markowitz model, an asset i is analyzed in terms of its expected return $E(R_i)$, defined as the sum of the expected dividend and change in price, and risk, measured by the variance of returns, $V(R_i)$. A high variance means a high risk that the actual return will deviate from the expected mean. An asset is pictured in a mean–variance graph where the horizontal axis measures risk and the vertical axis measures the expected yield (see Figure 7.1). Diversified portfolios that minimize risk for a given expected return or maximize return for a given risk are called efficient portfolios and are located on an efficient mean–variance frontier.

The diversification model has been extended to analyze diversification or capital allocation when there is a riskless asset, which has a risk-free return R^f, zero variance, and zero correlation with any risky asset or portfolio. The investor could hold his or her wealth in the risk-free asset or the risky portfolio, or in a combination of the two. The combined portfolio will have the following expected return and risk:

$$E(R_C) = w_F R^f + w_P E(R_p) \tag{1}$$

$$V(R_C) = \sigma_C^2 = w_F^2 \sigma_F^2 + w_P^2 \sigma_P^2 = w_P^2 \sigma_P^2 \quad \text{And} \quad w_F + w_P = 1 \tag{2}$$

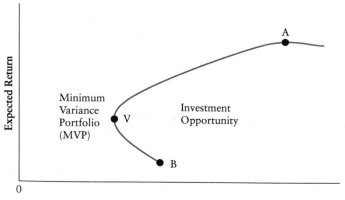

FIGURE 7.1   Mean–Variance Frontier

It follows that $\sigma_C = w_P \cdot \sigma_P$. Since σ_P is given, the risk of the combined portfolio is increased when w_P increases. The expected return of the combined portfolio is:

$$E(R_C) = (1 - w_P)R^f + w_P E(R_P) = R^f + w_P \left(E(R_P) - R^f \right)$$

$$E(R_C) = R^f + \frac{\sigma_C}{\sigma_P} \left(E(R_P) - R^f \right) \tag{3}$$

The equation for $E(R_c)$ in terms of the $E(R_p)$ line is called the capital allocation line (CAL). The excess return $E(R_C) - R^f$ is related to the excess return of the market portfolio $\left(E(R_p) - R^f \right)$ via the coefficient $\frac{\sigma_C}{\sigma_P}$. The return and variance of the combined portfolio are increased as the weight of the market portfolio is increased. The market allocation line is shown in Figure 7.2.

An Islamic economic system can be characterized as one in which there are no risk-free assets and where all financial arrangements are based on sharing risks and returns. An investor's preference for different classes of assets, portfolio composition, and asset allocation in such a system will be influenced by several factors. For instance, the investor's decision to form a portfolio will be determined mainly by the pool and diversity of instruments available in the market, his or her attitude toward risk, opportunities of diversification, and his or her preference for liquidity. In addition, degree of market completeness and information asymmetry in the market will influence portfolio choices.

An Islamic economic system offers several instruments that can serve as basic building blocks for a wide range of instruments with unique risk–return

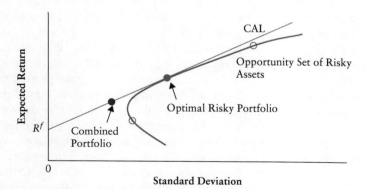

FIGURE 7.2   Expected Return–Risk in the Case of Riskless Assets and a Risky Portfolio

profiles and different maturity structures through spanning and the application of financial engineering (Iqbal, 1999). These basic building blocks can be divided into two broad categories of assets to appeal to different investors. The first category consists of securitized "asset-linked" securities, which are backed by a real asset—either through a sales or a lease contract; whereas the second category consists of financial claims that are based purely on equity partnership—for example, *musharakah*.[2] These two categories also represent two ends of the risk continuum in the Islamic economic system, from low-risk to high-risk securities. The entire fabric of the *Shari'ah* is contractual in its conceptualization, content, and application. Economic agents are given a wide freedom of contract, as long as the contract is not in violation of the *Shari'ah*, the agreement is based on the consent of the parties involved, and the shares of each are contingent upon uncertain gains. As a result of this freedom of contract, economic agents can apply innovative techniques to design complex securities.[3] Therefore, one can infer that with the availability of basic building blocks, the freedom of contract, and the application of financial engineering, investors will have access to a large set of assets with different risk–return characteristics to choose from in order to construct a diversified portfolio.

The Islamic admonition for risk sharing and equity participation is an implicit recognition of the acceptance of uncertainty regarding future events and outcomes.[4] In fact, the permissibility of *mudarabah* and *musharakah* makes sense only in the face of uncertainty regarding the magnitude and probability of expected return. Therefore, once risks associated with information disclosure and speculative behavior are eliminated, the investor will be concerned only with exposure to risks arising from the uncertainty of future outcomes, assuming that all business decision making conforms to the norms of social behavior expected by Islam. Given the attitude of Islam toward risk, and considering that a Muslim is expected to be a rational decision maker who is conscious of his or her obligations toward individuals and society and will comply with the rules of the system, it is fair to assume that an investor in the Islamic framework will be risk averse in his or her general behavior (Mirakhor, 1987). In terms of utility, an investor in the Islamic economic system will be one who is risk averse and prefers less risk to more risk, and maximizes the utility of wealth instead of wealth itself.

It is a general misconception that the removal of interest from an Islamic economy leads to the omission of the time value of money. Islam does recognize the time value of money, depending on the time value of resources and when and in what form it can be actually realized; that is, time value cannot be realized in an exchange of monetary resources, such as loans, but it can be realized in an exchange transaction of real goods and services, as an implicit part of the total return from the transaction (Khan, 1991). However, it cannot be realized explicitly and in isolation from the other components of the return from investment.[5] Therefore, an investor in the Islamic framework will construct the portfolio to optimize its return for a given level of risk by determining the expected returns and variances of future cash flows of an asset discounted at a rate which represents time value determined by returns on real goods and services.

Finally, the degree of market completeness and information asymmetry in the market will also influence an investor's decision on how to allocate funds among different classes of assets. Markets are considered incomplete when the sources of uncertainty affecting the fundamental asset–security are not spanned by traded securities. In the absence of a full set of contingent claims on basic assets, the pool of assets available for the investor will be limited and, thus, will limit his or her ability to construct securities and portfolios with unique risk–return profiles.[6] The degree of information asymmetry will determine the investor's preference for low-risk "asset-linked" securities over equity participation. Analytical models demonstrate that in the presence of information asymmetry between a lender and a borrower, the lender will prefer a debt contract to an equity contract in order to minimize monitoring costs (Diamond, 1984). The lower the degree of information asymmetry in the market, the more incentive there is for the investor to enter into an equity partnership.[7]

II. ASSET PRICING

How the risk of an asset should be measured, and what economic forces determine the price of risk (the additional return an investor gets for bearing additional risk), are two of the most fundamental questions in modern financial theory. A satisfactory model for risk and return must explain the magnitudes of the rewards that investors receive for bearing different kinds of risk. The primary role of asset-pricing models is to specify the appropriate measure(s) of risk and the appropriate risk–return profile, and to study the implications of competitive equilibrium in the securities market for the pricing of risk.

The literature on Islamic finance has paid little attention to the issue of pricing the risk of an asset in an interest-free system. In some cases, it is assumed that asset-pricing models in the conventional system are applicable in the Islamic system, provided a risk-free security can be designed in the Islamic system (Khan, 1999). However, the existence or non-existence of a risk-free security is not the only issue, as a number of the basic assumptions of the conventional asset-pricing model are not compatible with Islamic principles. Therefore, it is important to assess if the conventional asset-pricing models are applicable in the Islamic financial system—and if they are *not* applicable, to develop a model that is compatible.

Modern financial theory suggests several asset-pricing models, including the most popular model, the Capital Asset Pricing Model (CAPM), followed by the Arbitrage Pricing Theory (APT) and the Consumption Based CAPM (CCAPM). We examine the CAPM model to determine its compatibility with the Islamic financial system. The CAPM is based on an efficient frontier as developed by Markowitz's Modern Portfolio Theory (MPT) and Tobin's two-fund separation principle.[8] The model rests on eight assumptions. The first five are those that underlie the efficient market hypothesis, and thus underlie both MPT and CAPM. The last three assumptions are necessary to create the CAPM from MPT (Harrington, 1987).

1. Investors are risk averse and their objective is to maximize the utility of terminal wealth.
2. Investors make choices on the basis of risk and return.
3. Investors have homogeneous expectations of risk and return.
4. Investors have identical time horizons.
5. Information is freely and simultaneously available to all investors.
6. There is a risk-free asset, and investors can borrow and lend unlimited amounts at the risk-free rate.
7. There are no taxes, transaction costs, restrictions on selling short, or other market imperfections.
8. Total asset quantity is fixed, and all assets are marketable and divisible.

According to CAPM, in equilibrium a linear capital market line (CML) exists in the economy, which measures the price of risk in terms of covariance of a portfolio's return with the return of the market portfolio. As a result of diversification, all unsystematic risk associated with a security can be eliminated, and the only remaining risk will be systematic risk or market risk. Each security will fall on a security market line (SML) (see equation 1) derived from CML, where the price of the risk is the slope of the line, the difference between a risk-free rate and the expected rate of return on the market portfolio and the quantity of risk, commonly referred to as β.

$$E(R_i) = R_f + [E(R_m) - R_f] \frac{\sigma_{i,m}}{\sigma_m^2} \tag{4}$$

None of the assumptions of the Modern Portfolio Theory contradict any of the expected behaviors of investors in the Islamic financial system. However, two assumptions of CAPM need closer examination: (i) the existence of a system-wide, risk-free interest rate (R_f) and the ability of investors to borrow and lend an unlimited quantity of money at that rate; and (ii) the lack of any restrictions on short selling securities. CAPM's assumption of a risk-free rate has two important implications: (i) it expands the investment opportunity set for investors; and (ii) it results in a *linear* relationship between risk and return, as the risk-free interest rate simplifies the curved efficient frontier of MPT to the linear efficient frontier of the CAPM. Figure 7.3 shows how the introduction of R_f expands the investment opportunity set.

By introducing a risk-free interest rate with an efficient frontier (*EE'*), a linear relationship between the risk-free rate and the market rate is developed. Line R_fM represents the risk–return relationship when a portfolio consists of a risk-free security and a market portfolio in different combinations. Line *MZ* is only possible when an investor can borrow unlimited amounts at the risk-free rate and invest the proceeds in the market portfolio. Line *MZ* also offers a higher return for the same level of risk as compared to the efficient frontier. Line R_fL represents the relationship when the market portfolio is sold short and proceeds from short sales are invested in risk-free assets at the risk-free rate. Since the existence of a risk-free interest rate is so fundamental to the derivation of CAPM, at first glance it would appear that it would not be acceptable in the context of an Islamic financial system, which prohibits debt instruments with a predetermined rate of return and does not have a system-wide risk-free interest rate.

There has been much discussion in conventional finance on constructing a CAPM model without reference to a system-wide, risk-free rate of return. The assumption of a risk-free rate of interest is not essential for asset pricing, as long as there exists a risk-free asset in the economy or there are ways

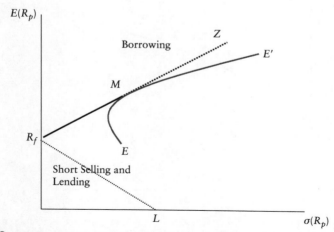

FIGURE 7.3 Capital Market Line and an Expanded Opportunity

to construct a portfolio of assets with zero risk. Black (1972) suggested that the minimum-risk asset required for derivation of CAPM is not in fact risk free, because it is subject to buffeting of inflation. Black created an alternative CAPM model using short selling as a proxy for the risk-free asset.[9] If investors can short sell assets, then short-sold assets, creating a riskless portfolio in any economic environment, can balance any portfolio of risky assets. Black's replacement for the risk-free asset was a portfolio that had no covariability with the market portfolio. Because the relevant risk in the CAPM is systematic risk, a risk-free asset would be one with no volatility relative to the market—that is, a portfolio with a beta of zero such that covariance between the portfolio and market returns is zero. All investor-preferred levels of risk could be obtained from various linear combinations of Black's zero-beta portfolio and the market portfolio (Harrington, 1987). Return on an asset will be expressed as follows:

$$E(R_i) = R_z + [E(R_m) - R_z]\frac{\sigma_{z,m}}{\sigma_m^2} \tag{5}$$

Figure 7.4 shows Black's version of CAPM, which is similar to Figure 7.3 except that a risk-free rate Rf is replaced with the return on zero beta asset R_z (Copeland and Weston, 1988). Portfolios A and B are uncorrelated with the market portfolio M and have the same expected return. However, only one of them, portfolio A, lies on the efficient frontier: the minimum variance zero-beta portfolio, which is unique. Portfolio B is also a zero-

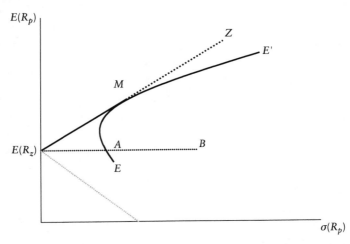

FIGURE 7.4   Capital Market Line with Zero-Beta Asset (Zero Covariance with the Market)

beta portfolio, but it has a higher variance and therefore does not lie on the minimum variance opportunity set. The remaining relationships are the same as in the conventional CAPM.

While Black's version of CAPM resolves the condition of the risk-free interest rate, it introduces another strong assumption of unlimited short-selling ability by investors, and this in turn requires close scrutiny. Investors exercise short selling when their market perception leads them to believe that security prices will decline in the future. Empirically, almost all asset returns have a positive correlation, which makes it impossible to construct a zero-beta portfolio composed of only long positions in securities.

Sourd (2010) sums up the doubts on the validity of CAPM:

Markowitz (2005) shows that when there is no risk-free asset, if there are constraints on short selling, or if it is not possible to borrow without limitations, the CAPM cannot be established. If borrowing capacity is limited and if it is not possible to sell short without restrictions, it is no longer possible to derive a portfolio with a risk suitable for each investor by combining the market portfolio and the risk-free rate. As a consequence, investors will choose a risky portfolio that corresponds to their appetite for risk, and different investors will hold different portfolios. In that case, investors still choose efficient portfolios, but we lose the convenient property that combinations of efficient portfolios are themselves efficient. So the market portfolio, a portfolio obtained by aggregating the efficient portfolios chosen by investors, is no longer efficient. The key conclusion of the CAPM, that all investors hold the same risky portfolio and combine it with holdings in the risk-free asset, is no longer valid. Likewise, Sharpe (1991) analyses asset pricing when short sales are not possible and comes to the conclusion that the market portfolio may not be efficient and that there may be no linear relationship between expected returns and CAPM beta. So, Markowitz, who laid the groundwork for the CAPM by introducing the concept of mean-variance portfolio choice in the 1950s, and Sharpe, who published the seminal paper on CAPM theory in the 1960s, have both concluded more recently that the market portfolio may not be efficient if risk-free lending and borrowing and short sales are restricted.

CAPM has also been criticized on the basis of other assumptions, such as the non-rationality of investor preferences and the impact of operational frictions such as taxes and transaction costs and the efficiency of market portfolio efficiency. With the growing complexity of financial systems, the applicability of CAPM to price assets is seriously questioned.

Turning to an examination of CAPM in the context of Islamic principles, Mirakhor (1988) demonstrates that the assumption of a fixed and predetermined rate of interest is not necessary for the determination of saving–investment behavior, or for the existence of a long-run equilibrium of the economy and, therefore, that the absence of interest-bearing assets does not hamper macroeconomic analysis or the workings of the economic system, in closed- or open-economy models. Standard macroeconomic analysis can be carried out to determine the conditions that must exist for a non-interest economy to reach its equilibrium.

Iqbal (2000) shows that the assumptions of borrowing and short sales limit the applicability of CAPM to price risk and the market price of securities. Prohibition of interest and elimination of debt security imposes constraints on creating leverage in the economy and therefore makes linearity of CAPM beyond the efficient market point impossible. The condition of short sales raises two questions. First, is borrowing a financial security or claim compatible with Islamic principles? And second, is the act of selling a financial security with the expectation of replacing it at a cheaper price in the future acceptable behavior for a Muslim investor? As far as borrowing a security is concerned, as a matter of principle, it can be argued that it is a simple *qard* (loan) from one party to another, and the contract stipulates returning the *qard* at face value without any additional reward attached to it; therefore, it could be acceptable by *Shari'ah*. However, the act of short selling with or without the permission of the owner of a security is speculative and high risk-taking behavior, and is done purely on the basis of the investor's expectations. Islam's position on risk taking, prohibiting speculation, and taking undue risks suggests that the act of short selling would not be permissible. *Shari'ah* also does not approve of short selling, arguing that it is not permissible to sell a stock that a seller does not possess, as it leads to unnecessary volatility in the market.[10]

In short, given that the principles of Islamic finance would not allow borrowing (or creating leverage) and short selling, one must conclude that any pricing model with a strong assumption of unlimited borrowing or lending or short selling will not hold.[11] Even if we assume that there exists an asset that has zero covariance with the market, a restriction on short selling will reduce the investment opportunity set and also affect the slope, intercept, and linearity of the capital market line. As a result, it will be impossible to maintain the linearity of CAPM for pricing assets in the Islamic financial system.

Mirakhor (1987) discussed the construction of diversified portfolios for Islamic banks to demonstrate that Modern Portfolio Theory can be applied to the portfolios of institutions holding Islamic financial instruments without resorting to the need for a risk-free asset. Although he used the analytical framework of MPT to evaluate the effect of bank regulation on the rate of return and risk of bank portfolios, the discussion laid the groundwork for the general use of investment and corporate finance analysis.[12] Mirakhor showed that in the absence of a risk-free rate of return, an investment opportunity set would exist for all securities in the Islamic economy, with varying degrees of risk. Investors would be risk averse but rational, and thus would make their portfolio selection based on their risk appetite.

Conventional finance, and especially CAPM, provides a framework for analyzing the price of riskiness of an asset with reference to a benchmark security, which happens to be a risk-free security. In an Islamic model, every corporation operates in a risky environment and is constantly reminded of the relationship between risk and expected return. Shareholders, or investors, invest in riskier assets only if they expect to receive higher returns. The management of risk is the essence of modern finance. In conventional finance, the benchmark rate of return is the risk-free rate R^f available to investors. In Islamic finance, there is no riskless asset; an investor is no longer interested in a risk premium, as his or her choice is between the menu of risky assets.

One may argue that, in an Islamic economy, a benchmark rate of return R^b could be used instead of the risk-free rate to price risk. Let R_i denote the required return on the $i - th$ stock, R^b the benchmark rate of return, R_M the market portfolio rate of return, and $RP_M = R_m - R^b$, the market risk premium. The risk–return relationship for the $i - th$ stock can then be expressed in terms of CAPM as:

$$R_i = R^b + \beta_i \left(R_M - R^b \right) = R^b + \beta_i RP_M \qquad (6)$$

However, using such a framework leads us to the same pitfalls identified in the earlier discussion of CAPM. For example, in an Islamic economy, there is no such thing as a "risk-free" rate (with zero variance), and there is no possibility of a zero-beta portfolio due to the constraints on short selling. Therefore, equation (6) can be immediately rejected. This leads to modifying the equation to accommodate the riskiness of the benchmark security. As soon as we treat the benchmark security as a risky security, equation (6) becomes a problem of constructing the portfolio using two risky assets, which takes us back to the investment opportunity set as described in Figure 7.5.

For the sake of discussion, even if one argues that one can have a security that is free of "credit risk"—that is, a securitized "asset-linked" security issued by the government with a low default or credit risk—we still run into the problem of a strong CAPM assumption of a risk-free asset not being correlated with market security. The net result is that any framework using

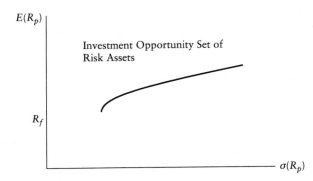

FIGURE 7.5   Diversified Investment Opportunity Set

a benchmark rate of return that has zero risk and zero correlation with the market does not hold.

III. THE EQUITY PREMIUM AND INTEREST RATE PUZZLES

The equity premium and risk-free interest rate puzzles are the inability of standard intertemporal economic models to rationalize the statistics that have characterized the US financial markets over the past century, namely the co-movements of three variables: the real return to the S&P 500; the real return to short-term, nominally risk-free bonds; and the growth rate of per capita real consumption (more precisely, non-durables and services). Mehra and Prescott (1985) noted that over the period from 1889 to 1978, the average real return to stocks in the United States has been about 6 percent per year, higher than that on Treasury bills (about 1 percent per year). Similarly, for post-war US data, real stock returns have averaged about 9 percent annually with a standard deviation of about 16 percent, while the real return on Treasury bills has been about 1 percent per year. Aggregate consumption growth has also been about 1 percent per year. Thus, the historical annual market Sharpe Ratio has been about 0.5. The slope of the mean-standard deviation frontier, or of expected return-beta lines, was much higher than the reasonable risk aversion and consumption volatility estimates suggested by the consumption model and data. The discrepancy between the model's prediction and empirical data has been coined the equity premium puzzle, while the low level of interest rates has been called the interest rate puzzle.

Real returns paid by different financial securities may differ considerably, even when averaged over long periods of time. These differences in average returns may be attributed to differences in the degree to which a security's return co-varies with the typical investor's consumption, as indicated by the price equation:

$$E(R_i) - R^b = -\frac{Cov(m, R_i)}{E(m)} = -\frac{\rho_{m,i}\sigma_i\sigma_m}{E(m)} \tag{7}$$

Stock returns co-vary more with consumption growth than do Treasury bills. Investors see stocks as a poorer hedge against consumption risk, and so stocks must afford higher average returns. The intertemporal consumer model that has led to equity premium and interest rates puzzles has three main assumptions regarding individual behavior and asset market structure. First, individuals have preferences associated with the "standard" utility function used in macroeconomics: they maximize the expected discounted value of a stream of utilities generated by a power utility function. Second, asset markets are complete: individuals can write insurance contracts against any possible contingency. Finally, asset trading is costless, so that taxes and brokerage fees are assumed to be insignificant. Mehra and Prescott found that for economies with such characteristics the average real annual yield on equity is a maximum of four-tenths of a percentage point higher than that on short-term debt, in contrast to the 6 percent premium observed.

The intertemporal representative consumer model can be summarized as follows:

$$\underset{c_t}{Max}\, E_0\left\{\sum_{t=0}^{\infty}\eta^t.U(c_t)\right\} \tag{8}$$

where $U(c_t) = \frac{c_t^{1-\gamma}}{1-\gamma}$; $\{c_t\}_{t=0}^{\infty}$ is a random consumption stream; E_0 represents an expectation conditional on information available to the individual at $t = 0$; the parameter η is a discount factor; and γ is a coefficient of constant relative risk aversion. The first order conditions for optimization are:

$$E_t\left\{\left(\frac{c_{t+1}}{c_t}\right)^{-\gamma}(R_{t+1}^m - R_{t+1}^D)\right\} = 0 \tag{9}$$

$$\eta.E_t\left\{\left(\frac{c_{t+1}}{c_t}\right)^{-\gamma}R_{t+1}^D\right\} = 1 \tag{10}$$

where R_{t+1}^m and R_{t+1}^D are the gross return to stocks and bonds from t to $t+1$, respectively. These conditions impose statistical restrictions on the co-movement between any person's pattern of consumption and asset returns. The prediction of the model for interest rates can be stated as:

$$R_t^D = 1 / E_t(m_{t+1}) = \frac{1}{\eta} E_t \left[\eta \cdot \left(\frac{c_{t+1}}{c_t} \right)^{\gamma} \right] \tag{11}$$

Assuming consumption growth is log normal, this condition can be approximated by:

$$r_t^D = v + \gamma E_t \left(\Delta \ln c_{t+1} \right) - \frac{\gamma^2}{2} \sigma_t^2 \left(\Delta \ln c_{t+1} \right) \tag{12}$$

where $r_t^D = \log R_t^D$ and $v = \log \eta$. Average real interest rates were about 1 percent. Thus, $\gamma = 50$ to 250 with a typical η such as $\eta = 0.01$ implies a very high benchmark rate of 50–250 percent. To get a reasonable interest rate, a subjective discount factor η has to be between –0.5 and –2.5, or –50 percent and –250 percent, which does not seem plausible; namely, consumers generally prefer present consumption to future consumption. Assuming the consumption growth rate to be log normally distributed, the prediction of the model for stock returns can be stated as:

$$\left| \frac{E\left(R^{mv}\right) - R^b}{\sigma_{mv}} \right| \approx \gamma \sigma \left(\Delta \ln c \right) \tag{13}$$

Given that over the last 50 years in the US, real stock returns have averaged 9 percent with a standard deviation of about 16 percent, while the real return on Treasury bills has been about 1 percent, the historical annual market Sharpe Ratio has been about 0.5. Aggregate consumption growth has been about 1 percent. Log utility implies $\sigma(m) = 1$ percent, which is far less than the 50 percent computed from historical data. To match the equity premium, the coefficient γ has to exceed 50, which seems a huge level of risk aversion. Plausible values were considered to be positive and less than 3.

The large equity premium has been rationalized in two ways: (i) either investors are highly averse to consumption risk; or (2) they find trading stocks to be much more costly than trading bonds. There is also a presumption that there is a large differential in the cost of trading between the stock and bond markets. Stocks imply risk sharing; they are contingent claims. Bonds, on the other hand, are fixed-income assets and imply risk shifting. Stocks have been subject to intense speculation ever since they became publicly held, such as in the South Sea stock crash of 1720. They have been among the most volatile assets and, therefore, exhibit high risk. Because of this high volatility, they may command a high-risk premium in excess of the risk-free rate. Moreover, the risk-free rate would be hardly thought of as a market-determined rate and may be directly set by the central bank. The Bank of England has had a direct role in the determination of interest rates in the past two centuries; while the US Fed has had a direct influence on interest rates since its establishment in 1913. The recent fixing of interest rates near zero provides a clear example of the role of the central bank and the creation of a large equity premium.

Black (1972) contended that the risk-free rate should not be the benchmark against which the equity premium should be estimated. The notion of a risk-free interest rate was seen to create a large market-excess return, called the equity premium puzzle. Black derived a more general version of the CAPM. In this Black version, the expected return of asset i in excess of the zero-beta return is linearly related to its beta. Specifically, for the expect return of asset i, $E(R^i)$, we have:

$$E(R^i) = E(R^{0m}) + \beta_{im}\left[E(R^{0m}) - E(R^{0m}) \right] \tag{14}$$

R^m is the return on the market portfolio, and R^{0m} is the return on the zero-beta portfolio associated with the market portfolio. The zero-beta portfolio is defined to be the portfolio that has minimum variance of all portfolios uncorrelated with the market portfolio frontier. In Islamic finance, the reference rate R^{0m} could be the average rate of return in the economy. It would be much higher than the risk-free interest rate and, therefore, the risk premium for holding an asset would be much smaller, since investors can only hold risky assets. Portfolio holders would have a choice between stocks and direct investment in equities. The rate of return for stocks should therefore be compared to the return of investment in the economy using an economic growth model. Economic growth could take place only with investment. The rate of return to capital, or the profit rate, should be the rate against which stock returns have to be assessed.

In this regard, the difference between Islamic finance and conventional finance is that in conventional finance there is essentially a wedge between the rate of interest and return to equities because of the availability of a riskless asset, whereas in Islamic finance the option of a risk-free asset does not exist. Thus, Islamic finance can exploit this wedge, or gap, because equities *do not* have to afford this higher return to compensate for risk over a riskless asset. In this sense, Islamic finance may be regarded as more efficient by relying on equity participation.

IV. THE EFFICIENCY HYPOTHESES OF STOCK MARKETS

The notion of market efficiency concerns all markets—not only stock markets, but also commodities and currency markets. For instance, parallel markets and price distortions are examples of market inefficiencies. However, the efficient-market hypothesis (EMH) has been especially assessed and tested for stock markets. EMH states that it is impossible to beat the market because stock market efficiency causes existing share prices to immediately incorporate and reflect all relevant information. According to the EMH, stocks always trade at their fair value on stock exchanges, and thus it is impossible for investors either to purchase undervalued stocks or to sell stocks for inflated prices. Thus, the crux of the EMH is that it should be impossible to outperform the overall market through expert stock selection or market timing, and that the only way an investor can possibly obtain higher returns is by purchasing riskier investments.

Louis Bachelier, a French mathematician, in his 1900 dissertation, "The Theory of Speculation," was the first person to express the efficient-market hypothesis. His work was largely ignored until the 1950s; however, beginning in the 1930s, other independent work corroborated his thesis. A small number of studies indicated that US stock prices and related financial series followed a random walk model. Alfred Cowles' research in the 1930s and 1940s suggested that professional investors were in general unable to outperform the market. But it was not until the mid-1960s, through the independent work of Paul A. Samuelson (1965) and Eugene Fama (1965), that EMH gained widespread acceptance. It was particularly the work of Fama (1965 and 1970) that conferred on the EMH prominence in stock market theory and applied research. Fama defined an efficient market as one where prices always reflect all the available information.

The notion of efficiency is closely related to the notion of a martingale, which is an even game that does not favor one player over the other. A martingale is a process $\{P_t\}$, which satisfies the following condition:

$$E\left[P_{t+1} \mid P_t, P_{t-1}, \ldots\right] = P_t$$

$$E\left[P_{t+1} - P_t \mid P_t, P_{t-1}, \ldots\right] = 0 \tag{15}$$

If P_t is an asset's price at time t, then the martingale hypothesis states that tomorrow's price is expected to be equal to today's price, given the asset's entire price history. In fact, the martingale was long considered to be a necessary condition for an efficient asset market, one in which the information contained in past prices is instantly and fully reflected in the asset's current price.

If the market is efficient, then it should not be possible to profit by trading on the information contained in the asset's price history. Fama (1965) formulated the notion of market efficiency as a random walk defined as:

$$P_{t+1} = P_{t-1} + \varepsilon_{t+1} \tag{16}$$

where ε_{t+1} is an independent and identically distributed random variable $(0, \sigma^2)$. The independence of the increments $\{\varepsilon_{t+1}\}$ implies that the random walk is a fair game, but in a much stronger sense than the martingale; independence implies not only that increments are uncorrelated, but also that any non-linear functions of the increments are uncorrelated.[13]

The EMH does not assume that all investors are rational. Instead, it assumes that stock prices reflect intrinsic values. New information causes a stock's current intrinsic value to move to a new intrinsic value based on that new information. Fama (1970) postulated three forms of market efficiency hypothesis: (i) weak-form efficiency, (ii) semi-strong-form efficiency, and (iii) strong-form efficiency. In weak-form efficiency, future prices cannot be predicted by analyzing prices from the past. Excess returns cannot be earned in the long run by using investment strategies based on historical share prices or other historical data. Technical analysis techniques will not consistently produce excess returns, though some forms of fundamental analysis may still provide excess returns. Weak-form efficiency implies that share prices exhibit no serial dependencies, meaning that there are no patterns to asset prices. This implies that future price movements are determined entirely by information not contained in the price series. Hence, prices must follow a random walk. The weak-form EMH does not require that prices remain at or near equilibrium, but only that market participants not be able to systematically profit from market inefficiencies. However, while EMH predicts that all price movement (in the absence of change in fundamental information) is random (that is, non-trending), many studies have shown a marked tendency for the stock markets to trend over time periods of weeks or longer and that, moreover, there is a positive correlation between degree of trending and length of time period studied. Various explanations for such large and apparently non-random price movements have been offered.

Semi-strong-form efficiency implies that share prices adjust to publicly available new information very rapidly and in an unbiased fashion, such that no excess returns can be earned by trading on that information. Semi-strong-form efficiency implies that neither fundamental analysis nor technical analysis techniques will reliably produce excess returns. To test for semi-strong-form efficiency, the adjustments to previously unknown news must be of a reasonable size and instantaneous. To test for this, consistent upward or downward adjustments after the initial change must be looked for. If there are any such adjustments it would suggest that investors had interpreted the information in a biased fashion and hence in an inefficient manner. In strong-form efficiency, share prices reflect all information, public and private, and no one can earn excess returns. If there are legal barriers to private information becoming public, as with insider trading laws, strong-form efficiency is impossible, except in the case where the laws are universally ignored. To test for strong-form efficiency, it must be the case that investors cannot consistently earn excess returns over a long period of time.

Numerous empirical studies have tested the validity of the three forms of market efficiency. Most empirical studies are joint tests of the EMH and a particular asset-pricing model, usually the CAPM or the Fama–French three-factor model (1996). They are joint tests in the sense that they examine whether a particular strategy can beat the market, where beating the market means getting a return higher than that predicted by the particular asset-pricing model. Most studies suggest that the stock market is highly efficient in the weak form and reasonably efficient in the semi-strong form, at least for larger and more widely followed stocks. The evidence suggests that the strong-form EMH does not hold, because those who possessed inside information could make abnormal profits.

However, many skeptics of the EMH point to the stock market bubble that burst in 2000 and suggest that at the height of the boom the prices of the stocks of many companies, particularly in the technology sector, vastly exceeded their intrinsic values. Speculative asset bubbles are an obvious anomaly, in that the market often appears to be driven by buyers operating on irrational exuberance, who take little notice of underlying value. These bubbles are typically followed by an over-reaction of frantic selling, allowing shrewd investors to buy stocks at bargain prices. Rational investors have difficulty profiting by shorting irrational bubbles because, as Keynes (1936) commented, "Markets can remain irrational far longer than you or I can remain solvent." Sudden market crashes as happened on Black Monday in 1987 are mysterious from the perspective of efficient markets, but are envisaged as rare statistical events under the weak-form EMH. More serious challenges to the EMH have emerged from research on long-term returns. Shiller (1981) argued that stock index returns are overly volatile relative to aggregate dividends, and many took this as support for Keynes's view that stock prices are driven more by speculators than by fundamentals. Related work by DeBondt and Thaler (1985) presented evidence of apparent over-reaction in individual stocks over long horizons of three to five years. Specifically, the prices of stocks that had performed relatively well over three- to five-year horizons tended to revert to their means over the subsequent three to five years, resulting in negative excess returns; the prices of stocks that had performed relatively poorly tended to revert to their means, resulting in positive excess returns. This is called "reversion to the mean" or "mean reversion." Summers (1986) showed that, in theory, prices could take long swings away from fundamentals that would be undetectable with short horizon returns. Additional empirical support for mispricing has come from Jegadeesh and Titman (1993), who found that stocks with relatively high or low returns over three- to 12-month intervals continued the trend over the subsequent three to 12 months.

Further empirical work has highlighted the impact of transaction costs on market efficiency, with evidence suggesting that any anomalies pertaining to market inefficiencies are the result of a cost-benefit analysis made by those willing to incur the cost of acquiring the valuable information in order to use it for trading purposes. Additionally, the concept of liquidity is a critical component of capturing "inefficiencies" in tests for abnormal returns. Any test of this proposition faces the joint hypothesis problem, where it is impossible to test for market efficiency, because it requires the use of a measuring norm against which abnormal returns are compared; one cannot know if the market is efficient if one does not know if a model correctly stipulates the required rate of return. Consequently, a situation arises where either the asset-pricing model is incorrect or the market is inefficient, but there is no way of knowing which is the case.

Tobin (1984) added to the debate the notions of fundamental-valuation efficiency, full-insurance efficiency, and functional efficiency. The first refers to the accuracy with which market valuations reflect fundamentals. The fundamentals for a stock are the expected future dividends or other payouts. The stock's value is the present discounted value of the expected future earnings. Causal observation suggests that the market moves up and down much more than can be justified by changes in rationally formed expectations, or in the rates at which they are discounted. The wide gyrations of stocks from fundamentals led Keynes (1936) to dub the stock market a "casino," and to express pessimism about the long-term rationality of securities markets. Although stock markets provide liquidity for shareholders, Keynes saw the liquidity provided by these markets as a mixed blessing, but concluded that illiquidity would be the worse evil, because it would push savers toward hoarding of money.

Regarding full-insurance efficiency, Tobin observed that as new financial markets and instruments have proliferated, it might be thought that the enlarged menu now spans more states of nature and moves us closer to the Arrow-Debreu vision of complete markets. Not much closer, he contended. The new options and futures contracts do not stretch very far into the future. They serve mainly to allow greater leverage to short-term speculators and arbitrageurs, and to limit losses in one direction or the other. Collectively, they contain considerable redundancy. Tobin concluded that any appraisal of the efficiency of the financial system must reach an equivocal and uncertain verdict. He invoked the casino aspect of the financial system, as only 5 percent of futures contracts entailed actual deliveries of the underlying commodities. He suspected that Keynes was right to suggest that there should be a greater deterrent to transient holdings of financial instruments and larger rewards for long-term investors.

V. THE THEORETICAL STABILITY OF AN ISLAMIC STOCK MARKET

Theoretically, an Islamic stock market operates according to the precepts of the *Qur'an* and the *sunnah*. In like manner to the theoretical stability of banks that operate on the basis of Islamic precepts, Islamic stock markets are free from two major sources of instability—namely, interest rates and speculation. A high degree of instability makes a market more inefficient, requiring large resources for trading and hedging risk. A high degree of instability will dissuade savers away from markets. Stock market crashes following stock market booms have often ruined household savings and caused economic disorders. A high degree of stability will encourage savers and enable stock markets to achieve maximum efficiency in financial intermediation, reduce trading cost, and enlarge participation.

Conventional markets have been characterized by high volatility. Keynes (1936) and Simons (1948) have underscored uncertainty in financial markets. Uncertainty, by definition, makes predictability difficult. The high degree of uncertainty has led to the development of hedging instruments to minimize losses arising from wide gyrations in asset prices and exchange rates. While uncertainty has been excessive in commodities and housing prices, it has been an inherent feature of conventional stock markets. Figure 7.6 portrays stock indices for the US, UK, and Japan over the period 1990M1–2009M4, as well as interest rates on US Treasury bills, UK Treasury bills, and Japan's financial bank rate. Both equity prices and interest rates displayed considerable fluctuations over the period under study. The Japanese stock index (Nikkei 225) displayed a long-term decline in equity prices following the boom in the 1980s, while the US Dow Jones and UK FTSE 100 indices illustrated consistent bubbles followed by dramatic crashes in equity share prices.

Numerous inferences can be made about stock markets in conventional finance from the behavior of stock indices. There is a considerable systemic risk in equity returns that cannot be diversified. Stock markets are arguably dominated by speculation. Most stocks tend to move in relation to the market when the market is bullish, creating a bubble. The price-earnings ratio (PER) increases tremendously and far exceeds interest rates, making equities

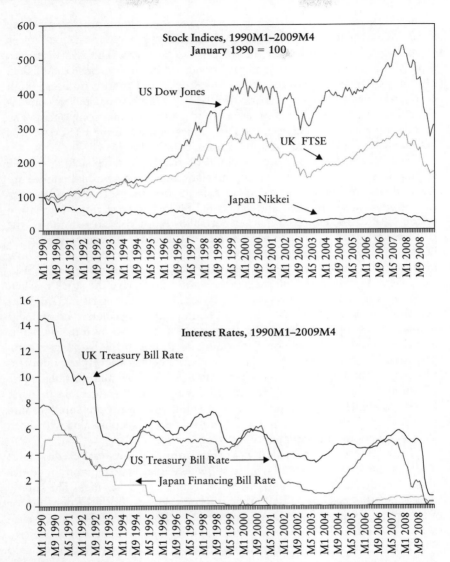

FIGURE 7.6 Stock Indices and Interest Rates in the US, UK, and Japan, 1990–2009
Source: International Monetary Fund, International Financial Statistics.

more attractive and intensifying speculation. Since shares are used as collateral, borrowers are encouraged to borrow in the upward phase. They create self-financing strategies and when equity shares drop, borrowers lose no capital value. Capital losses will be borne by the lenders who hold the equity share as collateral, as in the case of housing mortgages. Equity loans are non-recourse loans. When the sentiment is bearish or when bubbles burst, most stock prices experience the same downturn and record capital losses. The PER decreases rapidly and causes substitution toward bonds. Many studies have established a strong correlation between individual stocks and market indices. High correlation has been characteristic of all stock markets that reflect conventional finance. Correlation even has a broader international component. The correlation coefficient between the Dow Jones Index and the FTSE 100 was extremely high and estimated at 0.95 for 1990M1–2009M4.

The behavior of stock indices could be related to interest rates. While stock prices are market-determined, interest rates in conventional finance are set by the central bank and could cause large distortions; that is, a speculative boom can be preceded and supported by low interest rates. In relation to the CAPM, the expected market-portfolio return rises in relation to the risk-free rate and, therefore, encourages substitution of equity shares for bonds. Dramatic crashes in the stock indices are also accompanied by low interest rates, which can be explained by an increase in demand for risk-free assets. Very low interest rates in Japan did not revive the stock market. Similarly, very low interest rates in the US and UK after August 2007 did not prevent a crash in the stock market. The imploded speculative component in asset prices could not be fired up in view of large losses suffered by banks and the existence of large non-performing portfolios in the banking system. Moreover, when the interest rates are set at extremely low levels, the opportunity cost of holding bank reserves becomes very low. Low interest rates create a liquidity trap. Low interest rates reduce savings and, therefore, the demand for shares, which in turn contributes to keeping downward pressure on share prices. Empirically, low interest rates are found to be consistent with both asset-price booms and collapses.

In the absence of speculation arising from dysfunctional credit (debt) markets, equity prices would tend to show less volatility. Demand for equity shares would be driven essentially by dividends and by savings. The supply would be influenced by initial public offerings. Hence, both the demand for and supply of equity shares are influenced by stable variables in the absence of speculation, and equity prices would tend to display a stationary pattern. The behavior of the stock prices as exhibited in Figure 7.6 cannot be related to the real economy. For instance, the Dow Jones Index was appreciating at a rate of 10 percent a year during the period 1990–2007. It then depreciated by 50 percent from 2007M10 to 2009M4. Savings alone cannot explain the demand for shares. In particular, stock prices were experiencing a bubble when household saving rates were close to zero, and became depressed when they started to rise. Demand for shares seemed to be essentially financed by non-recourse loans from brokers or from banks. When interest rates are low, demand for loans increases, fueling a bubble. The supply of shares during the downturn was essentially in the form of portfolio liquidation by speculative hedge funds, money-market funds, and equity funds. The supply of shares can be increased in a downturn cycle by short selling, which may exacerbate downward pressure on equity prices.

Assuming that economic and financial relations in society are governed by the institutions (rules of behavior) prescribed by Islam, one would expect that there would be low probability of the emergence of speculative bubbles. Asset prices in Islamic finance would feature low correlation with the market portfolio and would be more influenced by idiosyncratic risks. Two elements explain the absence of systemic risk in the CAPM. First, the Sharpe Ratio is very low. Expected returns are compared to a beta-zero return or to the average rate of return in the economy. Such a rate of return would display a stable pattern over time and would not fluctuate in the same fashion as interest rates. Figure 7.6 shows large fluctuations in interest rates that played a role in equity markets. Interest rates on risk-free bonds cannot influence the Sharpe Ratio in Islamic finance. Consequently, the equity premium would be small, since households do not hold risk-free assets. The deviation between the expected return and the market return would be very small and result from non-systemic factors, such as the scale of the firm, the efficiency of its labor force, or its entrepreneurship. Second, the magnitude of beta coefficients would be small in Islamic finance. The performance of one firm would be influenced by its competitiveness, cost-efficiency, promotional efforts, and investment plans. In the absence of common systemic risks, the correlation of a firm's return with the market portfolio would be very low.

In Islamic finance, the pool of savings, rather than credit, would determine asset demand. The supply of equity shares would be determined by real investment plans. Hence, the demand for and supply of shares would tend to be stable. The rate of return would essentially comprise dividends, with very small changes in equity prices. Equity share prices would be stationary variables, with no persistent upward or downward trend.

VI. CONCLUSION

The primary role of asset-pricing models is to specify the appropriate measure(s) of risk and the appropriate risk–return profile, and to study the implications of competitive equilibrium in securities markets for the pricing of risk. The pricing of assets, and in particular of stocks, is an important area of finance and offers analytical tools for investors in an Islamic stock market.

In Islamic finance, there has been very little research into asset pricing and the pricing of risk in a system that excludes interest. As a result, most discussions of the pricing of risk in Islamic finance are almost exclusively based on conventional finance; and in some cases, it is even assumed that asset-pricing models in the conventional system are applicable in the Islamic system provided a risk-free security can be designed in that system.

Theoretically, an Islamic stock market operates according to the precepts of *Shari'ah*. Islamic stock markets are free from two major sources of instability—namely, interest rates and speculation. A high degree of instability makes a market more inefficient, requiring large resources for trading and hedging risk. A high degree of instability will dissuade savers away from markets. Stock market crashes following stock market booms have often ruined household savings and caused economic disorders. A high degree of stability will encourage savers and enable stock markets to achieve maximum efficiency in financial intermediation, reduce trading cost, and enlarge participation. In the absence of speculation arising from dysfunctional credit (debt) markets, equity prices would tend to show less volatility. Demand for equity shares would be driven essentially by dividends and by savings. The supply would be influenced by initial public offerings. Hence, both the demand for and supply of equity shares are influenced by stable variables in the absence of speculation, and equity prices would tend to display a stationary pattern. In Islamic finance, the pool of savings, rather than credit, would determine asset demand. The supply of equity shares would be determined by real investment plans. Hence, the demand for and supply of shares would tend to be stable. The rate of return would essentially comprise dividends, with very small changes in equity prices. Equity share prices would be stationary variables, with no persistent upward or downward trend.

ENDNOTES

1. Let the aggregate production function in the economy be denoted as $Y = F(K, L)$, where Y is real output, K is real capital stock, and L is labor; the marginal product of capital is then $R_K = \dfrac{\partial F}{\partial K}$. In an Islamic economy, the expected return on stocks should be assessed in relation to R_K and not to any interest rate.
2. Technically, every security in the Islamic economic system can be regarded as an "asset-linked" security because of a direct or indirect linkage to a real asset. However, securities as a result of a lease contract are stronger cases of "asset-inked" securities, since a real or tangible asset—as opposed to a financial claim—collateralizes these securities. It is often argued that instruments in this category resemble fixed-income debt securities, since the rate of return is predetermined or more certain than other instruments. Actually, in the context of the Islamic financial system, these instruments are not meant to be used to create a debt security. In the literature, such instruments are often referred to as "debt-like" securities, which is not an appropriate description.

3. Historically, *fuqaha* (Muslim religious scholars) did not define *a priori* the various methods of *riba*-free transactions available today. The practice was that the contracting parties would decide on a particular mode, and the *fuqaha* would rule on its permissibility (Iqbal and Mirakahor, 1999).
4. For example, see *Qur'an* (31:34): "No soul knoweth what it will earn tomorrow."
5. It is argued that acceptance of differences in spot and credit prices in instruments such as *bay' al-muajjal* and *bay' al-salam* are indicative that *Shari'ah* recognizes the time value of an asset. Differences in spot and future prices are attributed to expected changes in future demand and supply and not to the time value of money. See Khan (1991, 1994).
6. It is often argued that future sustainable growth of the Islamic financial markets will largely depend on innovating new securities to match investors' demand for well-diversified portfolios and securities for the extreme ends of the maturity structure. See Askari and Iqbal (1995), and Iqbal and Mirakhor (1999).
7. Empirical evidence based on 15 years of data from the Agricultural Bank of Iran (ABI) demonstrates that a reduction in information asymmetry and increased participation and monitoring by the lender lead to a preference for equity participation over debt, without sacrificing efficiency (see Sadr, 1999; and Sadr and Iqbal, 2000).
8. Markowitz considers an "efficient" frontier a portfolio that has either the highest expected return for a given risk or the lowest risk for a given expected return. Tobin demonstrated that by combining a risk-free security with the market portfolio, the composition of risky assets in an efficient portfolio is the same for every investor.
9. To short sell, the investor borrows securities and then sells them in anticipation of replacing them later at a lower price. Black assumed that short selling was a means of allowing market prices to be in equilibrium—that is, to be balanced between market pessimists and market optimists, buyers and sellers (see Harrington, 1987).
10. *Shari'ah* scholars find arguments against speculation and short sales on the basis of *nusus* (legal text) as well as *maslahah* or public interest (Chapra, 1985).
11. It is argued that selling an asset from one's own holding can also be viewed as short selling—that is, if an investor is holding an asset and decides to sell it with the expectation of buying at a lower price in the future. However, in such a case the short sale will not be unconstrained (a must for Black's model) and will be limited to the holdings of an investor.
12. Mirakhor demonstrated that the implementation of portfolio regulation through restrictions placed on high-risk, high-return asset acquisition through *musharakah* and *mudarabah* financing may produce results not intended by the authorities; that is, there is a distinct possibility that the risk of bank failures would increase. When the regulation takes the form of restricting the role of risk- and profit-sharing assets in the portfolio of banks, it has the effect of shifting the frontier downward. He considered a portfolio of two assets: one, a short-term investment in the form of trade financing called a mark-up sale; another, a *mudarabah* or *musharakah* long-term investment. The former asset could be considered as a low-yield, low-risk asset, and the second a higher-yield and higher-risk asset. Mirakhor

went on to show that the concentration of assets in a short-term investment would deprive the economy of long-term growth sustaining investment and would, in turn, increase the probability of bank failure. He suggested that an optimal allocation should be based on the expected return and risk of each asset and a correlation between assets as proposed in the MPT. A regulatory framework that unduly increases the share of short-term investment at the expense of long-term investment could inadvertently increase, as opposed to reduce, bank fragility.

13. A martingale has increments that are unpredictable—that is, the expected value of the increment is unpredictable. A random walk has independent increments—none of the moments are predictable. The popular "ARCH" class models in finance violate random walks because their variance is predictable, but most of the models are still martingales.

CHAPTER 8

Complementary Role of Intermediaries and Markets in Promoting Risk Sharing

Financial intermediation is at the heart of any financial system, providing the range of instruments that are demanded by savers and channeling savings to the most productive investments. This central function, which was historically carried out by financial intermediaries (commercial banks), has in recent years been increasingly supported by capital markets, with each playing a seemingly complementary role. But in the financial crisis of 2007–10, there was a clear breakdown of financial intermediation. While there was unprecedented reliance on markets, the required and essential regulatory scaffolding of credit screening, monitoring, and compliance was not in place. As a result, the financial markets froze and the needed resources for investment dried up. Also in play during a crisis are the range of risk-management tools being offered and the quality of regulations and monitoring of intermediaries.

Financial intermediaries are different from other economic agents. The acquisition and processing of information about economic agents, the packaging and repackaging of financial claims, and financial contracting are among the activities that differentiate financial intermediation from other economic activities. The primary functions of a financial intermediary are asset transformation, conducting of orderly payments, brokerage, and risk transformation. Asset transformation takes place in the form of matching the demand and supply of financial assets and liabilities (for example, deposits, equity, credit, loans, and insurance) and entails the transformation of maturity, scale, and place of the financial assets and liabilities of ultimate borrowers and lenders. The function of administration of an accounting and payments system (for example, check transfer, electronic funds transfer, settlement, and clearing) is considered another important intermediation function. Typically, financial intermediaries have also offered pure *brokerage* or matchmaking between the borrowers and lenders, and facilitated the demand and supply of non-tangible and contingent assets and liabilities, such as collateral, guarantees, financial advice, and custodial services (Scholtens, 1993). Financial intermediaries not only channel resources from capital-surplus agents (generally, households) to capital-deficit ones (the corporate sector), but also allow intertemporal smoothing of households' consumption and businesses' expenditures and thus allow both firms and households to share risks.[1]

In a risk-sharing financial system, financial intermediaries and markets play important and complementary roles. There is balance between financial intermediaries and markets. In such a system, there are two types of capital markets—(i) equity markets, and (ii) securitized "asset-linked" security markets—but there can be no bond or debt markets.

I. BACKGROUND

In a classical intermediary-based financial system (also referred to as a bank-based system), financial intermediaries borrow from savers and channel and lend to firms and entrepreneurs that have projects and are in need of resources for investment. In contrast, in a market-centered system, investors lend and invest directly in entities needing resources and create marketable securities that are generally tradable with prices that are observable. The question is which of these two systems is preferable for a system that is based exclusively on risk sharing, and can the two systems function side-by-side and be complementary? The answer requires an examination of a number of issues. Are their intermediation roles the same in attracting savings and financing, and in impacting economic growth? Are they both stable and should the government regulate them, and if so how? The development of bank-based and market-based financing, besides increasing access to financing for business and consumers, has enhanced the financial sector's ability to spread risk, presumably to entities who are better able to take on risk, and has increased the overall transfer and assumption of risk in economies. But has this increased risk taking, in turn, exposed economies to a higher risk of financial and economic turmoil? Namely, have intermediaries assumed excessive risk, and could their collective risk taking expose the financial sector to wider fluctuations and widespread instability? Could the excessive assumption of risk on the part of intermediaries encourage and impart higher risk taking in financial markets and threaten the financial system?

Historically, two types of financial systems have evolved, with an ongoing inconclusive debate as to which is preferable. A centralized or "bank-centered" financial system has been developed in countries such as

Germany and Japan, whereas a decentralized and "market-centered" system has emerged in Anglo-Saxon countries such as the United Kingdom and the United States.[2] The distinction between a bank-based and a market-based system is that agents within a bank-based system can cooperate and coordinate their actions, whereas agents in a market-based system compete (Boot and Thakor, 1997). A bank-centered financial system offers superior information processing by forming long-run relationships with firms to ease asymmetric information distortions and ameliorate moral hazard through effective monitoring, and thereby boosts economic growth.[3] Banks acting as delegated monitors make a long-term investment in acquiring information about firms and managers, and thereby improve their capital allocation and corporate goverance (Gorton and Winton, 2002).[4] Further positive contributions to development are made by intertemporal risk management as articulated by Allen and Gale (1999) and through the utilization of economies of scale. In contrast, the market-based or market-dominated view highlights the growth-enhancing role of well-functioning markets through: (i) fostering greater incentives to research new firms and to profit from this information by trading in large and liquid markets; (ii) facilitating corporate control by easing takeovers and linking managerial compensation to firm performance; and (iii) facilitating risk trading (Levine, 2002). Since the 19th century, many economists have argued that bank-based systems are better at mobilizing savings, identifying good investments, and exerting sound corporate control, particularly during the early stages of the economic development process and in a weak institutional environment. Others, however, emphasize the advantages of markets in allocating capital, providing risk-trading tools, and mitigating the problems associated with excessively powerful banks. Allen and Gale suggest that a bank-based system provides better intertemporal risk sharing, whereas markets provide better cross-sectional risk sharing.

The contrast between the market-based and bank-based financial systems suggests that markets and intermediaries are alternatives that perform more or less the same functions but in different ways, and perhaps with different degrees of success. This has led to the development of a middle ground position, which argues that the effectiveness of a particular financial architecture (either bank- or market-based) depends on a host of country-specific factors, such as the legal and contractual environment of the country, the informational structure of the participating economic agents, and the technological characteristics of the economy (Tadesse, 2002; Rajan and Zingales, 1998; Boot and Thakor, 1997). This perspective is drawn from the distinct differences, rather than the similarities, in the types of services provided by markets and banks. More formally known as the financial services view—as articulated by Merton and Bodie (1995), and Levine (1997)—it minimizes the importance of the bank-based versus market-based debate. In other words, financial arrangements arise to overcome market imperfections and provide financial services, such as assessing potential investment opportunities, exerting corporate control, facilitating risk management, enhancing liquidity, and easing saving mobilization. By providing these financial services more or less effectively, different financial systems promote economic growth to varying degrees. The issue is creating an environment where intermediaries and markets provide sound financial services. Conceptually, the financial services view is fully consistent with both the bank-based and market-based view. Nevertheless, the financial services perspective places the analytical spotlight on how to create better-functioning banks and markets, and relegates the banks-based versus market-based debate to the background (Levine, 2002).

Rajan (2006), in an insightful paper before the financial crisis of 2007, argues that increased risk sharing around the world has been greatly facilitated by: (i) technical change, such as lower communication and computation costs, the lower cost of gathering and processing information, academic research and the resulting financial innovations, and credit ratings and their availability; (ii) financial deregulation; and (iii) institutional change, creating new financial institutions and arrangements. It is precisely these changes that have facilitated and motivated the movement toward increasing reliance on market-based financing. Rajan notes that this movement toward market-based financing has expanded and broadened financial markets and allowed risk to be broadly spread. Yet, the process has been, perhaps misleadingly, coined as "disintermediation" in the literature. As individuals in a number of industrial countries have reduced the proportion of their deposits in banks in favor of indirectly investing in the market (through mutual funds, insurance companies, and pension funds) and in firms (through venture capital funds, hedge funds, and other forms of private equity), the managers of these entities have replaced banks and have in effect "re-intermediated" their institutions between individuals and markets. In the process, banks have been forced to acquire positions that are more illiquid and have been motivated to originate, transfer, and assume more risk. What do these developments mean for financial stability? Rajan goes on to elaborate:

> *The expansion in the variety of intermediaries and financial transactions has major benefits, including reducing the transactions costs of investing, expanding access to capital, allowing more diverse opinions to be expressed in the marketplace, and allowing better risk sharing. [For a discussion of the upsides, see Rajan and Zingales (2003), or Shiller (2002).] However, it has potential downsides . . .*

My main concern has to do with incentives. Any form of intermediation introduces a layer of management between the investor and the investment. A key question is how aligned are the incentives of managers with investors, and what distortions are created by misalignment . . .

. . . the incentive structure of investment managers today differs from the incentive structure of bank managers of the past in two important ways. First, the way compensation relates to returns implies there is typically less downside and more upside from generating investment returns. Managers therefore have greater incentive to take risk. Second, their performance relative to other peer managers matters, either because it is directly embedded in their compensation, or because investors exit or enter funds on that basis. The knowledge that managers are being evaluated against others can induce superior performance, but also a variety of perverse behavior.

One is the incentive to take risk that is concealed from investors—since risk and return are related, the manager then looks as if he outperforms peers given the risk he takes. Typically, the kinds of risks that can most easily be concealed, given the requirement of periodic reporting, are risks that generate severe adverse consequences with small probability but, in return, offer generous compensation the rest of the time. These risks are known as tail risks.

A second form of perverse behavior is the incentive to herd with other investment managers on investment choices, because herding provides insurance the manager will not under perform his peers. Herd behavior can move asset prices away from fundamentals.

Both behaviors can reinforce each other during an asset price boom, when investment managers are willing to bear the low probability "tail" risk that asset prices will revert to fundamentals abruptly, and the knowledge that many of their peers are herding on this risk gives them comfort that they will not under perform significantly if boom turns to bust. An environment of low interest rates following a period of high rates is particularly problematic, for not only does the incentive of some participants to "search for yield" go up, but also asset prices are given the initial impetus, which can lead to an upward spiral, creating the conditions for a sharp and messy realignment.

Will banks add to this behavior or restrain it? The compensation of bank managers, while not so tightly tied to returns, has not remained uninfluenced by competitive pressures. Banks make returns both by originating risks and by bearing them. . . .

> *But perhaps the most important concern is whether banks will be able to provide liquidity to financial markets so that if the tail risk does materialize, financial positions can be unwound and losses allocated so that the consequences to the real economy are minimized. Past episodes indicate that banks have played this role successfully. However, there is no assurance they will continue to be able to play the role. In particular, banks have been able to provide liquidity in the past, in part because their sound balance sheets have allowed them to attract the available spare liquidity in the market. However, banks today also require liquid markets to hedge some of the risks associated with complicated products they have created, or guarantees they have offered. Their greater reliance on market liquidity can make their balance sheets more suspect in times of crisis, making them less able to provide the liquidity assurance that they have provided in the past.*

In noting the increased dangers and risks associated with pro-cyclicality of bank lending, Rajan recommends intervention (while acknowledging that there are no guarantees that policymakers will be right where markets are not) to reduce the likelihood of a tail risk event and a financial meltdown. He advises that a higher capital requirement may not be the best policy given the implications of disintermediation and reintermediation. He recommends policies that affect incentive structure, prudential regulations that go beyond banks and investment banks in their coverage, and monetary policy that incorporates the impact of low interest rates on the behavior of managers of financial institutions.

In examining another dimension of stability, Wagner (2010) shows that systemic risk, which is the likelihood of several banks failing simultaneously, is not necessarily reduced when financial institutions become more diversified and reduce the risk of their own failure. Additionally, if the liquidation cost of systemic risk is high, then Wagner shows that in his model the optimal level of diversification is less than full diversification. De Jonghe (2010) provides recent empirical evidence on the impact of diversification (into non-traditional banking activities) on stability by estimating a bank's "tail beta," the probability that an extreme decline in the bank's stock price coincides with an extreme decline in the market. His results confirm the Wagner hypothesis that banks that diversified into non-traditional banking activities display greater tail betas. In other words, banks with a higher ratio of trading income and commission and fee income (and thus a lower proportion of traditional income from interest income from lending) display greater systemic risk, which indicates that the diversification of commercial banking into investment banking may have reduced financial system stability.

In a related article, Adrian and Shin (2010) provide an explanation for this somewhat unexpected result. Namely, when there is a general rise in security prices, on the one hand banks that invest in securities benefit from a rise in their capital, which initially reduces their marked-to-market leverage. However, to meet a leverage target, often determined by value at risk management, they increase their borrowing and purchases of securities. On the other hand, investment banks enhance their leverage by using repurchase agreements to buy securities. Thus, when security prices rise, banks purchase securities; and when they fall, banks sell securities; active leverage management by investment banks thus has the potential to magnify the volatility of security prices. Their empirical evidence shows that the growth in repurchase agreements is a lead indicator of market-wide volatility. In other words, diversification can be overdone.

While the impact of intermediation and financial development on financial stability is critical, its impact on economic growth is arguably as important. There is a vast literature advocating financial development (and enhanced intermediation) as an important input for economic growth—for instance, Beck and Levine (2002), Demirguc-Kunt and Levine (2001), and numerous other authors. (See Chapter 6 for a fuller discussion.) And in this empirical work, bank-based (that is, intermediaries) and financial market development are seen as complementary in their positive impact on economic growth and thus it is overall financial development, and not the relative proportions that are bank-based and market-based, that is important.

Deidda and Fattouh (2008) look into the impact on economic growth of moving from a financial system that is heavily based on financial intermediaries to one that is more reliant on capital markets. Using a model that assumes extreme behavior of intermediaries and markets, where banks monitor and screen borrowers, whereas markets do neither, screening and monitoring involves a cost for banks and, as a result, bank financing becomes more expensive than market financing, and hence less attractive. But not all firms can access market financing; to borrow in capital markets, they must have borrowed and been monitored by banks before. In their model, if we assume that capital markets require a sensible disclosure rule whereby firms disclose their source of financing, firms could reduce their recourse to bank financing. This, in turn, could reduce access to bank financing because as the demand for bank financing falls, screening and monitoring may no longer be viable for banks, reducing financing and thus having a negative impact on economic growth. That is, moving from a bank-based financial system to one that relies on both banks and capital markets could, under certain circumstances, be harmful to economic growth. This possibility, that bank-based and market financing are not complementary, contradicts the received theory that more developed and deeper financial systems support growth, no matter whether the system relies on markets or on intermediaries such as banks (see Beck and Levine, 2002; and Demirguc-Kunt and Levine, 2001). In the empirical testing of their model's unconventional prediction, Deidda and Fattouh use the same data used by Demirguc-Kunt and Levine and get the result that, although the development of bank-based and market financing supports economic growth, the development of bank-based financing by ameliorating market financing can reduce the demand for bank financing, in turn reducing bank screening and monitoring that could negatively impact market development, confirming the prediction of their model.

II. THE ROLE OF FINANCIAL INTERMEDIARIES IN A RISK-SHARING FINANCIAL SYSTEM

As discussed in Chapter 5, in Islamic finance, there is a set of available contracts that serve as the basis for financial intermediation. The role of intermediation contracts in Islam is to facilitate an efficient and transparent execution and financing of real sector economic activities (not financial sector activities, as may also be the case in conventional finance). Intermediation contracts provide economic agents a set of tools to perform the functions of financial intermediation through direct participation as partner or through indirect participation in the form of a principal-agent relationship.

A financial system comprises different sub-systems, such as the banking system, financial markets, capital markets, insurance system, and the legal institutions needed to support the financial sector. Given all the financial instruments sanctioned by the Islamic economic system, as discussed in Chapter 5, an Islamic financial intermediary can offer financial products and services for varied requirements, maturities, and degrees of risk to satisfy the needs of a diverse group of economic agents. By utilizing a set of inter-mediation contracts with respective functionality, IFIs will be able to offer a wide array of commercial- and investment-banking functionalities. The key distinction from the conventional system is the *risk-sharing* feature with the depositors and minimizing the financial intermediary's own exposure. This also puts additional responsibility on the financial intermediary to act prudently to retain and attract depositors or investors.

On the liabilities side, IFIs can accept demand deposits from customers with a 100 percent reserve requirement. This requirement is based on the presumption that the monies deposited as demand deposits are placed as *amanah* (for safekeeping), that they are repayable on demand and at par value, and that they are not invested; therefore, money creation through the multiplier effect would not be allowed. Whereas the liabilities side of an IFI has limited modes of mobilizing funds (*mudarabah*, *musharakah*, or *wikalah*), the asset side can carry a more diversified portfolio of heterogeneous asset classes representing a wider spectrum of risk and maturity profiles. For *short-term maturity, limited-risk investments*, there is a choice of holding financial claims against trade- and commodity-financed assets. The short-term maturity of these instruments and their backing by real assets minimizes their level of risk. A financial intermediary's basic service could be in the form of commercial banking, where the intermediary offers very low-risk, deposit-like investment accounts which are to be accepted on the basis of a *mudarabah* (principal–agent arrangement) or *wikalah* contract on behalf of the depositors. Depositors will be treated as investors and will share the profits as well as the losses with the financial intermediary. The financial intermediary may invest their funds to provide financing of low-risk and short-term trading activities such as commodity or trade financing. Since such trade- and commodity-financed assets would carry a very low risk—that is, the financial intermediary would be only exposed to credit risk while the other risks are hedged, and the financial intermediary will focus on minimizing credit risk by enhancing the selection and monitoring of borrowers. Depositors will be exposed to low risk, but will also earn low returns.

For *medium-term maturity investments*, IFIs have several choices. They can invest in *ijarah-* (lease) and *istisna'*-based assets held on the IFI's balance sheet, or investments in securities linked to leased assets.[5] By deploying permissible financial contracts, IFIs can set up special-purpose (customized) portfolios to invest in a particular asset class and sector, and can match these portfolios with the special-purpose *mudarabah* investments accepted on the liabilities side. In that sense, this segment of the assets side represents fund of funds, financed by matching *mudarabah* contracts on the liabilities side. The next level of financial service by an IFI could be in the form of investment funds to target specific risk and maturity profiles, and where the constraint of capital preservation is relaxed and the investor is willing to take additional risk. IFIs can offer this service by designing specialized funds on the assets side and then marketing the funds to investors utilizing restricted *mudarabah* or *musharakah* contracts.[6] This service can be catered to the next tier of investors with a higher risk appetite and can include high-net-worth individuals, institutional investors, and corporate clients who may have more tolerance for risk and are targeting medium- to long-term maturities. This class of financial service has considerable potential for designing and developing funds with specific risk–return profiles to offer individuals and institutional clients to manage portfolios and perform risk management.

For *longer-term maturity investments*, IFIs can engage in *musharakah*, venture capital, or private equity activities. In the absence of debt and markets, and the centrality of equity financing in the Islamic system, IFIs can focus on the development of well-established instruments of private equity and venture capital. Both private equity and venture capital can make a significant contribution to promote innovation, entry for new firms, and thus economic development. By offering these services, IFIs will be performing the functions of a conventional investment bank. In addition to asset and wealth management, IFIs can earn fee income by providing other commercial and investment banking services such as fund transfers, letters of credit, foreign exchange transactions, and investment management and advisory services to retail and corporate clients.

An IFI can attract depositors or investors in two modes: (i) it can invite investors to share profits and losses on a general pool of assets maintained by the financial intermediary itself; or (ii) it can act as a dealer or broker for third-party products. The general pool could be in the form of various funds specializing in specific sectors or geographical regions. In this case, an investor or depositor will be placing funds with the IFI in a "fund-of-funds," which would be a collection of diversified portfolios of financial assets. The relationship between the financial intermediary and the depositors or investors could be on the basis of either *mudarabah*, where the financial intermediary manages assets for a fee, or *musharakah*, where the financial intermediary shares profits and losses with the depositors or investors. In either case, there is risk sharing between the financial intermediary and the depositors or investors. On the other hand, IFIs can simply act as a dealer or broker and help the investor select and place funds in portfolios managed by independent fund managers who specialize in specific asset classes, investment styles, sectors, and maturity terms. In other words, in this second mode, the IFI acts as an intermediary to facilitate the purchase or sale of third-party products without any liability regarding the outcome or the performance of that financial product. However, the IFI may perform due diligence on the fund and its managers before recommending it to its customers.

The key to understanding the nature of financial intermediation in Islam is its nature of true intermediation, where the intermediary simply "passes through" the performance of its assets to the investors or depositors on its liabilities side. There is an element of risk sharing present in the contractual agreement between the financial intermediary and the depositors or investors. The assets on the assets side of the balance sheet could be in the form of over-the-counter assets financed by the IFI or direct investments in marketable securities of *Shari'ah*-compliant assets. It is important to note that the structure of a hypothetical Islamic financial intermediary combines the activities of commercial banking and investment banking. Figure 8.1 sets out the different functional components of an IFI from maturity and risk perspectives to show that an Islamic financial intermediary is able to offer the full spectrum of commercial and investment banking services in an efficient fashion. There is sufficient diversity on both the assets and liabilities sides to undertake all critical functions expected from an efficient financial intermediary. In this balance sheet, each box on the assets and liabilities sides represents a specialized function or financial service, whereas the arrows across liabilities and assets indicate how they can be matched. Each box separates assets and liabilities based on their function, risk profile, maturity structure, and targeted market. Similar to a conventional commercial bank, such a financial intermediary can raise funds as deposits and invest them in low-risk and high-quality investment-grade trade financing or real sector financing. Like an investment bank, it can offer underwriting services, asset management through specialized *mudarabah* funds, and other advisory services such as

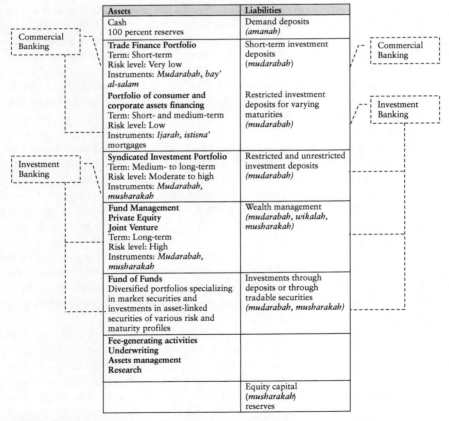

FIGURE 8.1 Functional Components of an Islamic Financial Intermediary

research about financial markets, maintenance of benchmarks, and portfolio and risk management.

III. EQUITY AND ASSET-LINKED MARKETS

While the critical role of a financial intermediary is evident, the significance of financial and capital markets cannot be ignored. Competitive capital markets play a positive role in aggregating information signals and effectively transmitting this information to investors, with beneficial implications for firms seeking financing and ultimately overall economic performance. Competition between the financial intermediary and the market in providing financial services may not be desirable, but both can perform complementary functions. For a financial intermediary, the absence of efficient and liquid financial markets can greatly hamper portfolio and risk management on its asset side. An organized market for financial securities co-existing with strong financial intermediaries will offer diversification opportunities, lower transaction costs, and improved liquidity, leading to enhanced efficiency in the financial system.

As discussed in Chapter 6, one can envision two types of capital markets in an Islamic financial system. As compared to conventional capital markets, which are dominated by debt securities, the market for equities and for securitized "asset-linked" certificates representing ownership in a pool of assets would dominate in Islamic capital markets. Vibrant asset-linked securities markets would replace debt markets. The role of asset-linked markets, where shares or certificates against some form of income-generating assets are traded, would be critical in the risk-sharing financial system. Such markets of "asset-linked" securities would provide a platform to securitize assets of different qualities, asset classes, and varying maturities. The notion in Islamic economics of binding capital closely and tightly to a real asset encourages the issuance of securities against an asset. For example, an asset financed through *ijarah* (lease) or *istisna'* can be used as collateral to issue securities linked to the payoffs and cash flows of underlying assets. Once the assets are securitized and a financial security is created, such securities can be traded on an organized capital market in the primary or secondary market.

The main difference between conventional securitization and that proposed in Chapter 6 is the way the end investor would have ownership rights to the securitized assets. Whereas in the conventional system there may be multiple layers of ownership, which may leave the final investor without any recourse, in the Islamic system, scholars have maintained strict requirements of clear ownership rights for the investor. This feature, in contrast to the conventional system, affords greater stability as the same underlying asset is not traded many times over, which could have a cascading effect in the case of liquidation. More importantly, in conventional securitization the underlying assets are debt-based, and thus have an implicit guarantee of the principal, whereas securitization in the Islamic system is based on risk sharing. Here, the return of the principal depends on the market value of the underlying asset, as opposed to securitization in a conventional system where the notion of market value is supposed to be reflected in the market price of the security, not of the underlying asset. Again, this is an important factor reinforcing financial stability.

An Islamic asset-linked securities market differs from the typical stock market in one crucial way. Whereas an equity share represents ownership in the equity capital of a firm and is therefore exposed to the general business of the firm, with an asset-linked security the investor's return is linked to the profit and loss of a pool of heterogeneous assets. Since the pool will be a portfolio of assets of the same type—for instance, leases—where the returns are driven by the performance of underlying assets, it will be relatively easy for the investor to forecast its future payoffs. As a result, it is expected that the volatility of such asset-linked securities will be lower than that of a simple stake in equity capital (that is, common stocks). Due to low volatility, it can cater to the needs of investors who would like more deterministic and low-risk returns. Finally, although both an equity stock and an asset-linked security will be based on equity sharing, an asset-linked security is expected to exhibit low risk and thus to occupy the vacuum in the risk spectrum of the financial system.

There is another compelling reason to encourage securitization and development of asset-linked securities. The financial intermediary's primary function is to intermediate between the savers and the users of funds. It can operate optimally when it performs the intermediation with the least degree of friction. However, if the financial intermediary takes on additional responsibilities of maintaining physical assets—that is, warehousing and trading of real assets—its attention will divert from intermediation and it may not do either task optimally. For example, it may not be efficient for the financial intermediary to operate leases or mortgages. One way of avoiding this problem would be for the financial intermediary to originate the assets and ultimately to pool them, securitize the pool, and issue marketable securities some of which the financial intermediary can hold on its balance sheet. This will free the financial intermediary from having to deal with operational issues pertaining to the assets and enable it to focus on intermediation.

With the prohibition of interest and a preference for sharing profits and losses, equity markets occupy a significant place in an Islamic financial system. Islamic scholars have pointed out the necessity, desirability, and permissibility of the existence of a stock market in the Islamic financial system, where transactions in capital instruments such as corporate stocks can take place. The operating conditions in markets for financial securities (either equity shares or asset-linked securities), in accordance with the rules of the *Shari'ah*, are much like those that must prevail in markets for goods and services. For example, in such markets the rules are intended to remove all factors inimical to catallactical justice and to yield prices that are considered fair and just. And prices are just or equitable not because they are based on any independent criterion of justice, but because they are the result of bargaining between equal, informed, free, and responsible economic agents. To ensure catallactical justice, the *Shari'ah* has provided a network of ethical and moral rules of behavior for all participants in the market and requires that these norms and rules be internalized and adhered to by all. Given that financial intermediaries act as underwriters of securities, firms could directly raise funds for their investment projects in the stock market, which would provide them a second source of funding in addition to banks.

A stock market operating strictly in accordance with Islamic rules is envisioned to be one in which the commitment of investible funds is based on the profit prospects of the enterprises, where relative profit rates reflect the efficiencies between firms and profit rates (as signals coming from the goods market) are not distorted by market imperfections. Such a market might be expected to allocate investible funds strictly in accordance with expected investment yields—that is, resources would be allocated in such a way as to first finance higher-return projects. Stock markets would also be capable of improving the allocation of savings by accumulating and disseminating vital information in order to facilitate comparisons between all available opportunities, thus reflecting the general efficiency in resource allocation expected from a system that operates primarily on the basis of productivity of an investment. The development of a secondary market is important and essential to the development of a primary market. All savers, to different degrees, have a liquidity preference. Liquidity preference, perhaps to a different extent and degree, can exist in an Islamic system as in any other system. Liquidity of an asset is an important attribute for its marketability. To the extent that savers can, if necessary, sell securities quickly and at low cost, they will be more willing to devote a higher portion of their savings to long-term instruments.

In the conventional interest-based system, the money market affords the vehicle for financial institutions to adjust their balance sheet and finance positions. Short-run cash positions, which exist as a result of imperfect synchronization in the payment period, become the essential ingredient for the presence of the money markets. The money market, in this case, becomes a source of temporary financing and a home for excess liquidity where transactions are mainly portfolio adjustments. In an Islamic financial system the liabilities that an economic unit generates are, by necessity, closely geared to the characteristics of its investment. Hence, given that debt instruments cannot exist, money market activities will have different characteristics from their counterparts in the conventional system. The existence of a poor money market combined with a poor structure of financial intermediation leads to a situation where money becomes more important as a repository of wealth than in a system with more active financial intermediation. Both individual and institutional investors may wish to allocate some portion of their savings in the form of very short-term—that is, 0–3 months' maturity—investments, especially if the conditions are conducive to the existence of a strong precautionary motive for liquidity needs. This would necessitate the development of a money market where the users of funds seeking short-term access to funding are matched with investors wishing to invest for the short term. Due to the prohibition of interest, a simple "I owe you" debt security would not be available. Instead, a money market that operates on the basis of exchanging claims on real assets would emerge, with the rate of return on such claims determined on the basis of profit and loss sharing. However, given that such a security traded in the money market would be linked to a real asset, the rate of return would be subject to low volatility. Given that the Islamic economic system emphasizes the tight coupling of the real and financial sectors, the system would have a large supply of short-term financial assets, which can be securitized to issue certificates traded for different maturities. A vibrant and liquid market for asset-linked securities would not only provide low-risk investment opportunities, but would also become the basis for developing a robust money market where securities are traded on the basis of profit and loss sharing.

In an Islamic system, perhaps more than in any other, both the primary and secondary markets require the active support of the government and the central bank, not only in their initial development and promotion but also in their supervision and control, in order to ensure their compliance with the rules of the *Shari'ah*. Particularly in the case of the secondary markets, traders and market makers need the support and supervision of the central bank for these markets to operate efficiently. For secondary markets to transform an asset into a reliable source of cash for an economic unit whenever the latter needs it, there must be dealer markets, where there are entities that take significant positions and trade significant amounts of assets. In the traditional interest-based system, these position takers are financed by borrowings from banks, financial intermediaries, and other private cash sources. Since in the Islamic system refinancing on the basis of debt is not permitted, reliable and adequate sources of funds would have to be provided by the central bank. There will have to be arrangements through which the central bank can, at least partially, finance secondary markets and fully supervise them.

IV. ISLAMIC AND CONVENTIONAL FINANCIAL INTERMEDIATION[7]

A financial intermediary in a risk-sharing financial system plays a very critical role, since it is required to screen and monitor good-quality assets in order to maximize the returns for depositors or investors. A financial system dominated by strong financial intermediaries is not necessarily an inefficient one. It is often said that Japan has sophisticated financial markets, but for most of the past 50 years, a concentrated banking system has played the dominant role in allocating resources and has contributed to economic development. A bank-centered financial system, where banks dominate the intermediation function, offers superior information processing by forming long-run relationships with firms to ease asymmetric information distortions, and ameliorates the moral hazard through effective monitoring, thereby boosting economic growth. Banks acting as delegated monitors make a long-term investment in acquiring information about firms and managers, and thereby improve capital allocation and corporate governance. Intertemporal risk management makes further positive contributions to development. Since the 19th century, many economists have argued that bank-based systems are better at mobilizing savings, identifying good investments, and exerting sound corporate control, particularly during the early stages of economic development and in a weak institutional environment.

As we have stressed earlier, the emerging financial services view clearly argues that it does not matter if the system is bank-based or market-based; the important issue is which institutions perform a particular function. The financial services view minimizes the importance of the bank-based versus market-based debate, stressing that financial arrangements—contracts, markets, and intermediaries—develop in order to ameliorate market imperfections and provide financial services. In a risk-sharing financial system, both financial intermediaries and financial markets play a complementary role. A financial intermediary without financial markets will not function efficiently; and similarly, financial markets without active participation by financial intermediaries will not survive. A financial intermediary will rely on financial markets, both equities and asset-linked securities, to provide access to liquid securities in order to construct diversified portfolios and manage risks for the depositors or investors. The important point to note is that the system will operate on a risk-sharing—and thus profit–loss-sharing—basis, which will result in enhanced financial stability.

A major difference between the conventional and Islamic systems is that, due to the prohibition of interest and the fact that they have to rely primarily on profit sharing, IFIs will have to offer their asset portfolios of primary securities to investors or depositors in the form of risky open-ended "mutual funds." In contrast to the Islamic system, banks in the conventional system finance the assets through issuing time-bound deposit contracts, a practice that results in solvency and liquidity risks, since their asset portfolios and loans entail risky payoffs and costs of liquidation prior to maturity, while their deposit contracts are liabilities that are often payable on demand and at par. In contrast, Islamic banks act as agents of investors or depositors and, therefore, create a pass-through intermediation between savers and entrepreneurs, eliminating the risk faced by conventional banks. Unlike conventional commercial banks that accept deposits with the assumption of capital preservation and a promised return, IFIs would not be able to offer such explicit guarantees but would have to ensure depositors that every opportunity will be taken to minimize the risks they face. Using the techniques of portfolio management and diversification, an optimal portfolio of trade-related and asset-linked securities can be designed. By deploying the funds in this fashion, the intermediary will not only be able to offer short-term time deposits with minimized financial risk and sufficient liquidity for the depositors, but will also facilitate a system-wide payment system that is backed by real assets.

The absence of risk-free assets in the system, and the reliance on trade-financing products with potential illiquidity, raises concerns about ensuring an efficient and smooth payment system. Acceptance of demand deposits that are not invested in any risky assets can address this issue.[8] Another alternative similar to narrow banking would be to have a portion of the demand and short-term deposits invested only in well-diversified portfolios of high-quality assets such as financial claims on trade and commodity assets and other asset-linked securities which have a liquid market and low credit risk, and are not exposed to market risk.

V. CONCLUSION

In any financial system, financial development is generally seen as supportive of economic growth. The simple reason is that those who invest are not necessarily the same as those that save. There is a need for financial intermediation to encourage and channel savings to the most productive investments. Financial intermediation is at the heart of any financial system. Its traditional function has been to transfer savings (real resources) to firms, entrepreneurs, and governments for investment, and increasingly in recent years to transfer risk to those who are better able to assume it and thus enhance risk sharing. Historically, financial intermediaries have provided these functions and services, but financial and capital markets have in recent years increasingly served the same functions. While intermediaries and markets could complement one another, competition may increase efficiency and risk taking. Under certain circumstances, the increased assumption of risk could threaten the overall financial system. Financial stability and risk transfer have become more important aspects of financial systems.

There is no doubt that well-developed political, economic, and legal institutions are essential to facilitate financial contracting and are a necessary element of a robust financial system. Better institutions promoting checks and balances and the quality of governance can affect financial markets in several ways.[9] Starting with the legal system, unless there is clarity with respect to creditors' and borrowers' rights, the protection of property rights, and access rights to collateral in the case of default, it would be difficult to build an efficient financial system. Prevailing legal systems are predominantly based on the conventional legal system, which may or may not have the provisions for handling specific treatment of *Shari'ah* rules. Furthermore, legal systems in place in Islamic countries are invariably plagued by enforcement shortcomings, a significant deterrent for any investor. Therefore, development of supportive legal and tax codes, and a harmonized regulatory framework based on Islamic law for the Islamic financial services industry, is critical for the efficient operation of the Islamic financial system.

Risk sharing and equity finance is the essence of Islamic finance. As stated in Chapters 4 and 5, the most sophisticated market-based risk-sharing mechanism is a vibrant stock market. Developing an efficient stock market can effectively complement and supplement the existing and to-be-developed array of other Islamic financial instruments. It would provide the means for business and industry to raise capital. Such an active market would reduce the dominance of banks and debt financing where risks become concentrated, creating system fragility. In the current evolution of Islamic finance, the emphasis should be on long-term investment contracts. Moreover, through holding diversified stock portfolios, investors can eliminate idiosyncratic risks specific to individual investors as well as to firms. Diversification can allow a reduction in portfolio risk. The model of Islamic financial intermediaries as presented in Chapter 5 and discussed briefly in this chapter is that of a specialized "funds" manager who acts as a buffer between the depositor who happens to be an investor and the market. IFIs specialize in processing information about markets and economic agents, and performing the functions of assets- and maturity-transformation on behalf of the depositor who is contractually an investor in the IFI. We have also argued that an IFI cannot function efficiently and effectively in the absence of vibrant capital markets and secondary and money markets. Therefore, the development of these markets is also necessary and vital for efficient financial intermediation. Financial intermediaries also play a special role in an Islamic financial system because in the absence of derivative markets the financial intermediary would also have to provide "risk-management" functionality, such as hedging for clients. Financial intermediaries will have to take on the responsibility of innovating risk-sharing mechanisms for hedging through collective cooperative-style schemes or through matching offsetting hedging needs. In sum, financial intermediation should and must play a critical role in a risk-sharing financial system, but it will require supporting markets and institutions if it is to perform effectively and efficiently and support the growth of the real sector.

ENDNOTES

1. Allen and Gale (1999) make a strong case for the role the financial intermediary plays in providing intertemporal risk-mitigating functionality in a financial system.
2. Baliga and Polak (2001) make an interesting observation that an important distinction between German and Anglo-Saxon financial systems concerns not the distinction between banks and the market, but between bank loans and bonds.
3. It is assumed that these benefits are achievable if the system is unhampered by regulatory restrictions on banks' activities.
4. For background, see Diamond (1984), and Ramakrishnan and Thakor (1984).
5. A benefit of *ijarah* contracts is that not only are they backed by an asset, but they can also have either a fixed or a floating rate feature, which can facilitate portfolio management. The common features of Islamic (*ijarah*) and conventional leasing provide additional investment opportunities for IFIs, since investing in conventional leases with appropriate modifications can be made consistent with *Shari'ah* principles. For a discussion of securitizing leases, see Iqbal (1999).
6. Restricted *mudarabah* is a special-purpose *mudarabah* where the intended usage of funds is agreed by the investor and the borrower.
7. For further discussions, see Askari et al. (2009b).
8. One alternative for addressing this issue in the conventional system is to consider narrow banking. The concept of narrow banking was originally presented by Fisher and is broadly referred to as one specializing in deposit-taking–payment activities, but which does not provide lending services. Stability and safety is achieved if deposits are invested only in short-term treasuries or their close equivalents.
9. For example, Akitoby and Stratmann (2009) show that better institutions lead to better fiscal policy, which reduces the default risk of a country and ultimately lowers its cost of borrowing. Significance of institutions increases with market integration and globalization, where economies with established institutions attract investors and capital, as opposed to economies where institutions are weak, ineffective, and inefficient.

Three

Moving Forward

Enhanced Access to Finance, Social Welfare, and Economic Development under a Risk-Sharing System

As has been emphasized throughout this volume, Islamic finance is based on sharing the investment risk between the entrepreneur and those that provide the other needed inputs, most importantly financing. That is, the financial system facilitates risk sharing. Thus in Islamic finance, financial access could be seen as the development of entrepreneurship, the capacity to promote projects, the development of capital markets, and the implementation of supervision and regulations that ensure the safety and soundness of capital markets. In other words, access to finance could be equated with increasing the role of risk sharing and capital markets in implementing projects and developing businesses. The more developed are the capital markets, the more significant the contributions of equity finance. Countries that have opted for a greater role of Islamic finance, such as Malaysia, have witnessed rising Islamic stock markets, with an increasing number of equity funds, mutual funds, real estate trust funds, and exchange-traded funds. The number of initial public offerings has also increased.

In conventional finance, financial access is especially an issue for the poorer members of society, including potential, or would-be, entrepreneurs. They are commonly referred to as "non-banked" or "non-bankable," and in the case of potential entrepreneurs they invariably lack adequate collateral to access conventional debt financing. While access to finance may be important for economic growth, the private sector may not be willing to provide financing to some areas because of the high cost associated with credit assessment and credit monitoring, and because of the lack of acceptable collateral. In essence, conventional financial institutions cannot provide financing on a profitable basis.

There is voluminous literature in economics and finance on the contributions of finance to economic growth and development. The main reason why finance matters is that financial development and intermediation has been shown empirically to be an important driver of economic growth and development. Finance (financial intermediation) motivates savers to save by offering them a range of instruments to fit their financial needs, channels savings to investors, and in the process broadens investment opportunities, increases investment, ameliorates risk sharing, increases growth of the real sector, enables individuals and business entities to smooth income and consumption profiles over time, and there is some evidence that it may reduce poverty and income inequality.

Although the thrust of research in this area is on the importance of finance for aggregate growth and development, there are secondary issues that cannot be overlooked. Do all businesses and individuals have access to finance and financial services, let alone the same or equal access? Is it important for all businesses and individuals to have access, or equal access, to finance? Should full financial services be available to every segment of an economy, such as all households and all businesses? What are the deficiencies in access to financial services in conventional finance? Should governments intervene to affect or enhance market access? In poor countries where savings rates are low, or even negative, and investment is financed through foreign aid, access to finance may be severely constrained by a shortage of savings, and the allocation of savings may be subject to stricter price rationing in comparison to countries that have high saving rates.

To assess the contributions of Islamic finance, there are additional considerations. Can Islamic finance, with its emphasis on risk sharing, ameliorate the gaps and deficiencies that are observed in conventional finance, and if so, how? Can Islamic finance in turn be as, or more, supportive of growth and development than conventional finance? Can Islamic finance promote the central goals of Islam—that is, equal opportunities for all in the broad context of establishing social and economic justice? While poverty reduction is not central to the financing activity in conventional finance, in Islam—given its emphasis on poverty eradication—access to finance must directly address the issue of poverty alleviation.

I. FINANCIAL ACCESS AND BARRIERS TO ACCESS

Although finance and the financial landscape have changed rapidly in recent years, the functions of financial services have remained remarkably constant: clearing and settling payments, pooling resources, transferring economic resources through time and space, managing risk, providing price information, and dealing with incentive problems. (See Merton, 1989, 1993, and Merton and Bodie, 1995, for a discussion of financial intermediation and the range of financial services that could be provided; and

Crane et al., 1995, for discussion of the stability of the functions of financial intermediation.) The major change in functions is a change in emphasis, specifically the increasing importance of risk management.

Financial access in countries and regions, however, changes as economies grow and develop. As a result, there is no universal definition of financial access. Differences in the definition of financial access may be due to several factors. There is the number of dimensions of access—services, providers, and environment—that are included in the definition (Claessens, 2005). Financial services include many different types of financial instruments (checking accounts, credit cards, debt financing, equity financing, traded shares, simple instruments, derivatives, etc.); these services can be provided by a number of different financial institutions (banks, investment banks, stock markets, etc.) and varied by the environment and structure (competitive private financial sector, public sector institutions such as post offices, globally integrated financial sector, and so on) where they are provided. Thus, access may be defined to include some or all of these instruments, provided by some or a number of institutions, within specific types of environments. Another dimension of financial access is the depth of such services that are available. The cost of financial services, their quality, and the ease of access are three more important dimensions of financial access. Thus, definitions of financial access may vary somewhat depending on the number of these factors that are included.

But access, no matter how defined, may be limited because of barriers. Claessens sums up the classifications of barriers as follows:

> *Explanations of the lack of access fall into two dimensions: financial institutions' specific constraints, and barriers arising from the overall institutional environment. In the terminology of Beck and de la Torre (2005), this means one can classify options to expand access in two groups: individual financial institutions' solutions, or what they call moving towards the country's access possibilities frontier; and government actions, or what they call expanding the country's access possibilities frontier.*

Individual financial institutions' constraints include: type of finance offered, minimum size, high fees, application cost, and implicit education barrier for application from formal institutions and collateral requirement. In response to some of these barriers, individuals may shun formal financial institutions and instead rely on family and friends to provide what may be called informal channels of financial services. If there is heavy reliance on informal channels, banks may in turn find the provision of financial services to the poor to be unprofitable (in part, because of the competition from informal coverage) and thus not provide it. Additionally, financial firms may find it unprofitable to offer services in rural areas, in areas with a low population density, and to borrowers with little financial capacity. As a result, providers of financial services may be unwilling to provide financial services, let alone the full range of services, in many areas of developing countries and even altogether in some small developing countries.

Market failure is normally seen as a possible reason when products and services of any kind are not provided. But after looking at the various studies and the facts, Claessens concluded that there is no evidence that the mismatch in supply and demand is due to market failure.

> *[But the] fact that they do not must mean that it is not profitable to do so given current technology and the institutional environment (legal, regulations and other requirements) they face in a particular market. Question is whether these mismatches between demand and supply need to and can be remedied.*

As to be expected, looking at cross-country comparisons it would appear that access to finance increases with GDP per capita, institutional quality, and market size. Moreover, the more competitive the conventional banking sector, the more access there is to microfinance in sparsely served areas. Distribution networks such as post offices and specialized savings banks have increased financial access in some areas. Thus, in some developing countries access may be more a result of networks and overall institutional environment than the quality of conventional banking. Because lenders need credit information on borrowers and legal support to recover their loans, good legal systems, contract enforcement and property rights, and the availability of reliable credit information may be important for access of business, and especially for small businesses as they may pose a bigger risk for lenders (Beck et al., 2005). In a more recent study, Kendall et al. (2010) used two financial access indicators (bank accounts and loans), five types of institutions that deliver financial services (commercial banks, specialized state-run savings and development banks, banks with a mutual ownership structure, microfinance institutions, and other) for 139 countries to estimate that there are 6.2 billion bank accounts in the world. For developed countries, they estimate that there are 3.2 bank accounts per adult, with 81 percent of adults banked; and in developing countries, they estimate 0.9 accounts per adult with 28 percent banked. In their cross-sectional analysis, they show a significant relationship between bank accounts, loans and branch penetration, and measures of economic development and physical infrastructure. For this and for other reasons, a number of countries have adopted universal access to finance as a goal—India, Pakistan, South Africa,

Mexico, Brazil, Colombia, Malaysia, and a number of European countries (Pearce, 2010).

Although there is no country-level study on financial access in Muslim countries, Pearce provides a recent assessment of financial inclusion in the Middle East and North Africa (MENA, a region of 20 countries and the Palestinian Authority (PA), including 18 Muslim countries and the PA region). Pearce concludes that there is still no comprehensive commitment across the region to enhance financial access. The MENA region has the second-lowest (after the OECD, which has the highest degree of inclusion) push to increase inclusion. Only five countries have adopted a strategy of financial inclusion, with three of these adopted since 2006 and financial inclusion is still not a priority item in the region. Banks are generally dissuaded from increasing financial access because of inadequate infrastructure, limited credit information, and uncertain regulatory policies such as caps on interest rates and contract enforcement. Because the region has the lowest score on the World Bank's "Doing Business Legal Rights" index, banks and other financial institutions face higher costs from information asymmetries and more credit and default risk for micro-lending, and are reluctant to increase inclusion by expanding their micro-lending activities. As a result, financial access, albeit on a low level, is largely supported by nongovernmental organizations dominated microcredit sectors, postal networks, and state banks. Pearce's broad recommendations for increasing financial access in the MENA region include the following:

> *[A] Financial Inclusion Strategy that is underpinned by improved data, that has both public and private sector commitment, and that scales up financial access on a large scale, principally through bank accounts. Secondly, . . . regulators should provide a legal and supervisory framework that enables access to finance to be expanded primarily through banks, but with regulatory space for the use of agents, mobile phone technology, and for a finance company model for microcredit and leasing. . . . removing interest rate caps on microloans, and instead strengthening consumer protection and supervisory capacity for microfinance, while stimulating competition between financial service providers. Thirdly, continued improvements to financial infrastructure are encouraged, particularly with regard to credit information and to secured transactions. Finally, . . .* the need to enable growth in Islamic financial services to meet market demand.[1]

On the latter point, namely the need for growth in Islamic financial services, Pearce cites the result of an International Finance Corporation (IFC) survey which found that 20–60 percent of those interviewed (microenterprises, low-income individuals) had a preference for *Shari'ah*-compliant products; and for some the lack of *Shari'ah*-compliant financial services was the binding constraint to access. Pearce states:

> *An innovation that is directly linked to financial inclusion is the introduction and adaptation of Islamic banking products for low income consumers and microenterprises. A lack of Shari'ah-compliant financial services is a constraint on financial inclusion to a proportion of the population. The growth of Islamic microfinance will depend to a large degree on whether financial institutions can develop sufficiently attractive financial products and services, which are competitive with conventional products in terms of pricing, transparency, processing time, and burden on the client. This will be determined in part by their capacity and systems, but regulators can also provide a more level playing field for Islamic microfinance. This extends beyond financial sector regulation to the tax code, as Islamic financing that involves additional transactions such as passing on a property title, has tax implications such as capital gains tax, which are not present in conventional deals. Practical measures that can be taken by regulators (as has been the case in Indonesia and Pakistan) include: licensing Islamic banks, supporting centers for training and certification on Islamic financial operations to staff and managers of financial service providers, and developing guidelines setting out requirements for licensing and appointment of Shari'ah advisers to rule on Shari'ah compliance. The political climate for Islamic finance also affects investor and lender decisions about whether to offer Shari'ah-compliant products, and acts as an incentive or disincentive to its growth.*

While there is less information and few studies available on the degree of financial access and its impact on development and growth of the real sector at the country level, there are some insights from the work that has been done. Banking and related regulations, usury laws, high capital requirements for banks, laws and legal requirements that impede new registration of new banks, restrictive accounting regulations, stifling regulation and supervision, high compliance cost, anti-money laundering initiatives, and customs that limit women from opening bank accounts appear to impede the development of small finance and microfinance institutions that could increase access for the under-served segments of society (Claessens). Because of the impact of regulations on access, as Claessens notes, there is usually a trade-off between more regulations (that are largely intended to protect consumers) and access to finance. However, there are measures that can increase access without reducing consumer protection. These include efforts to increase financial literacy, improvements in institutional infrastructure, better legal structure, measures to increase competition in the banking sector, improvements in the payments system, the introduction of new technologies (such as smart cards, pre-paid cards, the Internet, mobile phones, texting, ATM machines, alternative institutions for access, and so on). Entry of foreign banks can also be a positive force, both directly (as new providers of financial services) and indirectly (in fostering competition and introducing new technologies and know-how). Clark et al. (2003), in their review, conclude that foreign entry can bring enhanced financial stability and efficiency. All of these can be supportive of access, especially for smaller firms and the poorer members of society.

II. WHY FINANCIAL ACCESS MATTERS AND MAY BE SKEWED

The importance of finance as one of the important drivers of growth is confirmed at a number of levels, including country, sector, business, and household. Stated simplistically, in the absence of financing there can be no investment and without investment there can be little or no growth. Financial intermediation provides financing from savers to entrepreneurs and businesses. Claessens sums up the contributions of finance through a number of channels:

> *Financial deepening has been shown to "cause" growth (Rajan and Zingales, 1998; Demirguc-Kunt and Maksimovic, 1998; Levine, Loayza, and Beck, 1999; for an extensive review of this evidence, see Levine 2005). The channels why finance matters are multiple. Finance helps growth through raising and pooling funds, thereby allowing more and more risky investments to be undertaken, by allocating resources to their most productive use, by monitoring the usage of funds, and by providing instruments for risk mitigation. Interesting[ly], it is less the form in which these services come—whether from banks or capital markets— but more the fact that they are being provided in an efficient manner, i.e., being supported by a proper institutional and competitive environment, which matters for growth (Demirguc-Kunt and Levine, 2000; see also World Bank, 2001). As such, it is difficult to assert that particular types of financial systems are more or less conducive to growth, and possibly neither which type of system is more or less conducive to facilitate access to financial services.*

In addition to its contribution to overall economic growth, the most widely studied and supported attribute, finance has been shown to have other supportive and desirable effects that could also affect economic growth. First, finance can reduce poverty and thus improve income distribution, by raising overall growth, giving the less fortunate—individuals or small businesses—an opportunity to access funds and invest (Beck, et al., 2004). Honohan (2004a) has shown that financial deepening reduces poverty, defined as people with under US$1 or US$2 of daily income. A major channel for this result is that the availability of credit reduces child labor and increases education, thus raising incomes and reducing poverty. In addition, it is believed that financial access could be an important factor in attaining most of the Millennium Development Goals (Claessens). Collins et al. (2009), in their book using financial diaries, confirm the dependency of the poor on a few financial instruments, informal and formal, to manage the little money they have. And there are an increasing number of studies confirming the importance of financial access for the poor (Burgess and Pande, 2005; Karlan and Zinman, 2009; Dupas and Robinson, 2009; Banerjee et al. 2009; Bruhn and Love, 2009). Second, access to finance may be particularly important for small and medium-size enterprises (SMEs). Beck et al. (2004) argue that although the quality of the business environment (rule of law, property rights, contract enforcement, and so on) is the critical factor for the growth of all business enterprises, finance boosts the growth of SMEs more than that of large enterprises. In some sense, large firms already enjoy access to finance; however, for SMEs access to finance allows them to undertake bigger projects and investments, putting them on a more level footing with the big firms. Third, while access to finance may be a more important constraint for those who have no access, access tends to be skewed, especially in developing countries where SMEs and most individuals have little or no access. While financial development in general is beneficial for growth and poverty alleviation, this does not mean that finance is available on an equal basis for everyone. Finance can be allocated in a skewed or even perverse manner. There is some evidence that finance often benefits the few, especially in developing countries where access is determined by connections, relationships, and political clout. This has led to general failure of banks, and even to the disappearance of the banking system in countries where these practices have prevailed. As a result, it would appear that making financial access more generally, and equally, available would be helpful for economic growth and for economic equality and justice.

But as discussed in the previous section, the meaning of access is not clear-cut. As a result, it is difficult to decide what is the appropriate degree of access and in what form (for instance, access to checking accounts, credit cards, other credit, and so on). As Claessens notes:

Universal access is not necessarily the goal, different perhaps from basic health services, primary education, clean water, etc. There are [a] number of reasons. For one, we do not (yet) know at the micro-level sufficiently well what the benefits and impacts of access to finance are and whether there is a public goods argument to be made in favor of extending access more broadly. The gains of access to basic health care services such as immunization are better known today than the gains from access to financial services. Second, as for other good[s] and services, the demand for financial services may not exist. Many households even in developed countries choose not [to] have a bank account as they do not engage in enough financial transactions[—]e.g., write no checks, collect wages in cash or cash their checks[—]yet they may not [be] burdened by no "access." Firms without use of external credit may choose to remain so as their rates of return on capital are too low to justify formal finance or because they are not willing to provide the necessary information on their business to banks, and by implication to others, including tax authorities. Equally important, and even in the best financial systems[,] financial services providers may not wish to provide access to all customers as it is not profitable or sustainable to so. This does not reflect any market failures, but rather that finance, like other services, has its own demand and supply.

Answers to these questions are made all the more difficult because of inadequate data. Data for access is gathered through detailed household and business surveys. The coverage of these surveys is still quite limited (in terms of components of access, form of access, ease of access, cost of access, by socioeconomic breakdown, and geographically). The quality of this data is also generally questionable, and as important is the fact that complete surveys with full coverage are not even available for most advanced countries, let alone for developing countries. The surveys that exist are not always comparable across countries and over time. While there are more and more detailed surveys available on businesses than on households, generally indicating that access to credit and its cost may be the most important constraint to business growth, it is still difficult to assess what it costs business if credit is unavailable or is available only at a non-competitive price, and to what degree firm size is a factor in determining the availability and cost of credit. Given such information gaps, it is in turn difficult to decide to what degree and in what form access to finance should be enhanced. From our perspective—that is, the perspective of Islamic finance—it would be essential also to know the trade-offs between credit and equity finance for households and businesses. For reasons of social justice (see Section IV below), we would want detailed credit and cost information by the size of firm and political and economic clout.

While the traditional study of finance is focused on the efficient allocation of capital, today finance is arguably just as much, if not more, centered on risk allocation (Mason, 1995). Risk management and the cost of managing risk are one of the key, if not *the* key, functions of finance today. In the case of Islamic finance, the sharing and management of risk is its essence, as debt and predetermined interest are prohibited. While the allocation, management, sharing, and price of risk have become critical, risk sharing may be still in its infancy, even in the advanced nations. Risk sharing, even within countries, has not even begun to consider the menu of opportunities (Shiller, 2003).

III. GOVERNMENT INTERVENTION TO BROADEN AND ENHANCE ACCESS

From our discussions above, it would appear that government intervention may not always increase access (oppressive regulations, predatory lending, over-borrowing), and it may not be cost-effective or even desirable to adopt policies to afford all firms and all individuals equal access to finance. Claessen and others are, in our opinion, correct in concluding that the fundamental issue for the poor is not access to finance, but the fact that they are poor and all that goes with being poor. Instead of adopting policies to increase financial access, policies that may be costly and even counterproductive, governments should improve the educational system for all, increase economic growth to afford better jobs for anyone who can work, improve the quality of institutions, and strive for socioeconomic policies that are founded on justice and equity. Invariably, this may require a comprehensive social safety net to provide individuals and families with the basic requirements of life. In the pursuit of providing better education, jobs, and supportive institutions, most developing countries must acknowledge the fact that their institutions are woefully inadequate. Dysfunctional institutions may serve the short-term financial and political interests of those in power, but they will also stifle economic and social progress. In short, governments should focus on improving the overall quality of institutions, their infrastructure, and the quality of their policies before focusing on policies to increase access to finance as the primary input to alleviate poverty. Moreover, and in this regard, Claessens is correct in concluding that before government intervention to directly increase access can be determined, there is a need for more detailed and accurate surveys to determine exactly what the barriers to access are and if there are market imperfections and failures which would be alleviated by government intervention.

IV. SOCIAL AND ECONOMIC JUSTICE AND ECONOMIC DEVELOPMENT IN ISLAM, AND THE ROLE OF MICROFINANCE

With the pioneering contributions of Mahbub ul Haq and Amartya Sen, economics moved beyond the recognition that GDP is a poor measure of social welfare. Economists have begun to quantify other value systems that could replace GDP. They have conceptualized the well-being of humans as the end purpose of economic development, rather than as just an input in the process. Sen reintroduced the notions of equality and equity, and reconceptualized both in terms of the capabilities and functioning of human beings, forcing to the forefront of the discussion the question of life-options available to humans (capabilities) and what they actually do and achieve (functioning). Although Sen's and ul Haq's ideas were new to the world of conventional economics, many of them resonate with the Islamic value system introduced over 1,400 years ago.

Islam provides a rules-based system to guide a person in every aspect of life, including economic and business activities (Mirakhor and Askari, 2010). The concept of development in Islam has three dimensions: individual self-development, the physical development of the earth, and the development of the human collectivity, which includes both. The first specifies a dynamic process of the growth of the human person toward perfection. The second addresses the utilization of natural resources to develop the earth to provide for the material needs of the individual and all of humanity. The third dimension of development refers to the progress of the human collectivity toward full integration and unity. The most crucial element in development, and central to Islam's conception of development, is the progress humans make in developing the self. Without this, balanced and appropriate progress in the other two dimensions of development is not possible. Happiness and fulfillment in a person's life is not achieved by a mere increase in income, but rather with their full development along all three dimensions. At the same time, economic progress and prosperity is encouraged in Islam since this provides the means by which humans can satisfy their material needs and thus remove the economic barriers on the path to their spiritual progress. Economic transactions are based on freedom of choice and freedom of contract, which, in turn, require property rights over possessions to be exchanged. However, preferences in Islam are assumed to be different. A person is encouraged to satisfy his economic *needs, not wants*. Therefore, more money, more income, more material goods do not necessarily increase social welfare. Islam actually prohibits the accumulation of wealth proceeding from sale of property that exceeds the value of improvements from its original natural given state and imposes limits on consumption through its rules against over-spending, hoarding, and waste (Al-Hakimi et al., 1989).

It is widely recognized that the central economic tenet of Islam is to develop a prosperous, just, and egalitarian economic and social structure in which all members of society can maximize their intellectual capacity, preserve and promote their health, and actively contribute to the economic and social development of society. Economic development and growth, along with social justice, are the foundational elements of an Islamic economic system. All members of an Islamic society must be given the same opportunities to advance themselves; in other words, a level playing field, including access to the natural resources provided by Allah. For those for whom there is no work or who cannot work (such as the handicapped), society must afford the minimum requirements for a dignified life: shelter, food, healthcare, and education. The rights of future generations must be preserved. It is the duty of all generations to preserve what God has given to mankind (not absolute ownership, as in the West) for future generations. Specifically and importantly, this implies the preservation of the environment and the management of depletable resources in such a way as to afford all individuals across all generations equal benefits. In the case of depletable resources such as oil, one solution to the Islamic prescription is provided by the Solow (1974) formula—namely, that exhaustible resources should be optimally drawn down and replaced by reproducible capital (for future output) optimally for future generations.

Markets also play a crucial role in Islam, but with one major difference from that in conventional economics. Epistemologically, the difference is between the concept of the market as an ideology and as an instrument. This difference is profound. In societies known widely as "market economies," market norms are central to social relations. In turn, market norms are determined by self-interest, which dictates "rational" behavior as maximizing what interests the self, narrowly labeled as satisfaction (utility or profit). Market norms, in turn, determine the pattern of preferences of individuals. In Islam, by contrast, the market is an instrument. It is not an organism that determines the rules and norms of behavior, not even those of its own operation. Rules that determine the pattern of preferences of participants are determined outside the market. Participants internalize them before entering the market. The behavior of consumers, producers, and traders, informed by their preferences, is subject to rules determined outside the market. Rules such as no waste; no over-consumption or over-use; no opulence or extravagance; no harm or injury caused to anyone; and faithfulness to contracts, covenants, and promises, as well as trustworthiness, are general rules of behavior that are internalized by consumers, producers, and traders before they enter the market.

Moreover, there are rules specific to the exchange taking place in the market, such as no fraud, no cheating, no shortchanging of weights and measures, no interference with the flow of supply, no hoarding of commodities in the expectation of a price increase, and no restriction on the flow of information. All these rules permit the free and unrestricted interplay of demand and supply. They affect the pattern of preferences. Moreover, there are rules governing the legitimacy and permissibility of sources of income, demand, and supply, because not all sources of income, not all demands for goods and services, and not all supplies are permissible. For instance, income from interest, bribery, theft, or gambling, the confiscation of income belonging to others, and the demand and supply of certain goods and services are not permissible.

These values expressed in the *Qur'an* and operationalized by the Prophet (pbuh) are the multidimensional factors of well-being for society as a whole and contribute to the need for new indicators of economic output, economic development, and social welfare. Although these values have yet to be quantified, future research could explore how these rules and preferences would affect economic behavior and social welfare indicators. Briefly, some salient points of a human development index that could represent Islamic values would include GDP, but only as a measure of production of specific goods and services; and even then with appropriate adjustments for resource depletion and environmental preservation (Askari, 1990). In addition to the level of per capita income would be a measure of the overall welfare of society: economically, socially, and politically. As such, an Islamic index of development would place special emphasis on: the level of poverty in society and the concentration of wealth in the hands of a few; the availability of healthcare and education for all those that qualify; generally, the creation of a level playing field for all members of society to prosper through hard work; provision of the necessities of life for the handicapped and others who are unable to work; and the opportunity to work and earn a decent wage.

Given the emphasis on poverty alleviation in Islam, access to finance takes on a special importance for those who are poor. While access to finance may not be the most important input that the poor need to escape from the vicious cycle of poverty, in conventional finance microfinance has been seen as an important vehicle for improving financial access for the poor. While microfinance has been successful in conventional finance to afford the poor access to finance, there are limited cases of it operating under Islamic financial principles.

Microfinance is designed to address the absence of credit for those who are assessed as unbankable by the market in conventional finance—for whom it is too expensive to gather credit data, who have no acceptable collateral, and for whom it is too costly to monitor compliance. The innovation of microfinance is to resort to group lending. In its original form, as practiced by the Grameen Bank I, microfinance was restricted to the poor and no collateral was required, but a borrower had to be a member of a five-person group, who in turn had to be a member of an eight-group (that is, a total of 40 people) "center" in a village. Although loans are made to individuals for their own project, failure to repay by one individual would have a serious cost for all the other individual members of the "center." Specifically, every individual would lose his or her membership in the bank. Thus, each individual member has an incentive to make sure that the other members are honest, to help another member in their project, and to pay off the loan of a defaulting member in order not to lose (or to regain) their membership in the bank. While interest rates have been typically in the range of 20–30 percent per annum, high repayment rates attest to the success of microfinance. This innovative approach to providing financial access for the poor solved the two major obstacles for conventional financing—informational problems of adverse selection and moral hazard (to the selection of the group members) and monitoring (to the group). Grameen Bank II has made some modifications, but the essentials have remained the same.

The Islamic solution to afford financial access to the poor, or *qard-ul-hassan*, is a fundamentally different approach than microfinance. There is no interest on the loan and the borrower determines the term of the loan. While the borrower is obligated to repay the loan, the Prophet (pbuh) is reputed to have said that the lender should not press the borrower if he or she cannot repay the loan at the agreed-upon time. While microfinance has been growing rapidly, with 300–400 institutions providing financing, *qard-ul-hassan* is not formally supported by institutions in Muslim countries, with the possible exception of Iran (Askari et al., 2009b). The important similarities of *qard-ul-hassan* and microfinance are that they require no collateral and are targeted to benefit the poor. Their important innovation is that they get around informational and monitoring costs. But the differences are also striking: microfinance carries an interest expense and collective punishment in case of default, whereas *qard-ul-hassan* does not.

Obaidullah (2008) has looked into the contributions of microfinance in the context of Islamic finance. Drawing on the experience of three Muslim countries—Indonesia, Bangladesh, and Turkey—Obaidullah concludes that financing for the poor must be comprehensive and flexible from country to country to account for differences across countries. He offers the following advice:

- Credit is not always the most important element for success. (There are other elements, such as the market for a product and its marketing, product development, technology, and so on, that may be more important.)
- While studies in conventional finance conclude that financial access is the reason for non-participation of the poor in the development process, in Muslim societies a major reason for the observed absence

of access is the charging of interest associated with conventional finance.

- Conventional microfinance can expand its reach by offering Islamic financial services (void of interest expense).
- At the bottom of the ladder of the poor, the poorest cannot be helped by conventional microfinance as they need social safety nets for survival before they can access microfinance.
- There is a need to establish links between social safety net programs and microfinance—namely: Starting with grants to meet immediate consumption needs and build "micro-assets," these programs then provide skills training, business management training, savings services, and sometimes small credit to prepare clients for running microenterprises. Those who successfully move forward in this sequencing are likely to be ready to graduate to become microfinance clients. In the context of Islamic societies, a similar framework integrating *zakat* and *awqaf* with "for-profit" *Shari'ah*-compliant microfinance needs to be developed. Though traditionally these two institutions have been used as instruments of poverty alleviation and economic empowerment, their potential is vastly untapped.
- "Provision of the above financial services—microcredit, microsavings, microtransfers and microinsurance—to the poor is expected to lead to poverty alleviation. In the Islamic world provision of these services must also comply with Shariah so as to enhance financial inclusion."
- A number of policies are suggested for developing and promoting Islamic microfinance at the micro, meso, and macro levels.

While conventional finance has championed microfinance as an important channel to enhance financial access for the poor (unbanked in the conventional financial system) in order to reduce poverty, poverty in our opinion must be first addressed by broad programs to increase the universal availability of quality education, and to provide a social safety net to provide healthcare, shelter, and food to all those that are deprived. Access to finance cannot be a substitute for these. But access to finance for the poor, in addition to efficient institutions, could provide them with an important input for economic growth and job creation. While this can be handled in a variety of ways in Islam, what has been missing is an institutional structure to provide this interest-free financing; a structure that preserves all the Islamic attributes (no interest or lender-dictated term, and no pressure to repay). The institutional structure could be set up to accommodate poor borrowers that have small (microfinance) projects as well as those that have larger projects. When and if a workable and efficient institutional structure is developed, *qard-ul-hassan* in a microfinance framework could be much more supportive of growth and poverty alleviation because there would be no interest payments and the potential for longer-term loans may support projects that are currently not feasible under conventional microfinance.

Qard-ul-hassan could be established in a microfinance framework in a variety of forms. For instance, there would be a central *qard-ul-hassan* in a country (CQH), which would in turn divide the country into regional *qard-ul-hassan* (RQH) and sub-regional zones as necessary. The regions could be divided on the basis of income levels, population concentration, and private business activity; and the volume of loans going to each region would be dependent on these same variables. Although there are no charges and no pressure to pay back a loan before the agreed-upon date, loan volumes allocated to each region in subsequent years would depend on the mentioned variables and on the percentage of the loans that were repaid on schedule. While this latter condition may appear to be a violation of the Islamic intent, it could be seen instead as a system whereby total loan allocations to a region included late loans that would have been available to others had they been paid back. Thus, this would work just as envisaged in conventional microfinance, but with the added bonus that borrowers would not incur an interest charge and the term of the loans could be longer, accommodating a wider range of projects than is possible under conventional microfinance.

V. THE ROLE OF RISK SHARING IN BROADENING FINANCIAL ACCESS

How does risk sharing as compared to risk shifting affect access to finance? How can the emphasis on risk sharing and economic justice overcome the debt-based problems of conventional finance, including leveraging, risk shifting, and financial stability?

As discussed above, access to debt financing, especially in developing countries, is in large part driven by collateral and political connections. In contrast, access to equity financing requires good projects, good flow of information, business ventures, and hard work. Thus, those members of a community that are not rich (have no access to collateral) and those entrepreneurs who already have a business, though a small business but with no significant collateral, will be energized and motivated to conceive and develop businesses and projects that offer good risk–return profiles, and for those who have a small but ongoing business to expand. While equity financing would allow risk sharing for all businesses and projects, it may be especially important for smaller projects and businesses that would otherwise have no access to finance. This would be helpful for leveling the playing field, enhancing growth, reducing poverty, increasing employment, and improving income distribution.

Debt financing relies heavily on credit rating. If equity financing were to replace it, the need for credit rating would largely disappear. This again would benefit the poorer areas and regions where credit rating is not prevalent. Lester Thurow (1980), in referring to the unfairness of credit, said it somewhat differently (see Saleem, 2008):

> *Credit, therefore, tends to go to those who are lucky rather than smart or meritocratic. The banking system thus tends to reinforce the unequal distribution of capital. Even Morgan Guarantee Trust Company, [the] sixth largest bank in the U.S.[,] has admitted that the banking system has failed to "finance either maturing smaller companies or venture capitalist[s]" and "though awash with funds, is not encouraged to deliver competitively priced funding to any but the largest, most cash-rich companies." Hence, while deposits come from a broader cross-section of the population, their benefit goes mainly to the rich.*

As important, is the fact that debt financing is available for investment as well as for consumption. As a result, debt financing encourages excessive consumption, consumption beyond a person's means, magnifies differences between rich and poor, and as a result does not channel all of the economic resources to finance economic growth and development to create jobs. Lower potential growth unduly penalizes future generations. Moreover, the adverse effect on future generations is especially important when it comes to public expenditures. Governments have almost exclusively used debt financing to fund their consumption and investment expenditures that are beyond their current means (that is, in excess of tax and other revenues). In so doing, they penalize future generations, especially when debt financing is used to finance consumption. If governments were instead to rely exclusively on equity financing, financing would be only used for investment projects (roads, bridges, and other infrastructure). Also importantly, the risk for unproductive investments is borne by the current generation of investors, instead of having much of the risk shifted on to future generations.

While traditional intermediation is still important, academics are increasingly focusing on risk sharing as the premier function of intermediation. For example, Allen and Santomero (1996) comment:

> *. . . many current theories of intermediation are too heavily focused on functions of institutions that are no longer crucial in many*

developed financial systems. They focus on products and services that are of decreasing importance to the intermediaries, while they are unable to account for those activities which have become the central focus of many institutions. In short, we suggest that the literature's emphasis on the role of intermediaries as reducing the frictions of transaction costs and asymmetric information is too strong. The evidence we offer suggests that while these factors may once have been central to the role of intermediaries, they are increasingly less relevant.

We offer in its place a view of intermediaries that centers on two different roles that these firms currently play. These are facilitators of risk transfer and in dealing with the increasingly complex maze of financial instruments and markets. Risk management has become a key area of intermediary activity, though intermediation theory has offered little to explain why institutions should perform this function. In addition, we argue that the facilitation of participation in the sector is an important service provided by these firms. We suggest that reducing participation costs, which are the costs of learning about effectively using markets as well as participating in them on a day to day basis, play an important role in understanding the changes that have taken place.

Islamic finance promotes risk sharing. Increased risk sharing will encourage even more risk sharing and reduce the cost of risk management, further fueling economic growth.

VI. SUMMARY AND RECOMMENDATIONS

Access to finance, although not easily defined, matters. It matters for economic growth, for increasing income, for leveling the playing field between the rich (powerful) and the poor (powerless), for enabling SMEs to expand, for lifting up the poor and for reducing poverty. Access to finance invariably favors the powerful and the rich in developing countries. This is in part because the rich have collateral to access debt financing, and the powerful have the means to use their political connections to secure debt. Financial access is not equal for all regions and sectors in developing countries. Although access to finance helps the poor, it is not clear that equal access is what is called for. Before government intervention and specific policies are recommended, there is a need for much more data and analysis. But two things are for sure. First, there is an urgent need for economic and social justice in most developing countries, but this may be best promoted by a social safety net, rapid growth, and an increase in incomes of the poor, which depend on good institutions and sound policies. The increase in incomes and a reduction in poverty would in turn increase access to finance, as financial institutions would be motivated to provide services to individuals and entities who could meet their requirements. Second, in the specific case of Muslim countries, a significant percentage of Muslims have a clear preference for Islamic financial products and services; and for some Muslims it is more than a simple preference, it is a binding constraint—that is, financial access for them cannot be increased without the increased availability of Islamic financial products and services.

Islamic finance advocates risk sharing, and thus equity finance, while prohibiting debt financing and leveraging. We have argued that, as such, Islamic finance will promote financial access, increase the ratio of investment to consumption financing, enhance economic growth, provide more jobs, reduce government waste, and better protect the interests of future generations. Additionally, because of the focus on risk sharing, we would expect that, over time, risk sharing will be promoted and the cost of risk management reduced. Given the Islamic preoccupation with social and economic justice and the eradication of poverty, we would expect Islamic instruments that are targeted to address inequity, especially *qard-ul-hassan*, to play an important role if the required institutional structures are developed. The principles of microfinance can be combined with the structure of *qard-ul-hassan* to afford financial access to those who are currently underserved.

ENDNOTE

1. Emphasis on Islamic financial services added.

CHAPTER 10

The Role of Institutions and Governance in Risk Sharing

I. INTRODUCTION

Informational and agency problems have been discussed in the context of one risk–reward-sharing instrument, namely equity. On the one hand, for example, Stiglitz (1989) suggests that there are two informational problems in the case of equities: (i) an adverse signaling effect, which deters good firms from issuing equity for fear that it may signal poor quality; and (ii) an adverse incentive effect, which suggests that equity finance weakens the incentive for entrepreneurs or managers (agents) to exert their maximum effort for the highest maximum joint returns for themselves and their shareholders (principals). This happens because once the project is financed, the entrepreneur knows that the net return will have to be shared with the financier (the principal) and, therefore, may not have a strong motivation to work as hard as when the return is not shared. On the other hand, there are agency and informational problems in interest rate-based debt financing. Stiglitz points out that there is an inherent agency conflict in debt financing in that the entrepreneur (the agent) is interested in the high end of the risk–return distribution. The lender (the principal), on the other hand, who is interested in safety, focuses on the low end of the risk–return distribution, and therefore discourages risk taking. This, Stiglitz asserts, has "deleterious consequences for the economy." He further suggests that "from a social point of view equity has a distinct advantage: because risks are shared between the entrepreneur and the capital provider, the firm will not cut back production as much as it would with debt financing if there is [a] downturn in the economy." Moreover, we would add that in the case of an economic or financial crisis, a heavily debt-financed corporation may face withdrawal of short-term debt that could place its very existence in jeopardy, whereas an equity-financed company does not face such short-term withdrawals.

The agency problem has been generalized to bank lending. Banks, being highly leveraged institutions that borrow short (deposits) and lend long, are exposed to an asset–liability mismatch that creates potential for liquidity shocks and instability. Stiglitz suggests that to protect their financial resources, banks are generally discouraged from risk taking. Additionally, their behavior toward risk often creates informational problems that lead to phenomena that can be classified as market failure, such as credit rationing. In contrast to Stiglitz's position, Hellwig (1998) argues that there is an oft-neglected informational problem in the lending behavior of banks, which he refers to as "negative incentive effects on the choice of risk inherent in the moral hazard of riskiness of the lending strategy of banks." This risk materialized dramatically in the period of run up to the recent financial crisis (see Askari et al., 2010; Sheng, 2009).

Based on the above background, the central question is whether Islamic contracting (based on risk sharing and thus, in turn, equity finance) is better suited to solving this contractual dilemma under conditions that promote risk–reward sharing and prohibit interest-based debt financing. In the presence of informational problems such as asymmetric information (where only one side of the contract, usually the agent, has information not available to the other parties), there is transaction cost as well as cost of monitoring the agent's activities and the project(s) performance. It could be plausibly argued that in Islamic contracts asymmetric information issues would be minimized. This assertion is supported by the strict rules governing contracts, exchange, and trade enunciated in the *Qur'an* and in the Tradition of the Prophet (pbuh). These rules include the need for written contracts that fully and transparently stipulate terms and conditions, the direct and unequivocal admonition that commitments to the terms and conditions of contracts must be faithfully carried out, and strong emphasis on trust, cooperation, and consultation. Rules governing market behavior also create incentives—both positive and negative—to enforce honest, transparent, and compliant behavior on the part of participants. Hence, risk-sharing contracts designed under Islamic rules would mitigate informational problems (Khan and Mirakhor, 1987; Ul-Haque and Mirakhor, 1987; Presley and Sessions, 1994) and could be better structured than interest-based debt contracts with incentives to maximize both parties' expected joint rewards.

However, human nature being what it is, the rules of behavior established centuries ago are more likely to be followed if they are enforced. This requires the creation of financial and economic institutions that are based on and governed by Islamic teachings on economics, finance, and appropriate human behavior in business and financial dealings. In this chapter, we discuss the key institutions of Islam, which play a critical role in the economic system. We also discuss the required governance principles for developing economic institutions.

II. SIGNIFICANCE OF INSTITUTIONS AND THEIR DEVELOPMENT

Research has confirmed the critical role and importance of well-established and efficient institutions in the economic and social development of countries. Over the last 30 or so years, there has been a sea change in economic development theory. Whereas earlier economists used to stress the availability of national savings, foreign exchange earnings, and technology, today the foundation of sustained and rapid economic development is seen as good institutions, with education being the other critical element. Because of the distinct characteristics of financial contracts, the need for effective institutions in financial markets is most critical (Fergusson, 2006). As the financial markets grow, the significance of an appropriate legal framework and adequate enforcement of the rights and constraints (the "rule of law") of all the parties involved in the contract also grows. Beck and Levine (2003) show that the level of financial development is higher in countries where legal systems enforce private contracts and property rights, and where creditor rights are protected. If that is not the case, typical problems of moral hazard, adverse selection, and time inconsistency due to informational asymmetries can affect the smooth enforcement of contracts, and many of these problems can be mitigated through well-designed contracts and proper "institutions" (Fergusson, 2006). More simply stated, if financial markets and regulations are not well designed and rules of behavior are not supervised and enforced, individuals and corporations would be less likely to enter into financial contracts.

Fergusson undertook a detailed survey of the literature concerning the development of institutions and legal frameworks, and of their linkage with financial development. A condensed version of his main arguments and relevant empirical evidence is given in Table 10.1.

III. KEY ECONOMIC INSTITUTIONS OF ISLAM

An economic system is a collection of institutions set up by society to facilitate the allocation of resources, production and exchange of goods and services, and distribution of the resulting income and wealth, according to the society's social and moral priorities. What has been said can be directly applied to Islam with only a single exception—that is, instead of the word "society" in the definition of an economic system, we insert the words "the Law-Giver," to have a definition for an Islamic economic system as:

> *. . . a collection of institutions, i.e., formal and informal rules of conduct and their enforcement characteristics, designed by the Law-Giver, i.e.,* Allah *(swt) through the rules prescribed in the* Quran,

TABLE 10.1 Importance of Institutions and Legal Framework for Financial Systems

	Main Theoretical Arguments	Empirical Research
Institutions	Better protection of creditor rights increases the breadth and depth of capital markets.	Shareholder and creditor rights indices (for 49 countries with publicly traded companies) increase opportunities for external finance (La Porta et al., 1997a, 1998).
	Laws and their enforcement influence the extent to which insiders can expropriate outside investors who finance firms. Credibly pledging collateral reduces asymmetric information problems.	Creditor rights and law enforcement are also positively correlated with bank development (Levine, 1998, 1999), firms' ability to raise capital (Kumar et al., 2001; Beck et al., 2003), efficiency of equity markets (Morck et al., 2000), efficiency of capital reallocation (Beck and Levine, 2002; Wurgler, 2000), corporate and bank valuations (Claessens et al., 2000, 2003; La Porta et al., 2000) and ability to fund faster-growing firms (Demirguc-Kunt and Maksimovic, 1998), and firms with less collateral (Claessens and Laeven, 2003).
		Law enforcement and creditor protection also reduces credit cycles and currency and banking crises (Johnson et al., 2000; Galindo et al, 2001, 2004; Boucher, 2004).
Legal framework	Alternative view: strict protection of creditor rights (e.g., right to repossess collateral) might be inefficient and may impede continuation of efficient projects. Pro-creditor rights reduce risk-taking incentives for entrepreneurs. Protection of creditors reduces their incentives to screen projects and to discourage investment by overconfident entrepreneurs.	Extending La Porta et al.'s (2000) exercise by including additional macroeconomic controls, Padilla and Requejo (2000) find that, although an efficient judicial system improves the size and efficiency of the credit market, the effect of creditor protection is inconclusive. By extending the sample (15 additional developing countries), Galindo and Micco (2001) find that the positive effect of creditor protection does hold, even after controlling for macroeconomic variables.

		Countries with weak laws and enforcement tend to introduce remedial rules such as mandatory dividends and reserve requirements (La Porta et al., 1998), display more ownership concentration (Zingales, 1994; La Porta et al., 1998; Claessens et al., 2000; Himmelberg et al., 2000; Roe, 2000; Caprio et al., 2003; Dyck and Zingales, 2004), and invest more in tangible assets (Claessens and Laeven, 2003) and liquid assets (Pinkowitz et al., 2003).
Legal framework and corporate governance: by shaping firms' incentives, a weak protection of creditor rights and weak law enforcement might encourage adoption of remedial rules, higher ownership concentration, and excessive reliance on tangible and liquid assets.		
Other institutions (trust or social capital)	Trust: increasing the perception that others will cooperate facilitates cooperation in large and impersonal markets.	Social capital and financial development are strongly connected in Italy, according to household data (Guiso et al., 2000). Beyond Italy (in a sample of 48 countries), trust is positively correlated with the size and activity of financial intermediaries, bank efficiency, and stock and bond market development (Calderon et al., 2001).

Source: Fergusson (2006).

*operationalized by the practice (*Sunnah*) of the Prophet (*pbuh*) and extended to new situations by* ijtihad—*to deal with allocation of scarce resources, production and exchange of goods and services and distribution of resulting income and wealth.*[1]

More specifically, Islamic economics can be considered as a discipline concerned with: (a) the rules of behavior (institutions) prescribed by Islam as they relate to resource allocation, production, exchange, distribution, and redistribution; (b) economic implications of the operations of these rules; and (c) incentive structure and policy recommendations for achieving rule compliance that would facilitate the convergence of any workings of an economy to the ideal economic system as envisioned in Islam.

The key institutions are those that monitor and enforce Islam's rules concerning property rights, contracts, trust, market behavior, and distribution and redistribution of wealth. These rules are summarized below. (For more detail, see Iqbal and Mirakhor, 2011.)

Property rights

Rules defining property rights deal with the rights of ownership, acquisition, usage, and disposition of the property. Any violation of these rules is considered a transgression and leads to the disruption of social order. Interestingly, for Adam Smith property rights were sacred. He saw the major purpose of governments as being to provide protection for those that own property: "The property which every man has in his labour, as it is the original foundation of all other property, so it is the most sacred and inviolable" (Smith, 1776) and "Civil government, so far as it is instituted for the security of property, is in reality instituted for the defence of the rich against the poor, or of those who have some property against those who have none at all" (Smith, 1776). Islam's recognition and protection of rights is not limited to human beings but encompasses all forms of life, as well as the environment. Each element of creation has been endowed with certain rights, and each is obliged to respect and honor the rights of others. These rights are bundled with the responsibilities for which humans are held accountable. *Shari'ah* offers a comprehensive framework to identify, recognize, respect, and protect the rights of every individual, community, society, and state, including those of future generations.

The key principles of Islamic property rights can be summarized as follows:

1. The Supreme Creator is the ultimate owner of all properties and assets, but in order that humans become materially able to perform duties

and obligations prescribed by the Law Giver, they have been granted a conditional right of possession of property; this right is granted to the collectivity of humans.

2. The second principle establishes the right of collectivity to the created resources.
3. The third principle allows individuals to appropriate the products resulting from the combination of their labor utilizing these resources, *without* the collectivity losing its original rights either to the resources or to the goods and services by individuals.
4. The fourth principle recognizes only two ways in which individuals accrue rights to property: (i) through their own creative labor, and/or (ii) through transfers—via exchange, contracts, grants, or inheritance—from others who have gained property rights title to a property or an asset through their labor. Fundamentally, therefore, work is the basis of the acquisition of rights to property. Work, however, is not performed only for the purpose of satisfaction of wants or needs; it is considered a duty and obligation required from everyone who is able to do so.

Property acquired through non-permissible and unjustifiable means, such as gambling (*maysir*), bribing, stealing, cheating, forgery, coercion, or illegal trading, does not qualify as property (*al-mal*) as defined by *Shari'ah* and, therefore, is proscribed. Consequently, any property that is considered counter-productive or non-beneficial loses its legitimacy and its associated rights. Hoarding with the intention to create artificial scarcity and profiteering is considered an unacceptable means of building wealth and property. Similarly, property acquired through breach of trust, adulteration, non-compliance with weights and measures, or unethical means does not satisfy the definition of property and its ownership is, therefore, not considered legitimate.

Concomitant with property rights, the *Shari'ah* imposes responsibilities, among which are the obligations—severely incumbent upon the individual—not to waste, destroy, squander, or use the property for purposes not permitted by the *Shari'ah*.[2] Under such conditions, the legitimate authority is fully justified in withdrawing the rights of usage of that property in order to protect it from misuse by the owner.[3] This position of the *Shari'ah* is in conformity with the Islamic conception of justice (*al-adl* and *qist*) and the rights and responsibilities of the individual and the community.

Contracts

The significance of contractual obligations in economic and social relations cannot be over-emphasized. The whole fabric of Divine Law is contractual in its conception, content, and application. Islam recognizes only one status—that is, moral consciousness and virtue; all other status on any basis is obliterated. A contract in Islam is a time-bound instrument, which stipulates the obligations that each party is expected to fulfill in order to achieve the objective(s) of the contract. Contracts are considered binding and the *Shari'ah* protects their terms no less securely than the institution of property. The freedom to enter into contracts and the obligation to remain faithful to their stipulations has been so emphasized in Islam that a characteristic that distinguishes a Muslim is considered to be his faithfulness to the terms of his contracts. In the *Shari'ah*, the concept of justice, faithfulness (called *amanah*, whose antonym is *khiyanah*, meaning betrayal, faithlessness, and treachery), reward and punishment are linked with the fulfillment of obligations incurred under the stipulation of the contract.

The emphasis placed on contracts in Islam, by implication, makes the members of the society and economic agents aware of the obligations arising from their contractual agreements—verbal or written, explicit or implicit. In the case of explicit contracts, parties to the contract clearly stipulate the expected behavior and duties with respect to the terms of the contract. This contract is to be free of information asymmetry—that is, all parties are obligated to disclose any and all relevant information; parties intend to comply with the terms of the contract and are fully aware of their rights and obligations. Importantly, the state ensures enforceability of the contract in the case of violations by either party. On the other hand, implicit contracts are not formal contracts with clearly defined terms but are claims and obligations that come with the right to be part of a society. The principles of sharing and the rights of the collectivity to property are types of implicit contracts to preserve and protect the rights of others and thus establish a wide spectrum of implicit obligations. Within the property rights framework, one has contractual obligations to others, including the community and the society, according to the rules of the *Shari'ah*, and honoring these obligations is considered a sacred duty. This sacred duty to preserve the property rights of others is the moral, social, and legal foundation for recognizing and enforcing the obligations arising from implicit contracts.

Muslims are constantly reminded of the importance of contractual agreement, as they are required by their faith to honor their contracts. In a very terse, direct, and forceful verse, the *Qur'an* exhorts, "O you who believe, fulfill contracts." The Prophet (pbuh) also said: "Muslims honor their covenants." The *Qur'an* directs Muslims to reduce their contracts to writing and have witnesses to the conclusion of their agreements. The purpose of documenting a contract is to avoid any misunderstanding or ambiguity about the responsibilities of the parties to the contract. This also ensures that all parties to the contract have full knowledge of what they are committing to and what their respective responsibilities would be. *Shari'ah* scholars often point out that one of the reasons why the Islamic system of *mu'amalat* (transactions) is so highly articulated is that it is based on solid principles of contracts and the rights and obligations of the parties to the contract. The dynamic of contracts and the process of *ijtihad* inherent to *Shari'ah* have ensured that Muslim jurists continue to comment and build upon these theoretical constructs. It is worth noting that throughout the history of Islam, a body of rules, based on the *Qur'an* and the traditions of the Prophet (pbuh), constitute a general theory of contract. This body of rules covering all contracts has established the principle that any agreement not specifically prohibited by the law was valid and binding on the parties and must be enforced by the courts, which are to treat the parties to a contract as complete equals.

Trust

There is strong interdependence between contract and trust as reflected in the verse (23:8) above. Without trust, contracts become difficult to negotiate and conclude, and costly to monitor and enforce. When and where trust is weak, complex and expensive administrative devices are needed to enforce contracts. The *Qur'an* stresses the importance of trustworthiness as the benchmark that separates belief from disbelief (*Qur'an*, 2:282; 4:105; 4:107; 6:152; 8:27; 23:8). Trustworthiness and remaining faithful to one's promises and contracts are absolute. When a believer enters into a contract or is trusted with a commitment, money, pledge, or wealth by someone, the believer has to honor the obligation regardless of costs involved or whether the other party is a friend or a foe. A verse of the *Qur'an* commands the Messenger (*saw*) and his followers not to break a covenant existing between them and their enemies, and to fulfill their conditions to full term (*Qur'an*, 9:4). There is also a network of micro-level rules that ensure transparency and unhindered flow of information. This includes, *inter alia*, the requirement incumbent upon sellers that they must inform the buyers of prices, quantities, and qualities; a body of rules governing consumers' option of, under various circumstances, annulment of a transaction, the rule of non-interference with market supplies, the rule against hoarding, and the rule against collusion among market participants (Mirakhor, 2007; Iqbal and Mirakhor, 2007).

Market behavior

Rules governing the market relate to the appropriate behavior of all participants in the market. The *Qur'an* acknowledges the need for markets and affirms their existence, placing emphasis on contracts of exchange (*bayc*) and trade (*tijarah*). As a rule, the *Qur'an* places emphasis on market transactions based on mutual consent, and therefore on freedom of choice and freedom of contract, which, in turn, requires acknowledgement and affirmation of private property rights. The Messenger specified operational rules of conduct in the marketplace, appointed a market supervisor to ensure rule compliance, and encouraged internalization of these rules by participants before their entrance into the market. Compliance with the rules of market behavior ensures the emergence of prices that are fair and just. So long as market participants comply with the rules, no direct interference with the price mechanism is permitted, even though the legitimate authority has the power and the responsibility of supervision of market operations. Among the rules governing market conduct, five constitute the pillars of the market's institutional structure: (a) property rights, (b) free flow of information, (c) trust, (d) contract, and (e) the right not to be harmed by others, and the obligation not to harm anyone by one's activities. In combination, these five pillars reduce uncertainty and transaction costs as well as allow cooperation and collective action to proceed unhindered.

Distribution and redistribution

The most important economic institution that operationalizes the objective of achieving social justice is that of the distribution–redistribution rule of the Islamic economic paradigm. As was mentioned earlier, a crucial mission of all messengers and prophets is the establishment of social justice. As an aside, it should be noted that in the writings of Adam Smith (*The Theory of Moral Sentiments*, 1759, and *The Wealth of Nations*, 1776), arguably the father of capitalism, "a sense of justice" is seen as essential for the viable and long-term sustainability of any society. In practical terms, the *Qur'an* makes clear that this means creating a balanced society that avoids extremes of wealth and poverty, a society in which all understand that wealth is a blessing provided by the Creator for the sole purpose of providing support for the lives of all of mankind. The Islamic view holds that it is not possible to have many rich and wealthy people who continue to focus all their efforts on accumulating wealth without simultaneously creating a mass of economically deprived and destitute people. The rich consume opulently, while the poor suffer from deprivation because their rights to share in the wealth of the rich and powerful are not redeemed. To avoid this, Islam prohibits wealth accumulation, imposes limits on consumption through its rules prohibiting over-spending (*israf*), waste (*itlaf*), and ostentatious and opulent spending (*itraf*). It then ordains that the net surplus, after moderate spending necessary to maintain a modest living standard, must be returned to the members of the society who, for a variety of reasons, are unable to work; hence the resources they could have used to produce income and wealth were utilized by the more able. The *Qur'an* considers the more able as trustee–agents in using these resources on behalf of the less able. In this view, property is not a means of exclusion but rather inclusion, in which the rights of those less able to share in the income and wealth of the more able are redeemed. The result would be a balanced economy without extremes of wealth and poverty. The operational mechanism for redeeming the rights of the less able to share in the income and wealth of the more able is the network of mandatory and voluntary payments, such as *zakat* (2.5 percent of wealth), *khums* (20 percent of income), and payments referred to as *sadaqat*.

IV. CURRENT STATE OF INSTITUTIONS

To be effective, all institutions, Islamic or otherwise, must be built on a strong foundation. Unfortunately, countries that are generally classified as Muslim, such as those that belong to the Organization of the Islamic Conference (OIC), are generally underdeveloped and backward in most areas, including areas that would support institution building.[4] In a recent study (Rehman and Askari, 2010), countries were assessed as to their degree of "Islamicity." Islamic teachings were divided into four broad categories, with many sub-categories under each of these, a number of available indices were used to represent these teachings, and countries were ranked according to their adherence to these teachings. If one were to stand back and look at a collage of these teachings, they would represent a pattern of "good rules and good behavior," with the expectation that the advanced countries would score high on what is represented as an "Islamicity" Index. In Table 10.2, we report the summary results of the Islamicity Index disaggregated by country groupings and by four sub-groupings of Economic Islamicity (EI^2), Legal and Governance Islamicity (LGI^2), Human and Political Rights Islamicity (HPI^2), and International Relations Islamicity (IRI^2).

These preliminary results indicate that Islamic countries have not by-and-large adhered to Islamic principles, and to what we would generally classify as rules and attributes that would lead to good results. The average ranking of the 56 Islamic countries is 139; well below the average ranking of the 208 countries measured. If the Islamic countries (OIC) are compared with OECD countries, the disparities are even more pronounced. For example, the average I^2 rank among the OECD countries is 25, while (as mentioned above) it is 139 for the Islamic countries. One could argue that a fairer comparison would be to the group of non-OECD or Middle Income countries. However, even then the Islamic countries do not perform well as a group. When compared with the 178 non-OECD countries (average rank 118), the 41 Upper-Middle Income countries (average rank 85), and the

TABLE 10.2 Detailed Summary Results of the Islamicity Index (I^2)

Sub-Groups (# of Countries)	EI^2	LGI^2	HPI^2	IRI^2	Overall I^2 Rank
All Countries (208)	104	96	104	75	104
OECD[5] (30)	24	28	29	37	25
High-Income[6] (60)	60	40	84	40	60
Upper-Middle Income[7] (41)	83	84	88	87	85
Non-OECD Non-OIC (123)	111	101	110	89	108
Persian Gulf (7)	94	104	138	109	112
Lower-Middle Income[8] (55)	116	124	115	112	122
Non-OECD (178)	118	112	116	99	118
OIC[9] (56)	133	136	130	115	139
Low-Income[10] (54)	170	154	126	107	153

123 Non-OECD Non-OIC countries (average rank 108), the performance of the Islamic countries group (OIC) is the worst, with an average rank of 139. The degree of failure of the OIC countries' performance is most clearly demonstrated by the fact that the Islamic countries fared even worse on the ranking than the 55 Lower-Middle Income countries, which ranked at an average of 132. We are not unduly surprised by the fact that the OECD countries (and High-Income countries) have performed better in this ranking. The average overall I^2 ranking of OECD countries was 25, while the High-Income countries' average rank was 60 compared to the OIC average rank of 139. It is to be expected that the OECD countries would perform better in the index as Islamic principles are not only compatible with, but also promote, free markets and good economic governance, economic systems, and policies that encourage economic–social justice, legal systems, and governance that are fair to all members of society and which include global standards of human and political rights. Lastly, but equally importantly, they should promote and foster better international relations with the global community. In fact, only two Muslim countries make it into the top 50—Malaysia (38) and Kuwait (48).

Development of a risk-sharing financial system as advocated by Islam cannot take place unless such effort is accompanied by the development or pre-existence of key legal and economic institutions as prescribed by Islam. There are two issues with the state of institutions in countries interested in developing an Islamic financial system. First, in the case of a majority of Muslim countries, the institutional environment is generally weak. There is a small number of developing Muslim countries, such as Malaysia and Kuwait, where the institutional framework is growing, but at a slow pace. A second and more serious issue is that the prevailing legal system, which lays the foundation for the development of institutions, is derived from either common or English law, but without the necessary provisions for *Shari'ah* law. Key laws concerning insolvency or collateral or dispute resolution are not based on Islamic laws and, in some cases, may be in direct conflict with *Shari'ah*. Even where there is no conflict, the enforceability of law is in question. This poses a serious issue in the development of financial and economic institutions compatible with an Islamic financial system.

Development of insolvency laws is one example of how well the creditors' rights are protected in a financial system. If we look at insolvency laws in the Middle East and North Africa (MENA) region (a predominantly Muslim region), we find that the insolvency systems are by and large underdeveloped, as observed in a report by The World Bank (Uttamchandani, 2010):

> *In DoingBusiness 2010, the regional results for Closing a Business reflect the underdevelopment of insolvency in the MENA region. For MENA, the recovery rate on debt when closing a business is 29.9 cents on the dollar, compared to 68.6 cents for OECD countries. The time it takes to close a business is 3.5 years in MENA, compared to 1.7 in OECD, almost twice as long.[11] Many MENA countries report even longer time periods than 3.5 years. It also costs, on average, twice as much to close a business in MENA as in OECD— it costs 14.1 cents on the dollar in MENA, as opposed to 8.4 cents in OECD states. This is a reflection of, amongst other things, a region that has not made insolvency reform a policy priority.*

In Tables 10.3 to 10.5, we report a variety of financial development indices dealing with the MENA region, the GCC, and the non-GCC MENA region, and for the G-7 for the period 2005–10. In Table 10.3, we note that the "Strength of Legal Rights Index: Getting Credit" is much lower in the MENA countries than in the G-7 countries; the index for the GCC is higher than that for the rest of the MENA; and while the index for G-7 and the GCC has improved over the period, there has been no improvement for the rest of the MENA countries. In Table 10.4, we see that the "Extent of Disclosure Index: Protecting Investors" for the MENA and the GCC is much more in line with that of the G-7, and has improved over time; while for the G-7 there has been no change over time. Table 10.5 shows that the "Strength of Investor Protection Index: Protecting Investors" is low for the MENA region but is slightly better for the countries in the GCC grouping; and, as to be expected, both are low when compared to the average for the G-7 countries. Again as

TABLE 10.3   Strength of Legal Rights Index: Getting Credit

	2005	2006	2007	2008	2009	2010
Average MENA	2.93	2.93	3	3	3	3.13
Average GCC	3.75	3.75	3.67	3.67	3.67	4
Average Non-GCC	2.6	2.6	2.6	2.6	2.6	2.6
Average G-7	6.43	6.71	6.86	6.71	6.71	6.71

Source: *DoingBusiness* (Washington, D.C.: The World Bank).

TABLE 10.4   Extent of Disclosure Index: Protecting Investors

	2005	2006	2007	2008	2009	2010
Average MENA	5.86	5.86	5.94	6.13	6.44	6.56
Average GCC	6.5	6.5	6.5	6.83	6.83	6.83
Average Non-GCC	5.6	5.6	5.6	5.7	6.2	6.4
Average G-7	7.71	7.71	7.71	7.71	7.71	7.71

Source: *DoingBusiness* (Washington, D.C.: The World Bank).

TABLE 10.5   Strength of Investor Protection Index: Protecting Investors

	2005	2006	2007	2008	2009	2010
Average MENA	4.61	4.61	4.7	4.83	4.93	4.97
Average GCC	5.33	5.33	5.33	5.55	5.55	5.55
Average Non-GCC	4.32	4.32	4.32	4.39	4.55	4.62
Average G-7	6.8	6.8	6.8	6.8	6.8	6.8

Source: *DoingBusiness* (Washington, D.C.: The World Bank).

to be expected, while there has been less improvement for the G-7 average, there has been some improvement in the index for MENA countries since 2005 and less so for the GCC. All in all, the MENA region lags the G-7 in every area as measured by these financial development indicators, and in most areas highly significantly.

As emphasized above, the state of non-financial institutions in the MENA region and in Muslim countries is not that different; they are both significantly behind that of the advanced countries. Under such circumstances, attempts to develop an Islamic financial system in MENA and in Muslim countries more generally will be subject to tough challenges because the foundation is lacking. The superimposition of the Islamic financial system would without a doubt result in a sub-optimal representation and functioning of what would be considered an Islamic financial system. In reality, the resulting financial system might be a "half-baked" system with many more problems and issues than is the case today and one that bears little resemblance to what could be considered an Islamic financial system.

V. CORPORATE GOVERNANCE FRAMEWORK IN ISLAM

The issue of corporate governance and the search for an optimal governance structure has received considerable attention in the conventional economics literature and in public policy debates. This increased attention can be attributed to several factors, such as: (a) the growth of institutional investors (pension funds, insurance companies, mutual funds, and highly leveraged institutions), and the role they play in the financial sector, especially in the major industrial economies; (b) widely articulated concerns and criticisms that the current monitoring and control of publicly held corporations in Anglo-Saxon countries, especially the UK and the US, are seriously defective, leading to sub-optimal economic and social development (Kasey et al., 1997); (c) a shift away from a traditional "shareholder-value centered" view of corporate governance toward a corporate governance structure extended to a wide circle of stakeholders; and (d) the impact of the increased globalization of financial markets, the global trend toward the deregulation of financial sectors, and the liberalization of the activities of institutional investors, which have raised concerns over corporate governance.[12] Although each of the above-mentioned factors provides compelling reasons to examine corporate-governance structures, the current financial crisis has unearthed new governance issues, some of which were either ignored, or not taken seriously, or were never even discussed earlier.

Iqbal and Mirakhor (2002) developed a stakeholder-based framework of corporate governance in Islam. Key principles of Islam's perspective on governance can be understood in the light of its teachings on property rights, contracts, trust, and ethics, and are summarized below.[13]

Property rights

Preservation of the property rights of all members of society is essential in governance. The axioms of property rights as described earlier laid the foundation for good governance, which advocates that the rights of each member of society should be preserved over physical property, and that any misuse and misappropriation of others' rights should not be allowed. Business leaders and the holders of public office have an additional responsibility to ensure that the rights and responsibilities attached to the property given to them in trust are discharged according to their best ability and that the utmost care is taken in discharging this duty.

Whereas *Shari'ah* guarantees some basic property rights to individuals by virtue of them being members of society, the rights of a firm or a legal entity such as a corporation are earned and acquired. It is not the firm itself that accrues property rights, but the property acquired in the course of the firm's economic activity that has property rights and claims vested in it. Once a property is earned or acquired by the firm, it is subject to the same rules of sharing and the prohibition of waste as apply to the property of individuals. A firm's property rights also come with similar claims and responsibilities such that the firm is expected to preserve the property rights of the local community or society but also those of the people who have participated in the process of acquiring or earning the firm's property. No action of the firm that violates the basic property rights of those with whom it interacts is acceptable.

Contracts

The great emphasis placed on contracts for governance in Islam is to make individuals and economic agents aware of the obligations arising from their contractual agreements—verbal or written, explicit or implicit. In the case of explicit contracts, parties to the contract clearly stipulate the behavior and duties expected with respect to the terms of the contract. This contract is to be free of information asymmetry; parties intend to comply with the terms of the contract and are fully aware of their rights and obligations. Importantly, the state ensures the enforceability of the contract if either party violates the terms. On the other hand, implicit contracts are not formal contracts with clearly defined terms but are claims and obligations that come with the right to be part of a society.

Principles of sharing and the rights of collectivity to property rights are forms of implicit contracts which serve to preserve and protect the rights of others and thus establish a wide spectrum of implicit obligations. Within the property-rights framework, one has contractual obligations to others, including the community and society, according to the rules of *Shari'ah*, and the honoring of this obligation is considered a sacred duty. This sacred duty to preserve the property rights of others is the moral, social, and legal foundation for recognizing and enforcing obligations to explicit and implicit contracts. As such, it is one of the founding principles of the governance framework in Islam.

Trust

Trust brings responsibility and accountability. The *Qur'an* makes trust and trustworthiness, as well as keeping faith with contracts and promises, obligatory and inviolable except in the event of an explicitly permissible justification (Iqbal and Mirakhor, 2007; Habachy, 1962). Trust is important social capital, which plays a vital role in promoting good governance, especially in the case of institutions dealing with financial services, which are given property to manage in "trust." Therefore, preserving high trust should be an integral part of the governance goals of business leaders and the holders of public office.

Ethics

Islam demands high standards of ethical and moral behavior from everyone in society, but emphasizes these standards for those who govern or represent others in society. Islam expects excellence in moral values, truthfulness, and virtuous conduct from every member of society, particularly those who are involved in business.[14] For example, the *Qur'an* (3:110) says: "You are the best nation that has been raised up for mankind; you enjoin right conduct [rule compliance], forbid evil [rule violation] and believe in Allah (*swt*)." Also, there are several sayings of the Prophet (pbuh) to emphasise the significance of high morals and good conduct, such as the following:

> *I have been sent for the purpose of perfecting good morals.*
> —Ibn Hambal (No. 8595)

> *The truthful merchant [is rewarded by being ranked] on the Day of Resurrection with prophets, veracious souls, martyrs and pious people.*
> —Tirmidhi (No. 1130)

Within the framework of economic justice, emphasis is placed on being mindful to give full measure and weight in all business transactions. The verses which state "Woe unto those who give short measure, those who, when they are to receive their due from [other] people, demand that it be given in full but when they have to measure or weigh whatever they owe to others, give less than what is due!" (83:1–3) remind individuals against any negligence or cheating in determining what is owed to others. They refer not only to commercial dealings, but also encompass every aspect of social relations, both practical and moral, and apply to every individual's rights and obligations no less than to his or her physical possessions (Asad, 2004).

Inclusion

The governance framework is inclusive of a broad range of stakeholders. The principles governing property rights and contracts in Islam clearly justify the inclusion of stakeholders in the decision-making and governance structure. This inclusion is based on the principles that (a) the collectivity (community, society, state) shares the rights in the property acquired by either individuals or firms; (b) the exercising of property rights should not lead to any harm or damage to the property of others (including stakeholders); (c) the rights of others are considered as property and are therefore subject to the rules regarding the violation of property rights; and (d) any property leading to the denial of any valid claim or right by any member of society would not qualify to be recognized as *al mal* and, therefore, would be considered unlawful according to *Shari'ah*. Finally, the obligations accruing from explicit and implicit contracts broaden the range of stakeholders eligible for inclusion in the governance framework.

In the absence of rule compliance (that is, in a weak institutional environment), risk-sharing contracts require enhanced monitoring and a strengthened governance regulatory apparatus. The same principles of governance under which an individual or a ruler or a state should function apply also to firms. Iqbal and Mirakhor (2004) argue that within the Islamic framework a firm can be viewed as a "nexus of contracts" whose objective is to minimize transaction costs and maximize profits and returns to investors subject to constraints that these objectives do not violate the property rights of any party, whether it interacts with the firm directly or indirectly. In pursuit of these goals, the firm honors all implicit or explicit contractual obligations. As could be discerned from the discussions on contracts and trust, it is incumbent on individuals to preserve the sanctity of implicit contractual obligations no less than those of explicit contracts. By the same token, firms have to preserve the sanctity of implicit and explicit contractual obligations by recognizing and protecting the property rights of stakeholders, the community, society, and the state. Since the firm's behavior is shaped by that of its managers, it becomes their fiduciary duty to manage the firm as a trust for all stakeholders in ensuring that the behavior of the firm conforms to the rules and norms specified by the law (Iqbal and Mirakhor, 2011).

In sum, the governance framework, as defined by the principles of Islam, is focused on achieving the promotion of social justice, unity, and social cohesiveness; the curbing of counterproductive behavior such as greed, deceit, misrepresentation, and the misappropriation of property; a strong commitment to contractual obligations; establishment of trust; and transparency in decision making. The governance framework must be inclusive of the participation of all stakeholders in the decision-making process.

VI. SIGNIFICANCE OF ENHANCED MONITORING AND GOVERNANCE

The nature of risk-sharing contracts requires enhanced monitoring and governance. Certain characteristics of governance such as ownership structure, flow of financial information, stakeholder rights, and board structure are intended to reduce moral hazard and adverse selection problems present in publicly traded firms. Governance and a firm's capital structure are closely related. Studies have examined the impact of corporate governance on the value of the firm and have found that firms with weaker corporate governance mechanisms tend to have a higher debt level (Kumar, 2005). In the case of equity financing, dispersed shareholdings can also have a negative impact on the effectiveness of governance, since it is expensive for individual investors to monitor management activities on their own—a free rider problem (Skaife et al., 2004). However, as a shareholder accumulates more shares, his or her incentives for monitoring increase. This poses challenges for designing a governance structure and a monitoring mechanism to protect the rights of all stakeholders irrespective of the extent or the degree of their stake in a company or a project. The stakeholders-oriented governance structure as advocated by Islam can reduce or eliminate such governance issues.

The quality of financial information leading to greater disclosure and financial transparency reduces information asymmetries between the firm and its shareholders. Availability of credible information enhances monitoring and governance. Equity financing comes with unconditional monitoring rights, but debt holders' monitoring rights are contingent on the event of bankruptcy and depend on the implementation of a cost-effective and credible information flow to outside investors (Buehlmaier, 2011). One way to overcome the agency problem associated with debt has been to increase covenants that restrict borrowers' actions and indirectly grant control rights to the lender to reduce exposure to credit risk. Financial intermediaries and banks specialize in information gathering on borrowers and thus rely on monitoring and long-term relationships. Availability of transparent information becomes vital in determining an entrepreneur's preferred mode of financing. For example, a firm with less publicly available information is more likely to depend on lending from financial intermediaries such as banks at the expense of the firm's management's willingness to grant greater oversight to the financial intermediary. However, a firm with wider access to publicly accessible information will prefer to bypass a bank and access the capital markets directly (Whitehead, 2009).

Enhancing the quality and the flow of information is essential in enhancing the transparency and monitoring aspect of governance, especially for risk-sharing financial contracts. Access to information enables creditors to evaluate risk and the price of financial securities. Islam's emphasis on full disclosure of information through the prohibition of *gharar* (asymmetrical information) develops an environment conducive to reducing informational distortions in contracts and ultimately facilitates the monitoring and establishment of trust. With enhanced monitoring and trust in the quality of information, risk-sharing modes of financing become preferable to alternative debt-based risk-transferring contracts.

Access to credit information is provided through two channels: private credit bureaus (PCBs) and public credit registries (PCRs). These two institutions are at the core of a country's credit reporting system. A review of the status of credit reporting systems in the MENA region shows that, while the quality of credit reporting has improved in recent years, due largely to the introduction of new credit bureaus in some countries, much remains to be done, both in terms of design and coverage (Madeddu, 2010). It is disappointing to observe that two-thirds of MENA countries still rely entirely on PCRs. As shown in Table 10.6, three out of these six countries have developed their PCBs only in the past three years, while the oldest one was set up less than 10 years ago. Twelve MENA countries still rely entirely on PCRs, a higher percentage than those in all other regions except for Sub-Saharan Africa.

TABLE 10.6   Public Credit Registries and Private Credit Bureaus in MENA (year when PCB started operating in parentheses)

Both	Private Credit Bureau Only	Public Credit Registry Only
Egypt (2008)	Bahrain (2005)	Algeria
United Arab Emirates (2007)	Kuwait (2002)	Djibouti
	Morocco (2009)	Iran
	Saudi Arabia (2004)	Jordan
		Qatar
		Lebanon
		Oman
		Syria
		Tunisia
		West Bank and Gaza
		Yemen

Source: Madeddu (2010). Information on Iraq was not available or had negligible coverage.

TABLE 10.7 Depth of Credit Information Index: Getting Credit

	2005	2006	2007	2008	2009	2010
Average MENA	1.93	2.21	2.69	3.13	3.5	3.69
Average GCC	3	3	3.33	3.83	3.83	3.83
Average Non-GCC	1.5	1.9	2.3	2.7	3.3	3.6
Average G-7	5.71	5.57	5.57	5.57	5.57	5.57

Source: *DoingBusiness* (Washington, D.C.: The World Bank).

Table 10.7 shows the depth of credit information index for the MENA region. This index measures the rules and practices affecting the coverage, scope, and accessibility of credit information available through either a PCR or a PCB. The index shows relatively low levels compared to the developed economies of G-7. The trend has been improving over the last couple of years for the MENA region as a whole, which is a good sign for the development of financial markets.

The recent global financial crisis has emphasized and exposed serious lapses in the prevailing corporate governance framework, as expressed by the following two quotes:

> *Corporate governance is one of the most important failures behind the present financial crisis.*
> —De Larosière Group (2009)

> *This Report concludes that the financial crisis can be, to an important extent, attributed to failures and weaknesses in corporate governance arrangements.*
> —OECD Report (2009)

There are a number of lessons from this recent failure of governance. These include: (i) the growing realization that financial firms, capital markets, and other large corporations are driven by the sole objective of maximizing share value (and personal financial rewards), rather than by the long-term interests of their stakeholders; (ii) investors, and more pointedly ordinary people, lose "trust" (precious social capital) in business leaders and become critical of their irresponsible actions;[15] (iii) the role of the company board in effective oversight of all activities and in curbing the excessive risk-taking behavior of firms has failed its function; and (iv) a decline in the moral and ethical values of business leaders was evident. The managers and business leaders seemed to care more about circumventing regulatory constraints and finding loopholes in the law, than about morally correct behavior. Increasing greed and personal empire building became the norm on Wall Street, with little emphasis being placed on producing moral and ethical business leaders.

Of all the key lessons related to governance, one deserves further elaboration. While conventional finance expects business leaders to exhibit ethical behavior, its sole enforcement mechanism is market discipline, which has come under attack with the recent financial crisis. On the other hand, the Islamic financial system derives its values from the teachings of Islam and can expect ethical governance from the leaders, managers, and other stakeholders, who follow the rules prescribed by *Shari'ah*. Leaders who are fully conscious of their responsibilities, limitations, and obligations as expected in Islam could never fall into a behavior that would promote arrogance, ignorance, greed, deceitfulness, non-transparency, and delinquency. Islam governs the behavior of leaders at least no less stringently than that of individuals. Although each member of society is expected to exhibit high moral values in the observance of contracts and covenants, many scholars are of the view that these requirements apply with even greater force to the actions of leaders. Therefore, a breach of faith on the part of a leader is more heinous in its nature and more serious in its consequences than a similar breach by an ordinary individual. Research has demonstrated that since finance (particularly risk-sharing instruments such as equity) is trust-intensive, high-trust societies exhibit more developed and deeper financial systems. In Islam, the behavior expected of a firm is no different from than expected of any other member of society. Its managers acting on behalf of the owners shape the firm's economic and moral behavior, and it becomes their fiduciary duty to manage the firm as a *trust*. Consequently, it is incumbent upon managers to ensure that the firm's behavior conforms to the principles and the rules of *Shari'ah* and such compliance will ultimately lead to the development of trust, responsibility, and accountability.

While these are expectations of a truly Islamic financial system, where all market participants are devout Muslims and follow the spirit and the letter of the *Shari'ah* law, we are only too familiar with human frailties and with its many shortfalls. It is for this reason that efficient institutions, a governance structure that truly reflects Islamic values, and strict and just enforcement are essential for a truly Islamic financial system to be put into practice. Such a system is ethical and heavily based on Islamic values as elaborated in the *Qur'an* and interpreted in the tradition of the Prophet (pbuh). In the absence of this umbrella of ethical values, an Islamic financial system can only be a mirage.

VII. CONCLUSION

The development of efficient institutions, and of a sound governance framework, is important for the emergence and growth of a sound financial system. Institutions lay the foundation of the system, and the governance framework ensures that the rules are enforced so that the desired results are achieved.

The Islamic financial system is based and centered on risk sharing, affording equity finance a pre-eminent position in the financial system. Given the moral hazard and agency problems associated with equity-based financial contracts, institutions and governance become even more important in developing a risk-sharing financial system. Institutions governing economic transactions, such as property rights, trustworthiness, truthfulness, faithfulness to the terms and conditions of contracts, transparency, and non-interference with the workings of the markets and the price mechanism so long as market participants are rule-compliant, provide a reasonably strong economy where information flows unhindered and participants engage in transactions confidently with minimal concern for uncertainty regarding the actions and reactions of other participants. The result is that in such an economy with reduced uncertainty, economic agents will be encouraged to engage in risk-sharing contracts. As can be readily inferred, strict rule-compliance is absolutely essential for an Islamic financial system to live up to its expectations and billing. Human frailty being what it is, efficient institutions, especially the rule of law and all that it entails, are a prerequisite to success; and this must be accompanied by governance and effective enforcement. Unfortunately, data on the MENA region as defined by the World Bank, and information on countries belonging to the OIC, indicate that Muslim countries lack effective institutions and governance structures. In the next chapter, we will expand further on these "gaps."

ENDNOTES

1. Mirakhor (1989).
2. These rules are supported by various verses in the *Qur'an*, as follows:
   "And do not eat up your property among yourselves for vanities, nor use it as bait for the judges, with intent that ye may eat up wrongfully and knowingly a little of (other) people's property" (2:188).
   ". . . and who, whenever they spend on others, are neither wasteful nor niggardly but [remember that] there is always a just mean between those [two extremes]";
   "Those who when they spend are not extravagant and not niggardly, but hold a just (balance) between those (extremes)" (25:67). "Behold, the squanderers are, indeed, of the ilk of the satans" (17:27).

3. Bashir (1999) argues that Islam attaches great importance to protecting people from harm caused by others. The Prophet is reported to have said "to cause harm to others is not allowed in Islam."
4. OIC is comprised of Palestinian Authority and the following 56 countries: Afghanistan, Albania, Algeria, Azerbaijan, Bahrain, Bangladesh, Benin, Brunei, BurkinaFaso, Cameroon, Chad, Comoros, Cote d'Ivoire, Djibouti, Egypt, Gabon, Gambia, Guinea, Guinea-Bissau, Guyana, Indonesia, Iran, Iraq, Jordan, Kazakhstan, Kuwait, Kyrgyzstan, Lebanon, Libya, Malaysia, Maldives, Mali, Mauritania, Morocco, Mozambique, Niger, Nigeria, Oman, Pakistan, Qatar, Saudi Arabia, Senegal, Sierra Leone, Somalia, Sudan, Suriname, Syria, Tajikistan, Togo, Tunisia, Turkey, Turkmenistan, Uganda, United Arab Emirates, Uzbekistan, and Yemen.
5. They include: Australia, Austria, Belgium, Canada, Czech Republic, Denmark, Finland, France, Germany, Greece, Hungary, Iceland, Ireland, Italy, Japan, Luxembourg, Mexico, Netherlands, New Zealand, Norway, Poland, Portugal, Slovak Republic, South Korea, Spain, Sweden, Switzerland, Turkey, United Kingdom, and United States.
6. High-Income countries are classified as US$10,066 as per the World Bank.
7. Upper-Middle Income countries are classified as US$826–$10,065 as per the World Bank.
8. Lower-Middle Income countries are classified as US$826–$10,065 as per the World Bank.
9. Only 56 of the 57 OIC countries are included in this data set. Significant data on the Palestinian Authority was not available and, as such, it was not included.
10. Low-Income countries are classified as US$825 or less as per the World Bank.
11. "Closing a Business," *DoingBusiness 2010*, www.doingbusiness.org/Explore Topics/ClosingBusiness/.
12. For a detailed discussion, see Balling, et al. (1998); and Bloomestein (1998).
13. See Mirakhor (1989) for a detailed discussion of the notion of property rights and Islamic economics. Iqbal and Mirakhor (2004) applied these principles to corporate governance in Islam.
14. Dr. Sabahuddin Azmi, www.renaissance.com.pk/Mayviewpoint2y5.htm.
15. Richard Edelman, *The Edelman Trust Barometer* (2009), which tracks the level of trust in different countries, observed that, especially in the US, home to some of the largest corporate collapses, trust in business leaders dropped 20 percentage points as a result of the crisis.

CHAPTER 11

Gaps between the Theory and Practice of Islamic Finance

Since the 1970s, several institutions have been offering products and services compatible with the principles of *Shari'ah*. During its initial stages, the industry was limited to banking activities; however, as demand grew, other financial services began to emerge under the umbrella of "Islamic finance." Today, the Islamic financial industry is one of the fastest growing emerging markets and continues to enjoy high demand. According to some estimates, there are more than 300 institutions in over 65 jurisdictions engaged in Islamic finance and total assets under management exceeded US$1 trillion in 2010.[1]

In a broad sense, the Islamic financial industry consists of a number of very loosely connected components, such as Islamic banks, Islamic "windows" in conventional banks, Islamic insurance (*takaful*) and capital markets, and non-bank financial institutions offering *Shari'ah*-sanctioned products. Islamic banks are the largest segment of the market and perform the basic functions of financial intermediation, as described in Chapter 5. Islamic "windows" are special units within conventional banks, which specialize in offering Islamic finance products. Islamic insurance is another fast-growing segment of the industry. *Takaful* offers event, life, and health insurance by following the principles of "mutual guarantees" and by ensuring that all the funds are invested according to *Shari'ah*. In several countries, Islamic microfinance is being introduced and the initial assessment is that it is meeting with modest success. Islamic microfinance is structured on the basis of partnership, or on interest-free loans (*qard-e-hasan*), and all effort is made to keep the cost of funding low and the recovery rate high. A recent development in the market is the introduction of capital market products, which are mainly of two types. One product is in the form of Islamic funds, which are portfolios of either equities, commodities, or leases (*ijarah*), which are constructed by applying screening rules to conventional financial products. Currently, there are about 750 Islamic funds managing more than US$50 billion in assets. The other segment of the Islamic capital market is in the form of Islamic bonds (*sukuk*), which are securitized pools of underlying *Shari'ah*-compatible securities. The *sukuk* structure has also been used by conventional issuers to raise funds. During 2010, more than US$40 billion in *sukuk* bonds were issued.

Although Islamic finance started out in Muslim countries (principally Egypt and Malaysia), it has spread to all parts of the globe. One of the major developments in the past decade has been the "globalization" of Islamic finance, where the concept and practice of Islamic finance has been introduced to major international financial centers. Islamic finance has a long presence in Europe—particularly in the UK, Luxembourg and Germany—and has attracted attention from Japan, Hong Kong, and Korea. Although Islamic finance is practiced in the US, its practice is kept discreet for a number of reasons.

In earlier chapters, we presented the theoretical foundation of Islamic finance, which principally promotes risk sharing. In this chapter, we investigate the key divergences between the theory and the practice of Islamic finance and why the practice of Islamic finance falls short of expectations. In Section I, we discuss the institutional and macro-level impediments to the development of risk-sharing systems as envisioned in Islam. In Section II, we discuss issues that are directly relevant for the development of the Islamic financial industry.

I. GAPS IN INSTITUTIONS, MACROECONOMIC POLICIES, AND PERFORMANCE

Throughout the previous chapters, we have stressed the important reality that the truly Islamic financial system is not currently practiced today in any society or country around the world. Yes, Islamic financial products have been developed, packaged, marketed, and sold around the world; and even financial products that cannot be considered as Islamic are sold under the Islamic umbrella. Similarly, Islamically compliant banks and non-bank financial institutions have been operating side-by-side with conventional institutions under the banner of the conventional financial system. Yet, we do not find the complete Islamic financial system practiced anywhere today. Why? The reasons are many. In this chapter we summarize the various "gaps" that act as important impediments to the development of the Islamic financial system. We begin by expanding on our brief discussion in the previous chapter on the missing elements of a modern economic and financial system in Muslim countries.

In our discussion of an "Islamicity" index in the previous chapter, we recognized the fact that Islamic teachings on economics and governance are closely aligned with best practices as developed in the Western tradition, with the notable difference that Islam places much greater emphasis on social justice as the foundation of society. It is for this reason that the highest performers on the "Islamicity Index" were the advanced countries. In fact, the top 10 countries on the index are (see Table 11.1): New Zealand, Luxembourg, Ireland, Iceland, Finland, Denmark, Canada, the United Kingdom, Australia, and the Netherlands; with the top Muslim country, Malaysia, at number 38! Essentially, these results point to an indisputable fact: Muslim countries are not the best representatives of underlying Islamic values, especially when it comes to economics and economic justice. The absence of economic justice has become glaringly apparent with the unfolding of the "Arab Spring" in 2011. From a practical standpoint, Muslim countries lack the foundational elements of an efficient economic and financial system.

TABLE 11.1 "Islamicity Index" for Individual Countries (OIC countries in bold)

Countries	Overall Islamicity Index Rank	Countries	Overall Islamicity Index Rank
New Zealand	1	France	19
Luxembourg	2	Czech Republic	20
Ireland	3	Estonia	21
Iceland	4	Costa Rica	22
Finland	5	Spain	23
Denmark	6	Barbados	24
Canada	7	United States	25
United Kingdom	8	Slovenia	26
Australia	9	Hong Kong, China	27
Netherlands	9	Latvia	28
Austria	11	Japan	29
Norway	12	Malta	30
Switzerland	13	Hungary	31
Belgium	14	Slovak Republic	32
Sweden	15	Italy	33
Portugal	16	Chile	34
Germany	17	Lithuania	35
Bahamas	18	Cyprus	36

(Continued)

TABLE 11.1   Continued

Countries	Overall Islamicity Index Rank	Countries	Overall Islamicity Index Rank
Singapore	37	**Brunei**	65
Malaysia	38	Romania	66
Panama	39	**United Arab Emirates**	66
Trinidad and Tobago	40	Belize	68
Poland	41	Andorra	69
Mauritius	42	Cayman Islands	70
Croatia	43	Seychelles	71
St. Vincent and Grenadines	44	Fiji	72
Namibia	45	**Uganda**	73
Greece	46	Tanzania	74
Jamaica	47	Antigua and Barbuda	75
Kuwait	48	**Gabon**	75
Uruguay	48	**Jordan**	77
South Africa	50	Thailand	78
Botswana	51	Grenada	79
St. Lucia	52	San Marino	79
Ghana	53	China	81
Argentina	54	Nicaragua	81
Brazil	55	Cape Verde	83
Mexico	55	Macao, China	83
Bulgaria	57	**Tunisia**	83
El Salvador	58	Colombia	86
Philippines	59	Dominican Republic	87
Dominica	60	Peru	88
Israel	61	India	89
Monaco	62	Aruba	90
Lesotho	63	Russian Federation	91
Bahrain	64	Honduras	92

Countries	Overall Islamicity Index Rank	Countries	Overall Islamicity Index Rank
Greenland	93	Morocco	119
Guyana	94	Northern Mariana Islands	119
Netherlands Antilles	95	Papua New Guinea	119
Mozambique	96	Zambia	119
Mongolia	97	Bolivia	123
Macedonia, FYR	98	Gambia, The	124
Oman	99	Azerbaijan	125
Suriname	100	Ecuador	125
Bosnia and Herzegovina	101	Guatemala	127
Ukraine	102	Belarus	128
Turkey	103	Malawi	129
Maldives	104	Mali	130
Liechtenstein	105	Saudi Arabia	131
Korea, Rep.	106	Burkina Faso	132
Kazakhstan	107	Vanuatu	133
Timor-Leste	107	Vietnam	134
Senegal	109	Rwanda	135
Albania	110	Paraguay	136
Moldova	110	Kyrgyztan	137
Qatar	112	Korea, Dem. Rep.	138
Puerto Rico	113	Virgin Islands (US)	139
Armenia	114	Indonesia	140
Kiribati	115	Venezuela, RB	141
Sri Lanka	116	Madagascar	142
Georgia	117	Palau	143
St. Kitts and Nevis	117	Kenya	144

(Continued)

TABLE 11.1   Continued

Countries	Overall Islamicity Index Rank	Countries	Overall Islamicity Index Rank
Guinea	145	Congo, Dem. Rep.	171
Samoa	146	Togo	172
Benin	147	Turkmenistan	173
Pakistan	147	Nigeria	174
Cuba	149	Uzbekistan	174
New Caledonia	150	Haiti	176
Nepal	151	Tajikistan	176
Bangladesh	152	American Samoa	178
Egypt, Arab Rep.	153	Cote d'Ivoire	179
Cambodia	154	Ethiopia	180
Tonga	155	French Polynesia	181
Burundi	156	Congo, Rep.	182
Swaziland	156	Equatorial Guinea	183
Lebanon	158	Lao PDR	183
Zimbabwe	159	Serbia and Montenegro	185
Algeria	160	Syrian Arab Republic	186
Micronesia, Fed. Sts.	161	Marshall Islands	187
Cameroon	162	Faeroe Islands	188
Iran, Islamic Rep.	163	Niger	189
Myanmar	164	Guinea-Bissau	190
Central African Republic	165	Solomon Islands	190
Bermuda	166	Sao Tome and Principe	192
Bhutan	167	Djibouti	193
Sierra Leone	168	Liberia	194
Afghanistan	169	Mauritania	195
Guam	170	Libya	196

Countries	Overall Islamicity Index Rank	Countries	Overall Islamicity Index Rank
Chad	197	Sudan	202
Yemen, Rep.	198	Eritrea	204
Angola	199	Isle of Man	205
Comoros	200	Somalia	206
Iraq	201	West Bank and Gaza	207
Channel Islands	202	Mayotte	208

And as we have stated a number of times throughout this book, even if the Islamic financial system were to be adopted in a Muslim country today, it would not be representative of the "true" Islamic system because it would lack the important foundational elements of an economic and financial system. Some of these elements were incorporated (see Chapter 10, and Rehman and Askari, 2010) into the calculated "Islamicity Index," and included:

- UN International Convention on the Elimination of All Forms of Racial Discrimination;
- Ease of doing business (starting a business);
- Business and Market Freedom Indicator;
- Property and contractual rights;
- Transparency International Corruption Perception Index;
- Financial Freedom Index;
- Financial Information Infrastructure Index;
- Financial Market Risk Indicator; and
- Absence of Interest Indicator.

Islamic countries have low rankings on all these indicators. For a true risk-sharing financial system to have a fair chance of developing and producing the results that we envisage, Muslim countries have to tackle these glaring deficiencies in their economic systems. They require better institutions, better supervision, and better enforcement; and at the same time economic and financial policies must be more consistent and oriented toward economic growth. Additionally, while financial development is important for economic development and growth, so is economic development for financial development. There is a symbiotic relationship at work. How can finance develop in a stagnant economy where there is no growth and no savings? The performance of Islamic countries, though somewhat better, is hardly exemplary in performance indicators such as the UN Human Development Index, GDP growth rates, and GDP per capita (with the exception of the rich oil-exporting countries of the Gulf Cooperation Council).

Turning specifically to the state of financial practice in Muslim countries, the World Bank in 2010 completed a Financial Flagship study of the MENA region. Although our interest is in the development of Islamic finance, the state and practice of conventional finance in Muslim countries would afford us important insights into the elements of institutions, financial infrastructure, and financial policies that require attention as important elements of any financial system, including Islamic finance. These World Bank studies examine various aspects of financial development and afford policy recommendations to the authorities in these countries. In one of these papers, Pearce (2010b) assesses financial inclusion—or access to financial services such as credit, bank accounts, deposits, payment services, insurance, and pensions—in the MENA region. As discussed earlier in this book, financial access is generally accepted to be an important dimension of financial development. It brings enterprises into the formal economy, increasing investment and trade, and is ultimately supportive of more robust economic growth and development. While we discussed Pearce's results in Chapter 9, it may be useful to repeat his conclusions here.

Pearce concludes that:

> *Financial inclusion is a policy focus for several MENA countries, although it is not yet a priority objective alongside stability for MENA financial regulators and ministries of finance. Five MENA countries now have a financial inclusion strategy, and with three of these adopted since 2006 this seems to be a growing trend for [the] region. The enabling environment for financial inclusion in MENA has improved in the past two years, but is still weak overall. Deficiencies in financial infrastructure and regulatory frameworks make expanding access to finance costly and risky for banks. Lenders have to rely on collateral that is expensive to register and may not be readily enforceable. . . . [T]he priority recommendations are firstly to agree a Financial Inclusion Strategy that is underpinned by improved data, that has both public and private sector commitment, and that scales up financial access on a large scale, principally through bank accounts. Secondly, . . . that regulators should provide a legal and supervisory framework that enables access to finance to be expanded primarily through banks, but with regulatory space for the use of agents, mobile phone technology, and for a finance company model for microcredit*

and leasing. . . , removing interest rate caps on microloans, and instead strengthening consumer protection and supervisory capacity for microfinance, while stimulating competition between financial service providers. Thirdly, continued improvements to financial infrastructure are encouraged, particularly with regard to credit information and to secured transactions. Finally . . . [there is] the need to enable growth in Islamic financial services to meet market demand.

In another paper Anzoategui et al. (2010) examine the extent of bank competition in the MENA region during 1994–2008, using non-structural measures of competition. Their measures of competition (H-statistics and the Lerner Index) suggest that banking sector competition in MENA is less than that in other regions and, unfortunately, has not improved in recent years. Their analysis of the determinants of competition across countries indicates that lower competition in MENA can be attributed to the region's poor credit information environment and lower market contestability.

In yet another paper, Rocha et al. (2010) examine the status of bank lending to small and medium enterprises in MENA. Access to finance is important because SMEs are believed to account for a large percentage of manufacturing employment in developing countries.[2] The results of this study are as follows:

First, . . . MENA banks . . . regard the SME segment as potentially profitable, and most banks are already engaged in SME lending to some degree. The drivers that motivate banks to engage in SME lending include the potential profitability of the SME market, the saturation of the large corporate market, the need to enhance returns, and the desire to diversify risks. Larger banks (measured by total loans) have not played a more significant role in SME finance in MENA, but banks with a larger branch network do more SME lending, suggesting that relationship lending is still important in a region where financial infrastructure remains generally deficient.

Second, despite the interest in the SME sector, lending volumes are still not very impressive. The share of SME lending in total lending is only 8 percent, of which 2 percent [is] in the GCC (Gulf Cooperation Council) countries, and 14 percent in the non-GCC countries. The low share of SME lending in the GCC reflects largely the characteristics of concentrated oil economies. . . . Most importantly, the shares of SME lending in total lending in both the GCC and non-GCC regions are substantially below the banks' own long-run targets, also suggesting substantial room for further lending to

SMEs. Third, MENA banks quote the lack of SME transparency and the weak financial infrastructure (weak credit information, weak creditor rights and collateral infrastructure) as the main obstacles for further engagement in SME finance. Banks complain less about regulatory obstacles (e.g. interest rate ceilings), excessive competition in the SME market, or lack of demand for loans from SMEs. Within an overall environment of weak financial infrastructure, the countries that are able to strengthen creditor rights and provide more information to creditors succeed in inducing more SME lending overall or more long-term lending to SMEs. Fourth, state-owned banks in MENA still play an important role in providing finance to SMEs, with an average share of SME lending which is almost identical to that of private banks. . . . The generally weak quality of financial infrastructure in MENA is probably one of the main reasons why private banks have not engaged more in SME finance. . . . Fifth, state banks seem to be taking greater risks than private banks in their SME lending business. They are less selective in their strategies to target SMEs, have a lower ratio of collateralized loans to SMEs, and a higher share of investment lending in total SME lending. . . . Sixth, several MENA countries have introduced special interventions to induce banks to lend more to SMEs. In addition to the use of state banks, special programs have included exemptions on reserve requirements, credit subsidies and partial credit guarantee schemes. Guarantee schemes have proved particularly popular and are in operation in ten MENA countries.

While state banks and other interventions such as guarantee schemes may have played an important role in providing finance to SMEs . . . [s]trengthening credit information systems and creditor rights should remain the priority item in the legal/regulatory agenda.

In a fourth paper, Macko and Sourrouille (2010) examine the contribution and promise of investment funds in the MENA region. They conclude:

Privately managed funds that invest in a wide variety of asset classes are beginning to develop in MENA countries. In terms of assets under management/GDP, however, investment funds in MENA countries are still small relative to those in countries with similar economic and demographic characteristics. Well-run investment funds can offer individual investors (especially small ones) an efficient means of diversification. They may contribute to market liquidity, price discovery, and better corporate governance. MENA governments can do more to promote investment fund development—by raising investor protections to IOSCO [International Organization of Securities Commissions] standards; allowing funds to invest in additional asset classes (e.g., real estate securities); develop[ing] local bond markets; selling down residual government shareholdings in state-owned enterprises; further liberalizing capital flows as well as investment—both portfolio and directly in fund management operations—by foreign fund managers; selectively encouraging development of non-bank securities firms; and encouraging acquisition of smaller non-competitive funds and fund managers by larger peers.

In sum, we must stress the need for better institutions in general, better financial institutions, better regulations, better enforcement and more enlightened financial policies in most, if not all, of these countries to promote financial development. In the case of developing the Islamic financial system, there are a number of additional gaps that must be addressed.

II. GAPS IN THE ISLAMIC FINANCIAL INDUSTRY

Islamic financial markets are still emerging, and there is no shortage of literature pointing out the deficits in the current state of the industry and what needs to be done. In Table 11.2, we summarize some of the prescriptions given for enhancing various segments of the industry, such as banking, capital markets, regulation, and related areas. The next logical step would be to prioritize the steps to be taken and then prepare an action plan. A complete coverage of all the issues and challenges would be a lengthy and voluminous academic exercise. However, in this chapter we attempt to provide a short overview of some of the major challenges and focus on divergence from the "risk-sharing" aspect of the system.

Reluctance to promote risk-sharing finance

Risk sharing is the objective of Islamic finance. To foster the development of Islamic finance, there is a need to:

- emphasize its risk-sharing foundation;
- remove biases against equity finance;
- reduce the transaction costs of stock market participation;

TABLE 11.2   Some Suggestions for Enhancing the Islamic Financial Industry

Islamic Banking	Money, Capital Markets	Legal/Regulatory Issues	Others
Consolidation.	Develop liquidity-enhancing mechanisms.	Enhance and harmonize standards.	Social sector financing. Institutionalization of Islam's redistributive instruments.
Expand scope, services, products.	Develop asset-linked, rather than asset-based, products.	Enhance corporate governance.	Develop non-bank financial intermediation.
Enhance risk management.	Develop *sukuk* based on intangible assets such as services, rights, working capital, etc.	Enhance *Shari'ah* governance.	Reputational risk.
Lessen reliance on commodity/fixed-income-like products.	Develop partnership and risk-sharing products.	Supervision and monitoring.	Financial engineering. Ease of product development.
Reduce exposure to operational risk.	Develop *Shari'ah*-compliant securities/stock markets.	Financial sector development.	Hedging with or without derivatives.
Liquidity-enhancing products.	Develop Islamic benchmarks.	Investors' and creditors' rights.	Public finance.
Hedging products.	Public finance instruments.	Insolvency laws.	Monetary policy management.

Source: Iqbal (2010).

- create a market-based incentive structure to minimize speculative behavior; and
- develop long-term financing instruments as well as low-cost, efficient secondary markets for trading equity shares.

These secondary markets would enable better distribution of risk and achieve reduced risk with expected payoffs in line with the overall portfolio of stocks in the stock market. Absent true risk sharing, Islamic finance may provide a false impression of being all about developing debt-like, short-term, low-risk, and highly liquid financing without manifesting the most important dimension of Islamic finance: its ability to facilitate the high growth of employment and income with relatively low risk to individual investors and market participants.

One of the major criticisms of Islamic banks is their reluctance to hold risk-sharing assets. By design, because of Islam's economic principles—prohibition of interest and pure debt, and sharing of risks—Islamic banks should engage in partnerships and equity-sharing financial assets, but in practice the portion of such assets on the balance sheets of Islamic banks is minimal. For example, from Figure 11.1, which shows the percentage composition of various modes of financing across different countries in 2008, it is evident that Islamic banks' preference is for financing instruments that are generated through sale contracts and leasing instruments. Informal observation of more recent balance sheets shows a similar picture. Islamic banks' heavy usage of the sale-based financing instrument *murabahah* has earned this practice the title of "*Murabahah* syndrome" (Ali and Ahmad, 2006).

The reluctance of Islamic banks to embrace and promote risk-sharing instruments such as *musharakah* (equity partnership) and *mudarabah* (principal–agent partnership) is problematic for achieving the true potential

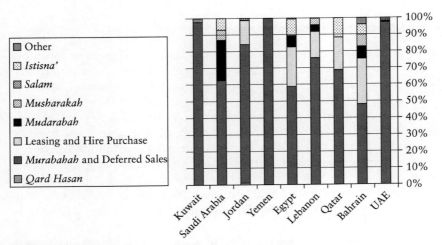

FIGURE 11.1 Asset Composition of Select Islamic Banks by Country
Source: Ali (2010).

and promise of the system. The reason for shying away from such instruments is a lack of appetite for riskier assets, which in turn is due to Islamic banks trying to emulate conventional commercial banks, whose foremost objective is preservation of depositors' principal. By investing in financing- and trade-related instruments, Islamic banks are able to provide low-risk and safe investment opportunities under an "Islamic umbrella." Islamic banks should change this business model and expand their portfolios to include risk-sharing instruments. Islamic banks often claim that their reluctance is a direct reflection of depositors' lack of appetite for risk-sharing instruments. However, it is possible that this low appetite is due to a lack of transparency and confidence in the ability of the banks as financial intermediaries. Therefore, Islamic banks should improve their selection and monitoring of risk-sharing assets and enhance the transparency of the investment process by providing depositors with good estimates of the risk exposure taken by the financial intermediary in investing in risk-sharing instruments.

In the long run, the design of a risk-sharing financial system requires that the necessary institutions, which must be based on Islamic economic tenets, are developed to act as the foundation for the system. Institutions to support risk sharing, partnership-based, and equity-style financing and investment are the most critical. By design, such instruments require close monitoring by the financial intermediary, which in turn results in additional costs. Therefore, there is a need to develop systemic-level mechanisms to perform collective monitoring of economic agents to reduce monitoring costs for individual financial intermediaries.

Limited market-based financial intermediation

Banks and financial markets play complementary roles. There is an increasing move toward transactions that are market based, as well as to institutions that have an arm's-length relationship with their clients. This has not, however, marginalized traditional institutions such as banks and their relationship-driven role as intermediaries. The changes have allowed such institutions to focus on their core business of intermediation, customization, and financial innovation, as well as risk management. Financial institutions are able to perform their core functionality more efficiently if there are supporting markets to provide liquidity, risk transfer, and insurance. As the "plain vanilla" transaction becomes more liquid and amenable to being traded in the market, banks wishing to be competitive will embrace more illiquid transactions (Rajan, 2006).

Institutions specializing in *Shari'ah*-compliant products have been functioning based on the same business model for some time and with very little innovation in their operational practice. Due to the lack of supporting money, capital, and derivative markets, financial intermediaries are retaining excessive exposure, especially exposure to liquidity risk, and are missing out on diversification opportunities. In order for the Islamic financial system to function properly, financial intermediaries need to specialize in mobilizing deposits, identifying investment opportunities, originating, structuring, and packaging securities, and managing risks, while allowing the complementary financial and capital markets to fill the remaining gaps and provide liquidity and risk sharing. Unless complementary financial markets are developed, financial intermediaries will continue on the same path as before—that is, with their limited scope and functionality.

Allen and Gale (2007) suggest that a successful, deep, and active stock market requires that information, enforcement, and governance costs be eliminated or at least minimized. Once this happens, the cost of entry into the equity market becomes low and "there is full participation in the market. All investors enter the market, the average amount of liquidity in the market is high, and asset prices are not excessively high." As mentioned earlier, if the Islamic rules of market behavior—such as faithfulness to the terms and conditions of contracts, trust, and trustworthiness—are in place in a society, the informational problems and transaction costs, governance, and enforcement issues either would not exist or would be at such low levels as not to create a deterrence to stock market entry.

There is, however, a paradigm gap between what Islam teaches and actual behavior in the market. For this reason, the actions governments take, and the institutions they create to remedy the deficit in informational, enforcement, and governance behavior in order to reduce the cost of participation in the stock markets, have to be stronger and more comprehensive than those that exist at present. These policies, actions, and institutions should have the competence, efficiency, and enforcement capabilities to elicit the kind of behavior that replicates or closely approximates those that would be expected if market participants were to behave in compliance with Islamic rules. Such actions, policies, and institutions would include, *inter alia*:

- policies to create a level playing field for equities to compete fairly with debt-based instruments; this means removing all legal, administrative, economic, financial, and regulatory biases that favor debt and place equity holding at a disadvantage;
- creating positive incentives for risk sharing via the stock market;
- investing in a massive public education campaign to familiarize the population with the benefits of stock market participation—the kind of campaign that, as we saw in an earlier chapter, Prime Minister Margaret Thatcher's government ran in the UK in the 1980s, which increased stock market participation substantially in a short span of time;

- investing in human capital to produce competent, well-educated, and well-trained reputational intermediaries—lawyers, accountants, financial journalists, and *Shari'ah* scholars—which means investing in the creation of world-class business and law schools that not only offer programs in economics and law, but also in Islamic economics, Islamic finance, and *Shari'ah* law, to graduate specialists who are experts in both Islamic and Western law and economics and finance;
- limiting leverage (including margin operations) of non-bank financial institutions and the credit-creation ability of banks through prudential rules that effectively cap the total credit the banking system can create;
- developing a strong and dynamic regulatory and supervisory system that not only continuously monitors the behavior of stock markets and participants but also stays a few steps ahead of those with the motivation to use regulatory arbitrage to get around rules and regulations;
- finding ways and means of regulating and supervising reputational intermediaries or, at least, mandating that they become self-regulating to ensure the minimization of false reporting or misreporting under the threat of liability to market participants;
- ensuring completely transparent and accurate reporting of the day's trade by all exchanges; and
- instituting legal requirements for the protection of the rights of minority shareholders.

The policies and actions listed above are by no means intended to be exhaustive, but even this limited list would help reduce the cost of market participation, give the financial markets enhanced credibility, and reduce the reliance on debt financing. Black (2001) asserts that just one element of the above list—namely, the legal protection of minority shareholders' rights—gives countries large stock market capitalization, larger minority shareholder participation in the stock market, more publicly listed firms relative to the total population, less concentrated ownership, higher dividend payout and lower cost of capital. Black also believes that a country will have the potential to develop a vibrant stock market if it can assure minority shareholders of good information about the true value of the activities the listed companies are engaged in, and that there is sufficient legal, regulatory, and supervisory protection against self-dealing transactions by companies, such as insider trading.

The absence of good information about the true value of firms, and the possibility of self-dealing on the part of companies, create problems of moral hazard and adverse selection. Both of these problems can be addressed by legal rules and procedures, as well as by the existence of efficient and credible public and private institutions that monitor the stock market and companies listed on the stock exchange. These laws and institutions can assure investors of the honesty of dealings by listed firms, and of the full transparency and accuracy of reporting and information. Effective laws covering financial disclosure and securities, coupled with oppressive fines and other penalties for all manner of misrepresentations, can be powerful tools for dissuading all those concerned from attempting to defraud investors. Requiring reputational intermediaries to be licensed by regulators, and revoking licenses or imposing heavy fines and initiating criminal proceedings against misbehavior, weakens the incentive structure for abuses in reporting, endorsing, and information processing. Strong listing standards, which stock exchanges enforce fully through the imposition of heavy fines, or even delisting of companies that violate disclosure rules, would discourage false information from reaching investors. The existence of an active, dynamic, well-informed financial press can also be valuable in creating a culture of disclosure. A strong, independent, and dynamic regulatory agency would be needed to monitor and supervise the stock market and the behavior of its participants, and to promote aggressively a culture of transparency by requiring prompt and accurate reporting on all trades in the market. Finally, it bears repeating that government must invest considerable resources in the development of world-class business and law schools to ensure a competent source of human capital to reputational intermediaries and with knowledge of Islam and *Shari'ah*.

While the above policies and institutions are crucial to reducing the cost of participation in stock markets, and thus to promoting widespread risk sharing, governments need to do more: they must lead by example. Generally, governments do share risks with their people, but they could choose to go one step further and finance part of their budget—at least their development spending—through risk sharing and direct ownership of development projects with their citizens through the stock market. In this way, they would reduce their budgetary debt burden. This reduction in government borrowing reduces the burden on monetary policy as well. Governments undertake public goods projects because the characteristics of these goods—importantly, indivisibility and non-exclusivity—prohibit their production by the private sector. However, their social rate of return is substantial and much higher than private rates of return. A recent popular proposal suggests that these projects should be undertaken jointly with the private sector—hence the Public Private Partnership (PPP) label. The proposal has a number of problems—market distortion, and informational and governance problems being just three of these.

Financial system, architecture, and infrastructure

In comparison to the conventional system, the currently practiced form of Islamic finance offers a very limited functionality of what would be expected from an efficient financial system. Table 11.3 provides a functional assessment of Islamic financial markets as they exist today. The deficiencies identified in the assessment call for serious efforts to develop the system in its holistic form if its full potential is to be achieved.

TABLE 11.3 Functional Assessments of Islamic Financial Markets

Function	Assessment
Capital mobilization	Limited set of instruments; concentration in short-term maturities; low depth and breadth of markets; and lack of liquidity.
Managing risk	No derivative markets or organized mechanism for risk mitigation. High geographic and sector concentration. Limited diversification opportunities.
Pooling and diverse ownership	Absence of or limited stock markets in Islamic countries, due to illiquid and poorly supervised stock markets, and limited opportunities for the pooling of ownership and the diversity of ownership. In non-Islamic countries, limited *Shari'ah*-compliant stocks are available to Islamic investors.
Efficient contracting	Lack of civil and commercial law based on Islamic law in several Islamic countries where the legal system is predominantly conventional limits efficient contracting. In non-Islamic countries, it may not be possible to replicate *Shari'ah* law in its intended form, which hinders efficient contracting.
Transparency and price discovery	Illiquid, shallow, and poorly supervised capital markets inhibit the process of price discovery and limit the ability to arbitrage.
Governance and control	Not all stakeholders participate in the governance of financial institutions offering Islamic financial services. There is lack of transparency in the governance of *Shari'ah* boards.
Operational efficiency	High perception of operational risk due to the lack of proper accounting standards, clearing and settlement processes, and trainer personnel.

Source: Adapted for Islamic financial markets based on Ul-Haque (2002).

The financial system infrastructure can be classified into three categories:

1. *Systemic liquidity infrastructure*, which covers institutional arrangements for money and government securities markets, payment settlement systems, monetary and foreign exchange operations, and liquidity risk management. Currently, the liquidity-management function is one of the weakest in the industry. There are very limited opportunities to access funding liquidity at short notice. Market liquidity is also poor due to large bid–ask spreads and low trading volumes.

2. *Information and governance infrastructure*, which includes accounting and disclosure standards and corporate governance arrangements for financial institutions. Although some progress has been made, there are still gaps. Governance mechanisms and standards are defined, but are not implemented. The current governance framework, including corporate social responsibility, is at quite a distance from the "stakeholders-oriented" governance model presented in Chapter 9.

3. *Insolvency regime and safety net infrastructure*, which includes lender of last resort arrangements, deposit insurance, and the legal framework governing bank insolvency, loan recovery, and creditors' rights (Martson and Sundararajan, 2006). As discussed in Chapter 9, the majority of Muslim countries do not have very well developed institutions to address these issues.

Sundararajan (2006), Martson and Sundararajan (2006), and IDB/IFSB (2006) provide a detailed discussion on the issues and the missing elements in developing architecture and infrastructure for the Islamic financial industry, which we summarize below:

- Whereas there are distinct differences in conventional and Islamic financial systems, significant parts of the conventional infrastructure elements are equally applicable and accessible to Islamic finance. Therefore, there is no need to duplicate components of infrastructure that can be shared with some adjustments to accommodate the specific operational requirements of Islamic finance.

- Financial architecture should be aligned with a vision for the industry, and it should start with a detailed policy designed to address issues of conforming financial sector laws—such as insolvency laws—with Islamic law (*Shari'ah*), strengthening the environment for risk sharing—that is, equity-based financial instruments and intermediation—and enhancing corporate governance of institutions offering Islamic products and services.

- At the national level, the financial architecture for Islamic finance is exposed to the same weaknesses as the conventional financial sector in many developing countries. Inadequate or non-existent legal frameworks for regulation, weak observance of base core principles (such as a lack of independence, weak risk management, weaknesses in disclosure), and ill-defined consolidated supervision affect both conventional and Islamic banks. In addition, there is a need for special treatment of the legal and institutional framework for the insolvency regime, investor rights, creditor rights, securitization, and judicial enforcement.

■ As part of the systemic liquidity infrastructure, the micro-structure of money and exchange and securities markets, payment settlement systems, and monetary and debt-management operations are not yet well adapted to accommodate and integrate Islamic financial institutions into the broader financial system. These factors limit the development of securities markets, which is critical for promoting product innovations, risk management, and effective supervision of Islamic finance generally. *Shari'ah*-compatible money and capital markets are essential for the implementation of monetary and fiscal policies.

■ The international architecture of Islamic finance needs to be strengthened, as there are still gaps and overlaps in the support structure provided by international infrastructure institutions. International infrastructure institutions can and should, therefore, play a key catalytic role in promoting the industry at the national level. In this respect, the Islamic Financial Services Board is expected to play the leading role in standards setting, and to coordinate with the Basel Committee on Banking Supervision (BCBS), the International Organization of Securities Commissions (IOSCO), and the International Accounting Standards Board (IASB). The Accounting and Auditing Organization for Islamic Financial Institutions should continue to realign work programs and promote greater adoption of AAOIFI standards at the national level. The International Islamic Financial Market (IIFM) should focus on market practices and contract standards and strengthen its role as an association of market players. The Liquidity Management Center (LMC), the Islamic investment banking firm in Bahrain, can play a role in promoting national and regional strategy for money market development. The Islamic International Rating Agency (IIRA) can play an important role in enhancing disclosure and transparency.

III. CONCLUSION

Although there are numerous gaps or impediments to the development of a truly Islamic financial system in Muslim countries—including developed economic and financial infrastructure, efficient and reliable institutions, sound economic and financial policies, institutions and policies required for the widespread practice of Islamic finance, and the required human capital to develop the regulatory, supervisory, and functioning aspects of a broad and complete Islamic financial system—the most difficult element to develop and put in place may be the high ethical and moral practices demanded by Islam. A society or country must be based on a foundation of social and economic justice, the government should be responsive to the needs of society as called for in the *Qur'an* and enunciated by the Prophet (pbuh) and individuals must adopt the expected ethical standards in all their dealings. Then, and only then, can the fully functioning risk-sharing financial system as envisaged in the *Qur'an* and interpreted by the Prophet (pbuh) be put into practice. In the meantime, the best we can hope for is a system that proceeds methodically based on the roadmap that we have tried to outline and with a strong commitment to ethical regulation, supervision and enforcement in order to develop its essential foundations.

ENDNOTES

1. For further details, see Iqbal and Mirakhor (2011).
2. Ayyagari et al. (2007) have reported that SMEs account for more than 60 percent of manufacturing employment across 76 developed and developing economies. See M. Ayyagari, T. Beck, and A. Demirgüç-Kunt, "Small and Medium Enterprises across the Globe," *Small Business Economics*, 29: 415–34.

CHAPTER 12

Concluding Remarks

Islamic finance has been touted in the financial press for its expansion and globalization. It has grown rapidly from a "cottage" industry practiced in a few Muslim countries to global recognition in London, New York, Paris, Kuala Lumpur, and Seoul, and with a presence in almost every corner of the world. Yes, financial products—more accurately *Shari'ah*-compliant financial products and sometimes even products that are not strictly *Shari'ah*-compliant—have been developed, marketed, and sold by all manner of financial institutions around the world as Islamic financial products largely to Muslim investors. More recently, conventional investors have also found value in *Shari'ah*-compliant products. Still, the Islamic financial system has not been established and demonstrated as the financial system of even a single country. What is behind these seemingly contradictory facts? What are the essential characteristics of the Islamic financial system? Is this system more or less stable than the conventional financial system? Can Islamic finance serve the important function of financial intermediation? Does it afford investors the choice of instruments to build efficient port-folios? What is needed before such a system can be established as the financial system of a country, a country that in all likelihood would be a Muslim country? Is it only a matter of time?

Before addressing these questions, which are at the center of our endeavor in this book, we examine the reasons for financial crises in the world of conventional finance to afford us the necessary basis of comparison of the conventional and Islamic financial systems. The suggested reasons for this financial crisis have been many: wholesale and foolhardy deregulation, inadequate and failed supervision, unregulated and unsupervised financial institutions, an inadequate level of capital, an extended episode of low interest rates, excessive risk taking, the emergence of a parallel banking sector (the repo market), rapid and uncontrolled financial innovations (derivatives), mark-to-market accounting, the consolidation of the financial sector and moral hazard or the emergence of institutions that are deemed "too big to fail," shortcomings of the credit rating agencies and especially the conflict of interest in their operations, excessive assumption of debt and leveraging, increased international capital mobility, and human greed and fraud.

We have argued that the conventional system is inherently unstable, often shaken by periodic crises and requiring massive bailouts, for essentially two reasons: (i) it is a debt and interest-based system; and (ii) it creates excessive debt and leveraging and, if faced with sudden withdrawal of deposits when confronted with default by borrowers on their payments, requires guarantee and support from the government. Simultaneously, the conventional financial system has been accompanied by financialization—that is: (i) fast expansion of financial institutions and products outside traditional banking and traditional instruments; (ii) a significant expansion of the financial sector relative to the real sector as reflected in a number of variables such as share in GDP, share of corporate profits, higher rate of return on equity, and the like; and (iii) an expansion that was not beneficial to the broader economy and may have even turned out to be harmful for longer-term economic growth. Needless to say, at the extreme, if the entire economy were to become finance, we would all starve to death! Financialization has illustrated the power of the financial system to create money, push debt, and create bubbles and volatility in the quest to earn greater wealth. It has created immense distortions in the economy that have led to changes in income distribution in favor of the financial sector and long-term economic stagnation as exemplified in Japan and in the drawn-out recession in the US and Europe during 2007–10. By creating speculative bubbles in assets and commodity markets, the financial sector could more readily excise real income at the expense of the real sector. The profits of the financial sector have remained private, but its losses have been socialized through massive government bailouts.

It is important, though maybe difficult given our mindsets, to recognize that there is nothing magical about the recent historical prominence of debt financing. Before the rise of debt financing, equity financing was pre-eminent. But a host of factors and developments catapulted debt financing to the forefront. Risk-sharing finance is trust-intensive, and trade financing during the Middle Ages was based on risk sharing, which, in turn, was based on mutual trust. Upheavals of the late Middle Ages in the 14th and 15th centuries, including the Black Death, strife within the Church and between the Church and hereditary rulers, and general economic decline contributed to the breakdown of trust in communities and among their members. While risk-sharing techniques continued to prevail in Europe until the mid-17th century, beginning in the mid-16th century the institution of interest-based debt financing also began to be used more widely and extensively. The catalyst for debt financing was primarily the breakdown of trust, in Europe and elsewhere, and the adoption of securitization in finance.

Over time, government deposit insurance schemes, tax treatments, rules, and regulations have all heavily favored debt-based contracts over risk-sharing contracts. Thus, risk sharing is still at an early stage of development in all countries, to say nothing of its even more modest international practice. These developments have helped the perpetuation of a system that a number of renowned economists, such as Keynes, have deemed detrimental to growth, development, and equitable income and wealth distribution. More recently, a growing literature and proposed reforms have argued that the stability of a financial system can only be assured by limiting credit expansion and leveraging; this, in turn, requires the elimination of implicit and explicit subsidies that fuel moral hazard, such as subsidized deposit insurance schemes and guarantees that support "too large to fail" institutions, and restrictions to limit the creation of money through the fractional reserve conventional banking system.

Islamic finance is basically a financial system structured on risk sharing and the prohibition of debt financing (leveraging). The central proposition of Islamic finance is the prohibition of transactions that embody rent for a specific period of time as a percentage of the loaned principle without the transfer of the property rights claims, thus shifting the entire risk of the transaction to the borrower. As the *Qur'an* prohibits interest rate-based debt contracts, it simultaneously ordains an alternative. The alternative to debt-based contracts is a mutual exchange in which one bundle of property rights is exchanged for another, thus allowing both parties to share production, transportation, and marketing risks. It further allows parties to an exchange to reduce the risk of income volatility and to allow consumption smoothing, which is a major outcome of risk sharing and increases the welfare of the parties to the exchange.

In order to fit into this framework, financial intermediation and banking in the Islamic financial system (and more generally in a risk-sharing system) has been proposed as having two tiers (i) a banking system that accepts deposits for safekeeping without accruing any return and requiring 100 percent reserves, thus protecting the payment system of the economy while concurrently limiting the credit-creating ability of the banking system and thus obviating the need for a deposit guarantee as in the conventional fractional reserve system; and (ii) an investment component that functions as a classical financial intermediary, channeling savings to investment projects, and where deposits in investment banks are considered as equity investments with no guarantees for their face value at maturity and subject to the sharing of profits and losses. Depositors are investors in the pool of assets maintained by the bank on the assets side of its balance sheet.

These banks invest directly in real projects in every segment of the economy (except activities that are prohibited, such as gambling and alcohol) and share in their attendant risks. An Islamic bank is assumed to match deposit maturities with investment maturities (with no need for asset–liability management). Short-term deposits may finance short-term trade operations, with the bank purchasing merchandise or raw materials and selling to other companies; liquidity is replenished as proceeds from sales operations are generated. For longer-term investment, longer-term deposits are used. In all these investments, an Islamic bank is a direct owner of the investment process, which is awarded through the normal due-diligence process. In such a system, a financial institution therefore participates directly in the evaluation, management, and monitoring of the investment process. Returns to invested funds arise *ex post* from the profits or losses of the operation, and are distributed to depositors as if they were shareholders of equity capital. Since loan default is absent, depositors do not face this risk of loss of their assets. From this discussion, it follows that in Islamic finance there is a one-to-one mapping between the growth of financial and real sector activities, meaning that credit cannot expand or contract independently of the real sector as in the conventional system. In other words, the real and the financial sectors are closely connected and cannot be decoupled as in conventional finance.

For the successful operation of the Islamic financial system, and specifically to fulfill its all-important mission of financial intermediation, it is essential that capital markets be developed and vibrant. Vibrant capital markets—including well-developed stock markets and other secondary capital markets for equity finance to motivate savers to provide financing and to supply entrepreneurs with sufficient resources for their projects—are essential for these institutions to fulfill their central role as intermediaries as envisaged in Islamic finance. There is no reason why governments should not also become active in stock markets for risk sharing. They could choose to finance part of their budget, at least development spending, through risk sharing and direct ownership of development projects with their citizens. In this way, they would also reduce their budgetary debt burden; the attendant reduction in government borrowing would in turn reduce the burden on monetary policy. Governments undertake public goods projects because the characteristics of these goods—especially their indivisibility and non-exclusivity characteristic—prohibit their production by the private sector.

In a risk-sharing financial system, debt is replaced by the securitized "asset-linked" securitized market. The main difference between the conventional securitization and our proposed Islamic securitization is the way the end investor would have ownership rights to the securitized assets. Whereas in the conventional system there may be multiple layers of ownership, which may leave the final investor without any recourse, in the case of the Islamic system, scholars have maintained strict requirements of clear ownership rights for the investor. This feature, in contrast with the conventional system, would afford an Islamic system more stability as the same underlying asset is not traded many times over, which could have a cascading effect in the case of liquidation. This is another feature of an Islamic system that promotes stability. More importantly, the underlying assets securitized in the conventional financial system are debt based and, therefore, have an implicit guarantee of principal. Securitization in the Islamic system would be based on risk sharing and, therefore, the principal return would depend on the market value of the underlying asset. Essentially, in the case of securitization in the conventional system market value is supposed to be reflected in the market price of the security, whereas in the Islamic system it is reflected in the market price of the underlying asset. Again, this is an important factor reinforcing financial stability.

An Islamic asset-linked security will complement the risk–return profile of a typical stock market security in one crucial way. Whereas an equity share represents ownership in the equity capital of a firm and is therefore exposed to the general business of the firm, an asset-linked security will represent a security where the investor's return would be linked to the profit and loss of a pool of heterogeneous assets. Since the pool will be a portfolio of assets of the same type—that is, leases where the returns are driven by the performance of the underlying assets—it would be relatively easy for the investor to forecast its future payoffs. As a result, it is expected that the volatility of such asset-linked securities will be lower than for a simple stake in equity capital (that is, common stocks) assuming no change in the creditworthiness of the asset owner. Due to low volatility, it can cater to the needs of investors who would like more deterministic and low-risk returns. Finally, although both an equity stock and an asset-linked security will be based on equity sharing, an asset-linked security is expected to exhibit low risk and thus occupies the vacuum in the risk spectrum of the financial system.

There is another compelling reason to encourage securitization and the development of asset-linked securities. The Islamic financial intermediary can operate optimally when it intermediates with the least degree of friction. However, if the financial intermediary takes on additional responsibilities of maintaining physical assets—that is, warehousing and trading of real assets— its attention will divert from intermediation and it may not do either task optimally. For example, it may not be efficient for the financial intermediary to operate leases or mortgages. One way of avoiding this problem would be for the financial intermediary to originate the assets but ultimately pool them, securitize the pool, and issue marketable securities some of which the financial intermediary can hold on its balance sheet. This will free the financial intermediary from operational issues of the assets and enable it to focus on intermediation. The recent financial crisis raised questions about the appropriate functions and roles of financial intermediaries and markets.

In the lead-up to the crisis, financial intermediaries whose primary role was to lend and finance the real sector were engaged in speculative activities, and the users of funds were left at the mercy of the markets. We maintain that the model of Islamic financial intermediaries as presented in this book is in fact that of a specialized funds manager who acts as a buffer between the depositor who happens to be an investor and the market. Islamic financial institutions specialize in processing information about markets and economic agents, and in performing the functions of assets- and maturity-transformation on behalf of the depositor who is contractually an investor in the Islamic institution.

Asset pricing and modern portfolio theory are at the core of modern conventional finance. In Islamic finance, there has been very little research into asset pricing and the pricing of risk in a system that excludes interest. As a result, most discussions of the pricing of risk in Islamic finance are almost exclusively based on conventional finance; and in some cases, it is even assumed that asset-pricing models in conventional systems are applicable in the Islamic system provided a risk-free security can be designed for the Islamic system. Conventional finance has developed a number of asset-pricing models. In the case of the popular CAPM model, two of its fundamental assumptions—(i) the existence of a risk-free interest rate, and the ability of investors to borrow and invest an unlimited amount of funds at this rate; and (ii) no restrictions on the short selling of securities—require careful examination before the model can be used in Islamic finance. Although the introduction of a risk-free rate leads to a linear relationship between the risk-free rate and the market rate, the assumption of a risk-free rate is not essential for asset pricing in CAPM as long as there exists a risk-free asset or there is a way to construct a portfolio with zero risk. To this end, Fischer Black developed a variant of the CAPM with short selling replacing the risk-free rate; the covariance between the zero-beta portfolio and the market return is zero, with the return on the zero-beta asset replacing the risk-free rate. However, in this variant the portfolio has a higher variance than the variance of the original CAPM portfolio and thus does not lie on the efficient frontier; all other relationships hold as in the original CAPM. While this variant of the CAPM solves the problems of the exclusion of the risk-free rate in Islamic finance, it introduces another issue—namely, short selling which is also prohibited in Islam, and the fact that a zero-beta portfolio cannot be constructed without short sales.

Considering that linear CAPM has serious issues, which have also been debated in conventional literature, does not mean that the concept of mean-variance analysis and pricing of risk should be discarded. To the contrary, in the absence of a risk-free interest rate, the ability to borrow (create leverage) and restrictions on short selling (a practice highly criticized and restricted even by regulators in advanced countries), a mean-variance efficient frontier would still be the framework to price risk and to manage portfolios. Similarly, investors in the Islamic financial system would be free to construct diversified portfolios within a mean-variance framework and would select a point on the efficient frontier representing their preference for the risk–reward trade-off.

In conventional finance, the equity premium and risk-free interest rate puzzles arise as a result of the inability of standard intertemporal economic models to rationalize the statistics that have characterized US financial markets over the past century—namely, the co-movements of three variables: (i) the real return to broad stock indices: (ii) the real return to short-term nominally risk-free bonds; and (iii) the growth rate of per capita real consumption (more precisely, non-durables and services). The large equity premium has been rationalized in two ways: (i) either investors are highly risk averse to consumption risk; or (ii) they find trading stocks to be much more costly than trading bonds. There is also a presumption that there is a large differential in the cost of trading between the stock and bond markets. Stocks imply risk sharing—they are contingent claims; bonds are fixed-income assets and imply risk shifting. In this regard, the difference between Islamic finance and conventional finance is that in conventional finance there is essentially a wedge between the rate of interest and return to equities because of the availability of a riskless asset, whereas in Islamic finance the option of a risk-free asset does not exist. Thus, Islamic finance can exploit this wedge, or gap, because equities *do not* have to afford this higher return to compensate for risk over a riskless asset. In this sense, Islamic finance may be regarded as more efficient by relying on equity participation.

To foster the development of what we have described as Islamic finance, there is a need to emphasize its risk-sharing foundation, remove biases against equity finance, reduce transaction costs of stock market participation, create a market-based incentive structure to minimize speculative behavior, and develop long-term financing instruments as well as low-cost efficient secondary markets for trading equity shares. These secondary markets would enable better distribution of risk and achieve reduced risk with expected payoffs in line with the overall stock market portfolio. Absent true risk sharing, Islamic finance may provide a false impression of being all about developing debt-like, short-term, low-risk, and highly liquid financing without manifesting the most important dimension of Islamic finance: its ability to facilitate high growth of employment and income with relatively low risk to individual investors and market participants.

Theoretically, an Islamic stock market operates according to the precepts of *Shari'ah*. Islamic stock markets are free from two major sources of instability—namely, interest rates and speculation. A high degree of instability makes a market more inefficient, requiring large resources for trading and hedging risk. A high degree of instability will dissuade savers away from markets, while stability will encourage savers and enable stock markets to achieve maximum efficiency in financial intermediation, reduce trading cost, and enlarge participation. In the absence of speculation arising from dysfunctional credit (debt) markets, equity prices would tend to show less volatility. Demand for equity shares would be driven essentially by dividends and by savings. The supply would be influenced by initial public offerings. Hence, both the demand for and supply of equity shares are influenced by stable variables in the absence of speculation, and equity prices would tend to display a stationary pattern. In Islamic finance, the pool of savings rather than credit would determine asset demand. The supply of equity shares would be determined by real investment plans. Hence, demand for and supply of shares would tend to be stable. The rate of return would essentially comprise dividends, with very small changes in equity prices. Equity share prices would be stationary variables, with no persistent upward or downward trend.

In any financial system, conventional or Islamic, financial development is seen as supportive of economic growth. The reason is that those who invest are not necessarily the same as those that save. There is a need for financial intermediation to encourage and channel savings to the most productive investments. Financial intermediation is at the heart of any financial system. Its traditional function has been to transfer savings (real resources) to firms, entrepreneurs, and governments for investment, and increasingly in recent years to transfer risk to those who are better able to assume it and thus enhance risk sharing. Historically, financial intermediaries have provided these functions and services, but financial and capital markets have in recent years increasingly served the same functions. While intermediaries and markets could complement one another, competition may increase efficiency and risk taking. We have argued that an Islamic financial institution cannot function efficiently and effectively in the absence of vibrant capital markets (including stocks and securitized assets), their respective secondary markets, and money markets. Therefore, the development of these markets is also necessary and vital for efficient financial intermediation. Financial intermediaries also play a special role in an Islamic financial system because in the absence of derivative markets the financial intermediary would also have to provide "risk-management" functionality, such as hedging for clients. Financial intermediaries will have to take on the responsibility of innovating risk-sharing mechanisms for hedging through collective cooperative-style schemes or through matching offsetting hedging needs.

We now turn to a final major theme of this volume—namely, what are the necessary developments and steps before the Islamic financial system can be established and practiced in a country? We have discussed the essentials of such a system (risk sharing and the prohibition of debt), its complementary institutional requirements for success (vibrant capital markets), and its characteristics (asset pricing and portfolio properties, intermediation, stability), but what is missing? If and when such a risk-sharing system is established, the first country where it would be established is likely to be a Muslim country. But we have seen that Muslim countries on the whole score quite low on the social and economic values and achievements that they *should* exhibit. Ironically, because these values and achievements in large part reflect best practices, advanced non-Muslim countries perform better, and Malaysia at number 38 is the highest-achieving Muslim country. But for the Islamic financial system to be successfully established and functioning, there are important prerequisites and complementary requirements.

A financial system, *ceteris paribus*, is more likely to thrive the healthier is the underlying economy. This obvious point deserves little discussion because if the real economy is moribund, savings are non-existent, and investment opportunities are not to be found, then the contribution of a financial system will be limited. Unfortunately, the economies of Muslim countries have not exhibited superior performance. While the level of per capita income and the United Nations Human Development Index (influenced by per capita income) is high in a few Muslim oil-exporting countries, the broad economic performance (sustained economic growth) of the great majority of Muslim countries has been quite disappointing. The common missing element in most Muslim countries has been quality institutions. Again, the only exception may be Malaysia. Thoughtful and consistent macroeconomic policies are another missing element in a number of Muslim countries. Good institutions are also essential for a thriving financial sector.

There is no doubt that well-developed political, economic, and legal institutions are essential to facilitate financial contracting and are a necessary element of a robust financial system. Better institutions promoting checks and balances and the quality of governance can affect financial markets in several ways. Starting with the legal system, unless there is clarity with respect to creditors' and borrowers' rights, the protection of property rights, and recourse to collateral in the case of default, it would be difficult to build an efficient financial system. Prevailing legal systems are predominantly based on the conventional legal system, which may or may not have the provisions for handling the specific treatment of *Shari'ah* rules. Furthermore and importantly, legal systems in place in Islamic countries are invariably plagued by enforcement shortcomings, a significant deterrent for any investor. Therefore, the development of supportive legal and tax codes, and a harmonized regulatory framework based on Islamic law for the Islamic financial services industry, is absolutely critical for the efficient operation of the Islamic financial system. Finance and financial intermediation should and must play a critical role in such a system but will require supporting markets and institutions if it is to perform effectively and efficiently and support the growth of the real sector.

Access to finance, although not easily defined, also matters for the performance of the financial sector and intermediation. It matters for economic growth, for increasing income, for leveling the playing field between the rich (powerful) and the poor (powerless), for enabling SMEs to expand, for lifting up the poor and for reducing poverty. Access to finance invariably favors the powerful and the rich in developing countries. This is in part because the rich have collateral to access debt financing and the powerful to use their political connections to secure debt. Financial access is not equal for all regions and sectors in developing countries. Although access to finance helps the poor, it is not clear that equal access is what is called for. Before government intervention and specific policies are recommended, there is a need for much more data and analysis.

Two facts should be emphasized in the case of most Muslim countries. First, economic and social justice is not what it should be in most Muslim countries, but this may be best promoted by a social safety net, rapid growth, and an increase in incomes of the poor, which depend on good institutions and sound policies. The increase in incomes and a reduction in poverty would in turn increase access to finance, as financial institutions would be motivated to provide services to individuals and entities who could meet their requirements. Second, in the specific case of Muslim countries, a significant percentage of Muslims have a clear preference for Islamic financial products and services; and for some Muslims it is more than simple preference: it is a binding constraint—that is, financial access for them cannot be increased without the increased availability of Islamic financial products and services.

Islamic finance advocates risk sharing and thus equity finance. We have argued that, as such, Islamic finance will promote financial access, increase the ratio of investment to consumption financing, enhance economic growth, provide more jobs, reduce government waste, and better protect the interests of future generations. Additionally, because of the focus on risk sharing, we would expect that, over time, risk sharing will be promoted and the cost of risk management reduced. Given the preoccupation of Islamic teachings with social and economic justice and the eradication of poverty, we would expect that Islamic instruments that are targeted to address inequity, especially *qard-ul-hassan* (literally "beautiful" loans), will play an important role if the required institutional structures are developed. The principles of microfinance can be combined with the structure of *qard-ul-hassan* to afford financial access to those who are currently underserved.

The development of efficient institutions and of a sound governance framework is important for the emergence and growth of a sound financial system. Institutions lay the foundation of the system, and the governance framework ensures that the rules are enforced so that the desired results are achieved. Given the moral hazard and agency problems associated with equity-based financial contracts, institutions and governance become even more important in developing a risk-sharing financial system. Institutions governing economic transactions, such as property rights, trustworthiness, truthfulness, faithfulness to the terms and conditions of contracts, transparency, and non-interference with the workings of the markets and the price mechanism so long as market participants are rule-compliant, provide a reasonably strong economy where information flows unhindered and participants engage in transactions confidently with minimal concern for uncertainty regarding the actions and reactions of other participants. The result is that in such an economy with reduced uncertainty, economic agents will be encouraged to engage in risk-sharing contracts. As can be readily inferred, strict rule-compliance is absolutely essential for an Islamic financial system to live up to its expectations and billing. Human frailty being what it is, efficient institutions, especially the rule of law and all that it entails, are a prerequisite to success; and this must be accompanied by governance and effective enforcement. Unfortunately, data on the MENA as defined by the World Bank, and information on countries belonging to the OIC, indicate that Muslim countries lack effective institutions and governance structure.

While in a truly Islamic financial system the "expectation" is that all market participants are devout Muslims and follow the spirit and the letter of the *Shari'ah* law, we are only too familiar with human frailties. It is for this reason that efficient institutions, governance that reflects Islamic values, and strict and just enforcement are essential for a truly Islamic financial system to flourish. Such a system is ethically based on Islamic values as elaborated in the *Qur'an* and interpreted in the tradition of the Prophet (pbuh). In the absence of this umbrella of ethical values, an Islamic financial system can be but a mirage.

Although there are numerous gaps or impediments to the development of a truly Islamic financial system in Muslim countries, the most difficult element to develop and put in place may be the high ethical and moral practices demanded by Islam. A society or country must be based on a foundation of social justice, with the government responsive to the needs of society as called for in the *Qur'an* and enunciated by the Prophet (pbuh) and individual members of society committed to ethical standards in all their dealings. Then, and only then, can the fully functioning Islamic financial system as envisaged in the *Qur'an* and interpreted by the Prophet (pbuh) be put into practice on this earth. In the meantime, the best we can hope for is a system that proceeds methodically on the roadmap that we have tried to outline and with a strong commitment to ethical regulation, supervision, and enforcement in order to develop the essential foundations.

References

Abed, G. T. and H. R. Davoodi, 2003, *Challenges of Growth and Globalization in the Middle East and North Africa* (Washington, DC: International Monetary Fund).

Abu-Lughod, J., 1994, "Discontinuities and Persistence," in *The World System: Five Hundred Years or Five Thousand?* (London and New York: Routledge).

Adelson, Howard L., 1960, "Early Medieval Trade Routes," *The American Historical Review,* 65(2): 271–87.

Adrian, Tobias and Hyun Song Shin, 2010, "Liquidity and Leverage," *Journal of Financial Intermediation*, 19(3): 418–37.

Ahmad, Mahmud, 1967, "Semantics of the Theory of Interest," *Islamic Studies*, 6(2): 171–96.

Akitoby, Bernardin and Thomas Stratmann, 2009, "The Value of Institutions for Financial Markets: Evidence from Emerging Markets," IMF Working Paper No. 09/27, February.

Al-Amine, Muhammad and Muhammad Al-Bashir, 2001, "The Islamic Bonds Market: Possibilities and Challenges," *International Journal of Islamic Financial Services*, 3(1).

Al-Dhareer, Siddiq Mohammad Al-Ameen, 1997, "Al-Gharar Contract and its Effects on Contemporary Transactions," Eminent Scholars' Lecture Series No. 16, Islamic Development Bank, Jeddah, Saudi Arabia.

Alesina, A. and E. La Ferrara, 2002, "Who Trusts Others?" *Journal of Public Economics*, 85: 207–34.

Al-Hakimi, M. R., M. Al-Hakimi, and Ali Al-Hakimi, 1989, *Al-Hayat* (Tehran: Maktab Nashr Al-Thaqrafa Al-Islamiyyah), 3: 211–14; 4: 203–73.

Al-Harran, Saad Abdul Sattar, 1993, *Islamic Finance: Partnership Financing* (Selangor Darul Ehsan, Malaysia: Pelanduk Publications).

Ali, Salman Syed, 2005, "Islamic Capital Market Products: Developments and Challenges," Occasional Paper No. 9 (Jeddah, Saudi Arabia: Islamic Development Bank).

Ali, Salman S. and Ausaf Ahmad, 2006, "An Overview," in Salman S. Ali and Ausaf Ahmad (eds.), *Islamic Banking and Finance: Fundamentals and Contemporary Issues* (Jeddah: IRTI).

Ali, Salman Syed, 2011, "Islamic Banking in the MENA Region," The World Bank, February.

Allais, Maurice, 1999, *La Crise Mondiale D'Aujourd'hui* (Paris: Clément Juglar).

Allen, F. and D. Gale, 1999, *Comparing Financial Systems* (Cambridge, MA: MIT Press).

Allen, F. and D. Gale, 2007, *Understanding Financial Crises* (Oxford: Oxford University Press).

Allen, Franklin and Anthony Santomero, 1996, "The Theory of Financial Intermediation," Working Paper No. 96-32 (The Wharton Financial Institutions Center).

Al-Saud, Mahmud Abu, 1993, "Islamic View of Riba (Usury and Interest)," in Saad Abdul Sattar Al-Harran (ed.), *Islamic Finance: Partnership Financing* (Selangor Darul Ehsan, Malaysia: Pelanduk Publications).

Al-Zarqa, Anas Muhammad, 1993, "An Islamic Perspective on the Economics of Discounting Project Evaluation," in Saad Abdul Sattar Al-Harran (ed.), *Islamic Finance: Partnership Financing* (Selangor Darul Ehsan, Malaysia: Pelanduk Publications).

Anderson, J. N. D. and N. J. Coulson, 1958, "The Moslem Ruler and Contractual Obligations," *NYV Law Review*, 33(7).

Anzoategui, Diego, María Soledad Martínez Pería, and Roberto Rocha, 2010, "Bank Competition in the Middle East and Northern Africa Region," The World Bank, June.

Archer, S. and T. Ahmed, 2003, "Emerging Standards for Islamic Financial Institutions: The Case of the Accounting and Auditing Organization for Islamic Financial Institutions," mimeo, The World Bank, Washington, DC.

Archer, Simon and Rifaat Abdel Karim, 2002, *Islamic Finance: Growth and Innovation* (London: Euromoney Books).

Arfoe, L., 1987, "Cedar Forest to Silver Mountain: Social Change and the Development of Long-Distance Trade in Early Near Eastern Societies," in M. Rowlands, M. Larsen, and K. Kristiansen (eds.), *Centre and Periphery in the Ancient World* (Cambridge, MA: Cambridge University Press), pp. 25–35.

Arrow, K., 1964, "The Role of Securities in the Optimal Allocation of Risk-Bearing," *Review of Economic Studies*, 31(2): 91–96.

Asad, Mohammad, 2004, *The Message of the Qur'an* (The Book Foundation), www.thebook.org/.

Ashtor, E., 1975, "The Volume of Levantine Trade in the Later Middle Ages," *Journal of European Economic History*, 4: 573–612.

Ashtor, E., 1976, *A Social and Economic History of the Near East in the Middle Ages* (London: Collins).

Ashtor, E., 1983, *Levant Trade in the Later Middle Ages* (Princeton, NJ: Princeton University Press), pp. 3–64.

Askari, Hossein, 1990, *Saudi Arabia and the Search for Economic Development* (Stamford, CT: JAI Press).

Askari, H. and Zamir Iqbal, 1995, "Opportunities for Western Institutions in Islamic Financial Markets," *The Banker*, 145(835).

Askari, H., Z. Iqbal, and A. Mirakhor, 2008, *New Issues in Islamic Finance and Economics: Progress and Challenges* (Singapore: John Wiley & Sons).

Askari, H., Z. Iqbal and A. Mirakhor, 2009, *Globalization and Islamic Finance: Convergence, Prospects, and Challenges* (Singapore: John Wiley & Sons).

Askari, H., Z. Iqbal, N. Krichene, and A. Mirakhor, 2010, *The Stability of Islamic Finance: Creating a Resilient Financial Environment for a Secure Future* (Singapore: John Wiley & Sons).

Ayoub, M., 2002, *Islamic Banking and Finance: Theory and Practice* (Karachi: State Bank of Pakistan).

Ayyagari, M., T. Beck, and A. Demirgüç-Kunt, 2007, "Small and Medium Enterprises across the Globe," *Small Business Economics*, 29: 415–34.

Azmi, Sabahuddin, www.renaissance.com.pk/Mayviewpoint2y5.htm.

Bachelier, L., 1900, *Théorie de la spéculation* (Paris: Gauthier-Villars).

Bagehot, Walter, 1873, *Lombard Street* (London: Henry S. King and Co.).

Baldwin, K., 2002, "Risk Management in Islamic Banks," in S. Archer and Rifaat Ahmed Abdel Karim (eds.), *Islamic Finance* (London: Euromoney).

Baliga, Sandeep and Ben Polak, 2001, "The Emergence and Persistence of the Anglo-Saxon and German Financial Systems," Working Paper (Yale University, Dept. of Economics).

Balling, M., E. Hennessy, and R. O'Brien, 1998, *Corporate Governance, Financial Markets and Global Convergence* (London: Kluwer Academic Publishers).

Banerjee, A., E. Duflos, R. Glennerster, and C. Kinnan, 2009, "The Miracle of Microfinance? Evidence from a Randomized Evaluation," mimeo.

Bashir, Abdel-Hameed M., 1999, "Property Rights in Islam," Conference Proceedings of the Third Harvard University Forum on Islamic Finance (Cambridge, MA: Harvard University), pp. 71–82.

Beck, Thorsten and Augusto de la Torre, 2005, "Broadening Access to Financial Services: Risks and Costs," PowerPoint presentation (Washington, DC: The World Bank).

Beck, Thorsten, Asli Demirguç-Kunt, and Ross Levine, 2004, "Finance and Poverty: Cross-Country Evidence," World Bank Policy Research Working Paper No. 3338.

Beck, Thorsten, Asli Demirgüç-Kunt, and Vojislav Maksimovic, 2005, "Financial and Legal Constraints to Firm Growth: Does Firm Size Matter?" *Journal of Finance*, 60: 137–77.

Beck, T. and Ross Levine, 2002, "Industry Growth and Capital Allocation: Does Having a Market or Bank-Based System Matter?" *Journal of Financial Economics*, 64: 147–80.

Beck, Thorsten and Ross Levine, 2003, "Legal Institutions and Financial Development," World Bank Policy Research Working Paper No. 3136.

Bergsten, Fred, 2009, "The Dollar and the Deficits," *Foreign Affairs*, 3(89).

Bhattacharya, S., 1982, "Aspects of Monetary and Banking Theory and Moral Hazard," *Journal of Finance*, 37(2): 371–84.

Black, Bernard, 2001, "The Legal and Institutional Preconditions for Strong Securities Markets," *UCLA Law Review,* 48: 781–858.

Black, F., 1972, "Capital Market Equilibrium with Restricted Borrowing," *Journal of Business*, 45: 444–54.

Black, Fischer and Myron Scholes, 1973, "The Pricing of Options and Corporate Liabilities," *Journal of Political Economy*, 81(3): 637–54.

Bloomestein, H. J., 1998, "The New Financial Landscape and its Impact on Corporate Governance," in M. Balling et al. (eds), *Corporate Governance, Financial Markets and Global Convergence* (London: Kluwer Academic Publishers).

Boot, Arnoud W. and Anjan V. Thakor, 1997, "Financial System Architecture," *The Review of Financial Studies*, 10(3): 693–733.

Brainard, W. and J. Tobin, 1977, "Asset Markets and the Cost of Capital," in B. Belassa and R. Nelson (eds.), *Economic Progress, Private Values, and Public Policy: Essays in Honor of William Fellner* (New York: North Holland).

Brav, Alon, George M. Constantinides, and Christopher C. Geczy, 2002, "Asset Pricing with Heterogeneous Consumers and Limited Participation: Empirical Evidence," *Journal of Political Economy*, 110(4): 793–824.

Brouwer, Maria, 2005, *Managing Uncertainty through Profit Sharing Contracts from Medieval Italy to Silicon Valley*, manuscript, University of Amsterdam, The Netherlands.

Bruhn, M. and I. Love, 2009, "The Economic Impact of Banking the Unbanked: Evidence from Mexico," World Bank Policy Research Working Paper No. 4981.

Buehlmaier, Matthias, 2011, "Debt, Equity, and Information" (April 11). Available at SSRN: http://ssm.com/abstract=1673132.

Burgess, R. and R. Pande, 2005, "Do Rural Banks Matter? Evidence from the Indian Social Banking Experiment," *American Economic Review*, 95(3): 780–95.

Byrne, E. H., 1920, "Genoese Trade with Syria in the Twelfth Century," *American Historical Review*, 25: 191–219.

Byrne, E. H., 1930, *Genoese Shipping in the Twelfth and Thirteenth Centuries* (doc. dated 1250) (Cambridge, MA), pp. 85–88.

Chapra M. Umer, 1985, *Towards a Just Monetary System: A Discussion of Money, Banking, and Monetary Policy in the Light of Islamic Teachings* (Leicester, UK: Islamic Foundation).

Chapra, M. Umer, 1989, "The Nature of *Riba*," *Journal of Islamic Banking and Finance (Pakistan)*, 6: 7–23.

Chapra, M. Umer, 2000, *The Future of Economics* (Leicester, UK: The Islamic Foundation).

Chapra, M. Umer and Ahmed Habib, 2002, "Corporate Governance in Islamic Financial Institutions," Occasional Paper No. 6 (Jeddah, Saudi Arabia: Islamic Research and Training Institute, Islamic Development Bank).

Chapra M. Umer and Tariqullah Khan, 2000, "Regulation and Supervision of Islamic Banks," Occasional Paper No. 3 (Jeddah, Saudi Arabia: Islamic Research and Training Institute, Islamic Development Bank).

Cho, Y. J., 1986, "Inefficiencies from Financial Liberalization in the Absence of Well-Functioning Equity Markets," *Journal of Money, Credit, and Banking*, 17(2): 191–200.

Choudhry, N. N. and A. Mirakhor, 1997, "Indirect Instruments of Monetary Control in an Islamic Financial System," *Islamic Economic Studies*, 4(2).

Cizakca, Murat, 1995, "Historical Background," *Encyclopedia of Islamic Banking and Insurance* (London: Institute of Islamic Banking and Insurance).

Claessens, Stijn, 2005, "Access to Financial Services: A Review of the Issues and Public Policy Objectives," World Bank Policy Research Working Paper No. 3589.

Clarke, George, Robert Cull, Maria Soledad Martinez Peria, and Susana M. Sánchez, 2003, "Foreign Bank Entry: Experience, Implications for Developing

Economies, and Agenda for Further Research," *World Bank Research Observer*, 18: 25–59.

Cochrane, John, 1991, "A Simple Test of Consumption Insurance," *Journal of Political Economy*, 99: 957–76.

Collins, D., J. Morduch, S. Rutherford, and O. Ruthven, 2009, *Portfolios of the Poor: How the World's Poor Live on $2 a Day* (Princeton, NJ: Princeton University Press).

Copeland, Thomas E. and J. Fred Weston, 1988, *Financial Theory and Corporate Policy* (New York: Addison-Wesley Publishing Co.)

Cowles, A., 1944, "Stock Market Forecasting," *Econometrica*, 12.

Crane, Dwight B., Kenneth A. Froot, Scott P. Mason, Andre F. Perold, Robert C. Merton, Zvi Bodie, Erik R. Sirri, and Peter Tufano, 1995, *The Global Financial System: A Functional Perspective* (Boston: Harvard Business School Press).

Creane, S., Rishi Goyal, A. Mushfiq Mobarak, and Randa Sab, 2003, *Financial Development in the Middle East and North Africa* (Washington, DC: International Monetary Agency).

Crotty, J., 2005, "The Neoliberal Paradox: The Impact of Destructive Product Market Competition and Modern Financial Markets on Non-Financial Corporations in the Neoliberal Era," in G. Epstein (ed.), *Financialization and the World Economy* (Cheltenham, UK: Edward Elgar Publishing).

Crucini, M., 1999, "On International and National Dimensions of Risk Sharing," *The Review of Economics and Statistics*, 81(1): 73–84.

Currie, Lauchlin, 1934, "The Failure of Monetary Policy to Prevent the Depression of 1929–32," *Journal of Political Economy*, 42: 143–77.

D'Arista, J., 2005, "The Role of the International Monetary System in Financialization," in G. Epstein (ed.), *Financialization and the World Economy* (Cheltenham, UK: Edward Elgar Publishing).

DeBondt, W. F. M. and R. H. Thaler, 1985, "Does the Stock Market Overreact?" *Journal of Finance*, 40: 557–8.

Deidda, L. and B. Fattouh, 2008, "Banks, Financial Markets and Growth," *Journal of Financial Intermediation*, 17: 6–36.

De Jonghe, Olivier, 2010, "Back to the Basics in Banking? A Micro-Analysis of Banking System Stability," *Journal of Financial Intermediation*, 19(3): 387–417.

De Larosière, 2009, *Report on the Future of Financial Supervision in the EU*, Brussels, February 25.

Demirgüç-Kunt, Asli and Ross Levine, 2001, *Financial Structure and Economic Growth: A Cross-Country Comparison of Banks, Markets, and Development* (Cambridge, MA: MIT Press).

Demirgüç-Kunt, Asli and Vojislav Maksimovic, 1998, "Law, Finance and Firm Growth," *Journal of Finance*, 53(6): 2107–37.

De Nicoló, Gianni, P. Bartholomew, J. Zaman, and M. Zephirin, 2003, "Bank Consolidation, Internationalization and Conglomeration: Trends and Implications for Financial Risk," International Monetary Fund Seminar Series (International), No. 2003-121: 1–49.

Diamond, Douglas W., 1984, "Financial Intermediation as Delegated Monitoring," *Review of Economic Studies*, 51 (July): 393–414.

Dickens, E., 2005, "The Eurodollar Market and the New Era of Global Financialization," in G. Epstein (ed.), *Financialization and the World Economy* (Cheltenham, UK: Edward Elgar Publishing).

Domar, E. D. and R. A. Musgrave, 1944, "Proportional Income Taxation and Risk Taking," *Quarterly Journal of Economics*, LVI (May).

Dupas, P. and J. Robinson, 2009, "Savings Constraints and Micro-Enterprise Development: Evidence from a Field Experiment in Kenya," NBER Working Paper No. 14693.

Edelman Trust Barometer, 2009, "Business Must Partner with Gov't to Regain Trust," www.edelman.com/trust/2009/.

El-Gamal, Mahmud, 2000, *A Basic Guide to Contemporary Islamic Banking and Finance* (Houston, TX: Rice University).

El-Hawary, Dahlia, Wafik Grais, and Zamir Iqbal, 2004, "Regulating Islamic Financial Institutions: The Nature of the Regulated," Policy Research Working Paper No. 3227 (Washington, DC: The World Bank).

Epstein, G. (ed.), 2005, *Financialization and the World Economy* (Cheltenham, UK: Edward Elgar Publishing).

Epstein, G. and A. Jayadev, 2005, "The Rise of Rentiers' Income in OECD Countries: Financialization, Central Banking, and Labor Solidarity," in G. Epstein (ed.), *Financialization and the World Economy* (Cheltenham, UK: Edward Elgar Publishing).

Erbas, N. and A. Mirakhor, 2007, "The Equity Premium Puzzle, Ambiguity Aversion and Institutional Quality," IMF Working Paper (Washington, DC: International Monetary Fund).

Errico, Luca and Mitra Farahbaksh, 1998, "Islamic Banking: Issues in Prudential Regulations and Supervision," IMF Working Paper No. WP/98/30 (Washington, DC: International Monetary Fund).

Exenberger, A., 2004, "The Cradle of Globalization: Venice's and Portugal's Contribution to a World Becoming Global," Working Papers in Economics 2004/02 (Austria: University of Innsbruck).

Fadeel, Mahmoud, 2002, "Legal Aspects of Islamic Finance," in Simon Archer and Rifaat Abdel Karim (eds.), *Islamic Finance: Growth and Innovation* (London: Euromoney Books).

Fama, E. F., 1965, "The Behavior of Stock Market Prices," *Journal of Business*, 38: 34–105.

Fama, E. F., 1970, "Efficient Capital Markets: A Review of Theory and Empirical Work," *Journal of Finance*, 25: 383–417.

Fama, E. F. and K. R. French, 1996, "A Multifactor Explanation of Asset-Pricing Anomalies," *Journal of Finance*, 47: 426–65.

Fama, Eugene F. and Jensen, Michael C., 1983, "Separation of Ownership and Control," in Michael C. Jensen, *Foundations of Organizational Strategy* (Harvard University Press).

Faria, A., P. Mauro, M. Minnoni, and A. Zaklan, 2006, "External Financing of Emerging Market Countries: Evidence from Two Waves of Financial

Globalization," IMF Working Paper No. WP/06/205 (Washington, DC: International Monetary Fund).

Fergusson, Leopoldo, 2006, Institutions for Financial Development: What Are They and Where Do They Come From?" *Journal of Economic Surveys*, 20(1): 27–70.

Fischel, W., 1933, "The Origin of Banking in Medieval Islam," *Journal of the Royal Asiatic Society*, 339–52 and 568–603.

Fischel, W., 1937, *Jews in the Economic and Political Life of Mediaeval Islam* (London).

Fisher, Irving, 1933, "The Debt Deflation Theory of Great Depressions," *Econometrica*, 1: 337–57.

Fisher, Irving, 1936, *100% Money* (New York: Adelphi Company).

Flood, R. P. and P. M. Garber, 1980, "Market Fundamentals versus Price Level Bubbles: The First Tests," *Journal of Political Economy*, 88: 745–70.

Frank, A. G., 1990, "The Thirteenth Century World System: A Review Essay," *Journal of World History*, 1(2): 249–56.

Fratzscher, M. and J. Imbs, 2009, "Risk Sharing, Finance, and Institutions in International Portfolios," *Journal of Financial Economics*, 94: 428–47.

Friedman, M., 1959, *A Program for Monetary Stability* (New York: Fordham University Press).

Friedman, Milton and Anna J. Schwartz, 1963, *A Monetary History of the United States, 1863–1960, A Study by the National Bureau of Economic Research, New York* (Princeton, NJ: Princeton University Press).

Fukuyama, Francis, 1996, *Trust: The Social Virtues and the Creation of Prosperity* (Free Press Paperbacks).

Garretsen, H., R. Lensink, and E. Sterken, 2003, "Growth, Financial Development, Societal Norms and Legal Institutions," *International Financial Markets Institutions and Money* (June).

Gills, B. K. and G. A. Frank (eds.), 1994a, "The Cumulation of Accumulation," *The World System: Five Hundred Years or Five Thousand?* (London and New York: Routledge), pp. 81–114.

Gills, B. K. and G. A. Frank, 1994b, "World System Cycles, Crises, and Hegemonic Shifts, 1700 BC to 1700 AD," *The World System: Five Hundred Years or Five Thousand?* (London and New York: Routledge), pp. 143–99.

Goitein, S. D., 1954, "From the Mediterranean to India," *Speculum*, 29: 181–97.

Goitein, S. D., 1955, "The Cairo Geniza as a Source for the History of Muslim Civilization," *Studia Islamica*, pp. 168–97.

Goitein, S. D., 1962, *Jewish Education in Muslim Countries, Based on Records of the Cairo Geniza* (Hebrew) (Jerusalem).

Goitein, S. D., 1964, "Commercial and Family Partnerships in the Countries of Medieval Islam," *Islamic Studies*, 3: 318–19.

Goitein, S. D., 1967, "A Mediterranean Society," *The Jewish Communities of the Arab World as Portrayed in the Documents of the Cairo Geniza*, Vol. I: Economic Foundations (Berkeley and Los Angeles).

Grais, Wafik and Zamir Iqbal, 2006, *"Corporate Governance Challenges of Islamic Financial Institutions,"* Seventh Harvard Forum on Islamic Finance, Boston, April 22–23.

Gray, Robert, 2005, *Islamic Capital Markets*, Presentation made to 10-Year Master Plan for Islamic Financial Services Industry, HSBC Bank plc, UK.

Gorton, Gary, 2010a, *Slapped by the Invisible Hand: The Panic of 2007* (New York: Oxford University Press).

Gorton, Gary, 2010b, "Questions and Answers about the Financial Crisis," prepared for the US Financial Crisis Inquiry Commission, Electronic copy available at: http://ssrn.com/abstract=1557279.

Gorton, Gary and Andrew Winton, 2002, "Financial Intermediation," NBER Working Paper Series No. 8928 (Cambridge, MA: National Bureau of Economic Research).

Guiso, L., P. Sapienza, and L. Zingales, 2005, "Trusting the Stock Market," NBER Working Paper No. 11648 (Cambridge, MA: National Bureau of Economic Research).

Guvenen, F., 2002, "Does Stockholding Provide Perfect Risk Sharing?" Working Paper No. 490 (Rochester Center for Economic Research, University of Rochester).

Habachy, S., 1962, "Property, Right, and Contract in Muslim Law," *Columbia Law Review I*, 62(3).

Haque, Zia-ul, 1995, *Riba—The Moral Economy of Usury, Interest, and Profit* Kuala Lumpur: Ikraq).

Harrington, Diana R., 1987, *Modern Portfolio Theory, The Capital Asset Pricing Model, and Arbitrage Pricing Theory: A User's Guide* (Englewood Cliffs, NJ: Prentice-Hall Inc.).

Hasanuzzaman, S. M., 1981, *The Economic Functions of the Early Islamic State* (Karachi: International Islamic Publishers).

Hasanuzzaman, S. M., 1993, *Indexation of Financial Assets: An Islamic Evaluation*, Research Monograph Series No. 4 (Islamabad, Pakistan: International Institute of Islamic Thought).

Hasanuzzaman, S. M., 1994, "Conceptual Foundations of Riba in Quran, Hadith and Fiqh," *Journal of Islamic Banking and Finance (Pakistan)*, 11: 7–15.

Hasanuzzaman, S. M., 2001, "What is Mudaraba?" *Journal of Islamic Banking and Finance (Pakistan)*, 18(3/4): 65–82.

Hayek, Friedrich, 1931, *Prices and Production* (New York: Augustus M. Kelly Publishers).

Hellwig, M., 1998, "Banks, Markets, and Allocation of Risks in an Economy," *Journal of Institutional and Theoretical Economics*, 154(1): 328–45.

Henry, James S. and Laurence J. Kotlikoff, 2010, "Financial Reform, R.I.P.," *Forbes*, July 15.

Hess, D. G and K. Shin, 1999, "Risk Sharing of Disaggregate Macroeconomic and Idiosyncratic Shocks," Working Paper No. 9915 (Federal Reserve Bank of Cleveland).

Hirshleifer, J., 1971, "The Private and Social Value of Information and the Reward to Inventive Activity," *American Economics Review*, 61: 561–74.

Hong, H., J. D. Kubik, and J. C. Stein, 2004, "Social Interaction and Stock-Market Participation," *The Journal of Finance*, 54(1): 137–63.

Honohan, Patrick, 2004a, "Financial Development, Growth and Poverty: How Close Are the Links?" World Bank Policy Research Working Paper No. 3203; also in Charles Goodhart (ed.), *Financial Development and Economic Growth: Explaining the Links* (London: Palgrave).

Honohan, Patrick, 2004b, "Financial Sector Policy and the Poor: Selected Findings and Issues," Working Paper No. 43 (Washington, DC: The World Bank).

Huberman, Gur, 2001, "Familiarity Breeds Investment," *The Review of Financial Studies*, 14(3): 659–80.

Hussein, K. A., 2003, "Operational Efficiency in Islamic Banking: The Sudanese Experience," Islamic Research and Training Institute (IRTI) Working Paper Series No. 1 (Jeddah, Saudi Arabia: Islamic Development Bank).

IFSB, 2005a, *Guiding Principles of Risk Management for Institutions (Other than Insurance Institutions) Offering Only Islamic Financial Services*, Exposure Draft No. 1 (Kuala Lumpur: Islamic Financial Services Board (IFSB)).

IFSB, 2005b, *Capital Adequacy Standard for Institutions (Other than Insurance Institutions) Offering Only Islamic Financial Services*, Exposure Draft No. 2 (Kuala Lumpur: Islamic Financial Services Board (IFSB)).

International Institute of Islamic Economics (IIIE), 1999, *IIIE's Blueprint of Islamic Financial System* (Islamabad, Pakistan: International Islamic University).

Iqbal, M., 2000, "Islamic and Conventional Banking in the Nineties: A Comparative Study," Islamic Economic Studies, 8(2) (April).

Iqbal, Zamir, 1997, "Islamic Financial Systems," *Finance and Development* (June) (Washington, DC: International Monetary Fund).

Iqbal, Zamir, 1999, "Financial Engineering in Islamic Finance," *Thunderbird International Business Review*, 41(4/5) (July–October): 541–60.

Iqbal, Zamir, 2004, "Financial Intermediation and Design of Financial System in Islam," International Seminar on Economics, Malaysia, September 22–24.

Iqbal, Zubair and Abbass Mirakhor, 1987, "Islamic Banking," Occasional Paper No. 49 (Washington, DC: International Monetary Fund).

Iqbal, Zamir and Abbas Mirakhor, 1999, "Progress and Challenges of Islamic Banking," *Thunderbird International Business Review*, 41(4/5) (July–October): 381–405.

Iqbal, Zamir and Abbas Mirakhor, 2002, "Development of Islamic Financial Institutions and Challenges Ahead," in Simon Archer and Rifaat Abdel Karim (eds.), *Islamic Finance: Growth and Innovation* (London: Euromoney Books).

Iqbal, Zamir and Abbas Mirakhor, 2004, "A Stakeholder's Model of Corporate Governance of Firm in Islamic Economic System," *Islamic Economic Studies*, 11(2) (March).

Iqbal, Z. and A. Mirakhor, 2007, *An Introduction to Islamic Finance: Theory and Practice* (Singapore: John Wiley & Sons).

Iqbal, Z. and A. Mirakhor, 2011, *An Introduction to Islamic Finance: Theory and Practice*, 2nd ed. (Singapore: John Wiley & Sons).

Iqbal, Zamir and Hiroshi Tsubota, 2005, "Emerging Islamic Markets," in *The Euromoney International Debt Capital Markets Handbook* (London: Euromoney Publishing).

Jegadeesh, N. and S. Titman, 1993, "Returns to Buying Winners and Selling Losers: Implications for Stock Market Efficiency," *Journal of Finance*, 48: 65–91.

Jensen, M. and W. Meckling, 1976, "Theory of the Firm: Managerial Behaviour, Agency Costs and Ownership Structure," *Journal of Financial Economics*, 3: 305–60.

Kahf, M., 1999, "Islamic Banks at the Threshold of the Third Millennium," *Thunderbird International Business Review*, 41(4/5) (July–October): 445–60.

Karlan, D. and J. Zinman, 2009, "Expanding Credit Access: Using Randomized Supply Decisions to Estimate the Impacts," *Review of Financial Studies*.

Kasey, K., S. Thompson, and M. Wright, 1997, *Corporate Governance: Economic and Financial Issues* (Oxford, UK: Oxford University Press).

Kendall, Jake, Nataliya Mylenko, and Alejandro Ponce, 2010, "Measuring Financial Access around the World," World Bank Policy Research Working Paper No. 5253.

Keynes, John Maynard, 1936, *The General Theory of Employment, Interest, and Money* (London: Macmillan, St. Martin's Press, 1970).

Keynes, J. M., 1943, "Proposals by British Experts for an International Clearing Union," reproduced in the Proceedings and Documents of the United Nations Monetary and Financial Conference, 1948, pp. 1548–73.

Khan, M. 1987, "Islamic Interest-Free Banking: A Theoretical Analysis," in M. Khan and A Mirakhor (eds.), *Theoretical Studies in Islamic Banking and Finance* (Houston, TX: IRIS Books).

Khan, M. Fahim, 1991, "Time Value of Money and Discounting in Islamic Perspective," *Review of Islamic Economics*, 1(2).

Khan, M. Fahim, 1994, "Comparative Economics of Some Islamic Financing Techniques," *Islamic Economic Studies*, 2(1) (December).

Khan, Mohsin, 1987, "Islamic Interest-Free Banking: A Theoretical Analysis," in M. Khan and A. Mirakhor (eds.), *Theoretical Studies in Islamic Banking and Finance* (Houston, TX: IRIS Books).

Khan, M. Fahim, 1999, "Islamic Benchmarks as Alternative to LIBOR/Interest Rates," Working Paper (Jeddah, Saudi Arabia: Islamic Development Bank).

Khan, Mohsin and Abbas Mirakhor, 1987, *Theoretical Studies in Islamic Banking and Finance* (Houston, TX: IRIS Books).

Khan, Mohsin S. and A. Mirakhor, 1992, "Islam and the Economic System," *Review of Islamic Economics*, 2(1): 1–29.

Khan, Tariqullah and Habib Ahmed, 2001, "Risk Management: An Analysis of Issues in Islamic Financial Industry," Occasional Paper No. 9 (Jeddah, Saudi Arabia: Islamic Development Bank).

Kim, S., S. H. Kim, and Y. Wang, 2005, "Regional versus Global Risk Sharing in East Asia," *Asian Economic Papers*, 3(3): 195–201.

Kindleberger, C. and R. Aliber, 2005, *Manias, Panics and Crashes* (New York: Basic Books).

Kotlikoff, Laurence J., 2010, *Stewart is Dead—Ending the World's Financial Plague with Limited Purpose Banking* (Hoboken, NJ: John Wiley & Sons).

Kourides, P. N., 1970, "The Influence of Islamic Law on Contemporary Middle Eastern Legal System: The Foundation and Binding Force of Contracts," *Columbia Journal of Transnational Law*, 9(2): 384–435.

Krippner, G., 2005, "The Financialization of the American Economy," *Socio-Economic Review*, 3: 173–208.

Kumar, Jayesh, 2005, "Debt vs. Equity: Role of Corporate Governance," 8th Capital Markets Conference, Indian Institute of Capital Markets Paper. Available at SSRN: http://ssrn.com/abstract=592521.

Labib, Subhi Y., 1969, "Capitalism in Medieval Islam," *The Journal of Economic History*, 29(1): 79–96.

Laiou, A. E., 1992, "The Byzantine Economy in the Mediterranean Trade System: Thirteenth–Fifteenth Centuries," in A. E. Laiou (ed.), *Gender, Society and Economic Life in Byzantium* (Hampshire, UK), pp. 177–223.

Laiou, A. E., 2002, "The Levant Trade in the Middle Ages, The Economic History of Byzantium: From the Seventh through the Fifteenth Century," *Dumbarton Oaks Research Library and Collection*, No. 39.

Levine, Ross, 1997, "Financial Development and Economic Growth: Views and Agenda," *Journal of Economic Literature*, 35(2): 688–726.

Levine, Ross, 2002, "Bank-Based or Market-Based Financial Systems: Which is Better?" *Journal of Financial Intermediation*, 11: 398–428.

Levine, Ross, 2005, "Finance and Growth: Theory, Evidence, and Mechanisms," in P. Aghion and S. Durlauf (eds.), *Handbook of Economic Growth* (Amsterdam: North-Holland Elsevier Publishers).

Levine, Ross, Norman Loayza, and Thorsten Beck, 1999, "Financial Intermediation and Growth: Causality and Causes," World Bank Policy Research Working Paper No. 2059.

Lewis, K., 1996, "What Can Explain the Apparent Lack of International Consumption Risk Sharing?" *Journal of Political Economy*, 104: 267–97.

Lewis, Mervyn K. and Latifa M. Algaoud, 2001, *Islamic Banking* (Cheltenham, UK: Edward Elgar).

Lieber, A. E., 1968, "Eastern Business Practice and Medieval European Commerce," *Economic History Review*, 2nd series, 21: 230–43.

London School of Economics, 2010, *The Future of Finance: The LSE Report*, London, July.

Lopez, R. S., 1951, "The Dollar of the Middle Ages," *Journal of Economic History*: 209–34.

Lopez, R. S., 1952, "The Trade of Medieval Europe: The South," *The Cambridge Economic History of Europe* (Cambridge), Vol. 2, pp. 257–354.

Lopez, R. S., 1955, "East and West in the Early Middle Ages: Economic Relations," *Relazioni del X Congresso Internazionale di Scienze Storiche* (6 vols., Florence), Vol. III, pp. 129–37.

Lucas, R. E., 1990, "Supply-Side Economics: An Analytical Review," *Oxford Economic Papers*, 42: 293–316.

Mace, Barbara, 1991, "Full Insurance in the Presence of Aggregate Uncertainty," *Journal of Political Economy*, 99: 928–56.

Macko, William and Diego Sourrouille, 2010, "Investment Funds in MENA," The World Bank, December.

Madeddu, Oscar, 2010, *The Status of Information Sharing and Credit Reporting Infrastructure in the Middle East and North Africa Region* (Washington, DC: The World Bank).

Majid, M. A., N. G. M. Nor, and F. F. Said, 2003, "Efficiency of Islamic Banks in Malaysia," Conference Proceedings: The Fifth International Conference on Islamic Economics and Finance, Vol. II, Bahrain, October 7–9.

Markowitz, H. M., 1952, "Portfolio Selection," *The Journal of Finance*, 7(1): 77–91.

Martson, David and V. Sundararajan, 2006, "Unique Risks of Islamic Banks: Implications for Systemic Stability," in Tariqullah Khan and Dadan Muljawan (eds.), *Islamic Financial Architecture: Risk Management and Financial Stability* (Jeddah, Saudi Arabia: IRTI).

Marx, Karl, 1894, *Capital*, Vol. III, based on the 1st edition. Frederick Engels (ed.) (Chicago: Charles H. Kerr and Co.).

Mason, Scott P., 1995, "The Allocation of Risk," in *The Global Financial System: A Functional Perspective* (Boston: Harvard Business School Press).

Mehra, Rajnish, 2004, "The Equity Premium: Why is it a Puzzle?" *Financial Analysts Journal*: 54–69.

Mehra, R. and E. C. Prescott, 1985, "The Equity Premium Puzzle," *Journal of Monetary Economics*, 15: 145–61.

Menkoff, L. and N. Tolkorof, 2001, *Financial Market Drift: Decoupling of the Financial Market from the Real Economy?* (Heidelberg-Berlin: Springer-Verlag).

Merton, R. C., 1989, "On the Application of the Continuous-Time Theory of Finance to Financial Intermediation and Insurance," *Geneva Papers on Risk and Insurance*, 14 (July): 225–62.

Merton, R. C., 1993, "Operation and Regulation in Financial Intermediation: A Functional Perspective," in P. England (ed.), *Operation and Regulation of Financial Markets* (Stockholm: The Economic Council).

Merton, Robert C. and Zvi Bodie, 1995, "A Conceptual Framework for Analyzing the Financial Environment," in Dwight B. Crane et al. (eds.), *The Global Financial System: A Functional Perspective* (Boston, MA: Harvard Business School Press), pp. 3–32.

Metawally, M. M., 1985, "The Role of the Exchange in an Islamic Economy," *Journal of Research in Islamic Economics*, 2(1): 21–30.

Michie, R. C., 2007, *The Global Securities Market: A History* (Oxford: Oxford University Press).

Mills, Paul S. and John R. Presley, 1999, *Islamic Finance: Theory and Practice* (Hampshire, UK: Palgrave Macmillan Ltd, Hampshire, UK.

Minsky, Hyman, 1982, *Inflation, Recession and Economic Policy* (London: Wheatsheaf Books).

Minsky, Hyman, 1986, *Stabilizing an Unstable Economy*, A Twentieth Century Fund report (New Haven, CT and London: Yale University Press).

Minsky, Hyman P., 1992, "The Financial Instability Hypothesis," Working Paper No. 74 (The Jerome Levy Economics Institute of Bard College).

Mirakhor, Abbas, 1983, "Muslim Contribution to Economics," first presented at the Midwest Economic Association Meeting, April 7–9, and reprinted in Baqir Al-Hassani and Abbas Mirakhor, *Essays on Iqtisad: The Islamic Approach to Economic Problems* (New York: Global Scholarly Publications).

Mirakhor, Abbas, 1987, "Analysis of Short-Term Asset Concentration in Islamic Banking," IMF Working Paper No. WP/87/67 (Washington, DC: International Monetary Fund).

Mirakhor, Abbas, 1988, "Equilibrium in a Non-Interest Open Economy," IMF Working Paper No. WP/88/111 (Washington, DC: International Monetary Fund).

Mirakhor, Abbas, 1989, "General Characteristics of an Islamic Economic System," in Baqir Al-Hassani and Abbas Mirakhor (eds.), *Essays on Iqtisad: The Islamic Approach to Economic Problems* (New York: Global Scholarly Publications), pp. 45–80.

Mirakhor, Abbas, 1989, "Theory of an Islamic Financial System," in Baqir Al-Hassani and Abbas Mirakhor (eds.), *Essays on Iqtisad: The Islamic Approach to Economic Problems* (New York: Global Scholarly Publications).

Mirakhor, Abbas, 1994, "Equilibrium in a noninterest open economy," *Journal of King Abdulaziz University: Islamic Economics*, 6: 3–24.

Mirakhor, Abbas, 1995, "Outline of an Islamic Economic System," *Zahid Husain Memorial Lecture Series No. 11*, State Bank of Pakistan, Islamabad, March.

Mirakhor, Abbas, 1996, "Cost of Capital and Investment in a Non-Interest Economy," *Islamic Economic Studies*, 4(1).

Mirakhor, Abbas, 1999, "The Design of Instruments for Government Finance in an Islamic Economy," *Islamic Economic Studies*, 6(2).

Mirakhor, Abbas, 2002, "Hopes for the Future of Islamic Finance," *New Horizon*, 121 (July–August): 5–8.

Mirakhor, Abbas, 2003, "Muslim Contribution to Economics," presented at the Annual Meeting of the South-Western Economic Association, March, and reproduced from Baqir Al-Hassani and Abbas Mirakhor (eds.), *Essays on Iqtisad: The Islamic Approach to Economic Problems* (New York: Global Scholarly Publications).

Mirakhor, Abbas, 2005a, "Globalization and Islamic Finance," Keynote lecture at the 6th International Conference on Islamic Economics and Finance, Jakarta, Indonesia, November 21–23.

Mirakhor, Abbas, 2005b, "A Note on Islamic Economics," Lecture delivered at the Islamic Development Bank for Research in Islamic Economics, Saudi Arabia, April.

Mirakhor, Abbas, 2007, "Islamic Finance and Globalization: A Convergence?" *Journal of Islamic Economics, Banking and Finance*, 3(2): 11–72.

Mirakhor, Abbas, 2010, "Whither Islamic Finance? Risk Sharing in an Age of Crises," Paper presented at the Inaugural Securities Commission Malaysia (SC)—Oxford Centre for Islamic Studies (OCIS) Roundtable, "Developing a Scientific Methodology on Shariah Governance for Positioning Islamic Finance Globally."

Mirakhor, Abbas and Hossein Askari, 2010, *Islam and the Path to Human and Economic Development* (New York: Palgrave Macmillan).

Mirakhor, A. and I. Zaidi, 2007, "Profit-and-Loss Sharing Contracts in Islamic Finance," in K. Hassan and M. Lewis (eds.), *Handbook of Islamic Banking* (Cheltenham, UK and Northampton, US: Edward Elgar), pp. 49–63.

Modigliani, F. and M. H. Miller, 1958, "The Cost of Capital, Corporate Finance, and the Theory of Investment," *American Economic Review*, 48(3): 261–97.

Munro, J., 2003, "The Late-Medieval Origins of the Modern Financial Revolution: Overcoming Impediments from Church and State," Working Paper No. 2. Online version: www.chass.utoronto.ca/ecipa/wpa.html (University of Toronto, Department of Economics and Institute for Policy Analysis).

Nyazee, Imran Ahsan Khan, 1995, *The Concept of Riba and Islamic Banking* (Islamabad, Pakistan: Niazi Publishing House).

Obaidullah, Mohammed, 2008, *Role of Microfinance in Poverty Alleviation: Lessons from the Experiences in Selected IDB Member Countries* (Jeddah: Islamic Research & Training Institute, Islamic Development Bank).

Obstfeld, M. and A. Taylor, 2003, *Global Capital Markets: Integration, Crisis and Growth* (Cambridge: Cambridge University Press).

OECD, 2009, *Corporate Governance and the Financial Crisis: Key Findings and Main Messages*, A Report by the OECD Steering Group on Corporate Governance, Paris, June.

Palley, Thomas J., 2007, "Financialization: What It Is and Why It Matters," Working Paper No. 525 (The Levy Economics Institute).

Payandeh, A., 1984, *Nahjulfasahah: Collected Short Sayings of the Messenger* (Tehran: Golestanian).

Pearce, Douglas, 2010a, *In the Middle East and North Africa: Analysis and Roadmap Recommendations* (Washington, DC: The World Bank).

Pearce, Douglas, 2010b, "Financial Inclusion in the Middle East and North Africa: Analysis and Roadmap Recommendations," The World Bank, June.

Posen, A. S., 2001, *A Strategy to Prevent Future Crises: Safety Shrink the Banking Sector* (Washington, DC: Peter G. Peterson Institute for International Economics).

Postan, M., 1928, "Credit in Medieval Trade," *The Economic History Review*, 1(2): 234–61.

Postan, M., 1957, "Partnership in English Medieval Commerce," *Studi in Onore Di A. Sapori* (Milan), Vol. 1, pp. 521–49.

Prescott, E. C. and Rajnish Mehra, 1985, "Equity Premium; A Puzzle," *Journal of Monetary Economics* (Netherlands), 15(2): 145–61.

Presley, John R. and John G. Sessions, 1994, "Islamic Economics: The Emergence of a New Paradigm," *Economic Journal*, 104(424) (May): 584–96.

Rajan, Raghuram G., 2005, "Has Financial Development Made the World Riskier?" NBER Working Paper No. 11728.

Rajan, Raghuram G., 2006, "Has Finance Made the World Riskier?" *European Financial Management*, 12(4): 499–533.

Rajan, Raghuram G. and Luigi Zingales, 1998, "Financial Development and Growth," *The American Economic Review*, 88: 559–86.

Rajan, R. G. and L. Zingales, 2003, "The Great Reversals: The Politics of Financial Development in the Twentieth Century," *Journal of Financial Economics*, 69: 5–50.

Ramakrishnan, R. T. S. and Anjan Thakor, 1984, "Information Reliability and a Theory of Financial Intermediation," *Review of Economic Studies*, 51: 415–32.

Rehman, S. and H. Askari, 2010, "How Islamic Are Islamic Countries?" *Global Economy Journal*, 10(2).

Reinhart, Carmen M., 2010, "This Time is Different: Chartbook: Country Histories on Debt, Default, and Financial Crises," National Bureau of Economic Research, Working Paper No. No. 15815, March.

Reinhart, Carmen M. and Rogoff, Kenneth S., 2009, *This Time is Different: Eight Centuries of Financial Folly* (Princeton, NJ: Princeton University Press).

Ricardo, David, 1817, *On the Principles of Political Economy and Taxation* (London: John Murray).

Rocha, Robert, Subika Farazi, Rania Khouri, and Douglas Pearce, 2010, "The Status of Bank Lending to SMEs in the Middle East and North Africa Region," The World Bank, June.

Ross, S. A., 1976, "The Arbitrage Theory of Capital Asset Pricing," *Journal of Economic Theory*, 13: 341–60.

Ross, S. A., 1978, "Mutual Fund Separation in Financial Theory—The Separating Distributions," *Journal of Economic Theory*, 47: 254–86.

Rueff, J., 1964, *The Age of Inflation, Gateway Editions* (Chicago: Henry Regnery Company).

Sadr, Kazim, 1999, "The Role of Musharakah Financing in the Agricultural Bank of Iran," *Arab Law Quarterly,* pp. 245–56.

Sadr, Kazim and Zamir Iqbal, 2000, "Debt v. Equity Contract under Asymmetrical Information: An Empirical Evidence," Conference Proceedings 4th International Conference on Islamic Economics and Finance, Loughborough, UK. August 13–15.

Saeed, Abdul, 1996, *Islamic Banking and Interest* (Leiden, Netherlands: E.J. Brill).

Saez, E., 2010, "Striking it Richer," www.docstoc.com/docs/48716353/Striking-it-Richer-The-Evolution-of-Top-Incomes-in-the-United-States.

Saint-Paul, G., 1992, "Technological Choice, Financial Markets and Economic Development," *European Economic Review*, 36: 763–81.

Saleem, Shahid, 2008, "Role of Islamic Banks in Economic Development," Working Paper (University of Punjab, Pakistan).

Saleh, Nabil A., 1992, *Unlawful Gain and Legitimate Profit in Islamic Law: Riba, Gharar, and Islamic Banking*, 2nd ed. (London: Graham & Trotman).

Samad, H. and M. K. Hassan, 1999, "The Performance of Malaysian Islamic Banks during 1984–1997: An Exploratory Study," *International Journal of Islamic Financial Services*, 1(3).

Samuelson, P., 1965, "Proof That Properly Anticipated Prices Fluctuate Randomly," *Industrial Management Review*, 6: 41–49.

Sauer, J. B., 2002, "Metaphysics and Economy—The Problem of Interest. A Comparison of the Practice and Ethics of Interest in Islamic and Christian Cultures," *International Journal of Social Economics*, 29(1/2): 97–118.

Scholtens, B., 1993, "On the Foundations of Financial Intermediation: A Review of the Literature," *Kredit Und Kapital* (Germany), 26(1): 112–41.

Shabsigh, Ghiath, 2002, "Comments: Regulation of the Stock Market in an Islamic Economy," in Munawar Iqbal (ed.), *Islamic Banking and Finance: Current Developments in Theory and Practice* (Leicester, UK: Islamic Foundation).

Sheng, Andrew, 2009, *From Asian to Global Financial Crisis* (Cambridge, UK: Cambridge University Press).

Shiller, R. J., 1981, "Do Stock Prices Move Too Much to Be Justified by Subsequent Changes in Dividends?" *American Economic Review*, 71: 421–35.

Shiller, R. J., 2003, *The New Financial Order: Risk in the 21st Century* (Princeton, NJ: Princeton University Press).

Siddique, Shahid Hasan, 1994, *Islamic Banking* (Karachi, Pakistan: Royal Book Co.).

Simons, H., 1948, *Economic Policy for a Free Society* (Chicago: University of Chicago Press).

Skaife, Hollis Ashbaugh, Daniel W. Collins, and Ryan LaFond, 2004, "Corporate Governance and the Cost of Equity Capital." Available at SSRN: http://ssm. com/abstract=639681.

Smith, Adam, 1776/1976. *An Inquiry into the Nature and Causes of the Wealth of Nations*. Edited in two volumes by W. B. Todd. See Vol. 2 of the *Glasgow Edition of the Works and Correspondence of Adam Smith* (Oxford: Clarendon Press).

Solow, Robert M., 1974, "Intergenerational Equity and Exhaustible Resources," *The Review of Economic Studies*, Vol. 41, Symposium on the Economics of Exhaustible Resources, p. 41.

Sourd, Véronique Le, 2010, "The Impact of Constraints on Short Sales and on Borrowing on the Efficiency of the Market Portfolio," July, www.edhec-risk. com/research_news/choice/RISKReview.2010-03-16.3815.

Stiglitz, J., 1988, "Money, Credit and Business Fluctuations," *Economic Record*, 64(187): 307–22.

Stiglitz, J., 1989, "Financial Markets and Development," *Oxford Review of Economic Policy*, 5(4).

Stiglitz, J. and A. Weiss, 1981, "Credit Rationing in Markets with Imperfect Information," *American Economic Review*, 71(3): 333–421.

Summers, L., 1986, "Does the Stock Market Rationally Reflect Fundamental Values?" *Journal of Finance*, 41: 591–601.

Sundararajan, V., 2004, "Risk Measurement, Risk Management, and Disclosure in Islamic Finance," Seminar on Comparative Supervision of Islamic and Conventional Finance, December 7–8, Beirut, Lebanon.

Sundararajan, V., 2006, "Islamic Financial Architecture and Infrastructure: Key Issues," 2nd International Research Conference on Islamic Banking—Risk Management, Regulation, and Supervision, Kuala Lumpur, February 7–8.

Sundararajan, V. and Luca Errico, 2002, "Islamic Financial Institutions and Products in the Global Financial System; Key Issues in Risk Management and Challenges Ahead," IMF Working Paper No. WP/02/192 (International Monetary Fund), November.

Tadesse, S., 2002, "Financial Architecture and Economic Performance: International Evidence," *Journal of Financial Intermediation*, 11: 429–54.

Taj El-Din, S. E. I., 2002, "Towards an Islamic Model of Stock Market," *Journal of King Abdul-Aziz University: Islamic Economics*, 14: 3–29.

Temin, Peter, 1991, *Lessons from the Great Depression* (Cambridge, MA: MIT Press).

Thornton, H., 1802, *An Inquiry into the Nature and Effects of the Paper Credit of Great Britain*. F. Hayek (ed.) (New York: Rinehart, 1939).

Thurow, Lester, 1980, *The Zero-Sum Society: Distribution and the Possibilities for Economic Change* (New York: Basic Books).

Tobin, J., 1984, "On the Efficiency of the Financial System," *Lloyds Bank Review*, 153: 15.

Townsend, R. M., 1994, "Risk and Insurance in Village India," *Econometrica*, 62: 539–91.

Triffin, R., 1960, *Gold and the Dollar Crisis: The Future of Convertibility* (New Haven, CT: Yale University Press).

Udovitch, A. L., 1962, *At the Origins of the Western Commenda: Islam, Israel, Byzantium?*, pp. 198–207.

Udovitch, A. L., 1967, "Credit as a Means of Investment in Medieval Islamic Trade," *Journal of the American Oriental Society*, 87(3) (July–September): 260–4.

Udovitch, A. L., 1970a, "Commercial Techniques in Early Medieval Islamic Trade," in D. Richards (ed.), *Islam and the Trade of Asia*, pp. 37–62.

Udovitch, A. L., 1970b, *Partnership and Profit in Medieval Islam* (Princeton, NJ: Princeton University Press).

Udovitch, Abraham L., 1981, "Bankers without Banks: Commerce, Banking and Society in the Islamic World of Middle Ages," Princeton Near East Paper No. 30 (Princeton, NJ: Princeton University Press).

Ul-Haque, Nadeem (2002), "On the Development of Financial Markets in Developing Economies," Republic commemoration lecture delivered on May 25, 2000 at the Center for Banking Studies, Sri Lanka.

Ul-Haque, Nadeem and Abbas Mirakhor, 1987, "Optimal Profit-Sharing Contracts and Investment in an Interest-Free Economy," in Mohsin Khan and Abbas Mirakhor (eds.), *Theoretical Studies in Islamic Banking* (Houston, TX: Institute for Research and Islamic Studies).

Ul-Haque, N. and A. Mirakhor, 1999, "The Design of Instruments for Government Finance in an Islamic Economy," *Islamic Economic Studies*, 6(2).

Usmani, Taqi, 1999, *An Introduction to Islamic Finance* (Karachi, Pakistan: Idaratul Ma'arif).

Uttamchandani, Mahesh, 2010, "'No Way Out': The Lack of Efficient Insolvency Regimes in the MENA Region," MENA Flagship, The World Bank, June.

Van Greuning, Hennie and Zamir Iqbal, 2006, "Banking and the Risk Environment," in S. Archer and R. A. Karim (eds.), *Islamic Finance: Regulatory Challenges* (Singapore: John Wiley & Sons).

Van Greuning, Hennie and Sonja Brajovic Bratanovic, 2003, *Analyzing and Managing Banking Risk: A Framework for Assessing Corporate Governance and Financial Risk*, 2nd ed. (Washington, DC: The World Bank).

Visser, Wayne A. M. and Alastair McIntosh, 1998, "A Short Review of the Historical Critique of Usury," *Accounting, Business & Financial History*, 8(2) (July): 175–89.

Vogel, F. E. and Samuel L. Hayes, 1998, *Islamic Law and Finance: Religion, Risk and Return* (Cambridge, MA: Kluwer Law International).

Wagner, Wolf, 2010, "Diversification at Financial Institutions and Systematic Crises," *Journal of Financial Intermediation*, 19(3): 373–86.

Warde, I., 2000, *Islamic Finance in the Global Economy* (Edinburgh: Edinburgh University Press).

Weber, Max, 2003, *The History of Commercial Partnerships in the Middle Ages.* Lutz Kaelber (transl. and intro.). (Rowman & Littlefield Publishers Inc.). The original title of the German edition was *Handelsgesellschaften im Mittelalter*, and was first published in 1889.

Whitehead, Charles K., 2009, "The Evolution of Debt: Covenants, the Credit Market, and Corporate Governance," *Journal of Corporation Law*, 34(3) (August 11): 641.

Wicksell, K., 1898, *Interest and Prices.* R. F. Kahn (transl.). (London: Macmillan, 1936; reprinted New York: A. M. Kelley, 1965).

World Bank, 2001, *Finance for Growth, Policy Choices in a Volatile World* (Washington, DC: Oxford University Press and The World Bank).

Yudistira, D., 2004, "Efficiency in Islamic Banking: An Empirical Analysis of Eighteen Banks," *Islamic Economic Studies*, 12(1) (August).

Index

A

ajar, xix
akhlaq, xix
akl amwal alnas bi al-batil, xix
al-adl, xix, 207
al-amal, xix
al-bay', xix, 50, 51
al-ihsan, xix
al-khiyar, khiyar, xix
allocation, 42, 53, 71, 73, 74, 95, 96, 109,
   120, 134, 135, 158, 161, 172, 174, 182,
   190, 203, 206
al-mal, xix, 207
al-Mo'meneen, xix
amanah, xix, 99–100, 102, 166, 169, 208
aqidah, xix
asset, xx, 4, 5, 6, 7, 8, 9, 11, 12, 13, 15–16,
   17, 18, 20, 23, 26, 28, 32, 33, 36, 37, 44,
   53, 61, 63, 64, 65, 71, 72, 74, 78, 80, 81,
   82, 84, 85, 89, 93, 97, 98, 100, 102, 103,
   104, 105, 106, 107, 108, 109, 113, 120,
   122, 124–130, 133–156, 159, 160, 167,
   168, 170–173, 174, 175, 202, 237, 239,
   251, 252, 253
asset–liability, x, 5, 28, 44, 85, 89, 102,
   104–105, 107, 202, 250
asset-linked, 108–109, 124–130, 136, 137,
   156n2, 170–175, 251
asymmetric, xx, 65, 66, 85, 86, 161, 174,
   198, 202, 204
asymmetry, 57, 79, 123, 135, 137,
   208, 216
awqaf, xix, xxiv, 195

B

bailouts, 10, 28n3
bai' bithamin ajil (BBA), xix
banking, x, xi, xii, xiv, 4–8, 9, 10, 11, 12,
   15, 18, 19–20, 21, 22, 23, 26, 31, 32, 34,
   59, 60, 65, 66, 86, 88, 89, 90, 98–101,
   113, 115, 130, 164, 166, 168, 174, 184,
   186, 236, 240, 247, 249
bankruptcy, 5, 7, 12, 15, 21, 88, 219
banks, x, xi, xiii, xiv, 4, 5, 6, 7, 9, 10, 12,
   14, 15, 16, 17, 18, 20, 21, 22, 23, 27,
   31, 32, 34, 41, 42, 43, 44, 49, 60, 61, 62,
   66, 85, 95, 100, 102, 103–109, 112, 113,
   115, 117, 122, 124, 127, 131, 132, 142,
   152, 154, 157, 159, 161–166, 172, 173,
   174, 175, 176, 177, 183, 184, 185, 186,
   187, 202, 219, 225, 226, 234, 237, 238,
   240, 244, 249
barakah, xix
bashar, xix, xxi
bay' al-arabun, xix
bay' al-dayn, xix
bay' al-istisna', xix
bay' al-muajjil, xix
bay' al-salam (also *salaf)*, xix, 157, 169
bay' xix,
benchmark, 133, 143–144, 146, 170, 209
borrowing, 14, 17, 19, 23, 28, 33, 35, 58,
   78, 118, 119, 139, 141, 142, 165, 177,
   190, 241, 250, 261, 274
bubbles, 4, 8, 11, 12, 16, 18, 23, 26, 36,
   37, 42, 44, 90, 124, 131, 150, 152, 154,
   155, 248

C

capital, ix, x, xiii, xiv, xv, xxii, 5, 6, 7, 8, 9,
   10, 11, 12, 14, 19, 24, 25, 26, 27, 32, 33,
   34, 35, 36, 37, 41, 43, 61, 62, 63, 65, 69,
   80, 81, 82, 85, 87, 88, 89, 90, 91, 92, 95,
   96, 97, 98, 99, 101, 103, 105, 108, 109,
   113, 115, 116, 117, 118, 119, 121, 122,
   123, 124, 125, 126, 127, 129, 130, 131,
   132, 133, 134, 135, 138, 139, 140, 142,
   147, 153, 154, 156, 159, 160, 161, 162,
   164, 165, 166, 167, 168, 169, 170, 171,
   172, 174, 175, 176, 177n9, 181, 186,

187, 189, 190, 192, 197, 201, 204, 205, 217, 219, 221, 225, 235, 236, 239, 240, 241, 242, 244, 245, 247, 248, 250, 251, 254, 255

CAPM, 64, 80, 138, 139, 140, 141, 142, 143, 147, 150, 154, 155, 252

central, xiv, 4, 5, 6, 10, 11, 12, 13, 15, 17, 18, 20, 22, 23, 24, 27, 31, 36, 38, 42, 44, 50, 52, 55, 63, 64, 83, 92, 111, 112, 113, 115, 124, 131, 147, 154, 159, 173, 182, 191, 192, 196, 198, 202, 249, 250

commenda, 49, 58

competition, xiv, 29, 32, 34, 39, 41, 51, 62, 69, 105, 170, 175, 184, 185, 187, 233, 234, 254

consumption, xv, 11, 24, 33, 35, 39, 40, 42, 51, 57, 70, 71, 75–83, 93n7, 103, 138, 144, 145, 146, 160, 182, 191, 192, 195, 197, 199, 210, 249, 253, 256

contract, xix, xxi, xxii, xxiii, xxiv, 51, 54, 55, 65, 70, 71, 84, 86, 87, 92, 98, 99, 100, 101, 102, 110, 111, 121, 128, 136, 137, 142, 167, 184, 185, 188, 191, 202, 203, 208, 209, 210, 216, 244

contractual, 49, 54, 55, 56, 70, 73, 86, 97, 106, 129, 136, 161, 168, 202, 207, 208, 216, 218, 231

conventional, ix, x, xiii, xiv, xv, xx, 3, 4–8, 26, 27, 28, 37, 43, 44, 50, 59, 60, 61, 62, 63, 64, 65, 66, 67, 70, 71, 72, 82, 83, 85, 86, 88, 89, 90, 92, 98, 100, 103, 104, 106, 107, 108, 110, 111, 112, 113, 115, 116, 118, 123, 125, 127, 128, 130, 131, 133, 137, 139, 141, 143, 147, 152, 154, 156, 166, 168, 169, 170, 171, 172, 173, 174, 175, 176, 181, 182, 184, 186, 191, 192, 193, 194, 195, 196, 215, 222, 225, 226, 232, 238, 242, 243, 244, 247, 248, 249, 250, 251, 252, 253, 254, 255

corporate, xii, 31, 33, 37, 44, 49, 53, 61, 64, 81, 108, 114, 116, 120, 126, 127, 143, 160, 161, 162, 167, 168, 169, 172, 174, 204, 205, 215, 219, 233, 235, 236, 243, 248

costs, x, xiii, 23, 34, 51, 56, 59, 65, 71, 78, 81, 82, 89, 92, 93, 95, 96, 100, 104, 107, 110, 115, 116, 121, 122, 131, 132, 137, 138, 141, 151, 162, 170, 175, 185, 189, 194, 198, 209, 210, 213, 218, 235, 238, 239, 253

credit, ix, xi, xv, 3, 4, 6, 7, 8, 9, 11, 12, 13, 14, 15, 16, 17, 20, 21, 23, 24, 25, 26, 27, 32, 33, 36, 37, 41, 42, 43, 58, 66, 67, 69, 85, 89, 90, 92, 103, 106, 109, 115, 120, 122, 123, 125, 127, 128, 129, 131, 143, 154, 155, 156, 157, 159, 162, 167, 168, 175, 181, 183, 184, 185, 188, 189, 190, 193, 194, 195, 197, 202, 204, 213, 214, 219, 220, 221, 232, 233, 234, 240, 247, 249, 250

crisis, crises, ix, 3–24, 25, 26, 27, 31, 35, 42, 43, 67, 86, 88, 95, 125, 159, 162, 201, 202, 215, 221, 222, 247, 251, 252

D

dayn, xix

debt, ix, x, xi, xii, xiii, xiv, xix, 3, 4, 7, 8, 9, 17, 19, 25, 26, 27, 30, 32, 33, 35, 36, 37, 40, 41, 42, 44, 49, 50, 51, 57, 58, 59, 61, 65, 66, 67, 70, 71, 83, 84, 85, 86, 87, 88, 91, 92, 98, 100, 104, 105, 107, 108, 109, 112, 113, 115, 116, 117, 118, 119, 120, 122, 127, 128, 130, 131, 132, 133, 137, 139, 142, 145, 154, 156, 157n7, 160, 167, 170, 171, 173, 176, 181, 183, 190, 196, 197, 198, 199, 201, 202, 213, 219, 220, 237, 239, 240, 241, 244, 248, 249, 250, 251, 253, 254, 255, 256

default, 3, 6, 8, 9, 17, 18, 19, 29, 32, 37, 73, 87, 89, 106, 111, 128, 143, 176, 177, 185, 194, 248, 250, 255

demand, xiii, 5, 7, 12, 14, 15, 16, 17, 23, 24, 28, 29, 36, 40, 41, 42, 43, 60, 61, 62, 65, 69, 87, 93, 100, 101, 102, 112, 121, 124, 132, 133, 154, 155, 156, 157, 159, 160, 165, 166, 169, 175, 184, 185, 189, 193, 217, 225, 233, 234, 254

depositors, 5, 7, 8, 9, 15, 20, 28, 29, 34, 89, 101, 102, 103, 104, 106, 107, 166, 167, 168, 174, 175, 238, 249, 250

deposits, x, xi, xiv, 3, 4, 5, 6, 7, 9, 10, 12, 15, 28, 29, 30, 32, 34, 42, 66, 85, 89, 91, 99, 100, 101, 102, 103, 104, 107, 115, 159, 162, 166, 169, 175, 177, 197, 202, 232, 239, 248, 249, 250

depression, ix, 5, 7, 9, 10, 12, 14, 15, 17, 18, 20, 21, 24, 31

derivatives, ix, x, xii, 7, 32, 35, 36, 40, 42, 44, 72, 76, 86, 90, 93, 109, 110, 111, 124, 125, 183, 236, 247 developed, developing, xiv, xv, 10, 11, 13, 19, 25, 27, 29, 40, 42, 44, 61, 62, 63, 64, 69, 70, 82, 90, 91, 95, 109, 113, 115, 117, 121, 122, 123, 124, 130, 134, 139, 165, 167, 173, 176, 181, 184, 189, 195, 196, 198, 199, 202, 212, 215, 220, 221, 223, 226, 231, 237, 238, 239, 240, 243, 245, 247, 250, 253, 255, 256, 257

development, 10, 16, 24, 32, 50, 52, 53, 57, 60, 61, 62, 63, 64, 65, 68, 71, 83, 92, 95, 96, 111, 113, 116, 118, 120, 121, 125, 131, 132, 152, 160, 161, 165, 166, 168, 171, 172, 173, 174, 175, 176, 181, 182, 183, 184, 185, 186, 187, 188, 189, 191, 192, 193, 194, 195, 197, 199, 203, 204, 205, 212, 213, 214, 215, 221, 222, 223, 225, 226, 231, 232, 235, 236, 241, 244, 249, 250, 251, 253, 254, 255, 257, 259, 260, 261, 262, 263, 264, 265, 267, 268, 269, 271, 272, 273, 274, 275

dharoora, xix

distortions, 4, 5, 23, 32, 35, 44, 131, 133, 148, 154, 161, 163, 174, 220, 248

distribution, 32, 33, 38, 40, 44, 49, 51, 79, 85, 92, 112, 184, 188, 197, 201, 203, 206, 210, 237, 248, 249, 253

diversification, 133

diversified, 169

E

economic, ix, xi, xii, xiii, xv, xxii, 3, 4, 5, 6, 7, 8, 10, 11, 12, 14, 15, 16, 17, 18, 19, 20, 21, 22, 23, 24, 25, 26, 27, 28, 30, 31, 32, 33, 35, 37, 39, 40, 42, 43, 44, 49, 50, 51, 52, 57, 58, 60, 67, 69, 71, 72, 79, 83, 84, 86, 87, 90, 91, 95, 96, 97, 98, 101, 102, 108, 109, 110, 112, 116, 117, 122, 123, 125, 130, 135, 136, 137, 140, 142, 144, 147, 152, 155, 156, 159, 160, 161, 162, 165, 166, 168, 170, 172, 173, 174, 175, 176, 181, 182, 183, 184, 185, 187, 188, 189, 190, 191, 192, 193, 195, 196, 197, 198, 199, 201, 202, 203, 206, 207, 208, 210, 211, 212, 213, 215, 216, 217, 222, 223, 226, 227, 231, 232, 234, 237, 238, 239, 244, 245, 248, 252, 253, 254, 255, 256, 257

economic development, 24, 50, 57, 60, 95, 96, 161, 168, 174, 181, 183, 184, 191, 192, 193, 203, 231

economic growth, xii, xiii, xxii, 3, 14, 17, 18, 20, 26, 27, 28, 31, 32, 35, 39, 42, 43, 50, 67, 71, 90, 91, 95, 110, 117, 130, 147, 160, 161, 162, 165, 166, 174, 175, 181, 182, 188, 190, 195, 197, 198, 199, 231, 232, 248, 254, 255, 256

economics, 60, 63, 65, 66, 122, 170, 181, 191, 192, 202, 206, 215, 224, 226, 227, 240

economy, x, xii, xiii, xiv, 4, 5, 6, 8, 10, 11, 13, 16, 19, 23, 24, 25, 26, 29, 30, 31, 32, 33, 35, 37, 39, 40, 41, 45, 51, 53, 63, 72, 73, 78, 79, 81, 85, 86, 88, 91, 93, 96, 100, 101, 104, 105, 113, 115, 116, 117, 120, 121, 123, 124, 131, 132, 133, 136, 138, 139, 142, 143, 147, 154, 155, 156, 158, 161, 164, 182, 201, 206, 211, 223, 232, 248, 249, 255, 257

efficiency, efficient, 29, 64, 77, 83, 84, 87, 90, 91, 95, 96, 97, 109, 113, 117, 120, 131, 134, 138, 139, 140, 148, 150, 166, 170, 175, 176, 187, 190, 195, 203, 223, 227, 236, 241, 242, 244, 247, 251, 255, 256

employment, xiii, xiv, 3, 6, 16, 22, 23, 24, 27, 30, 49, 90, 91, 92, 106, 116, 117, 197, 233, 237, 245, 253

enforcement, 34, 84, 90, 91, 116, 121, 122, 176, 184, 185, 188, 203, 204, 205, 222, 223, 231, 235, 239, 244, 245, 255, 257, 258

entrepreneurs, xiii, 7, 9, 36, 49, 59, 84, 85, 88, 101, 104, 107, 113, 121, 160, 175, 181, 187, 196, 201, 204, 250, 254

equilibrium, 35, 40, 72, 80, 93, 117, 133, 137, 138, 142, 149, 155, 157

equities, 23, 36, 43, 57, 61, 65, 81, 84, 85, 88, 106, 108, 122, 133, 147, 152, 170, 174, 201, 225, 239, 253

equity, x, xiii, xiv, xv, 3, 4, 7, 19, 22, 27, 31, 32, 33, 34, 35, 38, 42, 44, 49, 50, 52, 57, 61, 65, 66, 67, 71, 81, 82, 83, 84, 85, 88, 89, 90, 91, 92, 93, 98, 99, 101, 105, 107, 108, 113, 115, 116, 117, 118, 120, 121, 122, 124, 129, 131, 132, 133, 136, 137, 144, 145, 146, 147, 152, 153, 154, 155, 156, 157, 159, 160, 162, 167, 168, 169, 170, 171, 172, 176, 181, 183, 189, 190, 191, 196, 197, 199, 201, 202, 204, 219, 222, 223, 235, 236, 237, 238, 239, 248, 249, 250, 251, 253, 254, 256, 257

expansion, 6, 7, 10, 11, 12, 14–15, 17, 18,
21, 23, 24, 25, 26, 28, 31, 35, 36, 37, 41,
43, 59, 60, 82, 88, 89, 91, 92, 162, 247,
248, 249

F
fadl, xx
faqih (pl. *fuqaha'*), xx
fatwa, xx
finance, 20, 36, 49–68, 69–93, 115–132,
181–199, 225–245, 256, 258
financial crisis, 8
financial engineering, 236
financialization, 21, 31–44, 45, 248
financing, 88, 119, 153, 169
fiqh, xx, 58, 110, 266
fiqhi, xx
firms, 6, 8, 9, 11, 12, 20, 22, 25, 27, 35, 56,
64, 69, 90, 108, 110, 118, 120, 121, 124,
161, 165, 172, 174, 175, 184, 187, 188,
189, 198, 201, 204, 209, 218, 219, 221,
240, 254

G
GDP, xii, 9, 19, 31, 35, 36, 37, 80, 88, 184,
191, 193, 232, 234, 248
ghabun, xx
gharar, xx, 110, 220
global, 19, 31, 36, 37, 41, 57, 58, 61,
65, 66, 67, 82, 88, 105, 132, 212, 215,
221, 247
globalization, 39, 52, 95, 177, 215, 226, 247
governance, 33, 52, 56, 61, 66, 97, 115,
119, 122, 174, 176, 201, 202, 203, 205,
207, 209, 211, 212, 213, 215, 216, 217,
218, 219, 221, 222, 223, 224, 226, 235,
236, 239, 241, 242, 243, 255, 257
government, x, xi, xiii, 3, 4, 5, 7, 9, 10, 11,
13, 16, 19, 20, 21, 27, 28, 29, 30, 31, 34,
35, 43, 44, 62, 88, 92, 104, 111, 113,
116, 117, 118, 119, 120, 121, 122, 130,
132, 143, 160, 173, 183, 190, 198, 199,
206, 235, 239, 241, 243, 245, 248, 249,
250, 256, 257
growth, xii, xiii, xiv, xxii, xxiii, 3, 14, 17,
18, 20, 21, 22, 23, 24, 26, 27, 28, 31,
32, 35, 36, 37, 39, 40, 42, 43, 44, 50,
58, 59, 60, 61, 62, 65, 67, 70, 71, 76,
77, 78, 79, 80, 81, 86, 90, 91, 92, 95,
96, 110, 116, 117, 129, 130, 133, 144,

145, 146, 147, 157, 158, 160, 161, 162,
165, 166, 174, 175, 177, 181, 182, 185,
186, 187, 188, 189, 190, 191, 192, 195,
196, 197, 198, 199, 215, 223, 231, 232,
233, 237, 248, 249, 250, 253, 254, 255,
256, 257

H
hadia, hibah, xx
hadith (pl. *ahadith*), xx, xxi
hajj, umra, xx
hajr, xx
haram, xx
hawala, xx, 58
hifz al-mal, xx
hila (pl. *hiyal*), xx

I
'ibada (pl. *ibadat*), xx
ijarah, xx, 103, 124, 126, 167, 170, 177,
209, 225
ijarah sukuk, xx
ijarah wa "qtinah", xxi
ijma, xxi
ijtihad, xxi, 209
ikrah, xxi
iman, xxi
imperfections, 100, 103, 138, 168, 172,
174, 190
incentive, 33, 50, 59, 66, 85, 92, 96, 97,
121, 137, 163, 164, 182, 186, 194, 201,
202, 206, 236, 241, 253
income, xv, 6, 9, 14, 23, 32, 33, 35, 36, 37,
38, 39, 40, 44, 45, 50, 51, 52, 57, 61, 63,
73, 75, 77, 78, 79, 80, 81, 82, 84, 91, 92,
103, 112, 122, 125, 128, 146, 156, 164,
168, 170, 182, 186, 188, 191, 193, 196,
197, 198, 203, 206, 210, 211, 212, 224,
237, 248, 249, 253, 255, 256
index, 18, 64, 120, 150, 152, 154, 185, 193,
211, 212, 213, 214, 221, 226, 227, 228,
229, 230, 231, 232, 233
individuals, 14, 30, 37, 49, 52, 53, 54, 55,
56, 63, 66, 70, 71, 77, 78, 79, 81, 82, 84,
110, 116, 118, 119, 124, 127, 136, 145,
162, 167, 173, 182, 183, 186, 188, 190,
192, 194, 199, 203, 207, 216, 217, 218,
222, 245, 253, 256, 258
inflation, xi, 4, 5, 6, 11, 14, 15, 16, 17, 18,
19, 23, 25, 28

information, 36, 51, 57, 64, 65, 66, 75, 79, 81, 85, 86, 87, 95, 96, 97, 103, 109, 110, 114, 121, 122, 123, 132, 135, 136, 137, 138, 145, 148, 149, 150, 151, 157, 159, 161, 162, 170, 172, 174, 176, 182, 184, 185, 186, 189, 190, 193, 196, 198, 202, 204, 208, 209, 210, 216, 219, 220, 221, 223, 231, 233, 234, 239, 240, 241, 243, 252, 257

informational, 57, 65, 67, 85, 86, 87, 90, 91, 115, 119, 121, 122, 161, 194, 201, 202, 203, 220, 239, 241

insan, xxi

insolvency, 5, 213, 236, 243, 244

instability, x, xiii, 3, 4, 6, 8, 13, 17, 18, 20, 21, 22, 23, 24, 25, 26, 28, 33, 36, 41, 43, 44, 66, 67, 85, 86, 88, 104, 110, 116, 118, 131, 132, 152, 156, 160, 202, 253, 254

institutional, 7, 29, 32, 33, 36, 41, 65, 66, 82, 116, 121, 123, 125, 126, 127, 131, 133, 161, 162, 167, 173, 174, 183, 184, 187, 195, 199, 210, 212, 213, 215, 218, 226, 243, 244, 255, 257

institutions, ix, x, 4, 5, 7, 10, 14, 19, 22, 30, 31, 32, 33, 34, 35, 39, 41, 44, 49, 52, 54, 55, 56, 57, 58, 60, 61, 62, 67, 82, 85, 92, 96, 97, 99, 103, 104, 105, 108, 112, 115, 116, 122, 123, 142, 155, 162, 164, 166, 172, 174, 176, 177, 181, 183, 184, 185, 186, 187, 190, 194, 195, 197, 198, 199, 201, 202, 203, 204, 205, 206, 207, 209, 211, 212, 213, 214, 215, 217, 219, 220, 221, 222, 223, 225, 226, 231, 232, 235, 238, 239, 240, 241, 242, 243, 244, 245, 247, 248, 249, 250, 252, 255, 256, 257

instruments, xi, xv, 26, 31, 32, 33, 37, 43, 52, 58, 61, 63, 65, 67, 68, 71, 72, 83, 90, 91, 92, 100, 101, 102, 103, 107, 108, 109, 110, 111, 112, 113, 117, 120, 121, 122, 130, 132, 135, 139, 142, 151, 152, 156, 157, 159, 166, 167, 168, 169, 172, 173, 176, 182, 183, 187, 188, 195, 198, 199, 222, 236, 237, 238, 239, 242, 243, 247, 248, 253

insurance, xxiii, 5, 6, 20, 27, 28, 32, 34, 44, 57, 62, 69, 70, 71, 78, 79, 81, 82, 90, 92, 96, 120, 127, 145, 151, 159, 162, 163, 166, 215, 225, 232, 238, 243, 249

interest, ix, xi, xii, xiv, xv, 3, 4, 5, 6, 11, 12, 13, 14, 15, 16, 17, 18, 20, 22, 23, 24, 25, 26, 27, 28, 29, 30, 31, 33, 34, 36, 37, 50, 51, 56, 57, 58, 59, 60, 61, 62, 63, 65, 66, 67, 70, 71, 83, 84, 85, 86, 87, 88, 89, 93, 98, 102, 103, 105, 106, 108, 109, 112, 113, 115, 116, 120, 123, 127, 128, 131, 132, 133, 136, 137, 138, 139, 141, 142, 144, 145, 146, 147, 152, 153, 154, 155, 156, 157, 163, 164, 171, 172, 173, 174, 185, 190, 192, 193, 194, 195, 196, 201, 202, 225, 231, 232, 233, 234, 237, 247, 248, 249, 252, 253

intermediary, intermediaries, xi, xiv, 19, 32, 35, 36, 59, 60, 62, 65, 97, 99, 100, 101, 104, 106, 112, 115, 122, 123, 124, 159–177, 198, 219, 238, 249, 251, 254

intermediation, x, 10, 11, 12, 21, 32, 40, 61, 81, 90, 95, 96, 97, 98, 100, 101, 103, 104, 105, 106, 107, 112, 115, 152, 156, 159, 160, 163, 165, 166, 168, 171, 173, 174, 175, 176, 177, 181, 182, 183, 187, 197, 198, 225, 236, 238, 243, 247, 249, 250, 251, 254, 255, 256

international, ix, 3, 4, 10, 18, 19, 24, 25, 33, 41, 42, 44, 55, 60, 69, 78, 80, 81, 82, 92, 118, 119, 120, 121, 132, 153, 154, 185, 211, 212, 226, 231, 235, 244, 248, 249

investment, investments, x, xi, xiii, xiv, xx, 8, 10, 14, 20, 21, 24, 28, 30, 32, 33, 35, 36, 40, 42, 60, 61, 81, 82, , 84, 87, 89, 90, 91, 93, 97, 101, 102, 103, 104, 105, 106, 107, 109, 113, 115, 116, 117, 120, 123, 124, 129, 130, 131, 132, 134, 137, 142, 143, 147, 155, 157, 158, 159, 160, 163, 164, 165, 167, 168, 172, 173, 174, 175, 181, 182, 183, 197, 232, 234, 238, 239, 249, 250, 254

investor, investors, x, xi, xii, xiv, xx, 7, 10, 11, 12, 15, 27, 29, 32, 33, 36, 41, 49, 56, 62, 63, 66, 70, 78, 80, 85, 87, 92, 97, 98, 99, 101, 102, 103, 104, 105, 107, 111, 116, 121, 125, 126, 127, 128, 129, 130, 131, 132, 133, 134, 135, 136, 137, 138, 139, 140, 141, 142, 143, 145, 148, 149, 150, 152, 157, 163, 167, 168, 170, 173, 174, 175, 176, 182, 197, 213, 214, 215, 218, 219, 221, 234, 235, 237, 239, 241, 242, 244, 247, 249, 250, 251, 252, 253

Islam, xiv, xv, xx, xxiii, 27, 50, 52, 53, 54,
55, 56, 57, 62, 64, 70, 83, 87, 106, 110,
113, 122, 130, 131, 133, 136, 142, 155,
166, 168, 182, 191, 192, 193, 195, 202,
203, 206, 207, 208, 209, 210, 212, 215,
216, 217, 218, 219, 222, 224, 226, 227,
236, 237, 239, 241, 245, 252
israf, xxi, 210
istihsan, xxi
istisna' (short form for *bay' al-istisna'*), xxi,
103, 124, 167, 170, 237
itlaf, xxi, 210
itraf, xxi, 210

J
jo'alah, xxi
justice, 27, 57, 108, 172, 188, 189, 190,
191, 192, 196, 198, 199, 207, 208, 210,
212, 217, 218, 227, 256

K
kanz (pl. *konooz*), xxi
khalifa, xxi
khawf, xxi
khilafah, xxi
khisarah, xxi
khums, xxi, 211
kifala, 23, 100

L
law, 20, 22, 23, 54–55, 56, 57, 59, 123, 176,
188, 203, 204, 207, 209, 213, 218, 222,
223, 240, 241, 242, 243, 255, 257
legal, xiv, 55, 56, 57, 58, 65, 66, 96, 97, 98,
99, 119, 122, 123, 150, 161, 166, 176,
184, 186, 187, 203, 204–205, 208, 211,
212, 213, 214, 216, 236, 239, 240, 241,
242, 243, 244, 255
lending, x, 14, 28, 32, 58, 85, 142, 164,
177, 185, 190, 193, 202, 219, 233, 234
leverage, xii, xiii, 7, 9, 19, 21, 27, 37,
86, 90, 117, 122, 132, 142, 151, 165,
240, 252
liabilities, xii, 6, 8, 9, 21, 29, 35, 41, 53,
86, 89, 99, 101, 102, 103, 104, 107, 112,
159, 160, 166, 167, 168, 169, 172, 175
liquidity, x, 3, 5, 6, 8, 9, 10, 12, 15, 17, 22,
23, 28, 32, 33, 36, 37, 62, 75, 81, 85, 89,
90, 91, 104, 107, 109, 111, 112, 113,
116, 119, 120, 122, 124, 131, 135, 151,

154, 162, 164, 170, 172, 173, 175, 202,
235, 238, 239, 242, 243, 244
loans, x, xi, 5, 6, 9, 11, 12, 14, 15, 16, 20,
21, 24, 30, 32, 42, 43, 44, 58, 66, 81, 82,
89, 102, 104, 105, 107, 123, 136, 142,
154, 155, 159, 175, 177, 184, 194, 196,
225, 233, 234, 256

M
ma'aad, xxi
macroeconomic, 35, 36, 96, 142, 204,
226, 255
madhahib, xxi
manafaah al-ikhtiyarat, xxi
management, 11, 25, 28, 29, 39, 44, 49,
50, 61, 63, 64, 66, 71, 83, 89, 97, 98–99,
102, 103, 107, 109, 111, 117, 119, 127,
129, 130, 143, 161, 162, 163, 165, 167,
168, 169, 170, 174, 175, 176, 177, 183,
190, 192, 195, 198, 199, 219, 225, 236,
238, 243, 244, 250, 254, 256
manfaa maal, manfa' ah, xxi
maqasid al-Shari'ah, xxi
market, xiv, xv, 6, 7, 8, 9, 10, 11, 12, 13,
14, 15, 17, 18, 20, 24, 26, 28, 29, 30, 32,
33, 34, 36, 37, 38, 39, 41, 42, 43, 45, 51,
53, 54, 61, 62, 63, 64, 65, 66, 70, 71, 72,
73, 74, 77, 78, 79, 80, 82, 84, 85, 86,
90, 91, 92–93, 95, 96, 97–98, 108–113,
114, 115–132, 133, 135, 137, 138, 139,
140, 141, 142, 143, 144, 145, 146, 147,
148–155, 156, 157, 159–177, 182, 184,
185, 189, 190, 192, 193, 194, 202, 204,
205, 206, 209–210, 212, 222, 223, 225,
233, 235, 236, 237, 238–241, 243, 244,
247, 250, 251, 252, 253–254, 257
maslahah, x, 157
MENA, 185, 213–214, 220, 221, 223, 232,
233, 234, 235, 257
microfinance, 191–196
mithaq, xxii
monetary, 12, 13, 15, 16, 17, 18, 19, 21, 22,
23, 24, 25, 26, 28, 31, 34, 36, 41, 44, 54,
118, 119, 124, 131, 132, 136, 153, 164,
236, 241, 243, 244, 250
money, x, xi, xii, xiv, 4, 5, 6, 10, 11, 12, 13,
14, 15, 16, 17, 20, 21, 23, 27, 28, 29, 30,
31, 32, 34, 44, 51, 58, 62, 63, 73, 83, 84,
92, 95, 97, 99, 100, 102, 104, 111–113,
126, 132, 136, 139, 151, 155, 166, 172,

173, 176, 186, 188, 191, 209, 236, 239, 243, 244, 248, 249, 254

monitoring, 59, 65, 86, 89, 95, 96, 100, 106–107, 129, 130, 137, 157, 159, 161, 165, 166, 167, 174, 181, 194, 202, 215, 218, 219–222, 236, 238, 250

moral, x, 5, 11, 34, 44, 57, 66, 79, 85, 86, 87, 92, 104, 108, 161, 172, 174, 194, 202, 203, 208, 216, 217, 219, 221, 222, 223, 240, 245, 247, 249, 257

muamalat, xxii

mubaya'a, xxii

mudarabah, xxii, 58, 87, 92, 98–99, 101, 102, 103, 136, 157, 166, 167, 168, 169, 177, 237

mudarib, xxii, 98, 99, 101

muhtasib, xxii

murabahah, xxii, 103, 237

musharakah, xxii, 58, 98, 99, 103, 136, 157, 166, 167, 168, 237

musharakah mulk, xxii

musharakah mutanaqisah, xxii

musharakah 'aqd, xxii

Muslim, xiv, xv, 52, 54, 55, 57, 59–60, 61, 136, 142, 157, 185, 194, 199, 208, 209, 211, 212, 213, 214, 223, 226, 227, 231, 232, 243, 244, 247, 255, 256, 257

mysir, xxii

N

nafaqa, xxii

nafs, xxii

nisab, xxii

niyyah, xxii

O

OECD, 39, 61, 118, 185, 211, 212, 213

ownership, 10, 22, 49, 54, 90, 97, 118, 119, 125, 127, 128, 129, 131, 132, 170, 171, 184, 192, 205, 206, 207, 219, 240, 241, 242, 250, 251

P

policy, policies, x, 7, 12, 13, 16, 18, 20, 21, 22, 23, 24–25, 26, 28, 29, 31, 33, 34, 36, 40, 57, 65, 70, 82, 96, 118, 120, 122, 123, 124, 131, 164, 177, 185, 190, 198, 199, 212, 215, 231, 232, 235, 239–240, 241, 243, 245, 250, 256

poor, 5, 7, 10, 38, 50, 71, 78, 82, 85, 87, 88, 112, 118, 121, 173, 182, 183, 188, 190,

191, 193, 194, 195, 197, 198, 199, 206, 210, 233, 256

portfolio, porfolios, 11, 17, 28, 30, 61, 62, 64, 69, 70, 80, 81, 82, 90, 91, 103, 104, 107, 109, 111, 112, 113, 119, 124, 125, 127, 128, 129, 133–158, 167, 168, 170, 171, 174, 175, 176, 177, 235, 237, 247, 251, 252, 253, 255

poverty, 52, 88, 182, 188, 190, 193, 195, 196, 197, 198, 199, 210, 211, 256

pricing, x, 64, 69, 72, 74, 77, 78, 80, 83, 93, 127, 128, 129, 133, 137–144, 150, 151, 155–156, 157, 252, 255

private, xiii, 10, 19, 22, 26, 29, 30, 35, 44, 53, 54, 61, 83, 87, 88, 90, 93, 112, 118, 119, 121, 130, 131, 132, 150, 162, 167, 168, 173, 181, 183, 196, 203, 210, 220, 241, 248, 250

production, 7, 23, 33, 37, 39, 50, 51, 64, 70, 81, 84, 85, 87, 89, 90, 98, 116, 119, 131, 156, 193, 201, 203, 206, 241, 249, 250

profits, xxii, 4, 11, 12, 14, 15, 18, 19, 27, 30, 31, 32, 33, 34, 36, 38, 39, 40, 44, 52, 56, 63, 69, 88, 89, 90, 91, 98–99, 101–102, 106, 107, 108, 109, 113, 149, 150, 168, 171, 172, 173, 174, 192, 195, 218, 248, 249, 250

prohibited, 52, 70, 84, 86, 89, 115, 190, 209, 249, 252

property, 30, 40, 50, 51, 52–53, 54, 55, 56, 72, 74, 83, 84, 87, 89, 99, 116, 141, 176, 184, 186, 188, 191, 203, 206–207, 208, 210, 211, 215–216, 217, 218, 223, 249, 255, 257

public, 5, 10, 17, 19, 25, 35, 56, 58, 62, 82, 90, 108, 116, 118–119, 120, 122, 131, 132, 150, 154, 156, 181, 183, 189, 197, 215, 216, 217, 220, 232, 236, 239, 241, 250, 254

Q

qard, xxii

qard-ul-hassan, 194, 195, 196, 199, 256, 257

qimar, xxii

qist, xxii, 207

qiyas, xxii

Qur'an (also written as *al-Qur'an*), xxii, 28, 50, 51–52, 55–56, 57, 83, 84, 86, 88, 110, 152, 193, 202, 208, 209–210, 211, 217, 245, 249, 257, 258

R

rabb al-mal, xxiii

rahn, xxiii

rate, 3, 4, 9, 12, 13–14, 15, 17, 18, 20, 22, 23, 24, 25, 26, 27, 29, 30, 31, 33, 35, 36, 37, 40, 50, 59, 63, 65, 66, 76, 77, 79, 80, 83, 84, 85, 87, 88, 89, 90, 93, 106, 107, 109, 116, 119, 120, 124, 127, 133, 138–139, 141, 142, 143, 144, 146, 147, 151, 152, 155, 156, 173, 185, 201, 225, 241, 248, 252, 253, 254

recession, xi, 16, 17, 30, 33, 42, 44, 96, 116, 248

redistribution, 23, 39, 40, 51, 97, 109–110, 206, 210–211

regulations, 4, 8, 10, 19, 26, 34, 90, 92, 113, 123, 132, 159, 164, 181, 184, 186, 190, 203, 235, 240, 249

regulatory, 19, 22, 36, 37, 61, 96, 119, 122, 123, 124, 131, 132, 158, 159, 176, 177, 185, 218, 222, 236, 239, 240, 241, 245, 255

reserve, xi, 4, 9, 10, 15, 17, 21, 24, 25, 27, 28, 29, 30, 36, 41, 44, 59, 65, 66, 92, 101, 102, 103, 104, 105, 115, 166, 249

resources, 17, 21, 23, 28, 32, 37, 41, 42, 49, 53–54, 59, 70, 73, 82, 83–84, 85, 95, 97, 109, 113, 119, 121, 130, 131, 132, 136, 152, 156, 159, 160, 172, 174, 175, 182, 191, 192, 197, 202, 203, 207, 210, 211, 241, 250, 254

returns, 7, 11, 30, 36, 40, 56, 57, 63, 65, 66, 69, 84, 85, 88, 89, 93, 101, 104, 117, 119, 120, 122, 125, 129, 131, 134, 135, 137, 140, 141, 143, 144–145, 146, 147, 148, 149, 150, 151, 152, 155, 163, 171, 174, 201, 218, 250, 251

riba, xxiii, 51, 83, 98

ribh, xxiii

riskless, 63, 134, 135, 140, 143, 147, 253

risk–return, 64, 66, 85, 103, 104, 108, 113, 125, 126, 127, 129, 132, 135, 136, 137, 139, 143, 155, 167, 196, 201, 251

risks, x–xi, xii, xiii, 34, 50, 52, 57, 69, 70, 71, 72, 82, 85, 91, 95, 98, 104, 107, 109, 110, 111, 115, 117, 118, 119, 120, 124, 125, 128, 131, 135, 136, 142, 155, 160, 163, 164, 167, 174, 175, 176, 201, 234, 237, 239, 241, 249, 250

risk-sharing, xv, 27, 49–68, 71, 77, 80, 81, 84–85, 86, 87, 91, 92, 96, 98, 107, 108, 111, 115, 117, 118, 119, 120, 121, 132, 160, 166, 170, 174, 176, 177, 181, 196–198, 201–224, 226, 231, 235–238, 239, 241, 245, 248, 249, 250, 253, 255, 256, 257

risky, 5, 63, 69, 70, 72, 78, 84, 91, 103, 104, 107, 132, 134, 135, 140, 141, 143, 147, 157, 174–175

S

sadaqat, xxiii, 211

safih, xxiii

sarf, xxiii

sarrafs, xxiii

savings, 17, 21, 23, 28, 35, 36, 63, 89, 90, 95, 109, 111, 112, 115, 116, 131, 152, 154, 155, 156, 159, 160, 161, 172, 173, 174, 175, 182, 184, 195, 203, 249, 254, 255

sector, xii, 4, 8, 9, 10, 11, 12, 19, 21, 24, 27, 31, 32, 33, 34, 35–36, 38, 40, 43, 44, 62, 65, 67, 83, 86, 88, 92, 98, 105, 108, 110, 117, 118, 119, 121, 123, 129, 130, 131, 133, 150, 160, 166, 167, 169, 177, 181, 182, 183, 184, 185, 186, 187, 198, 215, 232, 233, 241, 242, 243, 247, 248, 250, 252, 255, 256

securities, 10, 15, 29, 32–33, 42, 43, 71, 72–74, 77, 78, 80, 91, 93, 104, 106, 108, 109, 110, 111, 118, 123, 124–130, 136, 137, 139, 141, 142, 143, 144, 151, 155, 156, 157, 160, 165, 167, 168, 170, 171, 172, 173, 174, 175, 219, 226, 235, 239, 241, 243, 244, 251, 252

securitization, 7, 15, 21, 29, 32, 35, 36, 43, 59, 61, 67, 125, 126, 127, 129, 170, 171, 244, 248, 250, 251

securitized, 32, 61, 98, 108, 109, 124–130, 136, 143, 160, 170, 173, 225, 250, 251, 254

share, 7, 10–11, 12, 15–16, 18, 25, 28, 30, 31, 32, 35, 38, 39, 40, 49, 62, 70, 71, 78, 87, 90, 101, 107, 115, 117, 118, 148, 149, 150, 152, 153, 154, 155, 156, 160, 167, 171, 211, 221, 233, 241, 248, 249, 250, 251, 254

shareholders, 5, 71, 85, 89, 91, 102, 116, 120, 123, 143, 151, 201, 219, 240, 250

Shari'ah, 56, 59, 60, 61, 62, 91, 98, 100, 106, 108, 110, 111, 113, 121, 122, 123, 136, 142, 156, 157, 168, 172, 173, 176, 177, 186, 195, 206, 207, 208, 209, 213, 216, 218, 222, 225, 226, 236, 238, 240, 241, 242, 243, 244, 247, 253, 255, 257

shirakah, xxiii, 99

social, 3–4, 21, 26, 27, 31, 32, 50, 52, 60, 71, 85, 86, 87, 118, 119, 120, 136, 182, 189, 190, 191–193, 195, 198–199, 201, 203, 206, 207, 208, 210, 212, 215, 216, 217, 218, 221, 227, 241, 243, 245, 255, 256, 257

society, 35, 53, 54, 57, 71, 87, 88, 110, 118, 120, 122, 136, 155, 181, 186, 187, 192, 193, 203, 206, 208, 210, 212, 215, 216, 217, 218, 222, 226, 227, 239, 245, 257, 258

speculation, 4, 5, 6, 7, 11, 14, 15, 16, 18, 19, 23, 25, 27, 32, 35, 36, 40, 63, 88, 90, 110, 116, 123, 124, 131, 142, 146, 148, 152, 153, 154, 156, 253, 254

speculative, 5, 7, 8, 9, 11, 12, 13, 14, 15, 18, 44, 63, 89, 90, 92, 110, 116, 123, 131, 136, 142, 150, 154, 155, 236, 248, 252, 253

stability, x, 3, 4, 12, 18, 20, 21, 22, 34, 92, 102, 104, 107, 116, 117, 119, 124, 131, 133, 152, 156, 164, 165, 170, 171, 174, 176, 177, 183, 187, 196, 249, 251, 254, 255

stable, 8, 27, 38, 61, 88, 90, 92, 95, 116, 131, 154, 155, 156, 160, 247, 254

stock, stocks, 7–12, 16, 18, 20, 23, 25, 28, 29, 30, 39, 52, 64, 69, 73, 79, 90, 91–93, 98, 108–109, 115–116, 117–124, 131–134, 145–156, 171–172, 176, 181, 240–242, 251, 253–254

structure, 3, 8, 23, 24, 28, 29, 40, 49, 50–57, 58, 64, 65, 67, 92, 101, 104, 112, 129, 131, 133, 145, 157, 161, 164, 168, 169, 173, 183, 184, 187, 192, 195, 199, 206, 210, 215, 218, 219, 222, 226, 236, 241, 244, 253, 257

sub-prime, 3, 8, 23, 25

suftaja, xxiii, 58

sukuk, xxiii, 61, 225, 226

sunnah, xxiii, 88, 152

surah, xxiii

system, 3–6, 8–9, 15, 17, 19, 20–30, 31–34, 36–37, 41–42, 44, 50, 52, 57–61, 63, 65, 66, 68–70, 86, 88–92, 95–100, 103–113, 115–118, 121, 123–125, 127, 130, 132–133, 135–139, 142, 151–152, 154–156, 159–161, 164–167, 170–177, 181, 187–188, 190–192, 195–196, 202–204, 206, 209, 212–215, 220, 222–223, 226–227, 231–232, 235, 238, 239, 240, 242–245, 247–258

T

tabdhir, xxiii

takaful, xxiii, 62, 70, 225

taqwa, xxiii

tawarruq, xxiii

tawhid, xxiii

taxpayers, 5, 21, 28, 31, 40

theory, 20, 36, 63, 64, 81, 226

tijaarah/tirajah, xxiii

transparency, ix, x, 33, 56, 66, 97, 209, 218, 219, 223, 231, 238, 241, 242, 244, 257

trust, 10, 51, 52, 54, 55, 56, 57, 58, 59, 61, 67, 86, 97, 99, 116, 121, 122, 181, 197, 202, 205, 206, 207, 209, 210, 215, 216, 217, 218, 220, 221, 222, 224, 239, 248

trustworthiness, 55, 122, 192, 209, 217, 223, 239, 257

U

unemployment, 10, 12, 22, 23, 24, 26, 28, 43, 69

urf, xxiii

V

volatility, 4, 19, 20, 21, 36, 44, 51, 129, 142, 144, 147, 152, 154, 156, 165, 171, 173, 248, 249, 251, 254

W

wadia, xxiii, 99–100, 102

wali, xxiv

waqf (pl. *awqaf*), xxiv

wa'd, xxiii

wealth, 5, 8, 11, 16, 21, 23, 26, 38, 39, 40, 41, 44, 45, 50, 52, 57, 75, 79, 84, 92, 112, 134, 136, 138, 168, 173, 191, 193, 203, 206, 207, 209, 210, 211, 248, 249

welfare, 21, 28, 51, 77, 80, 82, 83, 118, 191, 193, 249

wikalah, xxiv, 99, 102

Z

zakah, zakat, xxiv

MPM 011217
Printed in Singapore